WORD 2003
PERSONAL TRAINER

WORD 2003 PERSONAL TRAINER

CustomGuide, Inc.

O'REILLY®

Beijing • Cambridge • Farnham • Köln • Paris • Sebastopol • Taipei • Tokyo

Word 2003 Personal Trainer

by CustomGuide, Inc.

Cover illustration © 2005 Lou Brooks.

Published by O'Reilly Media, Inc., 1005 Gravenstein Highway North, Sebastopol, CA 95472.

O'Reilly books may be purchased for educational, business, or sales promotional use. Online editions are also available for most titles (*safari.oreilly.com*). For more information, contact our corporate/institutional sales department: (800) 998-9938 or *corporate@oreilly.com*.

Editor	Michele Filshie
Production Editor	Sarah Sherman
Art Director	Michele Wetherbee
Cover Designer	Emma Colby
Cover Illustrator	Lou Brooks
Interior Designer	Melanie Wang

Printing History

February 2005:   First Edition.

 This book uses RepKover™, a durable and flexible lay-flat binding.

ISBN: 0-596-00936-4

[C]

CONTENTS

Contents

About CustomGuide, Inc.

CustomGuide, Inc. (*http://www.customguide.com*) is a leading provider of training materials and e-learning for organizations; their client list includes Harvard, Yale, and Oxford universities. CustomGuide was founded by a small group of instructors who were dissatisfied by the dry and technical nature of computer training materials available to trainers and educators. They decided to write their own series of courseware that would be fun and user-friendly; and best of all, they would license it in electronic format so instructors could print only the topics they needed for a class or training session. Later, they found themselves unhappy with the e-learning industry and decided to create a new series of online, interactive training that matched their courseware. Today employees, students, and instructors at more than 2,000 organizations worldwide use CustomGuide courseware to help teach and learn about computers.

CustomGuide Inc, Staff and Contributors

Jonathan High	President	Jeremy Weaver	Senior Programmer
Daniel High	Vice President of Sales and Marketing	Luke Davidson	Programmer
		Lisa Price	Director of Business Development
Melissa Peterson	Senior Writer/Editor	Soda Rajsombath	Office Manager and Sales Representative
Kitty Rogers	Writer/Editor		
Kelly Waldrop	Writer/Editor	Megan Diemand	Sales Representative
Stephen Meinz	Writer/Editor	Hallie Stork	Sales Representative
Stan Keathly	Senior Developer	Sarah Saeger	Sales Support
Jeffrey High	Developer	Julie Geisler	Narrator
Chris Kannenman	Developer		

INTRODUCTION

About the Personal Trainer Series

Most software manuals are as hard to navigate as the programs they describe. They assume that you're going to read all 500 pages from start to finish, and that you can gain intimate familiarity with the program simply by reading about it. Some books give you sample files to practice on, but when you're finding your way around a new set of skills, it's all too easy to mess up program settings or delete data files and not know how to recover. Even if William Shakespeare and Bill Gates teamed up to write a book about Microsoft Word, their book would be frustrating to read because most people learn by doing the task.

While we don't claim to be rivals to either Bill, we think we have a winning formula in the Personal Trainer series. We've created a set of workouts that reflect the tasks you really want to do, whether as simple as resizing or as complex as integrating multimedia components. Each workout breaks a task into a series of simple steps, showing you exactly what to do to accomplish the task.

And instead of leaving you hanging, the interactive CD in the back of this book recreates the application for you to experiment in. In our unique simulator, there's no worry about permanently damaging your preferences, turning all your documents purple, losing data, or any of the other things that can go wrong when you're testing your new skills in the unforgiving world of the real application. It's fully interactive, giving you feedback and guidance as you work through the exercises—just like a real trainer!

Our friendly guides will help you buff up your skills in record time. You'll learn the secrets of the professionals in a safe environment, with exercises and homework for those of you who really want to break the pain barrier. You'll have your Word 2003 skills in shape in no time!

About This Book

We've aimed this book at Word 2003. Some features may look different or simply not exist if you're using another version of the program. If our simulator doesn't match your application, check the version number to make sure you're using the right version.

Since this is a hands-on course, each lesson contains an exercise with step-by-step instructions for you to follow.

To make learning easier, every exercise follows certain conventions:

* This book never assumes you know where (or what) something is. The first time you're told to click something, a picture of what you're supposed to click appears in the illustrations in the lesson.

* When you see a keyboard instruction like "press Ctrl + B," you should press and hold the first key ("Ctrl" in this example) while you press the second key ("B" in this example). Then, after you've pressed both keys, you can release them.

Our exclusive Quick Reference box appears at the end of every lesson. You can use it to review the skills you've learned in the lesson and as a handy reference—when you need to know how to do something fast and don't need to step through the sample exercises.

Conventions Used in This Book

The following is a list of typographical conventions used in this book:

Italic

Shows important terms the first time they are presented.

Constant Width

Shows anything you're actually supposed to type.

Color

Shows anything you're supposed to click, drag, or press.

≋ NOTE ≋ **Warns you of pitfalls that you could encounter if you're not careful.**

Indicates a suggestion or supplementary information to the topic at hand.

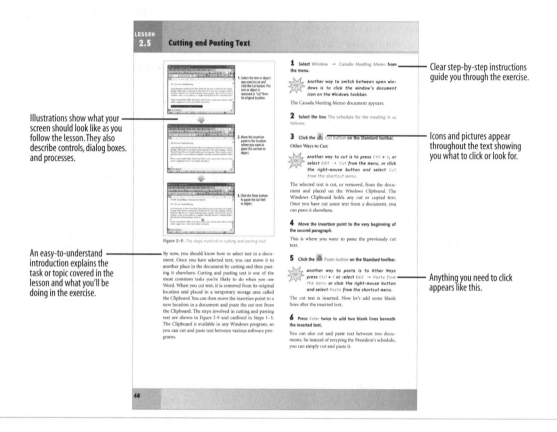

Illustrations show what your screen should look like as you follow the lesson. They also describe controls, dialog boxes, and processes.

An easy-to-understand introduction explains the task or topic covered in the lesson and what you'll be doing in the exercise.

Clear step-by-step instructions guide you through the exercise.

Icons and pictures appear throughout the text showing you what to click or look for.

Anything you need to click appears like this.

Using the Interactive Environment

Minimum Specs

- Windows 98 or better
- 64 MB RAM
- 150 MB Disk Space

Installation Instructions

Insert disc into CD-ROM drive. Click the Install button at the prompt. The installer will give you the option of installing the Interactive Content and the Practice Files. These are both installed by default. Practice files are also included on the CD in a directory called "Practice Files," which can be accessed without installing anything. If you select the installation item, the installer will then create a shortcut in your Start menu under the title "Personal Trainer," which you can use to access your installation selections.

Use of Interactive Content

Once you've installed the interactive content, placing the disc in your drive will cause the program to launch automatically. Then, once it has launched, just make your lesson selections and learn away!

How to Contact Us

We have tested and verified the information in this book to the best of our ability, but you might find that features have changed (or even that we have made mistakes!). As a reader of this book, you can help us to improve future editions by sending us your feedback. Please let us know about any errors, inaccuracies, bugs, misleading or confusing statements, and typos that you find anywhere in this book.

Please also let us know what we can do to make this book more useful to you. We take your comments seriously and will try to incorporate reasonable suggestions into future editions. You can write to us at:

O'Reilly Media, Inc.
1005 Gravenstein Highway North
Sebastopol, CA 95472
(800) 998-9938 (in the U.S. or Canada)
(707) 829-0515 (international or local)
(707) 829-0104 (fax)

To ask technical questions or to comment on the book, send e-mail to:

bookquestions@oreilly.com

The web site for *Outlook 2003 Personal Trainer* lists examples, errata, and plans for future editions. You can find this page at:

http://www.oreilly.com/catalog/wordpt/

For more information about this book and others, see the O'Reilly web site at:

http://www.oreilly.com

CHAPTER 1

THE FUNDAMENTALS

CHAPTER OBJECTIVES:

Starting Microsoft Word, Lesson 1.1

Giving commands, Lessons 1.4–1.7

Creating a new document, Lesson 1.8

Inserting and deleting text, Lessons 1.9 and 1.10

Naming and saving a document, Lesson 1.12

Printing and closing a document, Lesson 1.15

Exiting Word, Lesson 1.15

CHAPTER TASK: CREATE, PRINT, AND SAVE A SIMPLE MEMO

Prerequisites

- **A computer with Windows 2000 or XP and Word 2003 installed.**
- **An understanding of basic computer functions (how to use the mouse and keyboard).**

Welcome to your first Microsoft Word 2003 chapter. Microsoft Word is a powerful word-processing software program that gives its users the tools to create a variety of professional documents. Word automatically checks your spelling and grammar, and corrects common mistakes. For example, if one types *teh*, Word will automatically change it to *the*. It even lets you insert charts, tables, and pictures into your documents. Microsoft Word is the most widely used and, according to most reviews, the most powerful and user-friendly word-processor available. You have made a great choice by deciding to learn Microsoft Word 2003.

This chapter is an introduction to the Word basics—what you need to create, print, and save a document. If you've seen the Microsoft Word program before, you already know the screen is filled with cryptic-looking buttons, menus, and icons. By the time you've finished this chapter, you will know what many of them mean.

Your first task with Microsoft Word is an easy one: create a simple interoffice memo. Turn the page and let's get started!

Figure 1-1. The Windows Desktop.

Figure 1-2. Programs located under the Windows Start button.

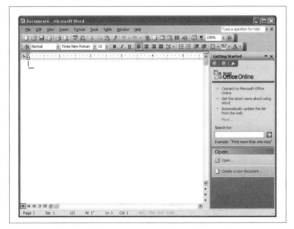

Figure 1-3. The Microsoft Word program screen.

Before starting Word 2003 (some people refer to starting a program as *opening* or *launching*), make sure your computer is on—if not, turn it on! Start Word 2003 the same as you would start any other program on your computer—use the Start button. Because every computer can be set up differently (some people like to rearrange and reorder their program menu), the procedure for starting Word might be different from the one listed here.

⸸ NOTE ⸸ *The method used to open Word may differ, depending on how your computer is organized.*

1 Make sure your computer is on and the Windows desktop is open.

Your computer screen should look similar to the one shown in Figure 1-1.

2 Click the Windows ▮ start Start button, located on the left-hand corner of the Windows taskbar at the bottom of the screen.

The Windows Start menu pops ups.

3 Move your mouse until the cursor points to All Programs.

A menu similar to the one shown in Figure 1-2 shoots out from the right side of All Programs. The programs and menus listed will depend on the programs installed on your computer, so your menu will probably look somewhat different from the illustration.

4 On the All Programs menu, point to Microsoft Office 2003. Then, point to and click Microsoft Office Word 2003.

Depending on how many programs are installed on your computer and how they are organized, it might be a little difficult to find the Microsoft Word program. Once you click on Microsoft Word, your computer's hard drive will whir for a moment while it loads the program. The Word program screen, then appears, as shown in Figure 1-3.

That's it! You are ready to start creating documents with Microsoft Word. In the next lesson, you will learn how to use all of those strange-looking buttons, bars, and menus.

QUICK REFERENCE

TO START THE MICROSOFT WORD PROGRAM:

1. CLICK THE WINDOWS START BUTTON.

2. SELECT ALL PROGRAMS → MICROSOFT OFFICE 2003 → MICROSOFT OFFICE WORD 2003.

What's New in Word 2003?

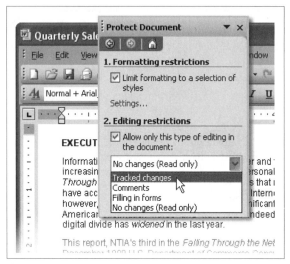

Figure 1-4. Word 2003 features enhanced editing tools.

If you're upgrading from a previous version of Word to Word 2003, you're in luck—in most respects, Word 2003 looks and works *almost* the same as previous versions. In fact, the upgrade from Word 2002 to Word 2003 probably saw the fewest changes from version to version. A handy new feature in Word 2003 is enhanced editing tools that give you more control over your documents, as shown in Figure 1-4. See Table 1-1 below for what's new in Word 2003 (and a review of some of the features from Word 2002):

Table 1-1. What's New

Feature	New in	Description
New User Interface and Task Panes	2003	Office 2003 has an open and energetic look and feel that organizes and focuses the page. Word also optimizes to the size and resolution of your screen. New task panes have been added as well: Getting Started, Help, Search Results, Shared Workspace, Document Updates, and Research.
Microsoft Office Online	2003	Online information is more integrated in Office 2003. You can access the Microsoft Office Online site through your Web browser or through links in the task panes to find templates, help topics, articles, clip art, tips, and more.
XML Support	2003	In a nutshell, XML makes the content of your document very easy to incorporate in your organization's database.
Reading Layout View	2003	This new view optimizes the program window for reading documents: unnecessary toolbars are hidden; page contents are scaled to fit on your screen so it's easy to read and browse; and the Reviewing toolbar lets you highlight sections and make changes.
Improved Document Protection	2003	Protecting a document has been fine-tuned in Word 2003. Now you can control formatting, content, or both. When protecting formatting, you can restrict which styles can be used in the document. When protecting content, you can designate which areas of the document are protected and even grant certain individuals access to restricted parts of the document.
Document Workspaces	2003	Avoid confusing copies of documents and e-mail attachments when reviewing and co-authoring documents. Use this feature to collaborate with others on a single document at the same time through SharePoint Services.
Compare Side by Side	2003	View the changes and differences between two documents side by side, without having to merge them into one document. Synchronized scrolling lets you scroll through both documents at the same time.
Research Task Pane	2003	With an Internet connection, the Research pane gives you access to a wealth of resource information. Conduct searches in an online encyclopedia, dictionary, or a third party's resources.

Table 1-1. What's New (Continued)

Feature	New in	Description
Ink Compatible	2003	Word 2003 is compatible with devices that support ink input, such as Tablet PC. This feature enables you to mark up a document in Word as you would on a printed document. Write handwritten comments, send a handwritten e-mail message, or blend Word document text with handwritten content.
Information Rights Management	2003	This new feature gives you complete control over your documents, so that sensitive information doesn't fall into the wrong hands. For example, you can create a document that only specified individuals can view, edit, print, or save. You can even set a time for the file to self-destruct, eliminating an electronic trail.
Smart Tags	2002	Context-sensitive smart tags are a set of buttons that provide speedy access to relevant information by alerting you to important actions, such as formatting options for pasted information, formula error correction, and more.
Task Panes	2002	The task pane appears on the right side of the screen and lets you quickly perform searches, open or start a new document, view the contents of the clipboard, format documents and presentations, or even access language translation and template services via the Web.
Document Recovery	2002	Document Recovery gives you the option to automatically save your current document at the time an application stops responding so you don't lose a moment's work. In the event of an error, Word keeps a backup of your work, giving you the chance to save and recover it so you don't lose valuable time or data.
Speech	2002	Word increases user productivity by supplementing traditional mouse and keyboard execution with voice commands. Users can dictate text, make direct formatting changes, and navigate menus using speech and voice commands.
Multilingual and International Support	2002	Word can automatically detect the language of text for a number of languages when you open a document or enter text. When Word detects a language, it shows the name of the language on the status bar and uses the spelling and grammar dictionaries, punctuation rules, and sorting conventions for that language. You can also enter, display, and edit text in all supported languages in any language version of Microsoft Office.
Multiple Cut, Copy, and Paste Clipboard		The Office 2003 clipboard lets you copy up to 24 pieces of information from all the Office applications on the Web and store them in the Office Clipboard task pane. The task pane gives you a visual representation of the copied data and a sample of the text, so you can easily distinguish clipboard items as they transfer to other documents.

Understanding the Word Screen

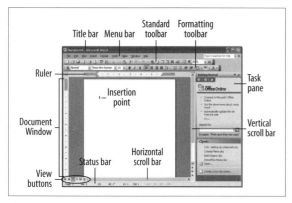

Figure 1-5. Elements of the Word program screen.

The Word 2003 program screen may seem confusing and overwhelming the first time you see it. What are all those buttons, icons, menus, and arrows for? This lesson will help you become familiar with the Word program screen. See Table 1-2 for Word program screen elements and uses. There are no step-by-step instructions for this lesson—all you have to do is look at Figure 1-5 to see what each element represents, and, most of all, relax! This lesson is only meant to help you get acquainted with the Word screen; you don't have to memorize anything.

By default, Word 2003 opens with the Standard and Formatting toolbars on the same line. In Figure 1-5, the toolbars are on two different rows. You'll learn how to change this in a later lesson regarding toolbars.

Table 1-2. The Word Program Screen

Element	What It's Used For
Title bar	Displays the name of the program you are currently using (Microsoft Word, of course) and the name of the document you are working on. A title bar appears at the top of all Windows programs.
Menu bar	Displays a list of menus used to give commands to Word. Clicking on a menu name displays a list of commands. For example, clicking the **Format** menu name would display different formatting commands.
Standard toolbar	Toolbars are shortcuts—they contain buttons for the most commonly used commands (instead of wading through several menus). The Standard toolbar contains buttons for the Word commands you use most frequently, such as saving, opening, and printing documents.
Formatting toolbar	Contains buttons for the most commonly used formatting commands, such as applying bold or italics to text.
Ruler	Displays left and right paragraph and document margins and tab stops.
Task pane	The task pane lists commands that are relevant to whatever it is that you're doing in Word. You can easily hide the task pane if you want to have more room to view a document: Simply click the Close button in the upper-right corner of the task pane.
Document window	This is where you type in text and work on your documents. You can have more than one document window open at a time, allowing you to work on several documents.
Insertion point	The small, blinking bar is where the text you type appears in the document. You can move the insertion point by moving your mouse to a new location in the document window (the pointer should change to ⌶ and clicking, or by using the arrow keys on the keyboard.
View buttons	The view buttons appear on the left-hand side of the horizontal scroll bar and are used to display documents in several different views: normal, online layout, print layout, and outline. You'll learn more about how these different views are used in a later lesson.
Scroll bars	There are both vertical and horizontal scroll bars—you use them to view and move around your document. The scroll box shows where you are in the document—for example, if the scroll box is located near the top of the scroll bar, you're at the beginning of a document.
Status bar	Displays various important types of information, such as the total number of pages in a document, which page you're currently working on, and the position of the insertion point.

Don't worry if you find some of these elements of the Word program screen confusing at first—they will make more sense after you've used them, which you will get to do in the next lesson.

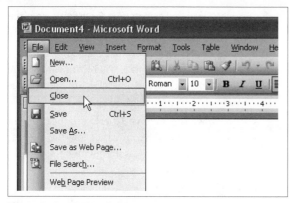

Figure 1-6. The File menu.

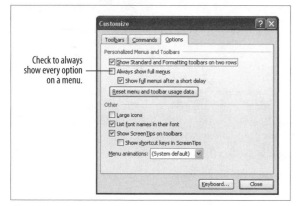

Check to always show every option on a menu.

Figure 1-7. The Customize dialog box.

This lesson explains the most common way to give commands to Word—by using *menus*. Menus for all Windows programs can be found at the top of a window, just beneath the program's title bar.

Word's *personalized menus* are unique. Microsoft Word 2003 displays its menu commands on the screen in three different ways:

- By displaying every command possible, like in earlier versions of Word.

- By hiding the commands you don't use as frequently (the more advanced commands) from view.

- By displaying the hidden commands by clicking the downward-pointing arrows at the bottom of the menu, or after waiting a couple seconds.

This lesson explains how to use Word 2003's new personalized menus.

1 Click the word File on the menu bar.

A menu drops down from the word File, as shown in Figure 1-6. The File menu contains a list of file-related commands, such as New, which creates a new file; Open, which opens or loads a saved file; Save, which saves the currently opened file; and Close, which closes the currently opened file. Move on to the next step to learn how to select a command from the File menu.

2 Click the word Close in the File menu.

The document window disappears because you have just closed the current document.

Notice each of the words in the menu has an underlined letter somewhere in them. For example, the F in the File menu is underlined. Holding down the Alt key and pressing the underlined letter in a menu produces the same effect as clicking the entire menu name or option. For example, pressing the Alt key and then the F key would also open the File menu. Move on to the next step and try it for yourself.

3 Press the Alt key then press the F key.

The File menu appears. Once you open a menu, you can navigate through the different menus using the mouse or by pressing the Alt key and then the letter that is underlined in the menu name.

4 Press the Right Arrow Key → .

The next menu to the right, the Edit menu, appears. If you open a menu and then change your mind, it's easy to close it without selecting any commands.

5 Click anywhere *outside* the menu or press the Esc key.

⋮ NOTE ⋮ *The procedure for using menus and the general order/layout of the menu is the same for most Windows programs. So, once you master Word's menus, you can handle just about any Windows-based program! Refer to Table 1-3 for a list of these menus.*

6 Click the word Tools on the menu bar.

The most common menu commands appear in the Tools menu. Some people feel intimidated by being confronted with so many menu options, so the menus display the more common commands at first. To display all of a menu's commands, either click on the downward-pointing arrows at the bottom of the menu, or keep the menu open for a few seconds.

7 If necessary, click the downward-pointing arrows at the bottom of the Tools menu.

All commands appear on the Tools menu.

If you're accustomed to working with earlier versions of Microsoft Office, you may find hiding the less frequently used commands disconcerting. If so, you can easily change how Word's menus work. Here's how:

8 Select View → Toolbars → Customize from the menu. Click the Options tab.

The Options tab of the Customize dialog box appears, as shown in Figure 1-7. This is where you can change how Word's menus work. There are two check boxes here that are important:

- **Always show full menus:** Check this box if you want to show all the commands on the menus, instead of hiding the less frequently used commands.

- **Show full menus after a short delay:** If checked, Word will wait a few seconds before displaying the less frequently used commands on a menu.

9 Click Close without making any changes.

Table 1-3. Menus Found in Microsoft Word

File	Description
File	File-related commands to open, save, close, print, and create new files.
Edit	Commands to copy, cut, paste, find, and replace text in a document.
View	Commands to change how the document is displayed on the screen.
Insert	Lists items that you can insert into a document.
Format	Commands to format text and paragraphs.
Tools	Lists tools such as the Thesaurus and Word Count.
Table	Table-related commands.
Window	Commands to display multiple windows.
Help	Get help using Microsoft Word.

QUICK REFERENCE

TO OPEN A MENU:

• CLICK THE MENU NAME WITH THE MOUSE.

OR...

• PRESS ALT AND THEN THE UNDERLINED LETTER IN THE MENU NAME.

TO DISPLAY A MENU'S HIDDEN COMMANDS:

• CLICK THE DOWNWARD-POINTING ARROWS AT THE BOTTOM OF THE MENU.

OR...

• OPEN THE MENU AND WAIT A FEW SECONDS.

TO CHANGE HOW MENUS WORK:

1. SELECT VIEW → TOOLBARS → CUSTOMIZE FROM THE MENU.

2. CHECK OR CLEAR EITHER THE ALWAYS SHOW FULL MENUS AND/OR SHOW FULL MENUS AFTER A SHORT DELAY OPTIONS, THEN CLICK CLOSE.

Using Toolbars and Creating a New Document

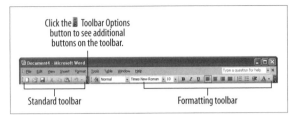

Figure 1-8. The Standard and Formatting toolbars squished together on the same row.

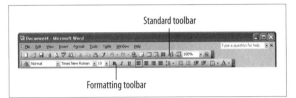

Figure 1-9. The Standard and Formatting toolbars stacked in two rows.

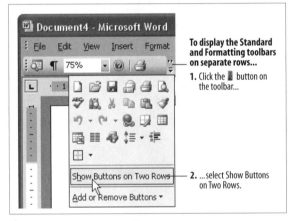

To display the Standard and Formatting toolbars on separate rows...

1. Click the button on the toolbar...

2. ...select Show Buttons on Two Rows.

Figure 1-10. Displaying toolbars on separate rows.

In this lesson, we will discuss another common way to give commands to Word—by using toolbars. Toolbars are shortcuts—they contain buttons for the most commonly used commands. Instead of wading through several menus to access a command, you can click a single button on a toolbar. Two toolbars appear by default when you start Word (see Figures 1-8 and 1-9):

- **Standard toolbar:** Located either to the left or on the top, the Standard toolbar contains buttons for the commands you'll use most frequently, such as Save and Print.

- **Formatting toolbar:** Located either to the right of or below the Standard toolbar, the Formatting toolbar

contains buttons for quickly formatting fonts and paragraphs.

1 Position the mouse pointer over the New Blank Document button on the Standard toolbar (but don't click the mouse yet!).

A ScreenTip appears over the button, briefly identifying what the button is. In this case, it's "New Blank Document." If you don't know what a button on a toolbar does, simply move the pointer over it, wait a second, and a ScreenTip will appear, telling you what it does.

2 Click the New Blank Document button on the Standard toolbar.

> *TIP*
>
> **Other Ways to Create a New Document: Select** File → New **from the menu. Click** Blank document **in the New Document task pane.**

A new, blank document appears. Now, not only have you learned how to use Microsoft Word's toolbars, you've also learned how to create a new blank document.

Word's toolbars have Toolbar Options buttons that work just like menus do. When you click a Toolbar Options button, it displays a drop-down menu of the remaining buttons and various toolbar-related options.

3 Click the Toolbar Options button on the far-right side of the Standard toolbar.

A list of the remaining buttons on the Standard toolbar appears, as shown in Figure 1-10. Just like personalized menus, Word remembers which toolbar buttons you use most often and displays them in a more prominent position on the toolbar.

Let's close this list without selecting any of its options.

4 Click anywhere outside the toolbar list.

The toolbar list closes.

Today, many computers have larger monitors, so Microsoft decided to save space on the screen in Office 2003 and squished both the Standard and Formatting toolbars together on the same bar, as shown in Figure 1-8. While squishing two toolbars together on the same bar gives you more space on the screen, it also makes the two toolbars look confusing—especially if you're used to working with a previous version of Microsoft Office. If you prefer, you can "unsquish" the Standard and Formatting toolbars and stack them on top of one another, as illustrated in Figure 1-9. Here's how…

5 Click the Toolbar Options button **on either the Standard or Formatting toolbar.**

> ⁞ NOTE ⁞ *If the button on the far-right side of the toolbar is a* ▮ *down arrow, the Show Buttons on Two Rows option has already been selected.*

6 Select Show Buttons on Two Rows **from the list.**

Microsoft Word displays the Standard and Formatting toolbars on two separate rows. You can display the Standard and Formatting toolbars on the same row using the same procedure.

7 Click the ▮ Toolbar Options button **on either the Standard or Formatting toolbar and select** Show Buttons on One Row **from the list.**

Word once again displays the Standard and Formatting toolbars on the same row.

So, should you display the Standard and Formatting toolbars on the same row, or should you give each toolbar its own row? The answer depends on the size and resolution of your computer's monitor and your own personal preference. If you have a large 17-inch monitor, you might want to display both toolbars on the same row. On the other hand, if you have a smaller monitor or are constantly clicking the Toolbar Options button to access hidden toolbar buttons, you may want to consider displaying the Standard and Formatting toolbars on separate rows.

QUICK REFERENCE

TO USE A TOOLBAR BUTTON:

- CLICK THE BUTTON YOU WANT TO USE.

TO DISPLAY A TOOLBAR BUTTON'S DESCRIPTION:

- POSITION THE POINTER OVER THE TOOLBAR BUTTON AND WAIT A SECOND. A SCREENTIP WILL APPEAR ABOVE THE BUTTON.

TO CREATE A NEW DOCUMENT:

- CLICK THE NEW BLANK DOCUMENT BUTTON ON THE STANDARD TOOLBAR.

OR…

- SELECT FILE → NEW FROM THE MENU.

TO STACK THE STANDARD AND FORMATTING TOOLBARS ON TWO SEPARATE ROWS:

- CLICK THE TOOLBAR OPTIONS BUTTON ON EITHER TOOLBAR AND SELECT SHOW BUTTONS ON TWO ROWS FROM THE LIST.

Filling Out Dialog Boxes

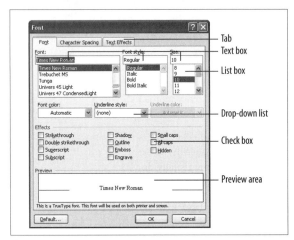

Figure 1-11. The Font dialog box.

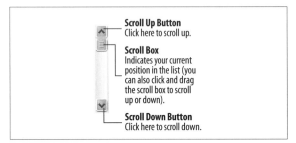

Figure 1-12. Using a Scroll Bar.

Some commands are more complicated than others. Saving a file is a simple process—you only need to select File → Save from the menu or click the Save button on the Standard toolbar. Other commands are more complex—for example, suppose you want to change the top margin of the current document to a half-inch. Whenever you want to do something relatively complicated, you must fill out a *dialog box*. Filling out a dialog box is usually very easy—if you've worked at all with Windows, you've undoubtedly encountered hundreds of dialog boxes. Dialog boxes usually contain several types of controls, including:

- Text boxes
- List boxes
- Check boxes
- Drop-down lists (also called Combo boxes)
- Buttons

It's important that you know the names of these controls, because this book will refer to them in just about every lesson. This lesson gives you a tour of a dialog box and

illustrates the common controls, so you will be able to identify them and know how to use them.

1 Click the word Format on the menu bar.

The Format menu appears. Take a look at the items listed in the Format menu—all of them are followed by ellipses (…). The ellipses indicate that there is a dialog box behind the menu item.

2 Select the word Font from the Format menu.

The Font dialog box appears, as shown in Figure 1-11. Remember: the purpose of this lesson is to learn about dialog boxes, not how to format fonts (we'll get to that later). We opened the Font dialog box because it is one of the most complex dialog boxes in Microsoft Word.

First, let's learn about text boxes. Look at the Font text box, as indicated in Figure 1-11. Text boxes are the most common component of a dialog box and are very similar to fill-in-the-blank sections found on paper forms. To use a text box, first select the text box by clicking it, or by pressing the Tab key until the insertion point appears in the text box. Then simply type the text into the text box.

3 Select the Font text box and type the word Arial.

You've just filled out the text box—nothing to it.

The next stop in our dialog box tour is the *list box*, and there's one located directly below the Font text box. A list box is a way of fitting several options into a small box. Sometimes list boxes contain so many options that they can't all be displayed at once, and you must use the list box's *scroll bar* to move up or down in the list.

4 Click and hold the Font list box's Scroll Down button until Times New Roman appears in the list. Figure 1-12 shows what the scroll box looks like.

5 Click the Times New Roman option in the list.

Our next destination is the *drop-down list* (also known as a combo box). The drop-down list is the list box's cousin. The only difference is that you must click the drop-down list's downward-pointing arrow in order to display its options.

6 Click the Underline style: list arrow.

A list of options appears.

7 Select Words only from the list.

Sometimes you need to select more than one item from a dialog box. For example, what if you want to add Shadow formatting *and* Small Caps formatting to the selected font? Use the *check box* control when you're presented with multiple choices.

8 In the Effects section of the Font dialog box, click the Shadow box and then click the Small Caps box.

The more complicated dialog boxes contain so many options that they can't all fit on the same screen. When this happens, Windows divides the dialog box into several related *tabs*, or sections. If you look near the top of the Font dialog box, you'll notice you're currently on the Font tab. To view a different tab, simply click on it.

9 Click the Character Spacing tab at the top of the dialog box.

The Character Spacing tab appears. The last destination on our dialog box tour is the *button*. Buttons found in dialog boxes are used to execute or cancel commands. Two buttons are usually found in every dialog box:

- **OK:** Applies and saves any changes you have made and, subsequently, closes the dialog box. Pressing the Enter key usually does the same thing as clicking the OK button.

- **Cancel:** Closes the dialog box without applying and saving any changes. Pressing the Esc key usually does the same thing as clicking the Cancel button.

10 Click the Cancel button to cancel the changes you made and to close the Font dialog box.

QUICK REFERENCE

TO SELECT A DIALOG BOX CONTROL:

- CLICK THE CONTROL WITH THE MOUSE.

OR...

- PRESS TAB TO MOVE TO THE NEXT CONTROL IN THE DIALOG BOX OR SHIFT + TAB TO MOVE TO THE PREVIOUS CONTROL UNTIL YOU ARRIVE AT THE DESIRED CONTROL.

TO VIEW A DIALOG BOX TAB:

- CLICK THE TAB YOU WANT TO VIEW.

TO SAVE YOUR CHANGES AND CLOSE A DIALOG BOX:

- CLICK THE OK BUTTON OR PRESS ENTER.

TO CLOSE A DIALOG BOX WITHOUT SAVING YOUR CHANGES:

- CLICK THE CANCEL BUTTON OR PRESS ESC.

Keystroke and Right Mouse Button Shortcuts

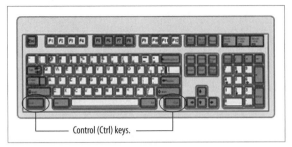

Figure 1-13. The Control (Ctrl) keys on a standard keyboard.

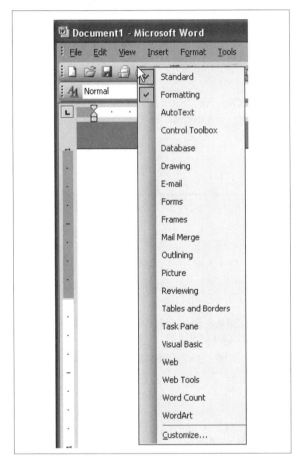

Figure 1-14. A shortcut menu for toolbars.

You are probably starting to realize that there are several methods for doing the same thing in Word. For example, to save a file, you can use the menu (select File → Save) or the toolbar (click the Save button). This lesson introduces you to two more methods of executing commands: right mouse button shortcut menus and keystroke shortcuts.

The left mouse button is the primary mouse button, used for clicking and double-clicking. It's the mouse button you will use over 95 percent of the time when you work with Word, so what's the right mouse button for? Well, whenever you *right-click* something, it brings up a shortcut menu that lists all actions you can perform on an object. Whenever you're unsure or curious about what you can do with an object, click it with the right mouse button. A shortcut menu will appear with a list of commands related to the object or area that you right-clicked.

Right mouse button shortcut menus are a great way to give commands to Word, because you don't have to wade through several levels of unfamiliar menus when you want to do something.

1 Click the right mouse button while the cursor is anywhere inside the document window.

 Right-click on an object to open a shortcut menu that lists the most important things you can do to the object.

A shortcut menu will appear where you clicked the mouse. Notice one of the items listed on the shortcut menu is Font. This is the same Font command you selected from the menu (Format → Font). Using the right mouse button shortcut method is slightly faster and usually easier to remember than using Word's menus. If you open a shortcut menu and then change your mind, you can close it without selecting anything. Here's how:

2 Move the mouse button anywhere outside the menu and click the left mouse button to close the shortcut menu.

Remember that the options listed in the shortcut menu will be different, depending on what or where you right-clicked.

3 Position the pointer over either the Standard or Formatting toolbar and click the right mouse button.

A shortcut menu appears listing all the toolbars you can view, as shown in Figure 1-14. Let's close this menu without selecting anything.

4 Move the mouse button anywhere outside the menu in the document window and click the left mouse button.

Now we'll discuss keystroke shortcuts. Without a doubt, keystroke shortcuts are the fastest way to give commands to Word, even if they are a little hard to remember at first. They're great time-savers for issuing common commands.

To issue a keystroke shortcut, press and hold the Ctrl key, press the shortcut key, and release both buttons. Figure 1-13 shows the location of the Control keys on the keyboard.

5 Press Ctrl + I at the same time.

This is the keystroke shortcut for Italics. Note that the Italics button on the Formatting toolbar appears pressed.

6 Type Italics.

The text appears italicized.

≋ NOTE ≋   *Although it won't be discussed in this lesson, Word's default keystroke shortcuts can be changed or remapped in order to execute other commands.*

Table 1-4 lists the most common keystroke shortcuts that you'll use in Microsoft Word.

Table 1-4. Common Keystroke Shortcuts

Keystroke	Description
Ctrl + B	Toggles (switches) bold font formatting.
Ctrl + I	Toggles italicized font formatting.
Ctrl + U	Toggles underline font formatting.
Ctrl + Spacebar	Returns the font formatting to the default setting.
Ctrl + O	Opens a document.
Ctrl + S	Saves the current document.
Ctrl + P	Sends the current document to the default printer.
Ctrl + C	Copies the selected text or object onto the Windows clipboard.
Ctrl + X	Cuts the selected text or object from its current location and places it on the Windows clipboard.
Ctrl + V	Pastes any copied or cut text or object to the current location.
Ctrl + Home	Moves the insertion point to the beginning of the document.
Ctrl + End	Moves the insertion point to the end of the document.

QUICK REFERENCE

TO OPEN A CONTEXT-SENSITIVE SHORTCUT MENU:

• RIGHT-CLICK THE OBJECT.

TO USE A KEYSTROKE SHORTCUT:

• PRESS CTRL + THE LETTER OF THE KEYSTROKE SHORTCUT YOU WANT TO PERFORM.

Closing a Document, Creating a New Document, and Entering Text

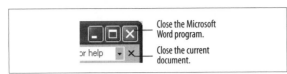

Close the Microsoft Word program.

Close the current document.

Figure 1-15. The Program and Document close buttons.

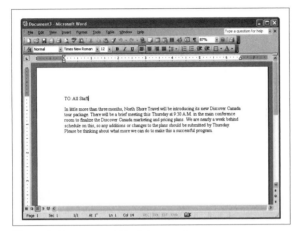

Figure 1-16. Text in a Word document.

You're finally ready to enter text and create your first document! Before you can start entering text and creating a new document, you need to get rid of the document you used in the previous lesson. To do this, close the current document and create a new, blank document.

1 Click the document window's Close button (the lower Close button).

> **TIP**
> **Other Ways to Close a Document: Select** File → Close **from the menu.**

There should be two Close buttons on your screen, as shown in Figure 1-15. The top-most Close button, located on the title bar of the Word program, closes Word entirely—*don't click this button!* The lower Close button closes the active document but won't exit Word—this is the button you should click.

Word will ask if you would like to save the document you created for later use. You don't need to save the document, so click No.

2 Click No.

> **NOTE**
> *If you have more than one document open in Word 2003, each document appears as an icon on the Windows taskbar. Additional document windows only have a single close button, located in the Word title bar. To close any additional documents, click the close button in the title bar.*

3 Click the New Blank Document button **on the Standard toolbar.**

> **TIP**
> **Other Ways to Create a New Document: Select** File → New **from the menu and click** Blank Document.

The document window reappears with a blank document you can work on.

4 Type the following: TO: All Staff

5 Press Enter twice.

Pressing Enter adds a new line and starts a new paragraph; therefore, pressing Enter twice adds two lines and separates your paragraphs.

6 If the Office Assistant appears (the Office Assistant is an annoying cartoon figure, usually an animated paper clip) click Cancel in the Office Assistant's speech-balloon dialog box.

Sometimes the Office Assistant asks if you want help creating a document using a wizard. Wizards can help you complete tasks by giving step-by-step instructions. Wizards are great for completing complicated tasks, such as creating a web page. For simpler tasks, however, like a memo or letter, they can be more troublesome than helpful.

7 Type the following paragraph:

In little more than three months, North Shore Travel will be introducing its new Discover Canada tour package. There will be a brief meeting this Thursday at 9:30 A.M. in the main conference room to finalize the Discover Canada marketing and pricing plans. We are nearly a week behind schedule on this, so any additions or changes to the plans should be submitted by Thursday. Please be thinking about what more we can do to make this a successful program.

Don't worry about spelling for now, and do not press Enter when you reach the end of a line—just keep typing. Notice how your typing automatically starts a new line when it reaches the edge of the computer screen? This feature is called *word-wrap*.

Great! You've created a document in Microsoft Word, which should look like Figure 1-16. In the next lesson, you will learn how to make changes to your document, and how to add and delete text.

QUICK REFERENCE

TO CLOSE A DOCUMENT:

• CLICK THE DOCUMENT WINDOW'S CLOSE BUTTON.

OR...

• SELECT FILE → CLOSE FROM THE MENU.

TO CREATE A NEW BLANK DOCUMENT:

• CLICK THE NEW BLANK DOCUMENT BUTTON ON THE STANDARD TOOLBAR.

OR...

1. SELECT FILE → NEW FROM THE MENU.

2. CLICK BLANK DOCUMENT.

Inserting and Deleting Text

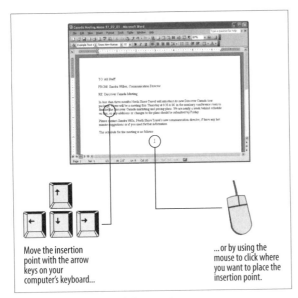

Move the insertion point with the arrow keys on your computer's keyboard...

...or by using the mouse to click where you want to place the insertion point.

Figure 1-17. The revised document.

After typing a document, you will often discover that you need to make several changes to your text—perhaps you want to delete or rephrase a sentence. Editing a document by inserting and deleting text couldn't be easier. To delete text, place the insertion point to the left or right of the text you want to delete, then press either the Backspace key (deletes text to the left) or the Delete key (deletes text to the right). Inserting text is just as simple—all you need to do is place the insertion point where you want to place the new text, and start typing.

In this lesson, you'll get practice inserting and deleting text so you can revise the memo you created in the previous lesson.

 You can also move the insertion point with the mouse. Move the I-beam pointer (ICON) with the mouse to the location you want and then click the left mouse button.

1 Press the Up Arrow Key to move the insertion point until it is one line below TO: All Staff.

2 Press Enter.

This will add a blank line under the "TO: All Staff" line.

 You can also move the insertion point with the mouse. Move the I-beam pointer (⌶) with the mouse to the location you want and then click the left mouse button.

3 Type FROM: Sandra Willes **and press** Enter **twice.**

4 Type RE: Discover Canada Meeting **and press** Enter.

5 Use the keyboard or mouse to move the insertion point to the very end of the line FROM: Sandra Willes **and type** , Communication Director.

You've just learned how to insert text in a document—pretty easy, huh? Now try deleting some text.

6 Move the insertion point to the very end of the document, after the sentence Please be thinking about what more we can do to make this a successful program.

Remember, you can move the insertion point by pressing the arrows on your keyboard, or by moving the I-beam (⌶) where you want to place the insertion point and then clicking the mouse button.

7 Press the Backspace **key several times.**

Pressing Backspace deletes one space to the left (backwards) of the insertion point.

8 Press and hold the Backspace **key until you have deleted the entire sentence** Please be thinking about what more we can do to make this a successful program. **Release the** Backspace **key when the sentence is deleted.**

Great! You've learned how to delete text using the Backspace key. The Delete key also deletes text, but in a slightly different way.

9 Move the insertion point right before the word main in the second sentence of the paragraph.

10 Press the Delete key.

Pressing Delete deletes one space to the right, or in front, of the insertion point.

11 Press and hold the Delete key until you have deleted the word main.

Now that you've deleted the word "main" add the word "auxiliary" so that the meeting will be held in the auxiliary conference room.

12 Type auxiliary.

Your revised document should look similar to Figure 1-17.

QUICK REFERENCE

TO MOVE THE INSERTION POINT:

- USE THE ARROW KEYS.

OR...

- WITH THE MOUSE, MOVE THE I-BEAM POINTER TO THE LOCATION YOU WANT AND THEN CLICK.

TO INSERT TEXT:

- MOVE THE INSERTION POINT WHERE YOU WANT TO INSERT THE TEXT AND THEN TYPE THE TEXT YOU WANT TO INSERT.

TO DELETE TEXT:

- THE BACKSPACE KEY DELETES TEXT BEFORE, OR TO THE LEFT OF, THE INSERTION POINT.
- THE DELETE KEY DELETES TEXT AFTER, OR TO THE RIGHT OF, THE INSERTION POINT.

Selecting and Replacing Text

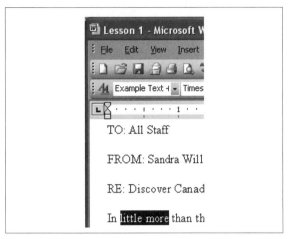

Figure 1-18. How to select text using the mouse.

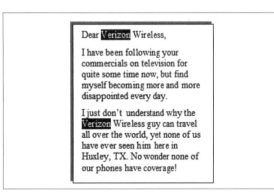

Figure 1-19. You can select a line of text using the Selection bar.

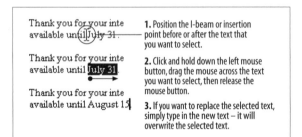

Figure 1-20. You can select more than one block of text by holding down the Ctrl key as you select the bits of text with the mouse.

When you want to edit more than one character at a time, you must *select* them first. Many other editing and formatting techniques, such as formatting text, also require that you select the text you want to modify. Actually, there are probably hundreds of reasons to select text in Word, so this is a task you have to learn.

1 Place the insertion point in front of the words little more in the first sentence of the paragraph.

2 Click and hold the left mouse button and drag the mouse across the words little more. When you're done (the words should be highlighted), release the left mouse button.

 TIP *You can also select text using the keyboard by pressing and holding the Shift key while using the arrow keys to select the text you want. To deselect text, point the mouse and click anywhere in the document.*

The words "little more" should be highlighted, as shown in Figure 1-18. Selecting text with the mouse can be a little tricky at first, especially if you don't have much experience using the mouse. While text is selected, anything you type will delete the existing selected text and replace it with the new text.

3 Type less.

The word "less" replaces the selected text "little more."

TIP *To replace text, select the text you want to replace, then type the new text to replace it.*

4 Double-click the word Thursday.

Double-clicking a single word is a quick way of selecting it.

5 Type Friday.

The word "Friday" replaces the word "Thursday."

6 Use the mouse to place the pointer to the very far left of the line TO: All Staff, until the pointer changes to a ⤢, then click the mouse button.

Positioning the pointer to the left of a line and then clicking selects the entire line, as shown in Figure 1-19.

7 Click anywhere in the document to deselect the text.

The line TO: All Staff is no longer selected.

Word 2003 can even select more than one bit of text at a time, as illustrated in Figure 1-20. Simply press and hold down the Ctrl key as you use the mouse to select the blocks of text.

8 Select the line TO: All Staff.

Now you can select additional blocks of text by holding down the Ctrl key.

9 Hold down the Ctrl key as you select the line RE: Discover Canada Meeting.

You've just selected two separate blocks of text.

You will not need to use this document again, so close it without saving changes.

10 Close the document without saving changes.

That's all there is to selecting text in Word. It can't be stressed enough how important it is for you to be an expert in selecting text. Knowing how to select text will make you more proficient and skillful at using Microsoft Word. People who haven't mastered selecting text treat Word as nothing more than a sophisticated typewriter, and never take advantage of the beneficial features Word has to offer.

Table 1-5 describes several shortcut techniques you can use to select text. You don't *have* to memorize these shortcuts, but if you do, it will certainly save you a lot of time.

Table 1-5. Text Selection Shortcuts

To select	Do this
A word	Double-click the word.
Several bits of text	Select the first block of text, then press and hold Ctrl as you select the remaining blocks of text.
A sentence	Press and hold Ctrl and click anywhere in the sentence.
A line of text	Click in the selection bar next to the line.
A paragraph	Triple-click in the paragraph, or double-click in the selection bar next to the paragraph.
The entire document	Triple-click in the selection bar, or press and hold Ctrl and click anywhere in the selection bar, or press Ctrl + A.

QUICK REFERENCE

TO SELECT TEXT:

1. MOVE THE INSERTION POINT TO THE BEGINNING OR END OF THE TEXT YOU WANT TO SELECT.

2. CLICK AND HOLD THE LEFT MOUSE BUTTON AND DRAG THE INSERTION POINT ACROSS THE TEXT, THEN RELEASE THE MOUSE BUTTON ONCE THE TEXT IS SELECTED.

TO SELECT MULTIPLE BLOCKS OF TEXT:

1. SELECT THE FIRST BLOCK OF TEXT.

2. HOLD DOWN THE CTRL KEY AS YOU SELECT THE REMAINING BLOCK(S) OF TEXT.

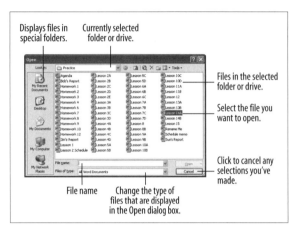

Figure 1-21. The Open dialog box.

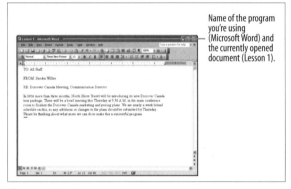

Figure 1-22. The Lesson 1 file appears in the document window.

When you work with Word, you will sometimes need to create a new document from scratch (something you hopefully learned to do when we talked about toolbars in a previous lesson); but, more often, you'll want to work on an existing document that you or someone else has previously saved. This lesson explains how to open, or retrieve, a saved document. Refer to Table 1-6 for the description of the special folders that appear in the left column of the Open and Save As dialog boxes (as shown in Figure 1-21).

1 Click the 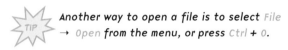 Open button on the Standard toolbar.

> *TIP* **Another way to open a file is to select** File → Open **from the menu, or press** Ctrl + O.

The Open dialog appears, as shown in Figure 1-21. Next, you have to tell Word where the file you want to open is located.

2 Navigate to and open your Practice folder.

Your computer stores information in files and folders, just like you store information in a filing cabinet. To open a file, you must first find and open the folder where it is saved. Normally new files are saved in a folder named "My Documents," but sometimes you will want to save or open files that are located in another folder.

The Open and Save dialog boxes both have their own toolbars that make it easy to browse through your computer's drives and folders. Two controls on this toolbar are particularly helpful:

- ⌐My Documents ▾ **Look In List:** Click to list the drives on your computer and the current folder, then select the drive and/or folder with the contents you want to display.

- 🔼 **Up One Level button:** Click to move up one folder.

3 Click the document named Lesson 1 in the file list box, then click Open.

Word opens the Lesson 1 file and displays it in the document window, as shown in Figure 1-22.

Table 1-6. Special Folders in the Open and Save As Dialog Boxes

Folder	Description
📄	Displays a list of files that you've recently worked on.
📄	Temporarily minimizes or hides all your programs so that you can see the Windows desktop.

Table 1-6. Special Folders in the Open and Save As Dialog Boxes (Continued)

Folder	Description
	Displays all the folders and files in the My Documents folder—the default location where Microsoft Office programs save their files.
	Displays a list of the different drives on your computer.
	If you have permission, My Network Places lets you browse through the folders and computers in your workgroup and on the network.

QUICK REFERENCE

TO OPEN A DOCUMENT:

- CLICK THE OPEN BUTTON ON THE STANDARD TOOLBAR.

OR...

- SELECT FILE → OPEN FROM THE MENU.

OR...

- PRESS CTRL + O.

Saving a Document

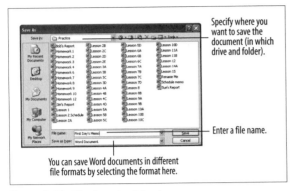

Specify where you want to save the document (in which drive and folder).

Enter a file name.

You can save Word documents in different file formats by selecting the format here.

Figure 1-23. The Save As dialog box.

After you've created a document, you need to save it if you intend to use it again. *Saving* a document stores it in a file on your computer's hard disk, similar to putting a file away in a filing cabinet so you can use it later. Once you have saved a document, it's a good idea to save it again from time to time as you work on it. You don't want to lose all your work if the power suddenly goes out or if your computer crashes! In this lesson, you will learn how to save an existing document under a different name without changing the original document. It's often easier and more efficient to create a document by modifying one that already exists, instead of having to retype a lot of information.

You want to use the information in the Lesson 1 document that we opened in the previous lesson to create a new document. Since you don't want to modify the original document, Lesson 1, let's save it as a new document and give it a different name.

1 Select File → Save As from the menu.

The Save As dialog box appears, as shown in Figure 1-23. This is where you can save the document with a new name. If you only want to save changes you've made to a document (instead of saving them in a new file), click the Save button on the Standard toolbar, or select File → Save from the menu, or press Ctrl + S.

First, you have to specify the drive and/or folder where you want to save your document.

2 If necessary, navigate to and open your Practice folder.

Next, specify a new name for the document.

3 In the File name text box, type First Day's Memo and click Save.

The Lesson 1 document is saved with the new name, First Day's Memo, and the original document, Lesson 1, closes. Now you can work on your new document without changing the original document.

When you make changes to your document, simply save your changes in the same file. Go ahead and try it.

4 Press Ctrl + End to move the insertion point to the end of the document, press Enter twice and type Thanks!

Now save your changes.

5 Click the 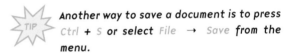 Save button on the Standard toolbar.

> *TIP* **Another way to save a document is to press** Ctrl + S **or select** File → Save **from the menu.**

Word saves the changes you've made to the First Day's Memo document.

Congratulations! You've just saved your first Word document.

QUICK REFERENCE

TO SAVE A DOCUMENT:

- CLICK THE SAVE BUTTON ON THE STANDARD TOOLBAR.

OR...

- SELECT FILE → SAVE FROM THE MENU.

OR...

- PRESS CTRL + S.

TO SAVE A DOCUMENT IN A NEW FILE WITH A DIFFERENT NAME:

1. SELECT FILE → SAVE AS FROM THE MENU.

2. TYPE A NEW NAME FOR THE DOCUMENT AND CLICK SAVE.

Figure 1-24. Asking a question in the Word Help task pane.

Figure 1-26. Help text for the selected topic.

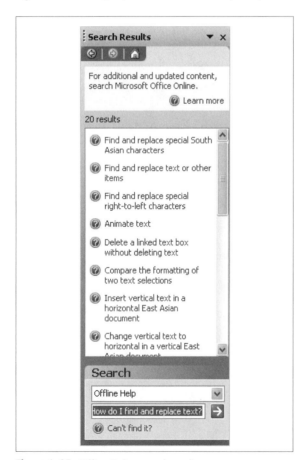

Figure 1-25. Office Online search results.

When you don't know how to do something in Windows or a Windows-based program, don't panic—just look up your question in the Word Help files. The Word Help files can answer your questions, offer tips, and provide help for all of Word's features. Many Word users forget to use Help, but this is unfortunate, because the Help files know more about Word than most reference books do!

You can make the Word Help files appear by pressing the F1 key. Then all you have to do is ask your question in normal English. This lesson will show you how you can get help using the Word Help files.

1 Press the F1 key.

The F1 key is the help key for all Windows-based programs.

Another way to get help is to type your question in the Type a question for help box on the menu bar and press Enter. The results appear in the Word Help task pane.

The Word Help task pane appears, as shown in Figure 1-24.

2 **Type** How do I find and replace text? **in the Search for: text box, as shown in Figure 1-24.**

You can ask Word Help questions in normal English, just as if you were asking a person instead of a computer. The program identifies keywords and phrases in your questions like "find," "replace," and "text."

≥ NOTE ≥ *Microsoft has totally changed the way Help works in Office 2003 with Office Online. Instead of searching for help in the files already stored on your computer, Office Online searches for the topic in their online database. The purpose of this feature is to provide current, up-to-date information on search topics. In their efforts to provide information on more advanced topics, however, they forgot the most basic and important ones—like finding and replacing text.*

3 **Click the** → **Start searching button.**

Office Online finds results like "Find and replace South Asian characters,"but nothing that will simply help you replace "Acme" and "Apex" in your document. We have to look in the trusty, old Offline Help files for that. Figure 1-25 shows an example of an Office Online search result. Office Online finds results like "Find and replace South Asian," but nothing that will simply help you replace "Acme" with "Apex" in your document. We have to look in the trusty old Offline Help files for that. Figure 1-25 shows an example of an Office Online Search result.

≥ NOTE ≥ *Fortunately, you can change your settings to perform Help searches without Office Online. Go to the "See also" section at the bottom of the Word Help task pane. Click the Online Content Settings option. Uncheck the "Search online content when connected" option and click OK.*

4 **Click the** Search **list arrow in the Search area at the bottom of the task pane. Select** Offline Help **from the list and click the** → **Start searching button.**

The Offline Help search results appear, including a topic that actually helps us out.

5 **Click the** Find and replace text or other items **help topic.**

Another window appears with more.

6 **Click the** Replace text **help topic.**

Word displays information on how to replace text, as shown in Figure 1-26.

Notice that the Microsoft Office Word Help task pane has a toolbar that looks like some of the buttons you might have seen on a Web browser. This lets you navigate through various help topics just as if you were browsing the Web. See Table 1-7 for a description of the help buttons.

7 **Click the Microsoft Office Word Help task pane's** Close button **to close the window.**

The Help task pane closes.

Table 1-7. Help Buttons

Button	Description
⊞	Tiles the Word program window and the Help window so you can see both at the same time.
⇐	Moves back to the previous help topic.
⇒	Moves forward to the next help topic.
🖨	Prints the current help topic.

QUICK REFERENCE

TO GET HELP:

1. PRESS THE F1 KEY.

2. TYPE YOUR QUESTION IN THE SEARCH FOR: TEXT BOX AND CLICK THE START SEARCHING BUTTON OR PRESS ENTER.

3. CLICK THE HELP TOPIC THAT BEST MATCHES WHAT YOU'RE LOOKING FOR (REPEAT THIS STEP AS NECESSARY).

TO TURN OFF OFFICE ONLINE:

1. CLICK THE ONLINE CONTENT SETTINGS OPTION IN THE WORD HELP TASK PANE.

2. UNCHECK THE SEARCH ONLINE CONTENT WHEN CONNECTED OPTION AND CLICK OK.

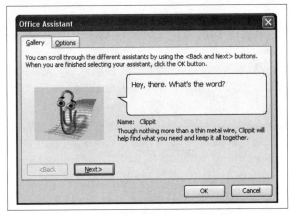

Figure 1-27. You can choose a new Office Assistant in the Office Assistant dialog box.

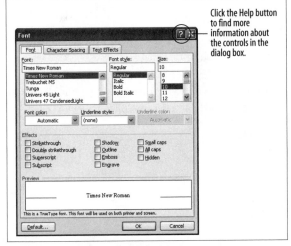

Click the Help button to find more information about the controls in the dialog box.

Figure 1-28. Click the Help button to view a brief description of the controls in a dialog box.

Figure 1-29. Click a link to find more information about the controls in the tab.

The Office Assistant is a cute animated character (a paper clip by default) that can answer your questions, offer tips, and provide help for all of Word's features. Many Word users don't use the Office Assistant, but it can be a very helpful tool. If you like using the Office Assistant but want a change of pace from Clippit's antics, you can choose one of eight different Office Assistants to guide you through Word. Of course, if you really hate the Office Assistant, you can always shut it off.

The other topic covered in this lesson is how to use the Help button. During your journey with Word, you will undoubtedly come across a dialog box or two with a number of confusing controls and options. To help you understand what the various controls and options in a dialog box are for, many dialog boxes contain a Help (**?**) button that explains the purpose of each of the dialog box's controls. This lesson will show you how to use the Help button, but first, let's start taming the Office Assistant.

1 Select Help → Show the Office Assistant from the menu.

The Office Assistant appears.

2 Right-click the Office Assistant and select Choose Assistant from the shortcut menu.

The Office Assistant dialog box appears, as shown in Figure 1-27.

3 Click the Back or Next button to see the available Office Assistants.

The Office Assistant you select is completely up to you. They all work the same—they just look and act different.

4 Click OK when you find an Office Assistant you like.

If you find the Office Assistant annoying (as many people do) and want to get rid of it altogether, here's how:

5 Right-click the Office Assistant.

A shortcut menu appears.

6 Select Hide from the shortcut menu.

You can always bring the Office Assistant back whenever you need its help.

Now, let's move on to how to use the Help button to discover the purpose of confusing dialog box controls.

7 Select Format → Font from the menu.

The Font dialog box appears, as shown in Figure 1-28. Notice the Help button located in the dialog box's title bar just to the left of the dialog box's close button.

8 Click the ？ Help button.

A Microsoft Office Word Help window appears, as shown in Figure 1-29.

9 Click the Font tab link.

A brief description of all the controls in the Font tab of the dialog box appears.

10 Click the Close button to close the Microsoft Office Word Help task pane. Click Cancel to close the Font dialog box.

QUICK REFERENCE

TO CHANGE OFFICE ASSISTANTS:

1. IF NECESSARY, SELECT HELP → SHOW THE OFFICE ASSISTANT FROM THE MENU.

2. RIGHT-CLICK THE OFFICE ASSISTANT AND SELECT CHOOSE ASSISTANT FROM THE SHORTCUT MENU.

3. CLICK THE NEXT OR BACK BUTTONS UNTIL YOU FIND AN OFFICE ASSISTANT YOU LIKE, THEN CLICK OK.

TO HIDE THE OFFICE ASSISTANT:

- RIGHT-CLICK THE OFFICE ASSISTANT AND SELECT HIDE FROM THE SHORTCUT MENU.

TO SEE WHAT A CONTROL IN A DIALOG BOX DOES:

1. CLICK THE DIALOG BOX HELP BUTTON (LOCATED RIGHT NEXT TO THE CLOSE BUTTON).

2. FIND THE CONTROL DESCRIPTION IN THE MICROSOFT OFFICE WORD HELP WINDOW.

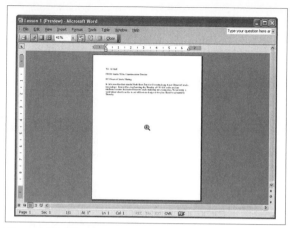

Figure 1-30. The Print Preview screen.

If you've been following the previous lessons in this book and aren't skipping ahead, you should know how to create, edit, and save a document. In this lesson, we're going to cover a lot of topics—previewing and printing a document, and exiting the Microsoft Word program—so get ready!

Once you have created a document, you can create a printed copy of it (if your computer is connected to a printer). Before you print a document, however, it's usually a good idea to preview it onscreen. You can preview a document by using Word's Print Preview feature.

1 Click the Print Preview button **on the Standard toolbar.**

> TIP *Another way to preview is to select* File → Print Preview *from the menu.*

Your document will be previewed on the screen, as shown in Figure 1-30. The preview looks fine, so you can move on to the next step to print your document.

2 Click the Print button **on the Print Preview toolbar.**

> TIP *Another way to print is to press* Ctrl + P *or select* File → Print *from the menu.*

The document is sent to the default printer connected to your computer.

3 Click the Close button **on the Print Preview toolbar.**

You return to the document where you can make any changes to the document.

You've finished both this lesson and the chapter, so move on to the next step to exit, or close, the Word program.

4 Click the Close button **on the Microsoft Word Title Bar.**

> TIP *Another way to exit Word is to select* File → Exit *from the menu.*

There are two close buttons on your screen—make sure you click the top Close button, located in the upper-right hand corner of the screen, to close Word. The Close button located underneath Word's Title Bar would close the document you are working on, not the Word program.

5 If a dialog box appears asking if you want to save changes to "First Day's Memo," click No.

The Word program closes and you should be back at the Windows desktop.

That's it! You are well on your way towards mastering Microsoft Word. You've already learned some very important things: how to start Word; how to create, preview, print, and save a document; how to get Help; and how to select, edit, insert, and delete text. You will use these skills regularly in your career with Microsoft Word.

QUICK REFERENCE

TO PREVIEW A DOCUMENT ONSCREEN:

- CLICK THE PRINT PREVIEW BUTTON ON THE STANDARD TOOLBAR.

OR...

- SELECT FILE → PRINT PREVIEW FROM THE MENU.

TO PRINT A DOCUMENT:

- CLICK THE PRINT BUTTON ON THE STANDARD TOOLBAR.

OR...

- SELECT FILE → PRINT FROM THE MENU.

OR...

- PRESS CTRL + P.

TO EXIT MICROSOFT WORD:

- CLICK THE WORD PROGRAM CLOSE BUTTON.

OR...

- SELECT FILE → EXIT FROM THE MENU.

Chapter One Review

Lesson Summary

Starting Word

Start Word by clicking the Start button and selecting All programs → Microsoft Office 2003 → Microsoft Office Word 2003 from the menu.

Understanding the Word Screen

Be able to identify the main components of the Word program screen.

Using Menus

To Use a Menu: Either click the menu name with the mouse pointer or press the Alt key and the letter that is underlined in the menu name.

Word 2003's personalized menus hide uncommon commands from view. To display a menu's hidden commands, click the downward-pointing arrow ⌄ at the bottom of the menu, or open the menu and wait a few seconds.

To Change How Menus Work: Select View → Toolbars → Customize from the menu, check or clear either the Always show full menus and/or Show full menus after a short delay options, then click Close.

Using Toolbars and Creating a New Document

To Use Word's Toolbars: Simply click the toolbar button you want to use. Leave the pointer over the button to display a screen tip of what the button does.

To Stack the Standard and Formatting toolbars in Two Separate Rows: Click the button on either toolbar and select Show Buttons on Two Rows from the list.

To Create a New Document: Click the New Blank Document button on the Standard toolbar or select File → New from the menu.

Filling Out Dialog Boxes

Be able to identify and use text boxes, list boxes, drop-down lists, check boxes, and sheet tabs.

Keystroke and Right Mouse Button Shortcuts

Keystroke shortcuts: Press Ctrl and the letter that corresponds to the shortcut command at the same time.

Right mouse button shortcut menus: Whenever you're unsure or curious about what you can do with an object, click it with the right mouse button to display a list of commands related to the object.

Closing a Document, Creating a New Document, and Entering Text

To Close a Document: Click the document window Close button or select File → Close from the menu.

To Create a New Document: Click the New Blank Document button on the Standard toolbar or select File → New from the menu, select Blank Document and click OK.

Inserting and Deleting Text

Moving the insertion point with the mouse: Click where you want to place the insertion point with the I pointer.

Moving the insertion point with the keyboard: Move the insertion point by pressing the keyboard arrow key that corresponds to the direction you want to move.

Insert text by using the keyboard arrow keys or the mouse to position the insertion point where you want to insert the text, and then begin typing.

The Backspace key deletes text before, or to the left of, the insertion point.

The Delete key deletes text after, or to the right of, the insertion point.

Selecting and Replacing Text

To Select Text: Move the insertion point to the beginning or end of the text you want to select, then click and hold the left mouse button and drag the insertion point across the text. Release the mouse button once the text is selected.

To Select Multiple Blocks of Text: Select the first block of text, then hold down the Ctrl key as you select the remaining block(s) of text.

To Replace Text: Replace text by selecting it and typing the new text.

Opening a Document

To Open a Document: Click the Open button on the Standard toolbar, or select File → Open from the menu, or press Ctrl + O.

Saving a Document

To Save a Document: Click the Save button on the Standard toolbar, or select File → Save from the menu, or press Ctrl + S.

To Save a Document in a New File with a Different Name: Select File → Save As from the menu, type a new name for the document, and click Save.

Getting Help from the Office Assistant

You can ask the Office Assistant (the cute animated character) your questions in conversational English. This is the easiest and most common method of getting help.

Press F1 to open the Office Assistant, type your question in normal English, and click the Start Searching button.

Changing the Office Assistant and Using the Help Button

To Change Office Assistants: If necessary, select Help → Show the Office Assistant from the menu. Right-click the Office Assistant and select Choose Assistant from the shortcut menu. Click the Next or Back buttons until you find an Office Assistant that you like, then click OK.

To Hide the Office Assistant: Right-click the Office Assistant and select Hide from the shortcut menu.

To See what a Control in a Dialog Box Does: Click the Dialog box Help button (located right next to the close button) and click the control you want more information on with the ▶? pointer.

Printing and Previewing a Document and Exiting Word

To Preview a Document on Screen: Click the Print Preview button on the Standard toolbar or select File → Print Preview from the menu.

To Print a Document: Click the Print button on the Standard toolbar, or select File → Print from the menu, or press Ctrl + P.

To Exit Microsoft Word: Click the Word Program Close button or select File → Exit from the menu.

Quiz

1. Right-clicking something in Word:
   A. Deletes the object.
   B. Opens a shortcut menu listing everything you can do to the object.
   C. Selects the object.
   D. Nothing—the right mouse button is there for left-handed people.

2. What keystroke combination selects the entire document?
   A. Alt + A.
   B. Shift + Ctrl + A.
   C. Ctrl + A.
   D. Alt + F8.

3. Which key deletes text behind, or to the left of, the insertion point?
   A. Page Up.
   B. Page Down.
   C. Delete.
   D. Backspace.

4. What is the fastest way to select a single word?
   A. Drag the pointer across the word using the mouse.
   B. Move the insertion point to the beginning of the word and hold down the Shift key as you use the arrow keys to highlight the word.
   C. Click the Select Word Wizard button on the toolbar and follow the on-screen instructions.
   D. Double-click the word.

5. Once a block of text is selected, you can replace the selected text with new text by:

   A. Simply typing the new text.

   B. Selecting File → Insert New Text from the menu.

   C. You can't replace selected text with new text.

   D. Clicking the Replace Text button on the Standard toolbar.

6. Which of the following are ways to save the current document? (Select all that apply.)

   A. Press Ctrl + S.

   B. Select File → Save from the menu.

   C. Click the Save button on the Standard toolbar.

   D. Click Save on the Windows Start button.

7. You can display how a document will look when it's printed onscreen by:

   A. Clicking the Print Preview button on the Standard toolbar.

   B. Selecting File → View Onscreen from the menu.

   C. Selecting View → WYSIWYG from the menu.

   D. Word is unable to display how documents will look when printed onscreen.

8. You want to manually spell check a document. You open the Tools menu but can't find the Spelling and Grammar command. What's wrong?

   A. The Spelling and Grammar command is in the Edit menu, silly!

   B. You need to display all the options in the Tools menu by clicking the downward-pointing arrow at the bottom of the menu.

   C. There isn't a Spelling and Grammar command.

   D. You need to display all the options in the Tools menu by pressing F2.

9. The fastest, easiest way you can get help in Word is by:

   A. Asking the Office Assistant your question in ordinary English.

   B. Reading the manual that came with the program.

   C. Spending your day on the phone with Microsoft Technical Support.

   D. Taking several classes on Word at your local technical college.

10. Office Online is: (Select all that apply.)

    A. A Microsoft service designed to provide current, up-to-date information on help topics.

    B. Not always a good substitute for the traditional offline help files that are installed with the program.

    C. A function that cannot be changed: you must always use this feature when looking for help.

    D. Another version of the Microsoft Office Suite.

11. What key can you press to get help in any Windows-based program?

    A. F12.

    B. Esc.

    C. Scroll Lock.

    D. F1.

Homework

1. Start Microsoft Word, open the Homework 7 document and save it as "Paper Games."

2. Go to Page 2. Click the Oval button on the Drawing toolbar. Position the pointer in the upper-left corner of the middle box, press and hold the Shift, and then drag down and to the right to create a circle that is the same size as the circle below it.

3. Click the Fill Color list arrow on the Drawing toolbar and select No Fill.

4. Go to Page 3. Select the yellowish rectangle, click the 3-D button on the Drawing toolbar, and select the first option.

5. Select all of the hangman objects (hold down the Shift key as you click each object or click or drag a

rectangle around the objects). Click the Draw menu button on the Drawing toolbar and select Group.

6. Select Insert → Picture → Clip Art from the menu. Search for a person for the hangman, and insert it in the document. Then close the Clip Art task pane.

7. Click the clip art picture to select it. Select Format → Picture from the menu. From the Layout tab, select Behind text and click OK.

8. Drag any of the cartoon's sizing handles until the figure is small enough to fit under the gallows.

9. Click and drag the cartoon figure under the gallows.

10. 1Save your work and exit Microsoft Word.

Quiz Answers

1. C. Of course you can format a text box's text!

2. B and D. Either of these methods will select multiple objects.

3. A, B, and C. You can format drawing objects using any of these methods.

4. False. You will have to summon the Picture toolbar to accomplish these tasks.

5. C. AutoShape categories.

6. False. Of course not! What a silly question!

7. B. Grouping all those ants will make them easier to work with.

8. C. That yellow diamond is the adjustment handle and is used to change an AutoShape's most prominent feature or angle.

9. A. You can ask the Office Assistant for help in everyday English. The other methods require a lot of scrolling, clicking, and selecting the appropriate help topic.

10. A and B. Office Online is a Microsoft service that provides current, up-to-date information on help topics, but it isn't always a good substitute for the traditional help files installed with the program.

11. D. The <F1> key brings up help in every Windows program.

CHAPTER 2
WORKING WITH AND EDITING TEXT

CHAPTER OBJECTIVES:

Opening a document and giving it a different name, Lesson 2.1

Understanding how to move through a document, Lesson 2.2

Viewing a document in different modes, Lessons 2.3 and 2.4

Cutting, copying, and pasting text, Lessons 2.5–2.7 and 2.9

Finding and replacing text, Lesson 2.8

Using spell checking, the thesaurus, and word count, Lessons 2.10 and 2.12

Understanding Smart tags, Lesson 2.11

Inserting special characters

Using undo, redo, and repeat, Lesson 2.14

Specifying which pages to print or printing multiple document copies, Lesson 2.17

Recovering your documents, Lesson 2.18

CHAPTER TASK: REVISE A SAVED MEMO

Prerequisites

- **How to start Word.**
- **How to use menus, toolbars, dialog boxes, and shortcut keystrokes.**
- **How to open and save a document.**

Now that you have the Microsoft Word basics down, this chapter will show you how to become a sophisticated Word user. This chapter explains many basic operations, such as how to open a document and save it under a different name; how to move around in a document; how to cut, copy and paste text; how to undo any mistakes you might have made; and how to correct spelling errors.

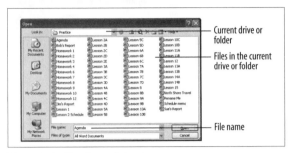

Current drive or folder

Files in the current drive or folder

File name

Figure 2-1. The Open dialog box.

You can save a lot of time and energy by using the text from an existing document to create a new document. Saving an existing document under a new name does just this. In this lesson, you will save an existing file named "Lesson 2A" as a new file named "Canada Meeting Memo."

1 Start the Microsoft Word program.

You learned how to start Word in the previous chapter.

2 Click the Open button on the Standard toolbar.

> TIP
> *Another way to open a document is to select File → Open from the menu or press Ctrl + O.*

The Open dialog box appears, as shown in Figure 2-1.

3 Navigate to and open your Practice folder.

Your computer stores information in files and folders, just like you store information in a filing cabinet. To open a file, you must first find and open the folder where it's saved. Microsoft Word normally saves new documents to a folder named "My Documents," but sometimes you will want to save or open documents in another folder.

Word's Open and Save dialog boxes both have their own toolbars that make it easy to browse through your computer's drives and folders. Two controls on this toolbar are particularly helpful:

- **Look In List:** Click to list the drives on your computer and the current folder, then select the drive and/or folder with the contents you want to display.

- **Up One Level button:** Click to move up one folder.

4 Click the document named Lesson 2A in the file list box and click Open.

> TIP
> *You can double-click a file name in the Open dialog box instead of selecting the file name and clicking Open.*

The Lesson 2A document opens and appears in Word's document window. You want to use the text from this document to create a new document. Since you don't want to make any changes to the Lesson 2A document, save it with a different name.

5 Select File → Save As from the menu.

The Save As dialog box appears. File → Save As lets you save a document in a new file under a different name.

6 In the File name text box, type Canada Meeting Memo and click Save.

The Lesson 2A document is saved in a new file, "Canada Meeting Memo," and the original Lesson 2A document closes. Now you can work on the new document, Canada Meeting Memo, without changing the original Lesson 2A document.

One important note about this document: if you're an English teacher, or just detail-oriented, you've probably already noticed it contains several spelling and grammatical errors. These errors should be obvious—Word highlights them with red and green underlining. Don't worry about these errors; we'll be fixing them later on in the chapter with Word's spell checker.

QUICK REFERENCE

TO OPEN A DOCUMENT:

- CLICK THE OPEN BUTTON ON THE STANDARD TOOLBAR.

OR...

- SELECT FILE → OPEN FROM THE MENU.

OR...

- PRESS CTRL + O.

Navigating through a Document

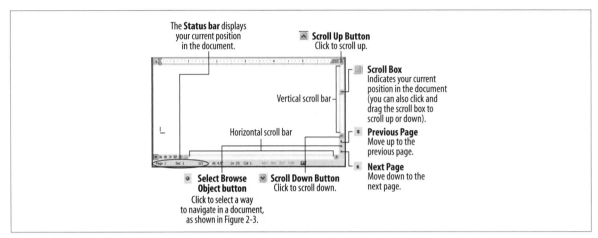

Figure 2-2. Use the scroll bars to move from place to place in a document.

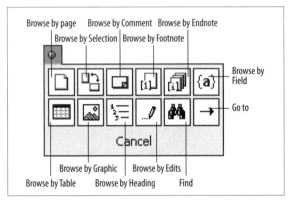

Figure 2-3. Use the Select Browse Object button to navigate a document.

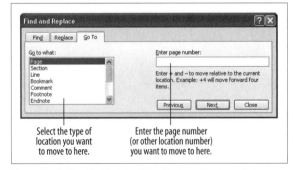

Figure 2-4. The Go To tab of the Find and Replace dialog box.

As a document gets longer, it gets harder and harder to navigate through it. For example, if you were working on a 200-page novel, how would you get to the very end of the document or to page 54? This lesson will show you how to move through a Word document.

1 **Open the document named** Lesson 10A.

This document is several pages long, so it will be great for learning how to move around in a document. Don't worry—the "Canada Meeting Memo" document is still there, it's just hidden behind the Lesson 10A document. We'll return to the "Canada Meeting Memo" document in the next lesson.

One way to get around in a document is by using Word's scroll bars. The *vertical scroll bar* is located along the right side of the window and is used to move up and down in a document. The *horizontal scroll bar* is located along the bottom of the window, and is used to move from left to right when a document doesn't fit entirely on the screen. Figure 2-2 shows both of these scroll bars.

2 **Click the scroll down button on the bottom of the vertical scroll bar several times.**

When you click the arrow, the screen scrolls down one line at a time.

3 **Click and hold the scroll down button.**

This causes the screen to move downward more rapidly.

4 **Click and drag the vertical** scroll box **to the top of the scroll bar.**

This takes you back to the beginning of the document.

5 Press the End key.

The insertion point moves to the end of the current line.

6 Press the Home key.

The insertion point moves to the beginning of the current line.

7 Press Ctrl + End.

The insertion point moves to the end of the document. Notice that the vertical scroll box appears near the end of the scroll bar, indicating your position in the document. You can also find your position in a document by looking at the status bar at the bottom of the screen—it states the page you're currently on.

8 Press the Page Up key to move up one screen.

9 Press the Page Down key to move down one screen.

10 Press Ctrl + Home to jump to the beginning of the document.

You can also move directly to a certain page number in a document. See Table 2-1 for a reminder of these helpful shortcuts.

 TIP Another way to navigate a document is by using the Select Browse Object button, as shown in Figure 2-3.

11 Select Edit → Go To from the menu.

 TIP Another way to open the Find and Replace dialog box is to press F5.

The Find and Replace dialog box appears with the Go To tab in front, as shown in Figure 2-4. Here you can jump to a particular page in a document. You can use the "Go To" command to jump to specific bookmarks, sections, and lines, concepts you will learn more about later on.

12 In the "Enter page number" box, type 3 and click Go To.

Word jumps to the third page in the document.

13 Click Close to close the Find and Replace dialog box, then close the Lesson 10A document by selecting File → Close from the menu or by clicking the document's Close button.

Table 2-1. Keyboard Shortcuts for Moving Around in a Document

Press	To Move
Home	To the start of the line.
End	To the end of the line.
Page Up	Up one screen.
Page Down	Down one screen.
Ctrl + Home	To the beginning of the document.
Ctrl + End	To the end of the document.

QUICK REFERENCE

TO MOVE TO THE BEGINNING OR END OF A LINE:

- PRESS HOME TO MOVE TO THE BEGINNING OF A LINE.
- PRESS END TO MOVE TO THE END OF A LINE.

TO MOVE UP OR DOWN ONE SCREEN:

- PRESS PAGE UP TO MOVE UP ONE SCREEN.
- PRESS PAGE DOWN TO MOVE DOWN ONE SCREEN.

TO MOVE TO THE BEGINNING OR END OF A DOCUMENT:

- PRESS CTRL + HOME TO MOVE TO THE BEGINNING OF THE DOCUMENT.
- PRESS CTRL + END TO MOVE TO THE END OF THE DOCUMENT.

TO JUMP TO A SPECIFIC PAGE IN A DOCUMENT:

1. SELECT EDIT → GO TO FROM THE MENU.
2. VERIFY THAT "PAGE" IS SELECTED IN THE "GO TO WHAT" BOX, TYPE THE PAGE NUMBER IN THE "ENTER PAGE NUMBER" TEXT BOX, AND CLICK GO TO.

Viewing a Document

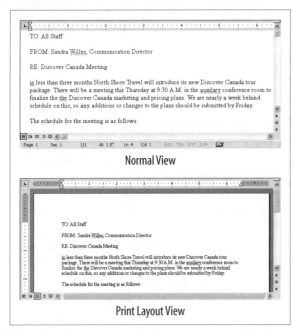
Normal View

Print Layout View

Figure 2-5. The same document in both Normal view and Print Layout view.

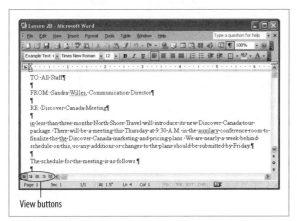
View buttons

Figure 2-6. Displaying hidden characters in a document and document view buttons.

Word can create a variety of different types of documents: letters, brochures, and flyers—even Web pages! When you work on various types of documents, you may find that you need to change how you view the document on the screen. Word offers several different ways to view the computer screen:

- **Normal View:** This view is good for most simple word-processing tasks, such as typing, editing, and formatting. This view does not display advanced formatting, such as page boundaries, headers and footers, or floating pictures.

- **Web Layout View:** You will work in Web Layout view when you are creating a Web page or a document that is viewed on the Web. In Web Layout view, you can see backgrounds, text is wrapped to fit inside the window, and graphics are positioned just as they are in a Web browser.

- **Print Layout View:** This view displays your document as it will appear when printed and is best for working in documents with images. Print Layout view uses more memory and can be slower on older computers. Figure 2-5 shows how Print Layout view differs from Normal view.

- **Outline View:** Displays your document in classic outline form. Work in Outline view when you need to organize and develop the content of your document.

- **Reading Layout:** This view is optimized for reading. Only necessary toolbars appear, making room for enlarged text and navigational tools.

In this lesson, you will learn how to use these view modes; zoom in or out of a document; and display characters you normally don't see, such as spaces, paragraph marks, and tabs.

If you closed the "Lesson 10A" document in the previous lesson, you should be looking at the "Canada Meeting Memo" document—the document you'll use for this lesson.

1 If necessary, find and open Lesson 2A from your Practice folder and save it as Canada Meeting Memo.

The first view we'll see is Normal view.

2 Click the Normal View button, located on the Horizontal scroll bar, as shown in Figure 2-6.

TIP *Another way to switch to Normal view is to select* View → Normal *from the menu.*

The document window changes to Normal view. Normal view optimizes the layout of a document to make it easier to read on the screen.

3 Click the Outline View button on the Horizontal scroll bar.

TIP *Another way to switch to Outline view is to select* View → Outline *from the menu.*

The document changes to a rather confusing-looking Outline view. Outline view is useful for creating outlines and long documents. It shows the headings of a document indented to represent its level in the document's structure. Outline view makes it easy to move quickly through a document, change the relative importance of headings, and rearrange large amounts of text by moving headings. We'll discuss how to actually use Outline view in an upcoming chapter.

4 Click the Reading Layout button on the Horizontal scroll bar.

The document changes to Reading Layout view. This view is great for when you are required to do a lot of reading in Word. The use of window space is maximized so that only necessary toolbars are shown, and the text is larger, making it very easy to read.

5 Select View → Print Layout from the menu.

Another way to switch to Print Layout View is to click the Print Layout button on the Horizontal scroll bar.

The document window changes to Print Layout view. Print Layout view displays your document as it will appear when you print it. Computer gurus sometimes refer to Print Layout view as a WYSIWYG view (pronounced Whiz-E-Wig and stands for What You See Is What You Get). Print Layout view is probably the best view to use when working on documents, especially if your computer has a large monitor and high (800 x 600 pixels or better) resolution.

Sometimes it is useful to see characters that are normally hidden, such as spaces, tabs, and returns.

6 Click the ¶ Show/Hide button on the Standard toolbar.

The hidden characters, or characters that normally don't print, appear in the document. Paragraph marks appears as ¶'s, tabs appear as → 's, and spaces appear as ♦'s. Notice the Show/Hide button on the Standard toolbar is highlighted orange, indicating that all the hidden characters in the document are visible.

7 Click the Show/Hide button on the Standard toolbar.

The hidden characters disappear. They're still there—you just can't see them.

Sometimes it is helpful to make a document appear larger on the computer's screen, especially if you have a small monitor or poor eyesight.

8 Click the 100% Zoom list arrow on the Standard toolbar and select 100%.

The document appears onscreen at a magnification level of 100%.

9 Click the Zoom list arrow on the Standard toolbar and select Page Width.

The document zooms out to a level optimal for viewing the page width of the document. This zoom level is an ideal setting for working with documents if you are working with a high resolution (800 x 600 pixels or better) and/or a large monitor.

You can also view a document in full screen mode, dedicating 100% of the screen to viewing the document.

10 Select View → Full Screen from the menu.

All the familiar title bars, menus, and toolbars disappear and the document appears in full screen mode. Full screen mode is useful if you want to view your document as a sheet of paper onscreen, but the disadvantage is that the Word tools—the toolbars and status bar—are not readily available. You can still access the menus, even though you can no longer see them, by clicking the mouse at the very top of the screen.

11 Click the Close Full Screen button floating over the document.

The full screen view closes and you are returned to the previous view.

QUICK REFERENCE

TO SWITCH BETWEEN VIEWS:

- CLICK THE VIEW BUTTON ON THE HORIZONTAL SCROLL BAR FOR THE VIEW YOU WANT.

OR...

- SELECT VIEW FROM THE MENU BAR AND SELECT THE VIEW YOU WANT.

TO DISPLAY/HIDE HIDDEN CHARACTERS (TABS, SPACES, AND PARAGRAPH MARKS):

- CLICK THE SHOW/HIDE BUTTON ON THE STANDARD TOOLBAR.

TO CHANGE THE ZOOM LEVEL OF A DOCUMENT:

- SELECT THE ZOOM LEVEL FROM THE ZOOM LIST ON THE STANDARD TOOLBAR.

OR...

- SELECT VIEW → ZOOM FROM THE MENU, SELECT THE ZOOM LEVEL YOU WANT, AND CLICK OK.

TO VIEW A DOCUMENT IN FULL SCREEN MODE:

- SELECT VIEW → FULL SCREEN FROM THE MENU.

Working with Multiple Documents and Windows

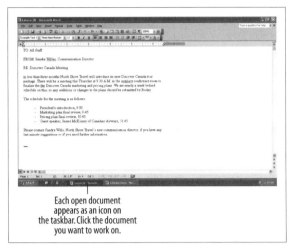

Each open document
appears as an icon on
the taskbar. Click the document
you want to work on.

Figure 2-7. Multiple documents appear as icons on the Windows taskbar.

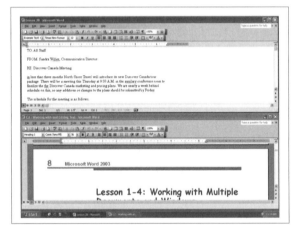

Figure 2-8. Displaying two documents at the same time.

One of the many benefits of Word is that you can open and work with several document files at the same time. Each document you open in Word has its own window. This lesson explains how to open and work with more than one document. You will also learn some tricks on changing the size of a window, moving a window, and arranging a window.

1 Click the Open button on the Standard toolbar, then find and open the Lesson 2 Schedule file in your Practice folder.

The Lesson 2 Schedule document appears, but where did the Canada Meeting Memo document go? Don't worry; it's still there in a window behind the Lesson 2 Schedule document. Each open document appears as

an icon on the Windows taskbar, as shown in Figure 2-7. To switch to a different document, click its icon on the taskbar.

2 Click the Canada Meeting Memo button on the Windows taskbar.

The Canada Meeting Memo document appears. The Lesson 2 Schedule document is still open, but you can't see it because it is located behind the Canada Meeting Memo document window.

Sometimes it can be helpful to view two or more documents onscreen at the same time.

3 Select Window → Arrange All from the menu.

Both documents—Lesson 2 Schedule and Canada Meeting Memo—appear in the program window, similar to Figure 2-8. Notice how the title bar of the Canada Meeting Memo window is darker than the title bar of the Lesson 2 Schedule window? That's because the Canada Meeting Memo window is *active*, meaning it's the window or document you're currently working on. The other window, Lesson 2 Schedule, is currently inactive.

4 Click anywhere in the Lesson 2 Schedule window.

The Lesson 2 Schedule window becomes active and the Canada Meeting Memo becomes inactive.

To make working with several programs at once easier, you can change the size of the windows. You can *maximize* or enlarge a window so it takes up the document window.

5 Click the 🔲 Maximize button in the Lesson 2 Schedule window's title bar.

The Lesson 2 Schedule window maximizes, filling the entire document window. You can change a maximized window back to its original size by clicking the Restore button. The Restore button replaces the Maximize button whenever a window is already maximized.

6 Click the 🗗 Restore button in the Lesson 2 Schedule window's title bar to restore the Lesson 2 Schedule window to its previous size.

The window returns to its previous size.

Besides Maximizing and Restoring a window, you can also manually fine-tune a window's size to meet your own specific needs. A window must not be in a maximized state if you want to manually size it.

7 Position the mouse pointer over the bottom edge of the Lesson 2 Schedule window, until it changes to a ↕.

NOTE: *The mouse is very picky about where you place the pointer, and it can sometimes be a little tricky finding the exact spot where the pointer changes.*

8 While the ↕ pointer is still over the bottom edge of the window, click and hold down the mouse button, drag the mouse down a half-inch to move the window border, and then release the mouse button.

Notice the window border follows as you drag the mouse. When the window is the size you want, you can release the mouse button to resize the window. You resized the window by adjusting the bottom edge of the window, but you can also adjust the left, right, and top edges of the window.

Sometimes, when you have more than one window open at the same time, you may find that one window covers another window or other items on your screen. When this happens, you can simply move a window to a new location on the screen—just like you would move a report or folder to a new location on your desk.

9 Click and drag the title bar of the Lesson 2 Schedule window to a new location on the screen. Release the mouse button to drop the window.

Remember that the title bar is at the top of the window or program, and displays the name of the program or window. An outline of the window follows your mouse as you drag the window, showing you where you are moving it.

10 Click the Maximize button in the Lesson 2 Schedule window's title bar.

QUICK REFERENCE

TO SWITCH BETWEEN MULTIPLE OPEN DOCUMENTS:

• CLICK THE DOCUMENT ON THE WINDOWS TASKBAR.

OR...

• SELECT WINDOW AND SELECT THE NAME OF THE DOCUMENT YOU WANT TO VIEW.

TO VIEW MULTIPLE WINDOWS AT THE SAME TIME:

• SELECT WINDOW → ARRANGE ALL.

TO MAXIMIZE A WINDOW:

• CLICK THE WINDOW'S MAXIMIZE BUTTON.

TO RESTORE A WINDOW:

• CLICK THE WINDOW'S RESTORE BUTTON.

TO MANUALLY RESIZE A WINDOW:

1. POSITION THE MOUSE POINTER OVER THE EDGE OF THE WINDOW.

2. HOLD DOWN THE MOUSE BUTTON AND DRAG THE MOUSE TO RESIZE THE WINDOW.

3. RELEASE THE MOUSE BUTTON.

TO MOVE A WINDOW:

• DRAG THE WINDOW'S TITLE BAR TO THE LOCATION WHERE YOU WANT TO POSITION THE WINDOW.

Cutting and Pasting Text

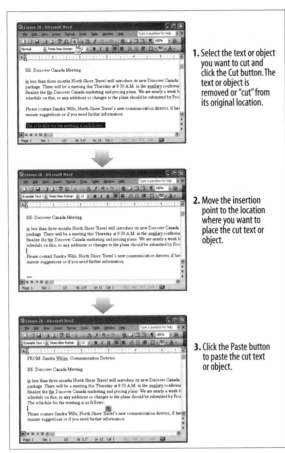

1. Select the text or object you want to cut and click the Cut button. The text or object is removed or "cut" from its original location.

2. Move the insertion point to the location where you want to place the cut text or object.

3. Click the Paste button to paste the cut text or object.

Figure 2-9. The steps involved in cutting and pasting text.

By now, you should know how to select text in a document. Once you have selected text, you can move it to another place in the document by cutting and then pasting it elsewhere. Cutting and pasting text is one of the most common tasks you're likely to do when you use Word. When you cut text, it is removed from its original location and placed in a temporary storage area called the *Clipboard*. You can then move the insertion point to a new location in a document and paste the cut text from the Clipboard. The steps involved in cutting and pasting text are shown in Figure 2-9 and outlined in Steps 1–3. The Clipboard is available in any Windows program, so you can cut and paste text between various software programs.

1 **Select** Window → Canada Meeting Memo **from the menu.**

 Another way to switch between open windows is to click the window's document icon on the Windows taskbar.

The Canada Meeting Memo document appears.

2 **Select the line** The schedule for the meeting is as follows:

3 **Click the** Cut button **on the Standard toolbar.**

Other Ways to Cut:

 Another way to cut is to press Ctrl + X, or select Edit → Cut from the menu, or click the right-mouse button and select Cut from the shortcut menu.

The selected text is cut, or removed, from the document and placed on the *Windows Clipboard*. The Windows Clipboard holds any cut or copied text. Once you have cut some text from a document, you can paste it elsewhere.

4 **Move the insertion point to the very beginning of the second paragraph.**

This is where you want to paste the previously cut text.

5 **Click the** Paste button **on the Standard toolbar.**

Another way to paste is to press Ctrl + V or select Edit → Paste from the menu or click the right-mouse button and select Paste from the shortcut menu.

The cut text is inserted. Now let's add some blank lines after the inserted text.

6 **Press** Enter **twice to add two blank lines beneath the inserted text.**

You can also cut and paste text between two documents. So instead of retyping the President's schedule, you can simply cut and paste it.

7 Select Window → Lesson 2 Schedule from the menu.

8 Select the four lines of the schedule, beginning with President's introduction, 9:30.

9 Click the Cut button on the Standard toolbar to cut these lines from the document.

The schedule is cut from the document, Lesson 2 Schedule, and placed on the Clipboard. Next, you will paste the schedule into the Canada Meeting Memo document.

10 Select Window → Canada Meeting Menu from the menu.

11 Make sure the insertion point is still located one line below The schedule for the meeting is as follows:

Make sure you leave a blank line between the "The schedule for the meeting is as follows:" line and the insertion point.

12 Click the Paste button on the Standard toolbar to paste the schedule into the document.

The schedule is pasted at the insertion point.

13 Save the document by clicking the Save button on the Standard toolbar.

Now that you know how to cut and paste text, you should be able to breeze through the next lesson: copying and pasting text.

QUICK REFERENCE

TO CUT SOMETHING:

1. SELECT THE TEXT OR OBJECT YOU WANT TO CUT.

2. CLICK THE CUT BUTTON ON THE STANDARD TOOLBAR.

   OR...

   SELECT EDIT → CUT FROM THE MENU.

   OR...

   PRESS CTRL + X.

TO PASTE A CLIPBOARD ITEM:

1. PLACE THE INSERTION POINT WHERE YOU WANT TO PASTE THE TEXT OR OBJECT.

2. CLICK THE PASTE BUTTON ON THE STANDARD TOOLBAR.

   OR...

   SELECT EDIT → PASTE FROM THE MENU.

   OR...

   PRESS CTRL + V.

Copying and Pasting Text and Comparing Documents Side by Side

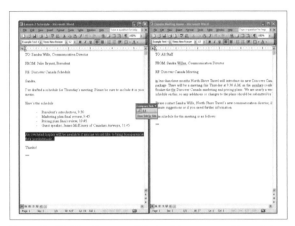

Figure 2-10. The Compare Side by Side command is useful when working with two documents.

Copying text is very similar to cutting and pasting text, except that you are duplicating the selected text instead of moving it. Copying text can save you a lot of time when you create documents—you can easily copy a paragraph from one document and then paste it into another one without having to retype it. You will practice working with multiple documents in this lesson.

You'll also learn about a new way to arrange windows: comparing them side by side.

1 If necessary, navigate to your Practice folder and open Lesson 2B. **Save the file as** Canada Meeting Memo. **Navigate to your Practice folder and open** Lesson 2 Schedule **as well.**

2 Select Window → Compare side by side with **from the menu.**

The two documents—Lesson 2 Schedule and Canada Meeting Memo—appear side by side in the program window, as shown in Figure 2-10.

3 Click anywhere in the Lesson 2 Schedule **window.**

The Lesson 2 Schedule window becomes active and the Canada Meeting Memo becomes inactive.

4 Select the entire sentence that begins with An overhead display will be available.

You may have to scroll the Lesson 2 Schedule document up or down to find the sentence.

5 Click the Copy button **on the Standard toolbar.**

TIP *Another way to copy is to press* Ctrl + C, *or select* Edit → Copy *from the menu, or click the right-mouse button and select* Copy *from the shortcut menu.*

Nothing appears to change, but the selected sentence has been copied to the Clipboard.

6 Click anywhere in the Canada Meeting Memo **to make it active.**

You need to place the insertion point where you want to paste the copied text.

7 Move the insertion point to the blank line at the very end of the document, about two lines beneath the last text in the document.

Okay! We're ready to paste the copied text.

8 Click the Paste button **on the Standard toolbar.**

TIP *Another way to paste is to press* Ctrl + V, *or select* Edit → Paste *from the menu, or click the right-mouse button and select* Paste *from the shortcut menu.*

The copied text is inserted. You won't need the Lesson 2 Schedule document anymore, so you can close it. But first, close the side by side command.

9 Click the Close Side by Side button **on the Compare Side by Side toolbar.**

The windows are back to their original size.

10 Activate the Lesson 2 Schedule window, and then select File → Close from the menu or else click the window's Close button.

You want to close the document without saving any of the changes you've made to it.

11 If a dialog box asks if you want to save your changes, click No to close the Lesson 2 Schedule document without saving any changes.

Maximize the Canada Meeting Memo window so it fills the entire document window.

12 Click the Canada Meeting Memo's Maximize button to maximize the window.

If the document appears empty at first, you'll have to scroll up or down until you see the document's text.

13 Save the document by clicking the Save button on the Standard toolbar.

You can also copy, cut, and paste text between two different Windows programs—for example, you could copy a name from a Word document and paste it into an Excel spreadsheet. The cut, copy, and paste commands you learned in Word (the toolbar buttons, menus, and/or keyboard shortcuts) will work with most Windows applications.

QUICK REFERENCE

TO COPY SOMETHING:

1. SELECT THE TEXT OR OBJECT YOU WANT TO COPY.

2. CLICK THE COPY BUTTON ON THE STANDARD TOOLBAR.

   OR...

   SELECT EDIT → COPY FROM THE MENU.

   OR...

   PRESS CTRL + C.

TO PASTE A CLIPBOARD ITEM:

1. PLACE THE INSERTION POINT WHERE YOU WANT TO PASTE THE TEXT OR OBJECT.

2. CLICK THE PASTE BUTTON ON THE STANDARD TOOLBAR.

   OR...

   SELECT EDIT → PASTE FROM THE MENU.

   OR...

   PRESS CTRL + V.

TO COMPARE DOCUMENTS SIDE BY SIDE:

1. OPEN TWO DOCUMENTS.

2. SELECT WINDOW → COMPARE SIDE BY SIDE WITH FROM THE MENU.

Moving and Copying Text with Drag and Drop

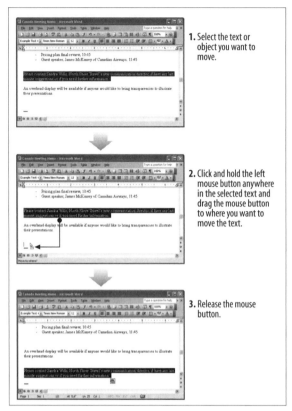

1. Select the text or object you want to move.

2. Click and hold the left mouse button anywhere in the selected text and drag the mouse button to where you want to move the text.

3. Release the mouse button.

Figure 2-11. The steps involved in moving text by using Drag and Drop.

A faster, more advanced method of moving and copying text in Word involves *dragging and dropping*. To drag and drop text, you must: (1) select the text you want to move, (2) click and hold the mouse button over the selected text, (3) while you are holding down the mouse button, move the mouse until the pointer is over the location where you want to place the text, and (4) release the mouse button.

Sound easy? Let's try it.

1 **Select the sentence that begins with** Please contact Sandra Wills.

The next three steps are tricky, especially if you're new to using a mouse. It might take you several tries before you get it right.

2 **Make sure the pointer is located over the selected text, then press and hold the left mouse button until the pointer changes from** ⌖ **to** **. Do not release the left mouse button!**

TIP

You can copy text using the Drag and Drop method by holding down the Ctrl key as you drag and drop the text.

Your document should appear similar to the second step in Figure 2-11.

3 **While still holding the left mouse button, drag the pointer down to the very end of the document.**

4 **Release the mouse button.**

The sentence is moved to the end of the document.

Moving selected text with the drag and drop method takes a lot of dexterity with the mouse, and many people accidentally drop their text in unintended areas. If you make a mistake using drag and drop, you can undo your action by clicking the Undo button on the Standard toolbar, or by pressing Ctrl + Z.

Here's something else you should know about drag and drop: Holding down the Ctrl key while using drag and drop *copies* the selected text instead of moving it.

QUICK REFERENCE

TO MOVE TEXT USING DRAG AND DROP:

1. SELECT THE TEXT YOU WANT TO MOVE.

2. POSITION THE POINTER ANYWHERE IN THE SELECTED TEXT, AND CLICK AND HOLD THE LEFT MOUSE BUTTON.

3. DRAG THE POINTER TO WHERE YOU WANT TO MOVE THE SELECTED TEXT, AND THEN RELEASE THE MOUSE BUTTON.

TO COPY TEXT USING DRAG AND DROP:

1. SELECT THE TEXT YOU WANT TO COPY.

2. POSITION THE POINTER ANYWHERE IN THE SELECTED TEXT, AND CLICK AND HOLD THE LEFT MOUSE BUTTON.

3. PRESS AND HOLD THE CTRL KEY.

4. DRAG THE POINTER TO WHERE YOU WANT TO MOVE THE SELECTED COPIED TEXT, AND THEN RELEASE THE MOUSE BUTTON AND THE CTRL KEY.

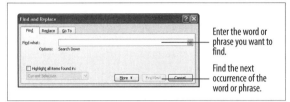

Figure 2-12. The Find tab of the Find and Replace dialog box.

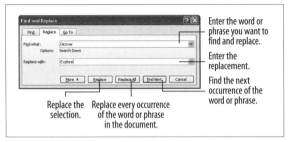

Figure 2-13. The Replace tab of the Find and Replace dialog box.

Imagine you are working on a very important 50-page report about flying squirrels. You're almost finished when you realize that you've mistakenly referred to flying squirrels not by their proper scientific name, "Sciuridae Glaucomys," but by the scientific name of the common gray squirrel, "Sciuridae Sciurus." Yikes! It will take hours to go back and find every instance of "Sciuridae Sciurus" and replace it with "Sciuridae Glaucomys." On the other hand, if you use Word's find and replace function it will take you less than a minute.

This lesson explains how to find specific words and phrases, and how to automatically replace words and phrases.

1 Press Ctrl + Home to move to the beginning, or top of the document.

If you only need to find a word but not replace it with another, select Edit → Find, as shown in Figure 2-12. Move on to the next step to learn how to find and replace.

2 Select Edit → Replace from the menu.

The Find and Replace dialog box opens with the Replace tab already selected, as shown in Figure 2-13.

3 In the Find what box, type Discover.

You want to replace every occurrence of the word "Discover" with the word "Explore" in the current document.

4 Click in the Replace with box.

5 Type Explore in the "Replace with" box.

6 Click the Replace All button.

⦂ NOTE ⦂ *Think carefully before using the Replace All button—you might not want it to replace every instance of a word! You can find and replace individual occurrences of a word or phrase by clicking the Find Next button and then clicking the Replace button to replace the text. Otherwise, click the Find Next button to leave the text alone and move on to the next occurrence.*

7 Click OK.

The dialog box closes and you're back at the Find and Replace dialog box.

8 Click the dialog box's Close button.

The Find and Replace dialog box disappears and you're back to your document. Notice that all occurrences of the word "Discover" have been replaced by "Explore."

QUICK REFERENCE

TO FIND TEXT:

1. SELECT EDIT → FIND FROM THE MENU.

2. TYPE THE TEXT YOU WANT TO FIND IN THE "FIND WHAT" BOX AND CLICK THE FIND NEXT BUTTON.

TO REPLACE TEXT:

1. SELECT EDIT → REPLACE FROM THE MENU.

2. TYPE THE TEXT YOU WANT TO FIND IN THE "FIND WHAT" BOX AND THE TEXT YOU WANT TO REPLACE IT WITH IN THE "REPLACE WITH" BOX.

3. CLICK EITHER FIND NEXT AND THEN REPLACE TO FIND AND THEN REPLACE EACH OCCURRENCE OF THE TEXT, OR CLICK REPLACE ALL TO REPLACE EVERY OCCURRENCE OF THE TEXT IN THE DOCUMENT ALL AT ONCE.

Collecting and Pasting Multiple Items

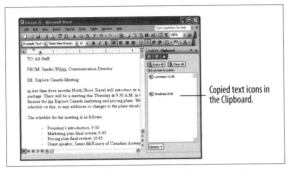

Copied text icons in the Clipboard.

Figure 2-14. The Clipboard task pane displays the cut or copied objects you've collected.

If you do a lot of cutting, copying, and pasting you will probably appreciate Word 2003's Office Clipboard, which holds not one, but *twenty-four* cut or copied objects.

You can use the Office Clipboard to collect and paste multiple items. For example, you can copy text in a Microsoft Word document, switch to Excel and copy a drawing object, switch to PowerPoint and copy a bulleted list, switch to Access and copy a datasheet, and then switch back to Word and paste the collection of copied items.

1 **If necessary, navigate to your Practice folder and open** Lesson 2C. **Save the file as** Canada Meeting Memo.

Next, we need to open the document that contains the text we want to copy.

2 **Find and open the** Schedule memo **document.**

This memo contains several new items that need to be copied and pasted into the "Canada Meeting Memo" document. Instead of switching between the two documents to copy and paste the items, you can use the Office Clipboard to copy and/or cut several items and then paste them all at once. In order to "collect and paste" multiple items, you may need to summon the task pane.

3 **Select** Edit → Office Clipboard **from the menu.**

Anything you cut or copy (up to 24 items) will appear in the Clipboard task pane.

The first item that needs to be copied is the schedule.

4 **Select the** Breakfast, 8:00 **line and click the** Copy button **on the Standard toolbar.**

Other Ways to Copy:

> **TIP** *Another way to copy is to press* Ctrl + C, *or select* Edit → Copy *from the menu.*

Word copies the text to the Office Clipboard and a Word icon appears in the task pane. Instead of switching back to the "Canada Meeting Memo" document to paste the copied text, here's how you can copy or cut several items to the Office Clipboard:

5 **Select the line** Luncheon, 12:00 **and click the** Copy button **on the Standard toolbar.**

Word copies the selected text to the Office Clipboard and another Word icon appears in the task pane, as shown in Figure 2-14. The type of icon indicates which program the object was collected from, as described in Table 2-2.

6 **Switch to the** Canada Meeting Memo **document by clicking its icon on the Windows taskbar. Select** Edit → Office Clipboard **from the menu.**

To paste an object from the Office Clipboard, simply click the object you want to paste.

7 **Place the insertion point immediately before the text** President's introduction, 9:30 **and click the** Breakfast, 8:00 icon **in the Clipboard task pane.**

Word pastes the selected contents of the Office Clipboard.

If the formatting doesn't match the list, you might have to use a Smart tag to fix it. Refer to Lesson 2-11 for help with Smart tags.

8 **Click the** Paste Options smart tag **and select** Paste List Without Merging **from the list.**

The pasted text's formatting matches the rest of the list.

9 **Following the same procedure, paste the** Luncheon, 12:00 **text as the last item in the schedule.**

Move on to the next step and close the Clipboard task pane.

10 **Click the Clipboard task pane's** Close button.

11 **Close the** Schedule memo **file.**

Table 2-2. Icons in the Clipboard

Icon	Description Contents
	Object cut or copied from a Microsoft Access database.
	Object cut or copied from a Microsoft Excel spreadsheet.
	Object cut or copied from a Microsoft PowerPoint presentation.
	Object cut or copied from a Microsoft Word document.
	Web page contents cut or copied from Microsoft Internet Explorer.
	Cut or copied graphic object.
	Object cut or copied from a program other than Microsoft Office.

QUICK REFERENCE

TO DISPLAY THE CLIPBOARD TASK PANE:

- SELECT EDIT → OFFICE CLIPBOARD FROM THE MENU.

TO ADD ITEMS TO THE OFFICE CLIPBOARD:

- COPY AND/OR CUT THE ITEMS AS YOU WOULD NORMALLY.

TO PASTE FROM THE OFFICE CLIPBOARD:

- IF NECESSARY, DISPLAY THE CLIPBOARD TASK PANE, THEN CLICK THE ITEM YOU WANT TO PASTE. CLICK THE PASTE ALL BUTTON TO PASTE ALL COLLECTED ITEMS.

- IF NECESSARY, USE THE PASTE OPTIONS SMART TAG TO FIX FORMATTING.

Correcting Your Spelling and Grammar

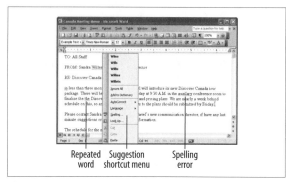

Figure 2-15. Spelling errors are underlined in red and grammar errors in green.

Repeated word · Suggestion shortcut menu · Spelling error

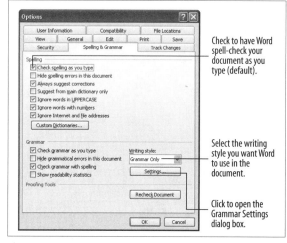

Figure 2-16. The Spelling & Grammar tab of the Options dialog box lets you specify which spelling and grammar errors you want to check.

Check to have Word spell-check your document as you type (default).

Select the writing style you want Word to use in the document.

Click to open the Grammar Settings dialog box.

Figure 2-17. The Grammar Settings dialog box lets you specify which types of grammar errors you want Word to check for.

In this lesson, you will learn how to use what many people think is the neatest feature of word processors: the spell checker. Word identifies spelling errors, grammar errors and repeated words as well. What's more, Word checks for these errors as you type, highlighting spelling errors with a red underline and grammar errors with a green underline.

1 **Right-click the red-underlined word,** Willes, **in the second line of the memo.**

A shortcut menu appears with suggestions for the correct spelling and several other options, as shown in Figure 2-15. "Willes" isn't misspelled—Word just can't find it in its dictionary. There are two things you can do when the spell checker doesn't recognize a correctly spelled word:

- **Ignore All:** Leaves the spelling as it is and ignores it throughout the rest of your document.

- **Add to Dictionary:** Adds the word to the spelling dictionary, so that Word won't nag you about it during future spell checks. Use this option for non-standard words you use often.

Since "Willes" isn't a spelling error, you can tell Word to ignore it.

2 Left-click Ignore All **on the shortcut menu.**

You can add your own words to the spelling dictionary so Word won't recognize them as spelling errors in the future. To do this, right-click the red-underlined word and select Add.

The squiggly red underline under the word "Willes" disappears. The next error in the document is a grammar error, indicated by a green underline under the word "in" in the first paragraph of the memo.

3 **Right-click the green-underlined word,** in, **at the beginning of the first body paragraph of the memo.**

Another shortcut menu appears, this time displaying any possible grammar corrections. Word only presents you with a single grammar suggestion—the properly capitalized word "In."

4 **Select the grammar suggestion** In **from the shortcut menu.**

Word capitalizes the word "In." The next error in the document is the misspelled word "auxilary."

5 **Right-click the red-underlined misspelled word** auxilary **and select the correct spelling,** auxiliary, **from the suggestion menu.**

Word makes the spelling correction. The next error is the repeated word "the."

6 **Right-click the red-underlined word** the **located near the end of the first paragraph in the memo.**

7 **Select** Delete Repeated Word **from the suggestion menu.**

Word deletes the extra word.

Unless your grandmother is an English professor, you would probably be less concerned about grammar in an informal letter than you would in a cover letter to a prospective employer. Microsoft recognizes that different types of documents use different writing styles, so you can specify the types of grammatical errors you want to have checked, as shown in Figure 2-17.

8 **Select** Tools → Options **from the menu and click the** Spelling & Grammar **tab.**

The Spelling & Grammar tab of the Options dialog box appears, as shown in Figure 2-16. Here you can specify which spelling and grammar "errors" you want Word to check. You can also specify whether or not you want Word to check your spelling as you type. You can specify the writing style you want Word to use by selecting it from the Writing style list.

⸝ NOTE ⸝ *Microsoft Word's grammar checking function isn't the greatest and should probably take a few remedial English courses. The grammar checker often mistakenly indicates grammar problems where there are none while ignoring blatantly obvious errors in the same sentence. Think of the grammar checker as a tool that sometimes catches simple grammar errors—don't expect it to be as accurate as the spelling checker.*

9 **Click** Cancel **to close the Options dialog box.**

No doubt about it, Word's spelling and grammar checker is a great tool to assist you in creating accurate documents. It's important to note, however, that Word will not catch all of your spelling and grammar errors. For example, if you mistyped the word "hat" when you meant to type "had" Word wouldn't catch it because "hat" is a correctly spelled word.

QUICK REFERENCE

TO CORRECT A SPELLING OR GRAMMAR ERROR:

- RIGHT-CLICK THE SPELLING OR GRAMMAR ERROR AND SELECT THE CORRECTION FROM THE SHORTCUT MENU.

OR...

- CORRECT THE SPELLING OR GRAMMAR ERROR BY RETYPING IT.

TO IGNORE A SPELLING OR GRAMMAR ERROR:

- RIGHT-CLICK THE SPELLING OR GRAMMAR ERROR AND SELECT IGNORE ALL FROM THE SHORTCUT MENU.

TO ADD A WORD TO THE SPELLING DICTIONARY:

- RIGHT-CLICK THE WORD YOU WANT TO ADD AND SELECT ADD TO DICTIONARY FROM THE SHORTCUT MENU.

TO CHANGE HOW WORD CHECKS FOR GRAMMAR AND SPELLING ERRORS:

- SELECT TOOLS → OPTIONS FROM THE MENU, CLICK THE SPELLING & GRAMMAR TAB, SPECIFY WHAT YOU WANT WORD TO CHECK, AND CLICK OK.

Understanding Smart Tags

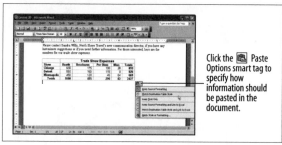

Click the 📋 Paste Options smart tag to specify how information should be pasted in the document.

Figure 2-18. Smart tags appear when you perform a particular task or when Word recognizes certain types of information.

Smart tags were new in Microsoft Office XP, and they make working with Word 2003 a lot easier. Smart tags are similar to right-mouse button shortcuts—you click smart tags to perform actions on various items. Smart tags appear when Word 2003 recognizes certain types of information, such as the name of a person in your Address Book. Word marks these items with a ⓘ smart tag indicator and/or a purple dotted underline. Clicking a ⓘ smart tag indicator displays a list of things that you can do to the smart tag, such as send an e-mail message. Other smart tag-like buttons appear when you paste information and use Word's AutoCorrect feature. Clicking these buttons specifies how Word pastes or corrects information.

In this lesson you will learn what smart tags look like and how to use them.

1 If you don't have the Canada Meeting Memo document open, find and open Lesson 2D and save it as Canada Meeting Memo.

First, let's make some changes to this document.

2 Press Ctrl + End to move to the end of the document, type For those interested, here are the numbers for our trade show expenses. and press Enter twice.

The trade show expense information is stored in a Microsoft Excel workbook, so we will have to start the Microsoft Excel program.

3 Click the Start button and select All Programs → Microsoft Office 2003 → Microsoft Office Excel 2003 from the menu.

You probably already know that the procedure for opening a file in Microsoft Excel is no different from opening a file in Microsoft Word.

4 In Excel, click the Open button on the Standard toolbar, browse to your Practice folder, then find and open the Trade Show Expenses file.

Next, you need to select and copy the information in this workbook.

5 Select the cell range A1:F8 by clicking cell A1, holding down the mouse button, and dragging to cell F8.

Now you can copy the selected cells to the Clipboard.

6 Click the Copy button on the Standard toolbar.

The information is copied to the Clipboard.

7 Close Microsoft Excel without saving changes.

You should be back in Microsoft Word. Let's paste the copied information.

8 Press Ctrl + End to ensure that you're at the end of the document, then click the Paste button on the Standard toolbar.

Word pastes the copied information into the document. Notice the 📋 Paste Options button appears next to the pasted worksheet. Click this button to specify how information is pasted, as shown in Figure 2-18.

9 Click the Paste Options button and select Match Destination Table Style from the drop-down list.

Word formats the Excel information into a Word table.

TIP

You can change the Smart Tag options by selecting Tools → AutoCorrect Options from the menu and clicking the Smart Tag tab. See Table 2-3 for Smart tag button icons and their descriptions.

Table 2-3. Smart Tags and Buttons

Smart Tag Button	Description
⑤	When Word recognizes certain types of data, such as the name of a person in your Address Book, the data is marked with a ⑤ smart tag indicator, or purple dotted underline. To find out what actions you can take with a smart tag, move the insertion point over the text with a smart tag indicator until the ⑤ smart tag button appears. Click the ⑤ button to see a menu of actions.
📋	The Paste Options button appears after you paste something. Click the Paste Options button to specify how information is pasted into your document. The available options depend on the type of content you are pasting, the program you are pasting from, and the format of the text into which you are pasting.
⚡	The AutoCorrect Options button appears after AutoCorrect automatically corrects a spelling error, such as changing "hte" to "the." If you find that you don't want text to be automatically corrected, you can undo a correction or turn AutoCorrect options on or off by clicking the AutoCorrect Options button and making a selection.

QUICK REFERENCE

UNDERSTANDING SMART TAGS:

- AS YOU ENTER INFORMATION IN A DOCUMENT, SMART TAG BUTTONS WILL APPEAR. CLICK THESE BUTTONS TO DISPLAY A LIST OF ACTIONS YOU CAN TAKE.

TO USE A SMART TAG:

- CLICK THE SMART TAG AND SELECT THE DESIRED ACTION OR OPTION.

TO VIEW/CHANGE SMART TAG OPTIONS:

- SELECT TOOLS → AUTOCORRECT OPTIONS FROM THE MENU AND CLICK THE SMART TAG TAB.

Using Thesaurus, Word Count, and Research Pane

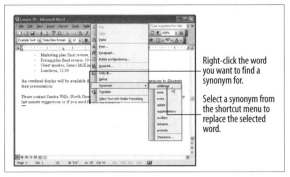

Right-click the word you want to find a synonym for.

Select a synonym from the shortcut menu to replace the selected word.

Figure 2-19. The Thesaurus makes it easy to find synonyms for a word.

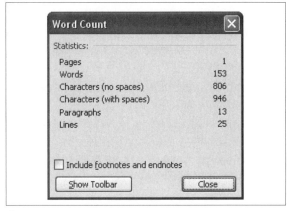

Figure 2-20. The Word Count dialog box.

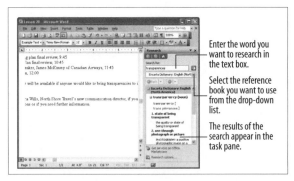

Enter the word you want to research in the text box.

Select the reference book you want to use from the drop-down list.

The results of the search appear in the task pane.

Figure 2-21. Looking up a definition in the Research task pane.

Use Word's built-in Thesaurus to help you find just the right word. The Thesaurus will look up synonyms for a selected word and allow you to replace that word with another. For example, you can use the Thesaurus to replace the ho-hum word "good" with "commendable," "capital," or "exemplary."

The Word Count feature counts all the words in your document, especially helpful for students who have been assigned a 500-word essay.

This lesson also explains how to use the Research task pane, a new feature that places reference material at your fingertips within the Word program.

1 Right-click the word further in the last body paragraph in the memo.

> **TIP** *Another way to use the Thesaurus is to select the word and press Shift + F7.*

A shortcut menu appears near the word. To look up a word in the Thesaurus, select Synonyms from the shortcut menu.

2 Select Synonyms from the shortcut menu.

Several synonyms for the word "further" appear in the shortcut menu, as shown in Figure 2-19. Now all you have to do is select the word you want to use.

3 Select the word additional from the synonym list box.

The word further is replaced with the new word, additional.

> **NOTE** *Just like the Grammar checker, Word's Thesaurus isn't the best—it doesn't offer enough synonyms (especially if you're a professional writer), but it's fast, convenient, and better than nothing. If you do a lot of professional writing, you can purchase a genuine Roget's Thesaurus to use with Microsoft Word, which offers significantly more words than Word's simple Thesaurus. Ask about it at your local computer store.*

Another important feature is Word Count. Word Count does exactly what it says it does: it counts how many words there are in a document. (It also counts the number of pages, lines, and characters.) This is an especially great feature if you're a student and need to know exactly when to quit on that 5,000-word report. Let's see how many words there are in the Canada Meeting Memo document.

4 Make sure no words are selected, and then select Tools → Word Count **from the menu.**

The Word Count dialog box appears, as shown in Figure 2-20. Here you can see how many words, pages, characters, and lines there are in the current document.

5 Click Close.

The Word Count dialog box closes.

The Research task pane is a new feature in Word 2003. It has a wealth of resource information, especially if you are connected to the Internet, such as a dictionary, encyclopedia, and translation service.

Let's try looking up a word using the dictionary in the Research task pane.

6 Click the  Research button **on the Standard toolbar.**

The Research task pane appears, as shown in Figure 2-21.

7 Click in the Search for **text box and type** transparencies.

Word will look up the definition of this word in the dictionary.

8 Click the Search for **list arrow in the task pane and select** Encarta Dictionary: English **from the list.**

Notice that there are many different reference books, research sites, and business and financial sites available in the "Search for" list.

You can perform a search using all of these resources by selecting "All Reference Books" in the task pane.

9 Click the Start Searching button **in the Research task pane.**

After searching for a moment, a definition of the word "transparency" appears in the task pane.

⫶ NOTE ⫶   *Since many of the Research task pane resources are accessed through the Internet, make sure you're connected before doing your research.*

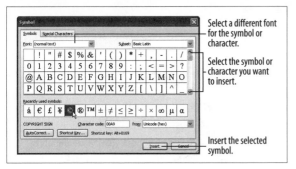

Select a different font
for the symbol or
character.

Select the symbol or
character you want
to insert.

Insert the selected
symbol.

Figure 2-22. The Symbol tab of the Symbol dialog box.

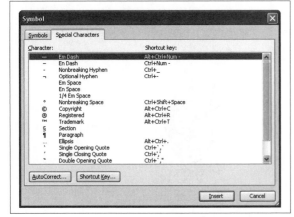

Figure 2-23. The Special Characters tab of the Symbol dialog box.

Believe it or not, you can enter many more characters and symbols in a document than can be found on the keyboard. For example, you can insert the copyright symbol (©), accented and foreign characters (β), silly characters (☺), and many more. In this lesson, you will learn how to insert several of these special symbols into a document.

1 Move the insertion point immediately after the first occurrence of the phrase, Explore Canada.

Make sure the insertion point is *immediately* after Explore Canada—don't even leave a space between the word Canada and the insertion point! You want to insert a copyright symbol (©) here, so nobody can copy North Shore Travel's new program name, *Explore Canada.*

2 Select Insert → Symbol from the menu.

The Symbol dialog box appears, as shown in Figure 2-22. Your computer has more than one set of fonts installed, so you need to select which font family the symbol you want to insert comes from. Most fonts contain mainly letters, numbers, and punctuation; however, there are several fonts that are made just for inserting symbols. Some of these fonts include:

- **Symbols:** Common typographical symbols, such as ©, ÷, µ, or →.
- **Wingdings:** Small typographical pictures suitable for bullets, such as ☑☺📖📕.
- **Webdings:** Small typographical pictures specifically designed to be used on Web pages, such as 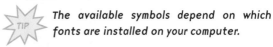.

TIP *The available symbols depend on which fonts are installed on your computer.*

3 Verify that Symbol appears in the Font box at the top of the dialog box. If it doesn't, click the Font list arrow, and scroll down the list to select Symbol.

4 Find and click the © symbol.

Be patient; you'll probably spend a few minutes looking for the tiny © symbol before you find it.

5 Click Insert.

The © symbol is inserted immediately after the word Canada. Now let anyone try to use our *Explore Canada* name! Add a © symbol behind the other occurrences of the phrase *Explore Canada.*

6 Scroll down the document (you don't have to close the Symbol dialog box), and add the © symbol behind every occurrence of Explore Canada.

Besides symbols, there are also some other special characters you can insert that can sometimes be useful. Let's take a look at these special characters.

7 **Click the** Special Characters **tab at the top of the Symbol dialog box.**

The Special Characters tab appears, as shown in Figure 2-23. We're just going to look here—you don't actually have to insert any of these symbols. Here you can find several useful characters, such as nonbreaking spaces and hyphens (both keep two words from being broken apart by word-wrap), various dashes, and also several of the most common symbols, like the © symbol. (Why didn't you send me here in the first place…?)

8 **Click** Cancel**.**

The Symbol dialog box closes.

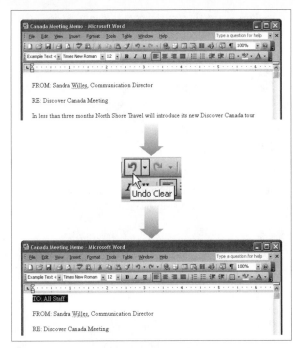

Figure 2-24. You can undo a text deletion.

You may not want to admit this, but you are going to make mistakes using Word. You might accidentally cut something you didn't really mean to cut, or replace something you didn't really mean to replace. Fortunately, Word has a wonderful feature called *undo* that does just that—it undoes any mistakes and actions, as though they never happened. You can almost think of undo as Word's "time machine" function, because it can take you back before you even made your mistake. This lesson explains how you can undo both single and multiple mistakes, and how to redo your actions in case you change your mind.

1 If necessary, open Lesson 2E from your Practice folder and save the file as Canada Meeting Memo.

2 Select the line TO: All Staff, then press the Delete key to erase the line.

The line TO: All Staff disappears. Whoops! You didn't really want to erase that! Watch how you can undo your "mistake."

3 Click the Undo button.

TIP — *Another way to undo is to press Ctrl + Z or select Edit → Undo from the menu.*

Poof! The deleted text "TO: All Staff" appears again (see Figure 2-24). Hmmm… maybe you did want to delete the line TO: All Staff, after all. Anything that can be undone can be redone in case you change your mind about something, or want to "undo an undo." Try redoing the text deletion.

4 Click the Redo button.

Other Ways to Redo:

TIP — *Another way to redo is to press Ctrl + Y or select Edit → Redo from the menu.*

The line "TO: All Staff" is deleted again.

If you're like most people, you will probably make not one, but several mistakes and it may be a minute or two before you've even realized you've made them. Fortunately, the programmers at Microsoft thought of us when they developed Word, because the undo feature is actually multileveled—meaning you can undo any of the previous things you did.

5 Select the word Sandra in the line FROM: Sandra Willes, Communication Director. Type Sandy to replace the word Sandra.

There's your second mistake (the first mistake was deleting the "TO: All Staff" text).

6 Select Edit → Replace from the menu.

The Find and Replace dialog box appears.

7 Type Explore in the Find what: text box, press the Tab key to move to the Replace with: text box, type Go and click Replace All. Click OK to confirm the Replace All. Click Close to close the dialog box.

Every occurrence of the word "Explore" in the document is replaced with the word "Go." Mistake number three.

8 **Change the time in the line** Guest speaker, James McKinsey of Canadian Airways, 11:45 **to** 11:30.

Mistake number four. You've made enough mistakes now to see how multilevel undo works. Try undoing all of your mistakes.

9 **Click the** Undo button **list arrow.**

A list of recent actions in Word appears immediately beneath the Undo button. Notice that there are more actions listed than your four recent "mistakes." If you wanted, you could undo everything you have worked on today on this document—but you don't want to do that—just undo the last four mistakes.

10 **Select the word** Clear **from the undo list (it should be the fourth action in the list).**

The last four changes we made to our document—deleting the first line of text, replacing some words, and changing the time—are all undone.

Besides correcting mistakes, undo and redo allows you to experiment with your documents by making changes, and then undoing them if you decide you don't like the changes.

The opposite of the Undo command is the Repeat command, which repeats your last command or action, if possible. Here's how to use it.

11 **Select the line** TO: All Staff, **then press the** Delete **key to erase the line.**

You've just deleted the recipient line. Now let's see how you can repeat your last command…

12 **Select the line** FROM: Sandra Willes, Communication Director **and press** Ctrl + Y.

Word repeats your last command and deletes the sender line.

13 **Click the** Undo button **on the Standard toolbar twice to undo your deletions, and then save your work.**

QUICK REFERENCE

TO UNDO:

• CLICK THE UNDO BUTTON ON THE STANDARD TOOLBAR.

OR…

• SELECT EDIT → UNDO FROM THE MENU.

OR…

• PRESS CTRL + Z.

TO REDO:

• CLICK THE REDO BUTTON ON THE STANDARD TOOLBAR.

OR…

• SELECT EDIT → REDO FROM THE MENU.

OR…

• PRESS CTRL + Y.

TO REPEAT:

• SELECT EDIT → REPEAT FROM THE MENU.

OR…

• PRESS CTRL + Y.

Word applies formatting (like tabs) automatically so you can begin typing once you've selected a location on the page.

Figure 2-25. Click and Type positions your text by adding the required number of paragraph marks and formatting.

Forget about pressing Enter or Spacebar to position text! Word 2003's *Click and Type* feature lets you quickly insert text in a blank area of a document. Just double-click in a blank area where you want to position your text, and start typing. Click and Type automatically applies the formatting necessary to position the item where you double-clicked. For example, you could use Click and Type to create a title page by double-clicking in the middle of a blank page and typing the centered title. Then you could double-click the lower-right margin of the page and type a right-aligned signature.

Click and Type is incredibly easy to use—here's how it works:

1 Make sure that you are in either Print Layout View or Web Layout View.

Click and Type works only if you're using one of these two views. Most people use Word in Print Layout view, so you are probably already in Print Layout view.

2 Move the mouse pointer near the bottom blank area of the document.

To use Click and Type, you merely need to move the mouse pointer and double-click where you want to start typing. The mouse pointer icon will change depending on where it is located on the screen, as illustrated in Table 2-4. Move on to the next step and see for yourself.

3 Slowly move the mouse pointer across the blank area at the bottom of the document, from left to right.

Notice how the pointer icon changes from a $I^{\equiv}$, to a $\underset{\equiv}{I}$, to a $^{\equiv}I$ as you move it across the page, indicating where text will be aligned when you double-click.

4 Double-click in the left of the blank area of the document.

The blinking insertion point should appear where you clicked in the left of the bottom of your document.

5 Type Sincerely, press Enter four times, and type your name.

Curious about how Click and Type does its magic in positioning text? Let's take a behind-the-scenes look…

6 Click the Show/Hide button on the Standard toolbar.

Word displays all nonprinting characters, as shown in Figure 2-25. Now you can see how Click and Type works—all Word does is insert a whole bunch of paragraph marks.

7 Click the Show/Hide button on the Standard toolbar to hide any nonprinting characters and then save your work.

Table 2-4. Click and Type Alignment Pointers

Mouse Pointer	Description
$I^{\equiv}$	Double-click near the left side of the page to align text to the left of the page.
$\underset{\equiv}{I}$	Double-click near the center of the page to center text on the page.
$^{\equiv}I$	Double-click near the right side of the page to align text to the right of the page.

QUICK REFERENCE

TO POSITION TEXT USING CLICK AND TYPE:

• DOUBLE-CLICK IN A BLANK AREA OF THE DOCUMENT WHERE YOU WANT TO POSITION YOUR TEXT AND START TYPING. THE POINTER CHANGES FROM ALIGN LEFT, CENTER, AND ALIGN RIGHT TO INDICATE HOW TEXT WILL BE ALIGNED.

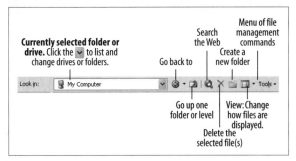

Figure 2-26. The Open and Save As dialog boxes' toolbar.

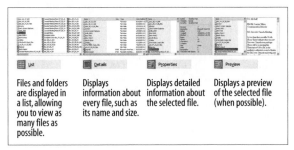

Figure 2-27. The View list button lets you change how files are displayed in the Open or Save As dialog boxes.

File management includes moving, copying, deleting, and renaming the files you've created. See Table 2-5 at the end of this lesson for File Shortcut Menu Commands. Although it's a little easier to work with and organize your files using Windows Explorer or My Computer, you can also perform a surprising number of file management chores right from inside Microsoft Word 2003—especially with its new and improved Open and Save dialog boxes.

1 Click the Open button on the Standard toolbar and you'll see something that looks like Figure 2-26.

The Open dialog box appears. The Open dialog box is normally used to open files, but you can also use it to perform several file management functions. There are two different ways to access file management commands from inside the Open or Save As dialog boxes:

- Select a file and then select the command you want from the dialog box's Tools menu.
- Right-click a file and select the command you want from the shortcut menu.

2 Right-click the Rename Me file.

A shortcut menu appears with a list of available file management commands for the selected file.

3 Select Rename from the shortcut menu, type Home Budget, and press Enter.

You have just changed the name of the selected file from "Rename Me" to "Home Budget." Instead of right-clicking the file, you could have selected it and then selected Rename from the Tools menu. Move on to the next step to learn how to delete a file.

4 Click the Home Budget file to select it and press the Delete key.

A dialog box appears, asking you to confirm the deletion of the Home Budget file.

5 Click Yes.

The Home Budget file is deleted. If you work with and create numerous files, you may find it difficult to remember what you named a file. To find the file(s) you're looking for, try previewing your files without opening them.

6 Click the View button list arrow and select Preview. See Figure 2-27 for information on the View list button.

The Open dialog box changes the display of Word files in the Practice folder from List view to Preview view. To see the contents of a file, select it in the file list on the left side of the dialog box, and it will appear in the Preview area to the right side of the dialog box. Try previewing the contents of a file now without opening it.

7 Click the Lesson 4A file.

The Lesson 4A file is selected and a preview of its contents appears in the Preview section. Change back to List view to display as many files in the window as possible.

8 Click the View button list arrow, select List to display the files in List view, and then close the dialog box by clicking Cancel.

Table 2-5. File Shortcut Menu Commands

Command	Description
Open	Opens the selected file.
Open Read-Only	Opens the selected file so that it can be read but not changed.
Open as Copy	Creates a copy of the selected file with the name "Copy of" and the name of the original file, and then opens the new, copied file.
Print	Sends the selected file to the default printer.
Quick View	Displays the contents of the selected file without opening the file.
Send To	Depending on how your computer is set up, it lets you send the selected file to a printer, to an email recipient, to a fax, or to a disk drive.
Cut	Used in conjunction with the Paste command to move files. It cuts, or removes, the selected file from its current folder or location.
Copy	Used in conjunction with the Paste command to copy files. It copies the selected file.
Paste	Pastes a cut or copied file or files.
Create Shortcut	Creates a shortcut—a quick way to a file or folder without having to go to its permanent location—to the file.
Delete	Deletes the selected file or files.
Rename	Renames the selected file.
Properties	Displays the properties of the selected file, such as when the file was created or last modified, or how large the file is.

QUICK REFERENCE

BASIC FILE MANAGEMENT IN THE OPEN DIALOG BOX:

1. OPEN THE OPEN OR SAVE AS DIALOG BOXES BY SELECTING OPEN OR SAVE AS FROM THE FILE MENU.

2. RIGHT-CLICK THE FILE AND REFER TO TABLE 2-5 FOR A LIST OF THINGS YOU CAN DO TO THE SELECTED FILE.

   OR...

   SELECT THE FILE AND SELECT A COMMAND FROM THE TOOLS LIST.

TO CHANGE HOW FILES ARE DISPLAYED:

- CLICK THE VIEW BUTTON LIST ARROW AND SELECT A VIEW.

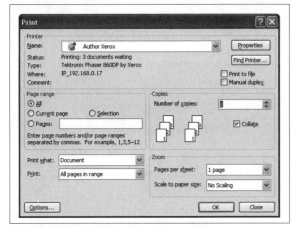

Figure 2-28. The Print dialog box.

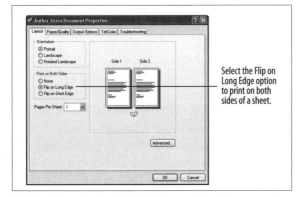

Select the Flip on Long Edge option to print on both sides of a sheet.

Figure 2-29. The Print Properties dialog box.

You already know how to print, but in this lesson you will become an expert at printing. This lesson explains how to print more than one copy of a document, send a document to a different printer, print on both sides of the page, and print specific pages of a document.

1 Select File → Print from the menu.

The Print dialog box appears, as shown in Figure 2-28.

The Print dialog box is where you can specify printing options when you print your document. Several frequently used print options you might specify would be how many pages to print, what pages to print, or what printer to use if your computer is attached to more than one printer. See Table 2-6 for a description of the available print options.

To print on both sides of a page or to print on the long edge rather than the short edge, click the Properties button and select the "Flip on Long Edge" option in the Properties dialog box, as shown in Figure 2-29.

2 In the Number of copies box, type 2.

3 Click OK.

The Print dialog box closes and Word prints two copies of your document (if your computer is attached to a printer).

Table 2-6 explains some of the other print options you can use when printing a document—for example, how to print a specific page or a range of pages.

Table 2-6. Print Dialog Box Options

Print option	Description
Name	Used to select what printer to send your document to when it prints. If you are connected to more than one printer, the currently selected printer is displayed.
Properties	Displays a dialog box with options available to your specific printer. The Properties dialog box will change according to the type of printer you use, but here are some common print properties: **Paper:** Change the size of the paper you're printing to, or the quality of the print, such as draft or professional mode. **Layout:** Change the paper orientation (portrait or landscape) or print on both sides of the sheet. **Color:** Print in black and white or choose how you want to print colors in your document. **Troubleshooting:** If your printer is having problems, you can try to solve the problem with the tools in this dialog box.
Print to file	Prints the document to a file instead of sending it to the printer.

Table 2-6. Print Dialog Box Options (Continued)

Print option	Description
Page range	Allows you to specify what pages you want printed. There are several options here: **All:** Prints the entire document. **Current page:** Prints only the page you're currently on. **Selection:** Prints only selected text. **Pages:** Prints only the pages you specify. Select a range of pages with a hyphen (5-8) and separate single pages with a comma (3,7).
Number of copies	Specifies the number of copies you want to print.
Print what	Allows you to select what to print: the document (the default, which you'll use 99.9% of the time) or only comments, annotations, or style.
Print	Specifies the print order for the page range: All Pages in Range, Odd Pages, and Even Pages.
Options	Lets you specify other printing options, such as printing a document in reverse order (from the last page to the first).

QUICK REFERENCE

TO CHANGE PRINTING OPTIONS:

1. SELECT FILE → PRINT FROM THE MENU.

2. REFER TO TABLE 2-6 FOR INFORMATION ON VARIOUS PRINTING OPTIONS.

FOR ADVANCED PRINTING OPTIONS:

1. SELECT FILE → PRINT FROM THE MENU.

2. CLICK THE PROPERTIES BUTTON FOR ADVANCED OPTIONS LIKE PRINTING ON BOTH SIDES OF THE PAGE, COLOR OPTIONS, AND PAPER SIZE.

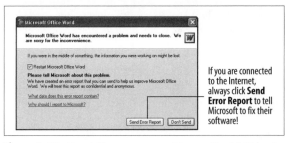

Figure 2-30. Oops! There goes your 50-page thesis! At least Microsoft is "sorry for the inconvenience."

If you are connected to the Internet, always click **Send Error Report** to tell Microsoft to fix their software!

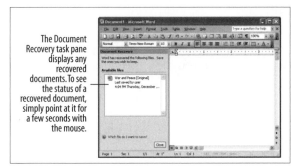

The Document Recovery task pane displays any recovered documents. To see the status of a recovered document, simply point at it for a few seconds with the mouse.

Figure 2-31. Review the recovered files listed in the Document Recovery pane and decide which one to keep.

If you haven't figured this out already, you're going to discover that computers don't always work the way they're supposed to. Nothing is more frustrating than when a program, for no apparent reason, decides to take a quick nap, locks up, and stops responding to your commands—especially if you lose the precious document that you're working on!

Fortunately, after more than ten years and roughly nine software versions, Microsoft has finally realized that people might want to recover their documents if Microsoft Word locks up or stops responding. If Word 2003 encounters a problem and stops responding (and after you finish swearing and hitting your computer's monitor), you can restart Microsoft Word or your computer and try to recover your lost documents. Sometimes Word will display a dialog box similar to the one shown in Figure 2-30 and automatically restart itself.

In this lesson, you will learn how to use Microsoft Word's new document recovery features should disaster strike.

1 If necessary, restart your computer and/or Microsoft Word.

You might not need to restart your computer or Word at all—Word will often display a dialog box, as shown in Figure 2-30, and automatically restart itself when it encounters a problem.

When you have restarted Microsoft Word, hopefully the Document Recovery pane will appear, as shown in Figure 2-31. If the Document Recovery pane doesn't appear, you're out of luck—Word didn't recover any of your documents. Hope you made a backup!

Sometimes Word will display several recovered documents in the Document Recovery task pane, such as the original document from the last manual save, and a recovered document that was automatically saved during an AutoRecover save process. You can see the status of any recovered document by simply pointing to the recovered document for a second or two. The Status Indicator appears in square brackets to the right of the document name (see Figure 2-31). Table 2-7 describes the status indicators.

2 To view details about any recovered document, simply point at the document in the Document Recovery task pane for a few seconds.

Hopefully you will find a version of your document—either original or recovered—that isn't missing too much of your work.

Here's how to select and save a recovered document…

3 Click the desired recovered document from the task pane.

The document appears in Word's document window.

4 Select File → Save As from the menu and save the document.

You can further protect your work by using the AutoRecover feature to periodically save a temporary copy of the document you're working on. To recover work after a power failure or similar problem, you must have turned on the AutoRecover feature before the problem occurred. You can set the AutoRecover save interval to occur more frequently than every 10 minutes (its default setting). For example, if you set it to save every 5 minutes, you'll recover more information than if you set it to save every 10 minutes. Here's how to change the AutoRecover save interval…

5 Select Tools → Options **from the menu and click the** Save **tab.**

The Save tab of the Options dialog box appears.

6 Ensure that the Save AutoRecovery info every **box is checked and specify the desired interval, in minutes, in the** minutes **box. Click** OK **when you're finished.**

Even with Word's document recovery features, the best way to ensure that you don't lose much information if your computer freezes up is to save your work regularly.

Table 2-7. Status Indicators in the Document Recovery Task Pane

Status Indicator	Description
Original	Original file based on last manual save.
Recovered	File recovered during recovery process or file saved during an AutoRecover save process.
Repaired	Word encountered problems while recovering the document and has attempted to repair them. Make sure that you double-check your document to make sure there isn't any corruption.

QUICK REFERENCE

TO RECOVER A DOCUMENT:

1. RESTART MICROSOFT WORD (IF IT DOESN'T RESTART BY ITSELF).

2. FIND AND THEN CLICK THE BEST RECOVERED DOCUMENT IN THE DOCUMENT RECOVERY TASK PANE.

3. SAVE THE DOCUMENT BY SELECTING FILE → SAVE AS FROM THE MENU.

TO CHANGE THE AUTORECOVERY SETTINGS:

1. SELECT TOOLS → OPTIONS FROM THE MENU AND CLICK THE SAVE TAB.

2. ENSURE THAT THE SAVE AUTORECOVERY INFO EVERY BOX IS CHECKED AND SPECIFY THE DESIRED INTERVAL, IN MINUTES, IN THE MINUTES BOX. CLICK OK WHEN YOU'RE FINISHED.

Chapter Two Review

Lesson Summary

Saving a Document with a Different Name

To Open a Document: Click the Open button on the Standard toolbar, or select File → Open from the menu, or press Ctrl + O.

To Save an Existing Document in a New File with a Different Name: Select File → Save As from the menu, type the new name for the file in the File name box and click OK.

Navigating through a Document

Press Home to move to the beginning of a line and End to move to the end of a line.

Press Page Up to move up one screen and Page Down to move down one screen.

Press Ctrl + Home to move to the beginning of a document and Ctrl + End to move to the end of a document.

To Jump to a Specific Page in a Document: Select Edit → Go To from the menu. Verify that "Page" is selected in the "Go to what" drop-down list, type the page number in the "Enter page number" text box, and click OK.

Viewing a Document

To Switch between Views: You can view a document in Normal, Web Layout, Print Layout, Outline and Reading Layout views. Change views by clicking one of the View buttons located on the horizontal scroll bar, or by selecting them from the View menu.

To Display/Hide Hidden Characters (Tabs, Spaces, and Paragraph Marks): Display/hide hidden characters by clicking the Show/Hide button on the Standard toolbar.

To Change the Zoom Level of a Document: Change the zoom level of a document view by using the Zoom box on the Standard toolbar.

To View a Document in Full Screen Mode: View a document in Full Screen mode by selecting View → Full Screen from the menu.

Working with Multiple Documents and Windows

You can open and work on several documents at the same time. To switch between documents, click the doc-ument icon on the Windows taskbar or select Window and select the name of the document you want to view.

To View Multiple Windows at the Same Time: Select Window → Arrange All.

Maximize a window (making it fill the entire screen) by clicking the window's Maximize button.

Restore a window (returning it to the previous size) by clicking the window's Restore button.

Resize a window by dragging it by its edges or corners.

Move a window by dragging the window's title bar to the location where you want to position the window.

Cutting and Pasting Text

To Cut Something: Select the text and cut it using one of the following methods:

- Click the Cut button on the Standard toolbar.
- Select Edit → Cut from the menu.
- Press Ctrl + X.

To Paste a Cut Object: Place the insertion point where you want to paste the text or object, and use one of the following methods to paste it:

- Click the Paste button on the Standard toolbar.
- Select Edit → Paste from the menu.
- Press Ctrl + V.

Copying and Pasting Text and Viewing Documents Side by Side

To Copy Something: Select the text and cut it using one of the following methods:

- Click the Copy button on the Standard toolbar
- Select Edit → Copy from the menu.
- Press Ctrl + C.

To Paste a Copied Object: Place the insertion point where you want to paste the text or object, and use one of the following methods to paste it:

- Click the Paste button on the Standard toolbar.
- Select Edit → Paste from the menu.
- Press Ctrl + V.

To Compare Documents Side by Side: Open two documents. Select Window → Compare Side by Side with from the menu.

Moving and Copying Text with Drag and Drop

To Move Text using Drag and Drop: Select the text you want to move, and drag the selected text to where you want to move it. Then, release the mouse button to drop the text.

To Copy Text using Drag and Drop: Select the text you want to copy. Position the pointer anywhere in the selected text and click and hold the mouse button. Press and hold the Ctrl key. Drag the pointer to where you want to move the selected text and then release the mouse button and the Ctrl key.

Finding and Replacing Text

To Find Text: Select Edit → Find from the menu, type the text you want to find in the "Find what" box and click the Find Next button.

To Replace Text: Select Edit → Replace from the menu, type the text you want to find in the "Find what" box and the text you want to replace it with in the "Replace with" box. Click either Find Next and then Replace to find each occurrence of the text or else Replace All to replace every occurrence of the text in the document at once.

Collecting and Pasting Multiple Items

To Display the Clipboard Task Pane: Select Edit → Office Clipboard from the menu.

To Add Items to the Office Clipboard: Copy and/or cut the items as you would normally.

To Paste from the Office Clipboard: If necessary, display the Clipboard task pane, then click the item you want to paste. Click the Paste All button to paste all collected items.

Correcting Your Spelling and Grammar

Word automatically underlines spelling errors in red, grammar errors in green, and possible formatting inconsistencies in blue.

To Correct a Spelling or Grammar Error: Right-click the spelling or grammar error and select the correction from the shortcut menu, or correct the spelling or grammar error by retyping it.

To Ignore a Spelling or Grammar Error: Right-click the spelling or grammar error and select Ignore All from the shortcut menu.

To Add a Word to the Spelling Dictionary: Right-click the word you want to add and select Add from the shortcut menu.

To Change How Word Checks for Grammar and Spelling Errors: Select Tools → Options from the menu, click the Spelling & Grammar tab, specify what you want Word to check, and click OK.

Understanding Smart Tags

As you enter information in a document, smart tag buttons will appear. Click these buttons to do something to the specified information.

To Use a Smart Tag: Click the Smart tag list arrow to select the desired action or option.

To View/Change Smart Tag Options: Select Tools → AutoCorrect Options from the menu and click the Smart tag tab.

Using Thesaurus, Word Count, and Research Pane

To Use the Thesaurus: Right-click the word you want to look up, select Synonyms from the shortcut menu and select a synonym from the list. Or, select the word you want to look up and select Tools → Language → Thesaurus from the menu, or press Shift + F7.

To Count the Number of Words in a Document: Select Tools → Word Count from the menu.

To Use the Research Task Pane: Click the Research button on the Standard toolbar. Enter the word you want to research in the Search for text box. Select the resource you want to use from the Search for drop-down list in the task pane. Click the Start searching button to begin the search.

Inserting Symbols and Special Characters

To Insert a Symbol or Special Character: Place the insertion point where you want to insert the character, select Insert → Symbol from the menu, select the symbol you want, and click INSERT.

Using Undo, Redo and Repeat

To Undo: Click the Undo button on the Standard toolbar, or select Edit → Undo from the menu, or press Ctrl + Z.

To Redo: Click the Redo button on the Standard toolbar, or select Edit → Redo from the menu, or press Ctrl + Y.

Multilevel Undo/Redo: Click the down arrows on the Undo or Redo buttons on the Standard toolbar to undo or redo several actions at once.

To Repeat a Command: Press Ctrl + Y or select Edit → Repeat from the menu.

Using Click and Type

To Position Text using Click and Type: Double-click a blank area of the document where you want to position your text and start typing. The pointer changes from ‖≡, ‖, ≡‖ to indicate how text will be aligned.

File Management

Basic File Management in the Open Dialog Box: You can perform most file management functions, such as delete, rename, and copy, from the Open File dialog box. Open the Open or Save As dialog boxes by selecting Open or Save As from the File menu. Right-click the file you want to manage, and select a file command from the shortcut menu. Or, select the file and select a command from the Tools menu

To Change How Files are Displayed: Click the View button list arrow and select a view.

Advanced Printing Options

To Change Printing Options: Open the Print Dialog box by selecting File → Print from the menu.

For Advanced Printing Options: Select File → Print from the menu. Click the Properties button for advanced options like printing on both sides, color options, and paper size.

Recovering Your Documents

To Recover a Document: Restart Microsoft Word (if it doesn't restart by itself). Find and then click the best recovered document in the Document Recovery task pane. Save the document by doing a File → Save As from the menu.

To Change the AutoRecovery Settings: Select Tools → Options from the menu and click the Save tab. Ensure that the Save AutoRecovery info every box is checked and specify the desired interval, in minutes, in the minutes box. Click OK when you're finished.

Quiz

1. 1.To save an existing document in a new file with a different name:
   - A. A.Click the Rename button on the Standard Toolbar.
   - B. Select File → New File Name Save from the menu.
   - C. Select File → Save As from the menu.
   - D. Word can't save documents in new files with different names.

2. To move to the end of a document press:
   - A. Ctrl + End
   - B. Ctrl + Page Down
   - C. End
   - D. Page Down

3. Which key or keystroke takes you to the beginning of the current line?
   - A. Ctrl + Home
   - B. Ctrl + Page Up
   - C. Home
   - D. There is no such key or keystroke.

4. To view a list of suggestions for a misspelled word:
   - A. Select the misspelled word and select Tools → Suggestions from the menu.
   - B. Press Ctrl + S
   - C. Select the misspelled word and click the Spelling Suggestion button on the Standard toolbar.
   - D. Right-click the misspelled word.

5. Word always marks your name as a spelling error. How can you get Word to stop saying your name is spelled incorrectly?

   A. Select Tools → Spelling and Grammar → Add from the menu.

   B. Right-click your name and select Add from the shortcut menu.

   C. Select Tools → Spelling and Grammar from the menu and click Add to Dictionary.

   D. You can't do anything about it.

6. You're working on your first novel and want to make it more dramatic. How can you replace every instance of the word "good" in your novel with "fantastic"?

   A. Select Edit → Replace from the menu, type "good" in the Find what box, type "fantastic" in the Replace with box and click Replace All.

   B. There isn't any easy way—you'll have to go through your novel and replace the words yourself.

   C. Click the Find and Replace button on the Standard toolbar, then follow the Find and Replace Wizard's on-screen instructions to replace the word.

   D. Select Tools → Replace from the menu, type "good" in the Find what box, type "fantastic" in the Replace with box and click Replace All.

7. In which color are grammar errors underlined?

   A. Red

   B. Blue

   C. Yellow

   D. Green

8. You want to see where the spaces, paragraphs, and tabs are in your document. How can you display these hidden characters?

   A. Select Tools → Reveal Codes from the menu.

   B. Click the Show/Hide button on the Standard Toolbar.

   C. Press Ctrl + R.

   D. Select Edit → Reveal Codes from the menu.

9. Which of the following is not a command to cut text or graphics?

   A. Click the Cut button on the Standard toolbar.

   B. Press Ctrl + C.

   C. Press Ctrl + X.

   D. Select Edit → Cut from the menu.

10. Click and type works only for left aligned paragraphs. (True or False)

11. How can you count how many words are in a document?

    A. Select Tools → Language → Word Count from the menu.

    B. Press Ctrl + W.

    C. Select Tools → Word Count from the menu.

    D. Click the Count Words button on the Standard toolbar.

12. You're working on a novel and want to go to page 144. What's the best way to do this?

    A. Select Edit → Go To from the menu.

    B. Click the Go To button on the Standard toolbar.

    C. Select Edit → Jump To from the menu.

    D. Select Edit → Find from the menu.

13. Which of these resources is available in the Research task pane?

    A. Encarta Dictionary.

    B. Factiva Search.

    C. Translation.

    D. Gale Company Profiles.

    E. All of the above.

14. How can you print three copies of a document?

    A. Select File → Print from the menu and type 3 in the Number of copies text box.

    B. Press Ctrl + P + 3.

    C. Select File → Properties from the menu and type 3 in the Copies to print text box.

    D. Click the Print button on the Standard toolbar to print the document and then take it to Kinko's and have 2 more copies made.

15. Which of the following statements is NOT true?

    A. You can add your own words to the spelling dictionary by right-clicking the unrecognized word and selecting Add from the shortcut menu.

    B. To find a word or phrase in a document, select Edit → Find from the menu.

    C. The Undo function can only undo one action— the last one that you performed.

    D. To find a synonym for a word, select the word and select Tools → Language → Thesaurus from the menu.

16. Why would you use the Save As option in the File menu instead of the Save option?

    A. To save a file under a new name and/or location.

    B. To send someone an e-mail of a file.

    C. To change how frequently Word saves AutoRecovery information about a file.

    D. To specify if Word should always create a backup copy of a file.

17. How many items can you copy to the Office Clipboard?

    A. 1.

    B. 6.

    C. 24.

    D. An unlimited number of items.

Homework

1. Start Microsoft Word by clicking the Windows Start button, pointing to All Programs and selecting Microsoft Office Word.

2. Click the Open button on the Standard toolbar. Navigate to your Practice folder or disk, click the Homework 2 file and click OK.

3. Press Ctrl + End to move to the end of the document.

4. Select the following sentences in the fourth paragraph:

5. Place the insertion point after the sentence "I don't have much experience writing books, but I like to write a lot of letters and I think I'm pretty funny." and paste the text by clicking the Paste button on the Standard toolbar or by pressing Ctrl + V.

6. Correct any spelling errors by right-clicking any words that are underlined with a red squiggly line and selecting a correction from the shortcut menu.

7. Correct any grammatical errors by right-clicking any words that are underlined with a green squiggly line and selecting a correction from the shortcut menu.

8. Press Ctrl + Home to move to the beginning of the document.

9. Select Edit → Find from the menu, type "ruckus," and click "Find Next" to find the word "ruckus" in the document.

10. While the word "ruckus" is still selected, select Tools → Language → Thesaurus from the menu or press Shift + F7 to find a synonym for the word "ruckus." In the Research task pane, click the "uproar" list arrow and select Insert from the menu.

11. Open the Print dialog box by selecting File → Print from the menu. How would you print three copies of this letter? Click Cancel to close the Print dialog box without printing anything.

12. Click the Save button on the Standard toolbar to save your changes and exit Microsoft Word.

Quiz Answers

1. C. Select File → Save As from the menu and enter a new name in File name box.

2. A. Press Ctrl + End to move to the end of a document.

3. C. Press the Home key to take you to the beginning of the current line.

4. D. Right-click a misspelled word to view a list of corrections.

5. B. Right-click your name and select Add from the shortcut menu to add your name to the dictionary.

6. A. Select Edit → Replace from the menu, type "good" in the Find what box, type "fantastic" in the Replace with box, and click Replace All.

7. D. Grammar errors are underlined in green.

8. B. Click the Show/Hide button on the Standard toolbar to display any hidden characters in a document.

9. B. Ctrl + C *copies* selected text or graphics, Ctrl + X *cuts* selected text or graphics.

10. False. Click and Type works for left align, center, and right align paragraphs.

11. C. Select Tools → Word Count from the menu to count the number of words in a document.

12. A. Select Edit → Go To from the menu to specify the page you want to view.

13. E. Encarta Dictionary, Factiva Search, Translation, and Gale Company Profiles are all resources available in the Research task pane.

14. A. You need to open the Print dialog box and specify the number of copies you want to print.

15. C. The Undo function can undo almost all of your actions.

16. A. You would use the Save As option in the File menu to save the file under a new name and/or location.

17. C. The Office Clipboard can hold up to 24 cut or copied items.

CHAPTER 3

FORMATTING CHARACTERS AND PARAGRAPHS

CHAPTER OBJECTIVES:

Formatting characters, Lessons 3.1–3.3

Changing a paragraph's alignment and spacing, Lessons 3.4 and 3.9

Indenting paragraphs, Lessons 3.5 and 3.6

Setting, changing, and removing tab stops, Lessons 3.7 and 3.8

Creating bulleted and numbered lists, Lessons 3.11

Adding borders and shading to a paragraph, Lessons 3.12 and 3.13

Understanding text flow and spacing before and after a paragraph, Lesson 3.10

CHAPTER TASK: CREATE, PRINT, AND SAVE A SIMPLE MEMO

Prerequisites

- **Windows basics: working with the mouse, menus, and dialog boxes.**
- **How to open and save a document.**
- **How to select text.**

You've probably seen documents created by several of your friends or work colleagues and envied their different fonts, italicized and boldfaced type, and fancy paragraph formatting. This chapter explains how to format both characters and paragraphs. You will learn how to change the appearance, size, and color of the characters in your documents. You will also learn the ins and outs of formatting paragraphs: aligning text to the left, right, and center of the page; increasing a paragraph's line spacing; and indenting paragraphs. This chapter also describes how to add borders to paragraphs and how to create bulleted and number lists.

Knowing how to format characters and paragraphs gives your documents more impact and makes them easier to read. Let's get started!

Formatting Characters Using the Toolbar

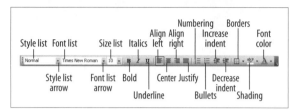

Figure 3-1. The Formatting toolbar.

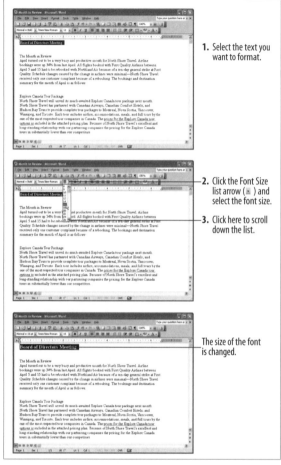

1. Select the text you want to format.

2. Click the Font Size list arrow (▪) and select the font size.

3. Click here to scroll down the list.

The size of the font is changed.

Figure 3-2. The procedure for changing font size.

You can emphasize text in a document by making the text darker and heavier (**bold**), slanted (*italics*), larger, or in a different typeface (or font). One of the easiest ways to apply character formatting is to use the Formatting toolbar. The Formatting toolbar includes buttons for applying the most common character and paragraph formatting options.

1 Start Microsoft Word.

2 Open the document named Lesson 3A, and save it as Month in Review.

The first thing you have to do is give this document a title so people can identify it.

3 Press Ctrl + Home to move the insertion point to the top of the document.

4 Click the Bold button on the Formatting toolbar. The Formatting toolbar is shown in Figure 3-1.

> **TIP**
> *Another way to bold is to press Ctrl + B, or select Format → Font from the menu, select Bold from the Font Style box, then click OK.*

The Bold button on the Formatting toolbar is now highlighted in orange, indicating that you are using bold character formatting. Anything you type while the Bold button is highlighted will be in boldface.

5 Type Board of Directors Meeting and press Enter twice.

Notice how the Bold button is still highlighted? You don't want to use bold character formatting anymore, so...

6 Click the Bold button on the Formatting toolbar.

The Bold button on the Formatting toolbar is no longer highlighted. You can also change the formatting of existing text by simply selecting the text and *then* formatting it. Let's try selecting some text and then formatting it.

7 In the first paragraph, select the text First Quality Airlines.

Now that the text has been selected, you can format it.

8 Click the Italics button on the Formatting toolbar.

> **TIP**
> *Another way to italicize text is to press Ctrl + I, or select Format → Font from the menu, select Italic from the Font Style box, then click OK.*

The selected text "First Quality Airlines" appears in Italics.

Besides applying Italics and Bold to text, you can also change the font type and font size. Let's make the headings in our summary stand out more by changing both the font and font size.

9 Select the text Board of Directors Meeting.

10 Click the Font list arrow on the formatting toolbar, then scroll to and click Arial in the list of fonts.

The selected text "Board of Directors Meeting" appears in Arial font. Arial and Times New Roman are two of the most commonly used fonts. Next, make the font size larger.

11 Keeping the same text selected, click the Font Size list arrow on the Formatting toolbar. Click 16.

The selected text "Board of Directors Meeting" appears in a larger font size (16 point type instead of the previous 12 point type), as shown in Figure 3-2. Wow! The new font formatting really makes the heading stand out from the rest of the document, doesn't it? Font sizes are measured in points (pt) which are 1/72 of an inch. The larger the number of points, the larger the font.

Now let's format the first subheading.

12 Select the subheading The Month in Review, and using the formatting techniques you have learned, apply the following font formatting to the selected heading: Arial, Bold, and 14 pt.

Table 3-1 outlines some common fonts and font sizes.

Table 3-1. Examples of Common Font Types and Sizes

Common Font Types	Common Font Sizes
Arial	Arial 8 point
Comic Sans MS	Arial 10 point
Courier New	Courier New
Times New Roman	Arial 12 point

QUICK REFERENCE

TO BOLD TEXT:

- CLICK THE BOLD BUTTON ON THE FORMATTING TOOLBAR OR PRESS CTRL + B.

TO ITALICIZE TEXT:

- CLICK THE ITALICS BUTTON ON THE FORMATTING TOOLBAR OR PRESS CTRL + I.

TO UNDERLINE TEXT:

- CLICK THE UNDERLINE BUTTON ON THE FORMATTING TOOLBAR OR PRESS CTRL + U.

TO CHANGE FONT SIZE:

- SELECT THE PT SIZE FROM THE FONT SIZE LIST ON THE FORMATTING TOOLBAR.

TO CHANGE FONT TYPE:

- SELECT THE FONT FROM THE FONT LIST ON THE FORMATTING TOOLBAR.

Using the Format Painter

Figure 3-3. First, select text with the formatting you want to copy…

Figure 3-4. …then apply the formatting using the Format Painter.

If you find yourself applying the same formatting to characters and/or paragraphs again and again, then you should familiarize yourself with the Format Painter tool. The Format Painter allows you to copy the formatting of text and apply it elsewhere. Sound confusing? It won't after you finish this lesson.

1 **Select the subheading** The Month in Review, **as shown in Figure 3-3.**

You want to use the same formatting in "The Month in Review" for the other two subheadings in the document.

2 **Double-click the** Format Painter button.

TIP

Single-click the Format Painter button to apply any copied formatting. Double-click the Format Painter button to apply copied formatting several times. Click the Format Painter button again when you're finished.

Double-clicking the Format Painter button allows you to copy the same formatting several times. If you had clicked the Format Painter button only once, it would only allow you to apply the copied formatting one time. Notice the pointer changes to a ![icon].

3 **Move the** ![icon] **pointer to the very beginning of the subheading,** Explore Canada Tour Package. **Click and hold the mouse button, and drag the pointer across the heading, as shown in Figure 3-4. Release the mouse button at the end of the heading.**

Like other mouse-intensive operations, this one can be a little tricky for some people the first time they try it. The formatting from the first heading should now be applied to the selected heading. Because you double-clicked the Format Painter button, you can keep applying the copied formatting to other paragraphs.

4 **Drag the** ![icon] **pointer across the remaining heading,** New Communications Director Position.

The formatting is applied to the last heading in the document.

5 Click the Format Painter button to deactivate the Format Painter.

6 Deselect the text (by clicking anywhere on the screen), and then save the document.

QUICK REFERENCE

TO COPY FORMATTING WITH THE FORMAT PAINTER:

1. SELECT THE TEXT OR PARAGRAPH WITH THE FORMATTING OPTIONS YOU WANT TO COPY.

2. CLICK THE FORMAT PAINTER BUTTON ON THE STANDARD TOOLBAR.

3. DRAG THE FORMAT PAINTER POINTER ACROSS THE TEXT OR PARAGRAPH WHERE YOU WANT TO APPLY THE COPIED FORMATTING.

TO COPY SELECTED FORMATTING TO SEVERAL LOCATIONS:

1. SELECT THE TEXT OR PARAGRAPH WITH THE FORMATTING OPTIONS YOU WANT TO COPY.

2. DOUBLE-CLICK THE FORMAT PAINTER BUTTON.

3. DRAG THE FORMAT PAINTER POINTER ACROSS THE TEXT OR PARAGRAPH WHERE YOU WANT TO APPLY THE COPIED FORMATTING.

4. CLICK THE FORMAT PAINTER BUTTON WHEN YOU'RE FINISHED.

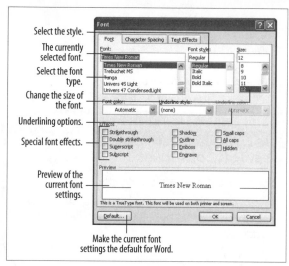

Select the style.

The currently
selected font.

Select the font
type.

Change the size of
the font.

Underlining options.

Special font effects.

Preview of the
current font
settings.

Make the current font
settings the default for Word.

Figure 3-5. The Font dialog box.

The Formatting toolbar is great for quickly applying the most common formatting options to characters, but it doesn't offer every formatting option available. To see and/or use every possible character formatting option, you need to use the Font dialog box—available by selecting Format → Font from the menu or by selecting Font from most shortcut menus. This lesson looks at how to format characters with the Font dialog box.

1 **Select the subheading** The Month in Review.

Remember that once you have selected a portion of text, you can format it. The Formatting toolbar is great for quick formatting, but the Font dialog box has additional, more advanced font formatting options.

Table 3-2. Font Formatting Options

2 Select Format → Font from the menu.

The Font dialog box appears, as shown in Figure 3-5. The line of text you selected will be a minor heading, so you need to make it stand out from the document.

3 **Scroll down the** Font: list box, and select Garamond.

Look at the Preview area at the bottom of the Font dialog box to see a sample or preview of how the selected text will look once it has been formatted.

4 **Scroll down the** Font style: box and select Bold Italic. **Click the** Font Color list arrow and select Blue.

> TIP
> *Another way to change the font color is to click the Font Color button on the Formatting toolbar.*

The selected text is colored blue.

5 **Click** OK and deselect the text.

The selected text appears in blue Garamond font, with bold and italics formatting.

6 **Click the** Undo button **to undo your font formatting changes.**

There are many other font formatting options available in the Font dialog box. The purpose of this lesson isn't to go through all of them, but to explain how to use the Font dialog box. Take a look at Table 3-2, which explains the different options in the Font dialog box.

Option	Description
Font	Allows you to change the font type.
Font style	Formats the style of the font: Regular (no emphasis), Italic, Bold, and Bold Italic.
Size	Allows you to increase or decrease the size of the font.
Underline style	Allows you to change font underlining options.
Font color	Allows you to change the font color.
Effects	Allows you to add special effects to fonts as follows:
	Underline
	Shadow
	Emboss
	^{Super}script
	$_{Sub}$script

Table 3-2. Font Formatting Options (Continued)

Option	Description
Default	Makes the current font formatting the default font. Word will use it automatically whenever you create a new document. (Be **very** careful when selecting this option!)

QUICK REFERENCE

TO OPEN THE FONT DIALOG BOX:

- SELECT FORMAT → FONT FROM THE MENU, SPECIFY THE FONT FORMATTING OPTIONS IN THE FONT DIALOG BOX, AND CLICK OK.

TO CHANGE A FONT'S COLOR:

- CLICK THE FONT COLOR BUTTON LIST ARROW ON THE FORMATTING TOOLBAR AND SELECT THE COLOR.

Changing Paragraph Alignment and Inserting the Current Date

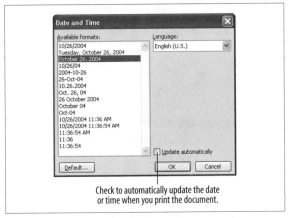

Check to automatically update the date
or time when you print the document.

Figure 3-6. The Date and Time dialog box.

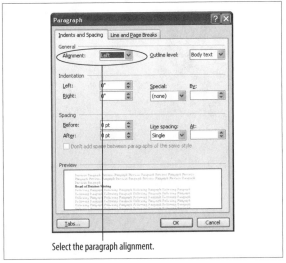

Figure 3-7. Left aligned, right aligned, centered, and justified paragraphs.

Select the paragraph alignment.

Figure 3-8. You can also change the alignment of the selected paragraph(s) by using the Paragraph dialog box.

This lesson moves on to paragraph formatting and how to align paragraphs to the left, right, center, or justified on a page. Figure 3-7 gives a better idea of what the various alignments—left, right, centered, and justified—look like. You will also learn how to do something that's not related to paragraph formatting at all, but is still useful: inserting the current date into a document.

1 If necessary, navigate to your Practice folder, open Lesson 3B and save the file as Month in Review.

2 Place the insertion point anywhere in the first line, Board of Directors Meeting.

3 Click the Center button on the Formatting toolbar.

TIP **Another way to center is to press** Ctrl + E.

The first line, the document's title, is centered between the left and right margins. Notice that you didn't have to select the text in the paragraph like you have to do when formatting fonts. Now let's add a new line with the date.

4 Press End to move the insertion point to the end of the current line and press Enter.

The new paragraph is also centered like the one above it. That's because when you press Enter, the new paragraph "inherits" the same formatting as the paragraph above it.

5 Select Insert → Date and Time from the menu.

TIP **You can have Word automatically insert today's date by selecting** Insert → Date and Time **from the menu.**

The Date and Time dialog box opens, as shown in Figure 3-6. Word automatically inserts the date, based on your computer's internal clock. Make sure that the "Update automatically" check box is not checked, or the date will change every time you save or print the document.

6 Click the third option from the list, as shown in Figure 3-6, and click OK.

Today's date (or the date your computer thinks it is) is inserted into the document.

7 Move the insertion point anywhere in the paragraph that starts with April turned out to be.

8 Click the Justify button on the Formatting toolbar.

> TIP
> *Another way to justify is to press Ctrl + J.*

The paragraph is justified—both the left and right edges of the paragraph are even.

9 Repeat Step 6 in the two other body paragraphs.

10 Press Ctrl + End to move the insertion point to the end of the document and press Enter twice.

11 Click the Align Right button on the Formatting toolbar.

> TIP
> *Another way to align right is to press Ctrl + R.*

12 Type Prepared by Sandra Willes.

The paragraph is formatted to the very right of the margin.

If you want to change the alignment of your paragraphs the hard way, you can also use the Paragraph dialog box.

13 Select Format → Paragraph from the menu.

The Paragraph dialog box appears, as shown in Figure 3-8. Here you can select paragraph alignment from the Alignment list. Although it's much easier and faster to use the Formatting toolbars to align paragraphs, if you are formatting another element of a paragraph, such as its spacing (more on that later!), you might as well use the Paragraph dialog box to adjust the paragraph alignment at the same time.

Now that you have aligned all the paragraphs in your document, you can close the Paragraph dialog box.

14 Click Cancel to close the Paragraph dialog box.

Indenting Paragraphs

Figure 3-9. An indented paragraph.

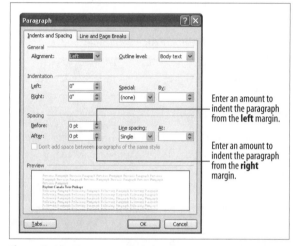

Figure 3-10. The Paragraph dialog box.

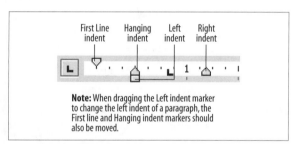

Figure 3-11. First line, Hanging, and Left indent markers on the ruler.

Indenting means to add blank space between the left and/ or right margin and the paragraph of text, as shown in Figure 3-9. Indenting paragraphs can emphasize the paragraphs and add organization to a document. Long quotations, numbered and bulleted lists, and bibliographies are a few examples of paragraphs that are often indented. You can indent paragraphs from the left and right margins.

1 Place the insertion point anywhere in the paragraph under the heading The Month in Review.

2 Click the Increase Indent button on the formatting toolbar.

> **TIP**
> *The Decrease Indent button is the opposite of the Increase Indent button—it moves the paragraph's left edge out towards the first tab stop.*

The Increase Indent button indents the paragraph a half-inch on the left.

3 Repeat Step 1 and indent the paragraph under the heading Explore Canada Tour Package.

4 Select the heading Explore Canada Tour Package and select Format → Paragraph from the menu.

The Paragraph dialog box appears, as shown in Figure 3-10.

5 Click in the Left indentation box and type 2.

You can also change the number by clicking the Left Indentation box's up arrow until 2 appears. This will make the paragraph indentation two inches (2"). Using the Paragraph dialog box allows you to indent paragraphs with greater precision than the Formatting toolbar. Click on the up and down arrows to increase and decrease paragraph indentation.

6 Click OK.

Word indents the selected paragraph two inches. Another way you can indent paragraphs is by using the Indent markers on the ruler.

7 Click the Undo button to undo your paragraph formatting changes.

The heading is no longer indented by 2 inches.

8 Place the insertion point anywhere in the last paragraph of the document under the heading New Communications Director Position and drag the Left indent marker on the ruler to the right so that it is at the half-inch mark.

Like other mouse-intensive operations, this one can be tricky for some people the first time they try it. It can also be confusing, because when you drag the Left indent marker, the Hanging Indent and First line indent markers also move, like this (see

Figure 3-11). The paragraph should have the same indentation as the two body paragraphs above it when you're finished.

You can also change the right indentation of a paragraph, just like the left.

9 Keeping the insertion point in the same sentence, select Format → Paragraph from the menu.

The Paragraph dialog box appears.

10 Click in the Right indentation box, type 1 and click OK.

The paragraph right indentation increases by one inch (1"). You can also increase a paragraph's right indentation by moving the Right Indent marker on the ruler:

11 Click and drag the Right indent marker on the ruler to the left another half-inch.

The paragraph's right edge is indented another half-inch.

12 Keeping the insertion point in the same sentence, select Format → Paragraph from the menu.

The Paragraph dialog box appears.

13 Type 0 in the Right indentation box and click OK.

The paragraph's right edge is no longer indented.

14 Save your work.

That concludes the lesson on indenting paragraphs. In the next lesson, you'll learn more specialized ways to indent paragraphs.

QUICK REFERENCE

TO INDENT A PARAGRAPH:

- CLICK THE INCREASE INDENT BUTTON ON THE FORMATTING TOOLBAR.

OR...

- CLICK AND DRAG THE LEFT INDENT MARKER ON THE RULER.

OR...

- SELECT FORMAT → PARAGRAPH FROM THE MENU AND ENTER HOW MUCH SPACE YOU WANT THE PARAGRAPH INDENTED BY.

TO DECREASE AN INDENT:

- CLICK THE DECREASE INDENT BUTTON ON THE FORMATTING TOOLBAR.

TO RIGHT INDENT A PARAGRAPH:

- CLICK AND DRAG THE △ RIGHT INDENT MARKER ON THE RULER.

OR...

- SELECT FORMAT → PARAGRAPH FROM THE MENU AND ENTER HOW MUCH SPACE YOU WANT THE PARAGRAPH INDENTED BY.

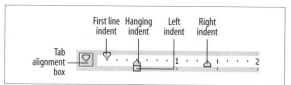

The Month in Review
    April turned out to be a very busy and productive month for North Shore Travel. Airline bookings were up 34% from last April. All flights booked with First Quality Airlines between April 5 and 15 had to be rebooked with Northland Air because of a ten-day general strike at First Quality. Schedule changes caused by the change in airlines were minimal—North Shore Travel received only one customer complaint because of a rebooking. The bookings and destination summary for the month of April is as follows:

The Month in Review
April turned out to be a very busy and productive month for North Shore Travel. Airline bookings were up 34% from last April. All flights booked with First Quality Airlines between April 5 and 15 had to be rebooked with Northland Air because of a ten-day general strike at First Quality. Schedule changes caused by the change in airlines were minimal—North Shore Travel received only one customer complaint because of a rebooking. The bookings and destination summary for the month of April is as follows:

Figure 3-12. First line indentation and Hanging indentation.

Figure 3-13. First line, Hanging, and Left and Right indent markers on the ruler.

Besides the standard left and right indentations, Word also lets you create two types of special indentations: First line indentations and Hanging indentations. A First line indentation lets you indent the first line of a paragraph independently of the other lines. Sometimes people indent the first line of their paragraphs by a half-inch by pressing the Tab key, but you can also format the paragraph so that the first line is automatically indented a half-inch. A Hanging indentation, on the other hand, is easier to understand by looking at it—see Figure 3-12 for an example. The first line in the paragraph stays put while the other lines in the paragraph are indented. Hanging indentations are often used in bibliographies.

1 Place the insertion point anywhere in the paragraph under the heading The Month in Review and select Format → Paragraph from the menu.

2 In the Indentation section, click the Special list arrow and select First line.

Notice 0.5" automatically appears in the "By" text box, which indicates that the first line of the paragraph will be indented a half-inch. If you wanted to indent the first line of the paragraph by an amount other than 0.5 inches, you would enter the amount in the "By" box.

3 Click OK.

The first line of the paragraph is indented an additional half-inch. You can also use the ruler to indent the first line instead of using the Paragraph dialog box. Let's try it!

4 Click the Undo button to undo the previous paragraph formatting.

The first line of the paragraph is no longer first line indented.

5 Drag the First line indent marker on the ruler to the right (ruler shown in Figure 3-13), moving it to the next half-inch mark.

Another way to insert a First line indent is to click the tab alignment box until you see the First line indent marker, then click where you want to insert the indent on the ruler.

The first line of the paragraph is indented a half-inch, just as it was in Step 3. Let's move on to the other type of special indentation—the Hanging indent.

6 Place the insertion point anywhere in the paragraph under the heading Explore Canada Tour Package and select Format → Paragraph from the menu.

The Paragraph dialog box appears.

7 Click the Special list arrow and select Hanging.

Another way to insert a Hanging indent is to click the tab alignment box until you see the Hanging indent marker, then click where you want to insert the indent on the ruler.

Again, 0.5" automatically appears in the "By" text box.

8 Click OK.

The paragraph is formatted with a Hanging indent, similar to the paragraph shown in Figure 3-12. You don't really need a hanging indent for this paragraph, so let's remove the special indent formatting.

9 Keeping the insertion point in the same paragraph, select Format → Paragraph from the menu.

The Paragraph dialog box appears.

10 Click the Special list arrow, select (none), then click OK.

QUICK REFERENCE

TO CREATE A HANGING INDENT:

1. SELECT FORMAT → PARAGRAPH FROM THE MENU.

2. SELECT HANGING FROM THE SPECIAL BOX IN THE INDENTATION SECTION.

3. ENTER THE DESIRED INDENT AMOUNT IN THE BY BOX, AND CLICK OK.

OR...

• CLICK AND DRAG THE ◯ HANGING INDENT MARKER ON THE RULER.

TO INDENT THE FIRST LINE OF A PARAGRAPH:

1. SELECT FORMAT → PARAGRAPH FROM THE MENU.

2. SELECT FIRST LINE FROM THE SPECIAL BOX IN THE INDENTATION SECTION.

3. ENTER THE DESIRED INDENT AMOUNT IN THE BY BOX, AND CLICK OK.

OR...

• CLICK AND DRAG THE ⸬WRD_103.06.01.⸬ FIRST LINE INDENT MARKER ON THE RULER.

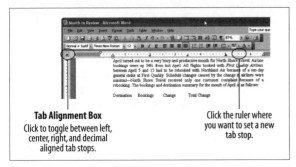

Tab Alignment Box
Click to toggle between left,
center, right, and decimal
aligned tab stops.

**Click the ruler where
you want to set a new
tab stop.**

Figure 3-14. Setting tab stops.

Tabs make it easy to align text. Many novice Word users mistakenly use the Spacebar to align text—don't! The Tab key is faster, more accurate, and much easier to change. Each time you press the Tab key, the insertion point moves to the next tab stop. Word's tab stops are set at every half-inch by default, but you can easily create your own. There are several different types of tab stops available: see Table 3-1 for their descriptions. Two methods can be used to add and modify tab stops: the horizontal ruler (which we will use in this lesson), and the Tabs dialog box (which we will use in the next lesson).

1 If necessary, navigate to your Practice folder, open Lesson 3C and save the file as Month in Review.

2 Click the ¶ Show/Hide button on the Standard toolbar.

All the hidden characters in the document (spaces, tabs, and paragraph marks) appear, making it easier for you to see any tab markers.

3 Place the insertion point at the beginning of the blank line underneath the first body paragraph and press Enter.

The default tab stops are normally left-aligned and located at every half-inch on the ruler.

4 Press Tab, type Destination, press Tab, type Bookings, press Tab, type Change, press Tab, and then type Total Change.

The headings you entered are all aligned with the default half-inch tab stops. You can change, add, and remove tab stops very easily. Here's how:

5 Click the 0.5″ mark on the ruler.

Word inserts a left-align tab stop where you click on the ruler. The "Destination" heading is aligned with the left-align tab stop.

Left-align tabs are the default type of tab stops—and they're the type you'll use 95 percent of the time. However, there are times when you may want to align text differently on a tab stop—so that it is centered or right-aligned, for example.

To change the type of tab stop Word uses, click the Tab alignment box until the tab stop you want appears, then click the ruler to add that type of tab stop.

6 Click the Tab alignment box so that the ⊥ Center Tab marker appears, then click the 2″ mark on the ruler.

See Figure 3-14 if you have trouble finding the Tab alignment box. The Tab alignment box cycles between four different types of tab stop alignment: left, center, right, and decimal. The "Bookings" heading is now aligned with the center-align tab stop.

7 Click the Tab alignment box until you see the ⌐ Right Tab marker, then click the 3.5″ mark on the ruler.

The "Change" heading is now aligned with the right-align tab stop.

The *decimal tab* is the most confusing of all the tab stops. It aligns numbers by their decimal point. If the number doesn't have a decimal point—or if it's not a number at all, but text—it will align to the left of the decimal tab stop.

8 Click the Tab alignment box until you see the ⊥ Decimal Tab marker, then click the 5″ mark on the ruler.

⋮ NOTE ⋮ *Tab stops are added to the current or selected paragraph(s)—not the entire document. If you want your entire document to have the same tab stops, you would have to select the entire document first (hold down the Ctrl key as you click the far left margin) and then add the tab stops.*

9 Press Enter and type the following text into the document. Make sure you press Tab as indicated, and remember to press Enter at the end of each line.

Tab Left Tab Center Tab Right Tab Decimal

Tab East Tab 9,417 Tab $968,723 Tab +32.38%

Tab West Tab 7,983 Tab $747,295 Tab +6.151%

Tab Central Tab 5,205 Tab $529,207 Tab +13.8%

When you press Enter, notice how each new paragraph has the new tab stops? That's because, as with paragraph formatting, each new paragraph "inherits" the tab stops in the paragraph above it.

Alignment	Mark	Example	Description
		`L · · · I · · · 1 · · · I · · · 2 · · I · · · 3 · · · I · · · 4 · · · I · · · 5`	
Left	`L`	1,000.00	Aligns the left side of text with the tab stop.
Center	`⊥`	1,000.00	Aligns the text so that it is centered over the tab stop.
Right	`⌐`	1,000.00	Aligns the right side of text with the tab stop.
Decimal	`⊥·`	1,000.00	Aligns text at the decimal point. Text and numbers before the decimal point appear to the left, and text and numbers after the decimal point appear to the right.
Bar	`I`			A vertical line character is inserted where the bar tab is located.

QUICK REFERENCE

TO ADD A TAB STOP:

• CLICK ON THE RULER WHERE YOU WANT TO ADD THE TAB STOP.

OR...

• SELECT FORMAT → TABS FROM THE MENU AND SPECIFY WHERE YOU WANT TO ADD THE TAB STOP(S).

TO CHANGE THE TAB ALIGNMENT:

• CLICK THE TAB ALIGNMENT BOX ON THE RULER UNTIL YOU SEE THE TYPE OF TAB YOU WANT TO USE (LEFT, CENTER, RIGHT, DECIMAL, OR BAR), AND THEN CLICK WHERE YOU WANT TO ADD THE TAB STOP.

TO ADJUST A TAB STOP:

• CLICK AND DRAG THE TAB STOP TO THE DESIRED POSITION ON THE RULER.

TO REMOVE A TAB STOP:

• CLICK AND DRAG THE TAB STOP OFF OF THE RULER.

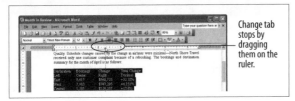

Change tab stops by dragging them on the ruler.

Figure 3-15. You can adjust a paragraph's tab settings by dragging the marker on the ruler.

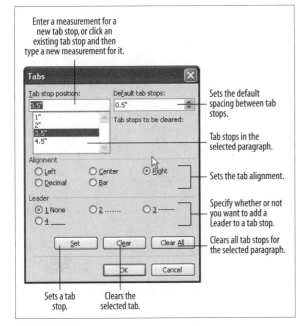

Enter a measurement for a new tab stop, or click an existing tab stop and then type a new measurement for it.

Sets the default spacing between tab stops.

Tab stops in the selected paragraph.

Sets the tab alignment.

Specify whether or not you want to add a Leader to a tab stop.

Clears all tab stops for the selected paragraph.

Sets a tab stop.

Clears the selected tab.

Figure 3-16. The Tabs dialog box.

The last lesson focused on setting tab stops by using the horizontal ruler. In this lesson, you'll learn how to add and modify tab stops by using the other method of setting tab stops: the Tabs dialog box. The Tabs dialog box is slightly slower to work with than setting tabs with the horizontal ruler, but it is more accurate and gives you more options. Enough talking—let's get started!

1 Select the entire list, as shown in Figure 3-15.

2 Carefully drag the Right Tab marker (above the "Change" heading) on the ruler from the 3.5" mark to the 3" mark.

The entire column moves to the left a half-inch. This is another mouse operation that requires some mouse dexterity—if you aren't extremely precise when you select and drag a tab, you may accidentally add a new tab stop.

Removing tabs is even easier than adjusting them—go ahead and try removing one:

3 With the text still selected, drag the Decimal Tab marker (above the "Total Change" heading) down and off the ruler.

When you remove a tab, the tabbed text moves to the nearest available tab stop. In this case, removing the decimal tab messes up your list quite a bit. Let's add a left-align tab to replace the decimal tab you just removed.

4 Click the Tab alignment box until you see the Left Tab marker, then click the 4" mark on the ruler.

The last column is aligned to the left of the new tab.

Another way to add, adjust, and remove tabs is to use the Tabs dialog box. The Tabs dialog box lets you add and adjust tabs by entering units of measurement, like 1.5", instead of sliding tab symbols on the ruler. The Tab dialog box allows you to be more precise when setting tab stops, and some people find it easier to use than setting tabs on the ruler.

5 Make sure the entire list is still selected and select Format → Tabs from the menu.

The Tabs dialog box appears, as shown in Figure 3-16.

 TIP *Clicking the Clear All button removes all tab stop settings for the selected paragraph(s).*

6 Select 2" from the Tab stop position list box and click the Clear button.

This will remove the 2" tab—the one above the "Bookings" heading. The Tabs dialog box is nice, because you can precisely enter where you want a tab stop, instead of eyeballing it on the ruler.

7 Type 1.8 in the Tab stop position text box, make sure the alignment option is set to Center, and click the Set button.

This will add a new, centered 1.8" tab.

8 Click OK.

The Tabs dialog box closes, and the "Bookings" column is aligned on the 1.8" centered tab.

The Tabs dialog box also offers a setting that is not available on the ruler: *leaders.* A leader is a set of periods or lines that run from one place to another. Leaders make reading lengthy lists and reference material easier and are usually used in the table of contents section of a report or book. Try adding a leader to one of your tab settings.

9 Keeping the same list selected, select Format → Tabs **from the menu.**

10 Select 1.8″ **from the** Tab stop position **list box.**

11 **In the Leader section, click the** 2 **option to place a dotted leader before the tab stop.**

You could have also chosen a dash leader (3) or a line leader (4).

12 **Click the** Set button **and click** OK **to close the dialog box.**

A dotted leader now precedes the "Bookings" column. You certainly don't need any leaders for the type of list you're working on, so let's go ahead and remove it.

13 **Click the** Undo button **to undo the last changes made to the tab settings.**

Since you're done working with tabs, you don't need to see the nonprinting characters (spaces, tabs, and paragraphs) anymore.

14 **Click the** Show/Hide button **on the Standard toolbar.**

The nonprinting characters are no longer displayed.

QUICK REFERENCE

TO ADJUST A TAB STOP:

- CLICK AND DRAG THE TAB STOP TO THE DESIRED LOCATION ON THE RULER.

TO REMOVE A TAB STOP:

- DRAG THE TAB STOP OFF OF THE RULER.

TO USE THE TABS DIALOG BOX:

- SELECT FORMAT → TABS FROM THE MENU.

TO ADD A LEADER TO A TAB STOP:

1. SELECT FORMAT → TABS FROM THE MENU TO OPEN THE TABS DIALOG BOX.

2. SELECT THE LEADER YOU WANT TO USE, CLICK THE SET BUTTON, AND CLICK OK.

Formatting Paragraph Line Spacing

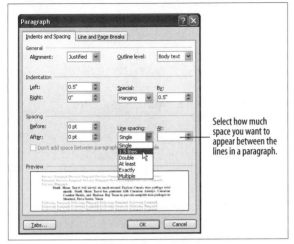

Figure 3-17. You can format line spacing in the Paragraph dialog box.

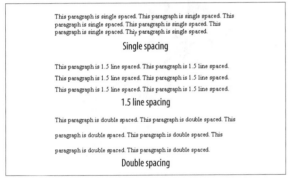

Figure 3-18. Line spacing example.

You've probably had a teacher, professor, or manager who would only accept reports that were double-spaced. Adding space between lines makes a document easier to read (and longer!). You can add as much or as little line spacing as you want. This lesson shows you how.

1 Place the insertion point anywhere in the first body paragraph and select Format → Paragraph from the menu.

The Paragraph dialog box appears, as shown in Figure 3-17. Look at the Line spacing text box—see how this paragraph's line spacing is currently single-spaced? You want to format this paragraph with 1.5 line spacing instead.

2 Click the Line spacing list arrow.

You have several line spacing choices (see Figure 3-18 for some of them):

• **Single:** Single spacing—line spacing that accommodates the largest font in that line, plus a small amount of extra space. This is the default setting for paragraphs.

• **1.5 Lines:** Space-and-a-half spacing—line spacing for each line that is one-and-one-half times that of single line spacing. For example, if 10-point text is spaced at 1.5 lines, the line spacing is approximately 15 points.

• **Double:** Double-spacing—line spacing for each line that is twice that of single line spacing. For example, in double-spaced lines of 10-point text, the line spacing is approximately 20 points

• **At least:** Minimum line spacing that Word can adjust to accommodate larger font sizes that would not otherwise fit within the specified spacing.

• **Exactly:** Fixed line spacing that Word does not adjust. This option makes all lines evenly spaced.

• **Multiple:** Line spacing that is increased or decreased by a percentage that you specify. For example, setting line spacing to a multiple of 1.2 would increase the space by 20 percent, while setting line spacing to a multiple of 0.8 would decrease the space by 20 percent. Setting the line spacing at a multiple of 2 is equivalent to setting the line spacing at Double. In the "At" box, type or select the line spacing you want. The default is three lines.

3 Select 1.5 lines from the list and click OK.

The Paragraph dialog disappears and the selected paragraph is formatted with 1.5 line spacing.

4 Repeat Steps 1–3 for the two remaining body paragraphs.

Of course there are other line spacing options besides single and 1.5 line spacing. Let's try formatting a paragraph with double spacing.

5 Place the insertion point anywhere in the first body paragraph and select Format → Paragraph from the menu.

The Paragraph dialog box appears.

6 Click the Line spacing list arrow and select Double from the list. Click OK.

The Paragraph dialog box disappears and the selected paragraph is formatted with double spacing. You don't want the line spacing to be double-spaced, so let's undo the previous formatting command.

7 Click the Undo button on the Standard toolbar.

The paragraph's line spacing returns to 1.5 line spacing.

What if you want to format your paragraph's line spacing with something that isn't available in the Line spacing list? For example, what if you want triple spacing?

8 Keeping the insertion point in the same paragraph, select Format → Paragraph from the menu.

The Paragraph dialog box appears.

9 Click the Line spacing list arrow and select Exactly from the list.

A number, probably 10 or 12 pt, will appear in the "At" text box to the right of the Line spacing list. The "At" text box allows you to specify the exact amount of line spacing that you want. We want to format the paragraph with triple line spacing, so enter 36 pt. (12 pt to a line × 3 = 36 pt).

10 In the At text box, type 36.

11 Click OK.

The selected paragraph is formatted with 36 pt line spacing.

12 Click the Undo button to undo the previous paragraph formatting command.

The selected paragraph's line spacing returns to 1.5 line spacing.

13 Save your work.

QUICK REFERENCE

TO CHANGE PARAGRAPH LINE SPACING:

1. SELECT FORMAT → PARAGRAPH FROM THE MENU TO OPEN THE PARAGRAPH DIALOG BOX.

2. CLICK THE LINE SPACING LIST ARROW AND SELECT THE SPACING OPTION YOU WANT TO USE (SINGLE, 1.5 LINES, DOUBLE, AT LEAST, EXACTLY, OR MULTIPLE).

Formatting Spacing Between Paragraphs

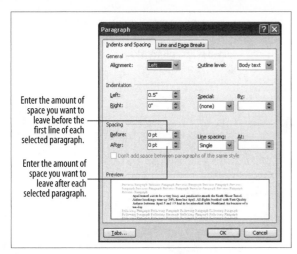

Figure 3-19. You can format spacing before and after paragraphs in the Paragraph dialog box.

Enter the amount of space you want to leave before the first line of each selected paragraph.

Enter the amount of space you want to leave after each selected paragraph.

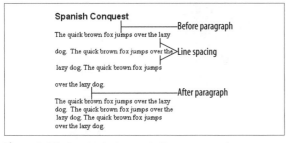

Figure 3-20. Spacing before and after a paragraph.

Adding space between the paragraphs in a document gives it structure and makes it easier to read. You're probably already thinking, "What's so hard about adding space between paragraphs? All I have to do is hit the Enter key a few times." This is true, but sometimes you might need more precise spacing than the Enter key can provide. For example, you might want to add just a tad more space above or below a paragraph, as illustrated in Figure 3-20. All you have to do is bring up the trusty Paragraph dialog box in order to adjust the spacing above or below the paragraph.

1 If necessary, navigate to your Practice folder, open Lesson 3D and save the file as Month in Review.

2 Place the insertion point anywhere in the first body paragraph.

Now we need to bring up the Paragraph dialog box.

3 Select Format → Paragraph from the menu.

The Paragraph dialog box appears, as shown in Figure 3-19. You need some space between this paragraph and the heading immediately above it. You could use the Enter key to add a blank line between the two paragraphs, but there's a better way.

4 In the Before text box, click the up arrow until 12 pt appears.

This will add 12 points of space before the selected paragraph. Since the font for the selected paragraph is 12 pt in size, 12 pt spacing would equal a single, blank line.

5 Click OK.

The Paragraph dialog box disappears, and the selected paragraph is formatted with 12 pt spacing immediately before, or above it.

6 Repeat Steps 3–5 for the two remaining body paragraphs.

You may have noticed that there is an "After" text box immediately below the "Before" text box in the Paragraph dialog box. That's right, Word can also add spacing *after* a paragraph.

7 Place the insertion point anywhere in the first paragraph heading, The Month in Review, and select Format → Paragraph from the menu.

8 In the After text box, click the up arrow until 6 pt appears.

This means you want 6 points of space to come *after* this paragraph.

9 Click OK.

The Paragraph dialog box closes, and the selected heading is formatted with 6 pt spacing immediately after, or below it.

10 Repeat Steps 7–9 for the two remaining headings.

Using the Paragraph dialog box to add space between paragraphs in a document is often easier than adding spacing with the Enter key—especially if you change your mind and want to modify how much space there is between paragraphs. You only need to select the paragraphs whose paragraph spacing you want to change, and then modify the paragraph spacing using the Paragraph dialog box. That way you don't have to hunt down each and every paragraph mark.

QUICK REFERENCE

TO ADJUST THE SPACE ABOVE A PARAGRAPH:

1. SELECT FORMAT → PARAGRAPH FROM THE MENU TO OPEN THE PARAGRAPH DIALOG BOX.

2. SPECIFY HOW MUCH SPACE YOU WANT IN THE SPACING BEFORE BOX.

TO ADJUST THE SPACE BELOW A PARAGRAPH:

1. SELECT FORMAT → PARAGRAPH FROM THE MENU TO OPEN THE PARAGRAPH DIALOG BOX.

2. SPECIFY HOW MUCH SPACE YOU WANT IN THE SPACING AFTER BOX.

Creating Bulleted and Numbered Lists

Things to buy:
• Peas
• Corn
• Cod-liver oil
Bulleted List

Figure 3-21. An example of a bulleted list.

How to turn on my computer:
1. Take a deep breath.
2. Press ON.
3. Wait.
Numbered List

Figure 3-22. An example of a numbered list.

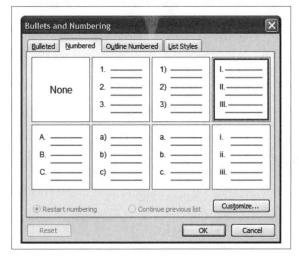

Figure 3-23. The Bulleted tab of the Bullets and Numbering dialog box.

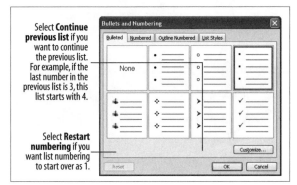

Select **Continue previous list** if you want to continue the previous list. For example, if the last number in the previous list is 3, this list starts with 4.

Select **Restart numbering** if you want list numbering to start over as 1.

Figure 3-24. The Numbered tab of the Bullets and Numbering dialog box.

You can make lists more attractive and easier to read by using bulleted lists. In a bulleted list, each paragraph is preceded by a *bullet*—a filled-in circle (•) or other character (an example of this is shown in Figure 3-21). Use bulleted lists when the order of items in a list doesn't matter.

When the order of items in a list *does* matter, however, try using a numbered list, as shown in Figure 3-22. Numbered lists are great when you want to present step-by-step instructions (like in this book!). When you work with a numbered list, Word takes care of the numbering for you—you can add or delete items in a list and they will always be numbered correctly.

1 Select the entire list at the end of the document, **beginning with** Written formal client correspondence, **and ending with** Updating North Shore Travel's future web site.

With the current formatting, it's difficult to distinguish this as a list. Let's add some bullets to make it more distinctive.

2 Click the ⬛ Bullets button on the Formatting toolbar.

Bullets appear in front of each listed item. Make the list stand out more by indenting it from the rest of the document.

3 Click the ⬛ Increase Indent button on the formatting toolbar.

The selected list (or paragraph) is indented to the right. Creating a numbered list is just as easy as creating a bulleted list.

4 Click the ⬛ Numbering button on the formatting toolbar.

Viola! The bulleted list is changed to a numbered list.

5 Place the insertion point at the end of the Updating North Shore Travel's future web site line.

6 Press Enter to start a new paragraph.

Notice how the new paragraph starts with the next number on the list and "inherits" the same formatting as the paragraph before it.

7 Type North Shore Travel's Monthly Newsletter.

8 Press Enter to start a new paragraph.

The paragraph starts with the next number on our list. Great, but hmmm…what if you've finished your list and want to type something else?

9 Press the Backspace key to stop adding to the list.

The paragraph no longer has a number in front of it and is no longer part of the list.

You can also create a bulleted or numbered list with the Bullets and Numbering dialog box. The Bullets and Numbering dialog box gives you many more formatting options than the Formatting toolbar does.

10 Select the entire list at the end of the document, beginning with Written formal client correspondence and ending with North Shore Travel's Monthly Newsletter.

11 Select Format → Bullets and Numbering from the menu.

The Bullets and Numbering dialog box appears with the Bulleted tab selected, as shown in Figure 3-23. Here, you can select the type of bullets you want to appear in your list. We don't want to change bullets in this lesson, so…

12 Click the Numbered tab.

The Numbered tab appears. Here you can select the type of numbering you would like to use to format your list.

13 Click the Roman numeral numbering option, as shown in Figure 3-24, and click OK.

The list is numbered with Roman numerals.

14 Save your work.

QUICK REFERENCE

TO CREATE A BULLETED LIST:

- CLICK THE BULLETS BUTTON ON THE FORMATTING TOOLBAR.

OR…

1. SELECT FORMAT → BULLETS AND NUMBERING FROM THE MENU AND CLICK THE BULLETED TAB.

2. SELECT THE BULLETING OPTION YOU WANT TO USE.

TO CREATE A NUMBERED LIST:

- CLICK THE NUMBERING BUTTON ON THE FORMATTING TOOLBAR.

OR…

1. SELECT FORMAT → BULLETS AND NUMBERING FROM THE MENU AND CLICK THE NUMBERED TAB.

2. SELECT THE NUMBERING OPTION YOU WANT TO USE.

Adding Borders to Your Paragraphs

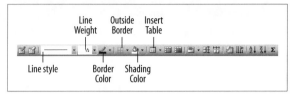

Figure 3-25. The Tables and Borders toolbar has several buttons for adding and formatting borders.

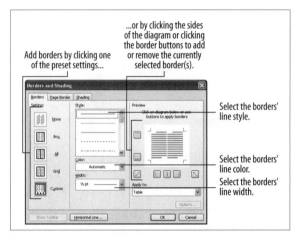

Figure 3-26. The Borders and Shading dialog box.

Borders are lines that you can add to the top, bottom, left, or right of paragraphs. Borders make paragraphs stand out and are great for emphasizing headings. Like just about every formatting command in Microsoft Word, you can add borders to your documents in one of two ways: By using the Formatting or Tables and Borders toolbar (fast and easy method), or by selecting Format → Borders and Shading from the menu (a slow but powerful method). We'll format several paragraphs using both methods in this lesson.

1 Select the heading The Month in Review.

Here's how to add a border to the selected paragraph…

2 Click the [icon] Border button list arrow on the Formatting toolbar, and select the Bottom Border (located in the third column of the second row).

TIP

Another way to add a border to a paragraph is to select Format → Borders and Shading from the menu and click where you want to add the border on Preview diagram.

A single, thin border appears at the bottom of the selected paragraph.

If you want to do anything more than add a simple line to a paragraph, you will need to summon the Tables and Borders toolbar or open the Borders and Shading dialog box. Let's try using the Tables and Borders toolbar to format the border we just added.

3 Right-click any toolbar, and select Tables and Borders from the shortcut menu.

You could have also selected View → Toolbars → Tables and Borders from the menu to display the toolbar. The Tables and Borders toolbar appears, as shown in Figure 3-25. The Tables and Borders toolbar has an Outsider Border button (just like the Formatting toolbar) that you can use to add or remove borders from your paragraphs. It also has several additional buttons you can use to change the style, size, and color of a border.

⁞ NOTE ⁞ *If your pointer changes to a pencil (✐), it means you have to turn off the Draw Table tool. Just click the [icon] Draw Table button on the Tables and Borders toolbar.*

4 With the heading still selected, click the Line Weight list arrow on the Tables and Borders toolbar and select the 3 pt option.

Reapply the bottom border and see what happens.

5 With the heading still selected, click the Border button list arrow on the Tables and Borders toolbar and select the Bottom Border option.

The heading's border changes to the thicker 3 point line weight.

We'll add a border to the next heading with the other method for adding and formatting paragraph borders—by using the Borders and Shading dialog box.

6 Select the Explore Canada Tour Package text and select Format → Borders and Shading from the menu.

The Borders and Shading dialog box appears with the Borders tab selected, as shown in Figure 3-26.

7 Click the Width list arrow and select 1 1/2 pt.

This will give you a thinner border. Notice that there are also lists in the Borders and Shading dialog box that let you change the style and color of a border.

On the right side of the Borders and Shading dialog box is the Preview diagram. The Preview diagram is a "model" paragraph. By clicking the top, bottom, left, and/or right sides of the "model," you can add borders above, below, and to the left and right of your paragraph.

8 Click the bottom of the paragraph in the Preview diagram.

A line appears under the model paragraph, showing you how the selected paragraph will look once it has a border below it.

9 Click OK to close the dialog box.

The selected paragraph, "Explore Canada Tour Package," now has a border underneath it. Let's add a border to the remaining heading.

10 Select the heading New Communications Director Position, and select Format → Borders and Shading from the menu.

So far, you've been adding borders underneath paragraphs. You can also add borders to the left, right, and/or top of a paragraph by clicking on the Preview diagram where you want to add the borders—or you can select one of the preset border settings:

11 Click the Box option in the Setting section, then click OK.

The selected paragraph is surrounded by a box—borders on the left, right, top, and bottom.

QUICK REFERENCE

TO ADD A BORDER TO A PARAGRAPH:

1. SELECT FORMAT → BORDERS AND SHADING FROM THE MENU AND CLICK THE BORDERS TAB.

2. CLICK THE SIDE(S) (TOP, BOTTOM, LEFT, AND/OR RIGHT) OF THE PARAGRAPH IN THE PREVIEW DIAGRAM WHERE YOU WANT TO APPLY THE BORDERS.

OR...

• CLICK THE BORDER BUTTON LIST ARROW ON THE FORMATTING TOOLBAR AND SELECT THE BORDER YOU WISH TO ADD.

TO SUMMON THE TABLES AND BORDERS TOOLBAR:

• RIGHT-CLICK ANY TOOLBAR AND SELECT TABLES AND BORDERS FROM THE SHORTCUT MENU, OR SELECT VIEW → TOOLBARS → TABLES AND BORDERS FROM THE MENU.

TO FORMAT THE STYLE OF A BORDER LINE:

• SELECT FORMAT → BORDERS AND SHADING FROM THE MENU AND SELECT THE FORMATTING OPTIONS.

OR...

• FORMAT THE BORDER USING THE TABLES AND BORDERS TOOLBAR.

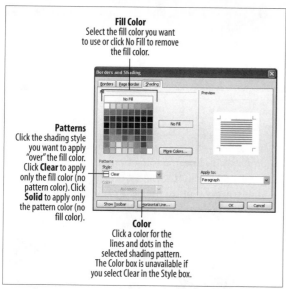

Fill Color
Select the fill color you want to use or click No Fill to remove the fill color.

Patterns
Click the shading style you want to apply "over" the fill color. Click **Clear** to apply only the fill color (no pattern color). Click **Solid** to apply only the pattern color (no fill color).

Color
Click a color for the lines and dots in the selected shading pattern. The Color box is unavailable if you select Clear in the Style box.

Figure 3-27. The Shading tab of the Borders and Shading dialog box.

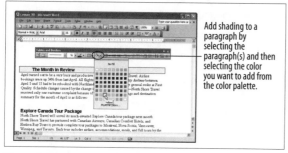

Add shading to a paragraph by selecting the paragraph(s) and then selecting the color you want to add from the color palette.

Figure 3-28. A paragraph with shaded formatting.

Adding shading, colors, and patterns to a paragraph is similar to adding borders. Just select the paragraph, and then select the shading options you want to apply from either the Tables and Borders toolbar or from the Borders and Shading dialog box. This lesson will give you some practice adding colors, shading, and patterns to your paragraphs.

1 Select the first heading, The Month in Review.

This is where you want to apply shading.

2 Click the Shading Color button **list arrow on the Tables and Borders toolbar.**

> **TIP** *Another way to apply shading is to select Format → Borders and Shading from the menu, click the Shading tab, and specify the shading options.*

A color palette appears below the Shading Color button.

3 Select the yellow color, as shown in Figure 3-28.

The selected paragraph is shaded with a yellow color. As with adding borders, you can also apply shading to a paragraph using the Borders and Shading dialog box.

4 Select the Explore Canada Tour Package heading, select Format → Borders and Shading from the menu, and click the Shading tab.

The Shading tab of the Borders and Shading dialog box appears, as shown in Figure 3-27. The Borders and Shading dialog box gives you more colors, patterns, and shading options than the Tables and Borders toolbar does.

5 Click the Style list arrow, scroll all the way down to familiarize yourself with the available shadings and patterns, and then scroll back up. Select the 10% option and click OK.

The Borders and Shading dialog box closes, and Word formats the selected paragraph with the specified 10 percent shading.

Now that you understand how to apply shading to a paragraph, let's undo the shading you added to the paragraphs.

6 Click the Undo button **twice to undo your last shading commands.**

Since we're finished working with borders and shading for now, you can hide the Tables and Borders toolbar.

7 Right-click any toolbar and select Tables and Borders from the shortcut menu.

The Tables and Borders toolbar disappears.

8 Save your work and close the Month in Review document.

QUICK REFERENCE

TO ADD SHADING TO A PARAGRAPH:

1. SELECT THE PARAGRAPH(S) TO WHICH YOU WANT TO APPLY THE SHADING AND/OR PATTERNS.

2. CLICK THE SHADING COLOR BUTTON LIST ARROW ON THE TABLES AND BORDERS TOOLBAR, AND SELECT THE COLOR YOU WANT TO APPLY.

OR...

SELECT FORMAT → BORDERS AND SHADING FROM THE MENU, CLICK THE SHADING TAB, AND SELECT A SHADING OPTION.

Lesson Summary

Formatting Characters using the Toolbar

To Bold Text: Click the Bold button on the Formatting toolbar or press Ctrl + B.

To Italicize Text: Click the Italics button on the Formatting toolbar or press Ctrl + I.

To Underline Text: Click the Underline button on the Formatting toolbar or press Ctrl + U.

To Change Font Size: Select the pt size from the Font Size list on the Formatting toolbar.

To Change Font Type: Select the font from the Font list on the Formatting toolbar.

Using the Format Painter

The Format Painter lets you copy character and paragraph formatting and apply or paste the formatting to other characters and paragraphs.

To Copy Formatting with the Format Painter: Select the text, paragraph, or object with the formatting options you want to copy. Click the Format Painter button on the Standard toolbar, and drag the Format Painter pointer across the text or paragraph where you want to apply the copied formatting.

To Copy Selected Formatting to Several Locations: Select the text, paragraph, or object with the formatting options you want to copy. Double-click the Format Painter button to apply formatting to several locations. Drag the Format Painter pointer across the text or paragraph where you want to apply the copied formatting. Click the Format Painter button again when you're finished.

Using the Font Dialog Box

Formatting characters with the Font dialog box isn't as fast or as easy as using the Formatting toolbar, but it offers more formatting options.

To Open the Font Dialog Box: Select Format → Font from the menu. Specify the font formatting options in the Font dialog box and click OK.

To Change a Font's Color: Click the Font Color button list arrow on the Formatting toolbar and select the color.

Changing Paragraph Alignment

To Left-Align a Paragraph: Click the Align Left button on the Formatting toolbar or press Ctrl + L.

To Center a Paragraph: Click the Center button on the Formatting toolbar or press Ctrl + E.

To Right-Align a Paragraph: Click the Align Right button on the Formatting toolbar or press Ctrl + R.

To Justify a Paragraph: Click the Justify button on the Formatting toolbar or press Ctrl + J.

To Align a Paragraph with the Paragraph dialog box: Select Format → Paragraph from the menu and select the paragraph alignment from the Alignment list.

Indenting Paragraphs

To Indent a Paragraph: Click the Increase Indent button on the Formatting toolbar, or click and drag the Left indent marker on the ruler, or select Format → Paragraph from the menu and enter how much space you want the paragraph indented by.

To Decrease an Indent: Click the Decrease Indent button on the Formatting toolbar.

To Right Indent a Paragraph: Click and drag the Right indent marker on the ruler, or select Format → Paragraph from the menu and enter how much space you want the paragraph indented by.

Special Indents

Hanging Indents (Using the Paragraph Dialog Box): Select Format → Paragraph from the menu, and select Hanging from the Special box in the Indentation section. Enter the desired indent amount in the By box, and click OK.

Hanging Indents (Using the Ruler): Click and drag the Hanging indent marker on the ruler.

To Indent Only the First Line of a Paragraph (Using the Paragraph Dialog Box): Select Format → Paragraph from the menu, and select First line from the Special box in the Indentation section. Enter the desired indent amount in the By box, and click OK.

To Indent Only the First Line of a Paragraph (Using the Ruler): Click and drag the First line indent marker on the ruler.

Setting Tab Stops with the Ruler

Tab stops can be aligned to the left, center, right, and to decimal points.

To Add a Tab Stop: Click on the ruler where you want to add the tab stop or select Format → Tabs from the menu and specify where you want to add the tab stop(s).

To Change the Tab Alignment: Click the Tab alignment box on the ruler until you see the type of tab you want to use (left, center, right, decimal, or bar), and then click where you want to add the tab stop.

To Adjust a Tab Stop: Click and drag the tab stop to the desired position on the ruler.

To Remove a Tab Stop: Drag the tab stop off of the ruler.

Adjusting and Removing Tabs, and Using the Tabs Dialog Box

To Adjust a Tab Stop: Click and drag the tab stop to the desired position on the ruler.

To Remove a Tab Stop: Drag the tab stop off of the ruler.

To Use the Tabs Dialog box: Select Format → Tabs from the menu.

To Add a Leader to a Tab Stop: Select Format → Tabs from the menu to open the Tabs dialog box and select the Leader you want to use. Click the Set button and click OK.

Formatting Paragraph Line Spacing

To Change Paragraph Line Spacing: Select Format → Paragraph from the menu, click the Line Spacing list arrow and select the spacing option you want to use (Single, 1.5 lines, Double, At least, Exactly, or Multiple).

Formatting Spacing between Paragraphs

To Adjust the Space Above a Paragraph: Select Format → Paragraph from the menu, and specify how much space you want in the Spacing Before box.

To Adjust the Space Below a Paragraph: Select Format → Paragraph from the menu, and specify how much space you want in the Spacing After box.

Creating Bulleted and Numbered Lists

To Create a Bulleted List: Click the Bullets button on the Formatting toolbar, or select Format → Bullets and Numbering from the menu, click the Bulleted tab, and select the bulleting option you want to use.

To Create a Numbered List: Click the Numbering button on the Formatting toolbar, or select Format → Bullets and Numbering from the menu, click the Numbered tab, and select the numbering option you want to use.

Adding Borders to Your Paragraphs

To Add a Border to a Paragraph: Select Format → Borders and Shading from the menu, click the Borders tab, and click the side(s) (top, bottom, left, and/or right) of the paragraph in the Preview diagram where you want the borders to appear. You can also add borders by clicking the Border button list arrow on the Formatting toolbar and selecting the border you wish to add.

To Summon the Tables and Borders toolbar: Right-click any toolbar and select Tables and Borders from the shortcut menu, or select View → Toolbars → Tables and Borders from the menu.

To Format the Style of a Border Line: Select Format → Borders and Shading from the menu and select the formatting options. Or, format the border using the Tables and Borders toolbar.

Adding Shading and Patterns

To Add a Shading to a Paragraph (Toolbar): Select the paragraph(s) where you want to apply the shading and/or patterns, click the Shading Color button list arrow on the Tables and Borders toolbar, and select the color you want to apply.

To Add a Shading to a Paragraph (Menu): Select Format → Borders and Shading from the menu, click the Shading tab, and select a shading option.

Quiz

1. Which of the following procedures can you use to change the size of a font?

    A. Select the text and select the font size from the Font Size list on the Formatting toolbar.

    B. Select the text, right-click it, choose Font from the shortcut menu, select the font size and click OK.

    C. Select the text, select Format → Font from the menu, select the font size and click OK.

    D. All of the above.

2. To copy character and paragraph formatting from one area in a document and apply it to another area you would use:

    A. The Edit → Copy Format and Edit → Paste Format commands from the menu.

    B. The Format Painter button on the Standard toolbar.

    C. There isn't a way to copy and apply formatting in Word.

    D. Open the Copy and Apply Formatting dialog box by selecting Format → Copy Formatting from the menu.

3. You want to use the Format Painter to apply formatting to multiple lines of a document that are not next to each other. How can you do this?

    A. Click the Format Painter button on the Standard toolbar.

    B. Double-click the Format Painter button on the Standard toolbar.

    C. This isn't possible.

    D. Open the Copy and Apply Formatting dialog box by selecting Format → Copy Formatting from the menu.

4. Which statement is NOT true?

    A. Clicking the Center button on the Formatting toolbar centers the current or selected paragraph(s) on the page.

    B. The default tab stop settings for Word are at every half-inch.

    C. When you set a tab stop, it is available in every paragraph in the document.

    D. First Line and Hanging are two special types of indents.

5. Which of the following is NOT a method for indenting a paragraph?

    A. Move the pointer to the left or right edge of the paragraph, and then drag the mouse to where you want the paragraph indented.

    B. Click the Increase Indent button on the Formatting toolbar.

    C. Click and drag the Indent marker on the ruler.

    D. Select Format → Paragraph from the menu and specify how much you would like the paragraph indented in the Indentation section.

6. Which is NOT a method for applying boldface to a selected block of text?

    A. Select Format → Font from the menu and select Bold from the Font style list.

    B. Press Ctrl + B.

    C. Right-click the text and select Boldface from the shortcut menu.

    D. Click the Bold button on the Formatting toolbar.

7. When you press Enter to start a new paragraph in Word, the new paragraph is formatted exactly like the paragraph before it. (True or False?)

8. Your research paper isn't long enough. How can you double-space it to make it longer?

    A. Select Tools → Format from the menu, click the Line Spacing arrow, and select Double.

    B. Select Tools → Paragraph Formatting from the menu, click the Line Spacing arrow, and select Double.

    C. Select Format → Paragraph from the menu, click the Line Spacing arrow, and select Double.

    D. Click the Paragraph Spacing arrow on the Formatting toolbar and select Double.

9. How do you center a paragraph?

    A. Click the Center button on the Formatting toolbar.

B. Click the Alignment arrow on the toolbar and select Center.

C. Press Ctrl + C.

D. Select Edit → Center from the menu.

10. In the context of word processing and publishing, what is a leader?

   A. A solid, dotted, or dashed line that fills the space used by a tab character.

   B. A location or selection of text that you name for reference purposes.

   C. A person you admire who taught you the basics of using a word processor.

   D. The area of white space above a paragraph.

11. Which of the following are types of tab stops? (Select all that apply.)

   A. Left

   B. Center

   C. Right

   D. Decimal

12. How can you change the bullet character that is used in a bulleted list?

   A. Click the Bullets arrow on the Formatting toolbar and select the character.

   B. You can't change the bullet character.

   C. Select Edit → Bullet Symbol from the menu, select the bulleted list you want to use, click Customize, and select the character you want to use.

   D. Select Format → Bullets and Numbering from the menu, select the bulleted list you want to use, click Customize, and select the character you want to use.

13. You want to add a border at the bottom of the paragraph. How can you do this?

   A. Click the Border button arrow on the Formatting toolbar and select the bottom option.

   B. Select the paragraph and click the Underline button on the Formatting toolbars.

   C. Select Edit → Border from the menu and click where you want to add the border on the paragraph diagram.

   D. Select Insert → Border from the menu.

Homework

1. Start Microsoft Word, open the "Homework 3" document, and save it as "Vikings."

2. Select the sentence "Thanks very much!" in the last paragraph and click the Bold button and the Italics button on the Formatting toolbar.

3. Center the sender's address (the first address) by selecting the entire address and clicking the Center button on the Formatting toolbar.

4. Change the font style and size of sender's address: With the sender's address still selected, select Arial from the Font List on the Formatting toolbar and 14 from the Font Size list on the Formatting toolbar.

5. Add a border below the sender's address: Place the insertion point in the last line of the address, click the Border list and select the Bottom Border option.

6. Create a bulleted list: Select the paragraphs beginning with "I've noticed that there have been some bad injuries in recent years…" and ending with "Now that's a good time!" Click the bullets button on the Formatting toolbar.

7. Create a numbered list: With the same paragraphs still selected, click the Numbering button on the formatting toolbar.

8. Indent the selected paragraphs: With the same paragraphs still selected, indent the numbered list by clicking the Increase Indent button on the Formatting toolbar.

9. Add spacing before the selected paragraph: With the same paragraphs still selected, select Format → Paragraph from the menu, type "6" in the Before box (in the spacing section) and click OK.

10. Set a left tab stop: Select the closing paragraphs, starting with "Don't give up," and ending with "P.S. Do you have any spare (XXL) jerseys?" Click the 2.5" mark on the ruler.

11. Place the insertion point at the very beginning of the "Don't give up," paragraph and press the Tab key. Repeat this for the two remaining paragraph lines ("Dave Eggey" and "P.S. Do you have any spare (XXL) jerseys?")

12. Adjust an existing tab stop: Select the closing paragraphs, starting with "Don't give up," and ending with "P.S. Do you have any spare (XXL) jerseys?" Click and place the ⌞ tab marker to the 3" mark.

13. Delete a tab stop: With the closing paragraphs still selected, drag the ⌞ tab marker off the ruler.

14. Save your work and exit Microsoft Word.

Quiz Answers

1. D. All of these procedures change the font size.

2. B. The Format Painter tool copies formatting properties from the selected item to another item in the document.

3. B. Double-click the Format Painter button to apply formatting to multiple areas of a document. Click the Format Painter button when you're finished.

4. C. Tab stops are only available in the paragraph in which they were formatted. To apply tab stops throughout the entire document, select the entire document and then add the tab stops.

5. A. The other three methods are valid ways to indent a paragraph.

6. C. You can use the other three methods to apply bold to text.

7. True. In most styles, paragraphs 'inherit' the formatting from the paragraphs above them. However, some styles are formatted so that the next paragraph does not inherit the paragraph's formatting when Enter is pressed.

8. C. Select Format → Paragraph from the menu, click the Line Spacing arrow, and select Double to double-space a paragraph.

9. A. Click the Center button on the Formatting toolbar to center a paragraph.

10. A. A leader is a solid, dotted, or dashed line that fills the space used by a tab character.

11. A, B, C, and D. All of these are types of tab stops.

12. D. To change the bullet character used in a bulleted list, select Format → Bullets and Numbering from the menu, select the bulleted list you want to use, click Customize, and select the character you want to use.

13. A. Click the Border button arrow on the Formatting toolbar and select the bottom option to add a border to the bottom of a paragraph.

CHAPTER 4
FORMATTING PAGES

CHAPTER OBJECTIVES:

Changing a document's margins, Lesson 4.1

Creating headers and footers, Lesson 4.2

Changing page orientation between portrait and landscape, Lesson 4.3

Previewing a document, Lesson 4.4

Controlling where the page breaks, Lesson 4.5

Adding section breaks and applying multiple page formats, Lesson 4.6

Printing envelopes, Lesson 4.7

CHAPTER TASK: EDIT A RESPONSE LETTER TO A CUSTOMER COMPLAINT

Prerequisites

- Windows basics: working with the mouse, menus, and dialog boxes.
- How to select text.
- How to switch between Normal and Print Layout view.

Instead of working with characters and paragraphs, this chapter takes a step back and looks at how to change the appearance of entire pages. When you format a page, you determine the margins between the text and the edge of the page, the orientation of the page, and the size of the paper. These topics are covered in this chapter. This chapter also explains how to add a header or footer that appears at the top or bottom of every page in your document, how to control where the page breaks, and how to use multiple page formats. Since you will be mastering page formatting in this chapter, you will also learn some neat Print Preview tricks, such as how to view multiple pages of a document simultaneously.

Page formatting is pretty straightforward, so this chapter isn't very long. Let's get started…

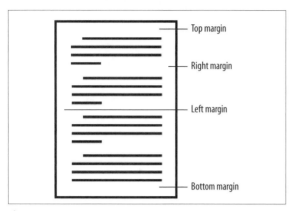

Top margin

Right margin

Left margin

Bottom margin

Figure 4-1. A document's margins.

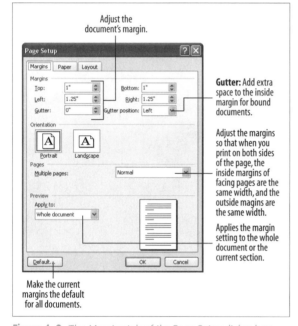

Adjust the document's margin.

Gutter: Add extra space to the inside margin for bound documents.

Adjust the margins so that when you print on both sides of the page, the inside margins of facing pages are the same width, and the outside margins are the same width.

Applies the margin setting to the whole document or the current section.

Make the current margins the default for all documents.

Figure 4-2. The Margins tab of the Page Setup dialog box.

You're probably already aware that *margins* are the empty space between a document's text and the left, right, top, and bottom edges of a page. Figure 4-1 shows the margins. Word's default margins are 1-inch margins at the top and bottom, and 1.25 inch margins to the left and right. You can also change the default margins if Word's are not to your liking—for example, many people have their default margins all set at 1 inch.

This lesson explains how to change a document's margins. There are many reasons to change the margins for a document: to make more text fit on a page, for binding documents, or for leaving a blank area on a document for notes. It's important that you don't confuse adjusting a

document's margins with adjusting a paragraph's indentation. Changing a document's margins effects the entire document and every paragraph in it. Changing a paragraph's Indentation indents only the selected paragraph(s)—it doesn't affect the rest of the document.

1 Start Microsoft Word, open the document named Lesson 4A, and save it as Complaint Letter.

Word is a little bit inconsistent when you format pages, because the Page Setup dialog box is located under the File menu, not the Format menu.

2 Select File → Page Setup from the menu. Click the Margins tab if it is not currently in front.

Word's default margins are 1 inch on the top and bottom and 1.25 inches on the left and right.

The Page Setup dialog box appears, as shown in Figure 4-2. This is where you can view and adjust the margin sizes for your document. Notice there are margin settings in the Top, Left, Right, and Gutter boxes.

3 Type .8 in the Top Margin box or click the Top Margin box down arrow until .8″ appears in the box.

This will change the size of the top margin from 1.0 inch to 0.8 inches. Notice that the Preview area of the Page Setup dialog box gives you a preview of what your document will look like with your new margin settings. Now change the bottom margin.

4 Type .8 in the Bottom Margin box or press the Bottom Margin box down arrow until .8″ appears in the box, then click OK.

The Page Setup dialog box closes and the top and bottom margins are changed from 1.0 inch to 0.8 inches.

If you intend to bind a document and require extra space for the plastic bindings, use the Gutter setting on the Margins tab.

You probably have already realized the importance of margins and knowing how to adjust them. What you may not know is that many other Windows programs, such as Microsoft Excel and PowerPoint, also use margins. Once you have mastered changing the margins in

one program, the procedure is almost the same in other
Windows programs.

QUICK REFERENCE

TO CHANGE A DOCUMENT'S MARGINS:

1. SELECT FILE → PAGE SETUP FROM THE MENU,
   AND CLICK THE MARGINS TAB.

2. ADJUST THE TOP, BOTTOM, LEFT, AND/OR RIGHT
   MARGINS AS NECESSARY.

OR...

• CLICK AND DRAG THE LEFT OR RIGHT MARGIN LINE
  ON THE RULER.

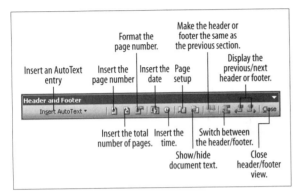

Figure 4-4. The Header and Footer toolbar, which lets you insert the date, time, and page number.

Documents with several pages often have information—such as the page number, the document's title, or the date—located at the top or bottom of every page. Text that appears at the top of every page in a document is called a *header*, while text appearing at the bottom of each page is called a *footer*. In this lesson, you will learn how to use both while you create a customer complaint letter. Here's how to edit a document's header and footer…

1 **Select** View → Header and Footer **from the menu.**

Word displays the Header area and the Header and Footer toolbar, as shown in Figure 4-3. Anything you type in the Header area (the outlined rectangle) will appear at the top of every page in your document. Notice that the text outside the header is dimmed, meaning you can't edit it while viewing the Header or the Footer.

Let's apply a company letterhead by typing North Shore Travel's address in the document's header.

2 **Click the** Center button **on the Formatting toolbar, and then click the** Bold button. **Type the following:** North Shore Travel, **click the Bold button, and press** Enter.

3 **Type North Shore Travel's address:**
502 Caribou Avenue Enter
Duluth, MN 55802

The lines of text you typed in the Header section will appear at the top of each page in the document. Next, let's add some text to the document's footer.

4 **Click the** ⬚ Switch Between Header and Footer button **(see Figure 4-4) on the Header and Footer toolbar to view the document's footer.**

The Switch Between Header and Footer button takes you back and forth between a document's header and footer. Word now displays the document's footer. In the footer area, you can type the text you want to appear at the bottom of every page.

5 **Click the** ⬚ Insert Date button **on the Header and Footer toolbar.**

Clicking the Insert Date button inserts the current date at the insertion point. Don't like how the date is formatted? Then instead of clicking the Insert Date button, select Insert → Date and Time from the menu, and select the date format you want.

6 **Press** Tab **twice, type** Page, **then press** Spacebar.

There are preset tab stops at the center and right of both headers and footers. By pressing the Tab key twice, you've moved the insertion point to the preset tab stop at the far right margin. Now insert a page number.

7 **Click the** ⬚ Insert Page Number button **on the Header and Footer toolbar.**

Word inserts the current page number. Now try something a little more advanced—inserting the total number of pages in the document.

8 Press the Spacebar to add a space, type of, and then press the Spacebar once more.

9 Click the Insert Number of Pages button on the Header and Footer toolbar.

The Insert Number of Pages button inserts the total number of pages in a document.

10 Scroll to the next page.

Notice how the header and footer we added appears on the next page of the document. You've finished working with headers and footers for now, so you can close the header/footer view and return to your document.

11 Click the Close button to return to your document.

The Header/Footer view of the document closes and you return to the document's text area.

Great! Now you know how to add headers and footers to your documents—something very important if you work with multiple page documents, and even more important if you have a supervisor that reads them.

QUICK REFERENCE

TO ADD OR VIEW A DOCUMENT HEADER OR FOOTER:

* SELECT VIEW → HEADER AND FOOTER FROM THE MENU.

TO SWITCH BETWEEN THE HEADER AND FOOTER:

* CLICK THE SWITCH BETWEEN HEADER AND FOOTER BUTTON ON THE HEADER AND FOOTER TOOLBAR.

TO INSERT A PAGE NUMBER INTO A HEADER OR FOOTER:

1. DISPLAY THE HEADER OR FOOTER AND POSITION THE INSERTION POINT WHERE YOU WANT TO INSERT THE PAGE NUMBER.

2. CLICK THE INSERT PAGE NUMBER BUTTON ON THE HEADER AND FOOTER TOOLBAR.

Changing the Paper Orientation and Size

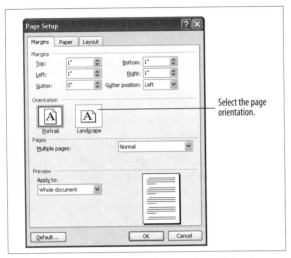

Select the page orientation.

Figure 4-5. The Margins tab in the Page Setup dialog box.

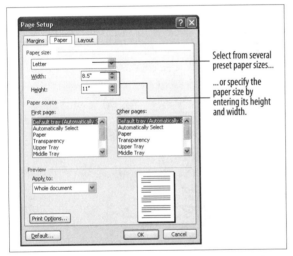

Select from several preset paper sizes...

...or specify the paper size by entering its height and width.

Figure 4-6. The Paper size options in the Page Setup dialog box.

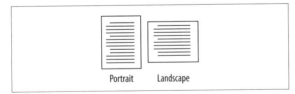

Portrait   Landscape

Figure 4-7. A comparison of Portrait and Landscape orientations.

Every document you print uses one of two different types of paper orientations: Portrait and Landscape. In Portrait orientation, the paper is taller than it is wide—like a portrait painting. In Landscape orientation, the paper is wider than it is tall—like a painting of a landscape.

Figure 4-7 shows the difference between Portrait and Landscape printing. Most documents are printed using Portrait orientation. However, there are times you may want to use landscape orientation for your documents, like if you want to display a sign or a large, complex table.

In this lesson, you will also learn how to print on different paper sizes. People normally print on standard Letter-sized (8 1/2 × 11) paper, but Word can also print on other paper sizes, such as Legal-sized (8 1/2 × 14) and other custom-sized paper. This means that you can use Word not only to print letters, but also postcards, tickets, flyers, and any other documents that use a nonstandard paper size. Here's how to change a document's paper orientation and size…

1 Select File → Page Setup **from the menu.**

The Page Setup dialog box appears. The page orientation settings are located on the Margins tab.

2 **If necessary, click the** Margins **tab.**

The Margin tab appears, as shown in Figure 4-5.

3 **In the Orientation area, click the** Landscape **option.**

Notice how the preview area displays how your document will look with the new page orientation settings.

4 **Click** OK.

The Page Setup dialog box closes, and the document is changed from portrait to landscape orientation. Since this is a business letter, it really should be formatted in portrait orientation, so undo your paper orientation changes:

5 **Click the** Undo button **to undo your orientation changes.**

Most documents and letters are Letter (8 1/2 × 11) sized. There are times, however, when you may find it necessary to create a document on irregular sized paper. You can adjust the page size on the Paper tab of the Page Setup dialog box.

6 Select File → Page Setup **from the menu and click the** Paper **tab.**

The Page Setup dialog box appears, as shown in Figure 4-6.

7 Click the Paper size list arrow and select Legal.

Notice how the Preview section displays what our paper size changes will look like. If you had clicked OK at this point, your document would be reformatted for Legal (8 1/2×14) paper size. You may have already noticed that the most common paper size options are listed in the Paper size list, but what if you're working with a paper size that isn't listed? Say, for example, a card? No problem—Word lets you enter the paper's width and height for custom paper sizes.

8 Click the Width text box down arrow until it displays 5.0".

Notice how the Preview area shows how our document will look on paper that is 5 inches wide. Now try adjusting the paper's height:

9 Click the Height text box down arrow until it displays 4.5".

⚡ NOTE ⚡   *Word may support all kinds of paper sizes, but your printer may not. Make sure your printer can handle the paper size you're using before printing, unless you want to cause a paper jam (or worse).*

Since you are working with a standard business letter in this lesson, Letter (8.5"×11") is fine, so cancel your paper size changes:

10 Click Cancel to cancel the paper size changes.

Knowing how to change the orientation of a document is another skill that can be used with many other Windows-based programs. Word documents normally use Portrait orientation, but other Windows programs may use Landscape orientation as their default, such as Microsoft PowerPoint.

TO CHANGE A PAGE'S ORIENTATION:

1. SELECT FILE → PAGE SETUP FROM THE MENU, AND CLICK THE MARGINS TAB.

2. IN THE ORIENTATION SECTION SELECT EITHER THE PORTRAIT OR LANDSCAPE OPTION.

TO CHANGE THE PAPER SIZE:

1. SELECT FILE → PAGE SETUP FROM THE MENU, AND CLICK THE PAPER TAB.

2. CLICK THE PAPER SIZE LIST ARROW TO SELECT FROM A LIST OF COMMON PAPER SIZES.

   OR...

   ADJUST THE PAPER SIZE MANUALLY BY ENTERING THE PAPER'S SIZE IN THE WIDTH AND HEIGHT TEXT BOXES.

QUICK REFERENCE

Previewing a Document

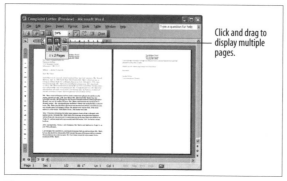

Figure 4-8. You can view multiple pages in Print Preview mode.

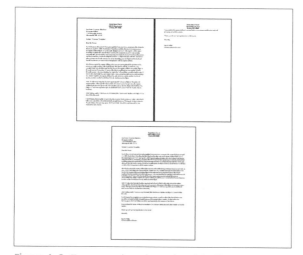

Figure 4-9. Two pages have been shrunk to fit on one page.

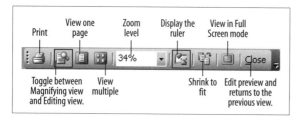

Figure 4-10. The Print Preview toolbar.

Before sending a document to the printer, it is a good idea to display the document on the computer screen using the Print Preview command. Print Preview allows you to check how your document will look before it is printed. You may catch some mistakes you didn't realize you had—for example, if your document is two pages long instead of one. Therefore, you can correct them before you waste time, paper, and your printer's ink by printing your document.

This lesson examines the Print Preview command in-depth. You will learn how to view multiple pages at once, how to edit a document in Print Preview mode, and how to use the Print Preview's neat *Shrink to Fit* feature to prevent a document from overflowing onto an additional printed page. Here's how to preview a document…

1 Click the Print Preview button on the Standard toolbar.

TIP *Another way to preview a document is to select* File → Print Preview *from the menu.*

The document appears in Print Preview mode. So far, you have only previewed a single page at a time. You can preview multiple pages at the same time by clicking the Multiple Pages button.

2 Click the Multiple Pages button on the Print Preview toolbar and drag to the grid to display two pages.

Two pages of the document are displayed, as shown in Figure 4-8. Do you find the previewed pages too small to read? You can get a close-up view of any page by using the magnifier button.

3 Click the top of the first page with the 🔍 pointer.

Word magnifies the top of the first page of the document, allowing you to read the text. If you see a mistake, you can edit the document in the Preview window.

4 Click the Magnifier button on the Print Preview toolbar to enter editing mode.

The Magnifier button un-shades and the 🔍 pointer changes to a 🔍, indicating that you can now edit text.

5 Move the insertion point to the very end of the line Subject: Customer Complaint.

Now return to Magnifying mode.

6 Click the Magnifier button on the Print Preview toolbar to exit editing mode.

The Magnifier button shades and the pointer changes to a 🔍.

7 Move the 🔍 pointer anywhere over the page and click the left mouse button.

The Preview window zooms back so that you can see both pages of the letter again. Notice how there are only a few lines on the second page? Sandra would like her letter to fit on only one page.

8 Click the ⊞ Shrink to Fit button on the Print Preview toolbar (Print Preview toolbar is shown in Figure 4-10).

The font size in our letter is slightly reduced so it will fit on a single page, as shown in Figure 4-9.

⫶ NOTE ⫶ *Using Shrink to Fit to adjust two pages so they fit on one page works great when there are only a few lines of text on the second page. Shrink to Fit doesn't work as well or may not work at all when there is a large amount of text on the second page.*

Since there is only one page in the document, it doesn't make sense to view Sandra's letter in Multiple Page mode.

9 Click the 🔲 One Page button on the Print Preview toolbar to preview a single page at a time.

10 Click the Close button to exit Print Preview mode.

11 Save your changes and close the Complaint Letter.

QUICK REFERENCE

TO PREVIEW MULTIPLE PAGES ON THE SCREEN:

1. CLICK THE PRINT PREVIEW BUTTON ON THE STANDARD TOOLBAR.

   OR...

   SELECT FILE → PRINT PREVIEW FROM THE MENU.

2. CLICK THE MULTIPLE PAGES BUTTON AND DRAG TO SELECT HOW MANY PAGES YOU WANT TO PREVIEW.

TO PREVENT A DOCUMENT FROM OVERFLOWING ONTO AN ADDITIONAL PRINTED PAGE (SHRINK TO FIT):

1. CLICK THE PRINT PREVIEW BUTTON ON THE STANDARD TOOLBAR.

   OR...

   SELECT FILE → PRINT PREVIEW FROM THE MENU.

2. CLICK THE SHRINK TO FIT BUTTON WHILE IN PRINT PREVIEW MODE.

REMEMBER: SHRINK TO FIT WILL ONLY WORK IF A SMALL AMOUNT OF TEXT APPEARS ON THE LAST PAGE OF A SHORT DOCUMENT.

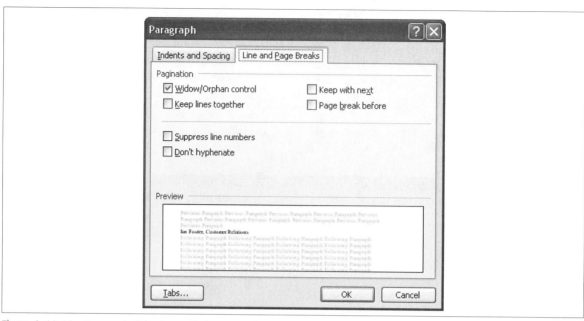

Figure 4-11. The Paragraph dialog box with the Line and Page Breaks tab displayed.

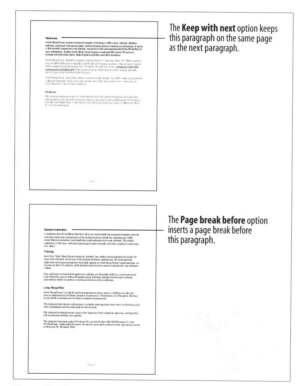

The **Keep with next** option keeps this paragraph on the same page as the next paragraph.

The **Page break before** option inserts a page break before this paragraph.

Figure 4-12. Examples of different line and page break options.

This lesson explains how to control exactly where the page breaks in a document.

1 Open the document named Lesson 4B and save it as Page Breaks.

Let's try inserting a manual page break.

2 Move the insertion point to the very beginning of the Assessment heading and insert a page break by pressing Ctrl + Enter.

Word inserts a page break at the insertion point, and the Assessment heading appears at the top of the second page in the document. Look at the end of the second page—the Hardware subheading is orphaned from the paragraph it belongs with, which appears on the third page. You can fix this problem by telling Word to keep the heading with the following paragraph—here's how:

3 Place the insertion point in the Hardware heading, select Format → Paragraph from the menu, and click the Line and Page Breaks tab.

The Paragraph dialog box appears with the Line and Page Breaks tab in front, as shown in Figure 4-11. The Line and Page Breaks tab lets you control how the page breaks. Table 4-1 describes the various options listed on the Line and Page Break Options tab.

4 Click the Keep with next **check box and click** OK.

The Keep with next option prevents a page break between the selected paragraph and the following paragraph.

You can also use the Line and Page Breaks tab of the Paragraph dialog box to insert a page break before a selected paragraph. This is especially useful for headings.

5 Place the insertion point in the System Strategies **heading at the end of the first page, and select** Format → Paragraph **from the menu.**

We're back at the Line and Page Breaks tab of the Paragraph dialog box.

6 Click the Page break before **check box and click** OK.

The dialog box closes and a page break appears before the System Strategies heading, so now it appears at the top of the document's third page. Figure 4-12 illustrates the Keep with Next option and the Page Break Before option.

It's easy to remove a paragraph's line and page break options—simply select the paragraph, select For-

mat → Paragraph from the menu, click the Line and Page Breaks tab and add or remove the checks from the appropriate check boxes. Removing a manual page break, like the one we inserted back in Step 2, isn't much harder—here's how to delete a manual page break.

7 Switch to Normal View by clicking the Normal View button, **found on the horizontal scroll bar at the bottom of the document window.**

Although you don't necessarily have to be in Normal view to delete a page break, page breaks are visible in Normal view—and and are therefore much easier to delete.

8 Press Ctrl + Home **to move to the beginning of the document.**

Since you're in Normal view, you can easily remove the manual page break you inserted.

9 Place the insertion point on the line that contains the Page Break **and press the** Delete **key.**

The page break is deleted.

10 Switch back to Print Layout view by clicking the Print Layout View button **at the bottom of the screen.**

Table 4-1. Paragraph Line and Page Break Options

Option	Description
Widow/Orphan control	Prevents Word from printing the last line of a paragraph by itself at the top of a page (widow) or the first line of a paragraph by itself at the bottom of a page (orphan). This option is selected by default.
Keep with next	Prevents the page from breaking between the selected paragraph and the following paragraph.
Keep lines together	Prevents the page from breaking within a paragraph.
Page break before	Inserts a page break before the selected paragraph. This is a good option for major headings.
Suppress line numbers	This prevents line numbers from appearing next to selected paragraphs if the Line Numbering option is on. This setting has no effect in documents or sections with no line numbers.
Don't hyphenate	Excludes a paragraph from automatic hyphenation.

QUICK REFERENCE

TO INSERT A MANUAL PAGE BREAK:

- PLACE THE INSERTION POINT WHERE YOU WANT TO INSERT THE PAGE BREAK AND PRESS CTRL + ENTER.

TO DELETE A PAGE BREAK:

- PLACE THE INSERTION POINT ON THE LINE THAT CONTAINS THE PAGE BREAK AND PRESS THE DELETE KEY.

- IT'S EASIER TO DELETE A PAGE BREAK IF YOU'RE IN NORMAL VIEW.

TO ADJUST THE LINE AND/OR PAGE BREAK SETTINGS FOR A PARAGRAPH:

1. SELECT THE PARAGRAPH AND SELECT FORMAT → PARAGRAPH FROM THE MENU AND CLICK THE LINE AND PAGE BREAK TAB.

2. SELECT THE LINE AND/OR PAGE BREAK OPTIONS FOR THE SELECTED PARAGRAPH AND CLICK OK.

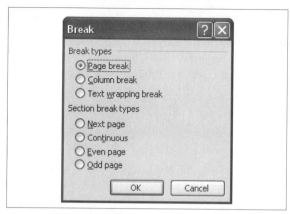

Figure 4-13. The Break dialog box.

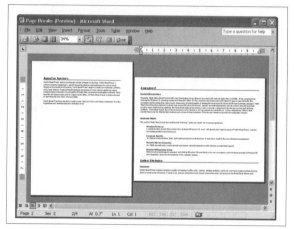

Figure 4-14. You can apply different page formats to the same document using section breaks.

By now, you should know how to adjust a document's margins, paper orientation (portrait or landscape), and paper size. What happens if you want to use different margin or orientation settings in the *same document*? For example, what do you do if you want one page of your document to appear in portrait orientation and another to appear in landscape orientation? You can apply different page formatting in the same document by using a *section break*. A section break allows you to use different page formatting elements—such as the margins, page orientation, headers and footers, and sequence of page numbers—in the same document. This lesson explains how to apply section breaks to use different page formats in the same document.

First, you need to specify where you want to insert a section break.

1 Move the insertion point to the very beginning of the Assessment heading.

This is where you want to insert a section break.

2 Select Insert → Break from the menu.

The Break dialog box appears, as shown in Figure 4-13. The Break dialog box lets you insert page, column, and section breaks. You need to insert a section break, so you can apply multiple page formats in the same document.

3 Under "Section break types," select Next Page, and then click OK.

Selecting the Next Page option will create a page break before the new section. See Table 4-2 for other break options. Now that you have two sections, you can add different headers, footers, and page formatting to each section. You will be changing the page orientation of the second section (where the insertion point is currently located).

4 Make sure the insertion point is located on the second page of the document and select File → Page Setup from the menu. Click the Margins tab if it isn't currently in front.

The Page Setup dialog box appears with the Margins tab in front. Change the orientation of the page in the second section from portrait to landscape.

5 Under the Orientation section, select Landscape. Make sure the Apply To text box says This Section.

All the pages in the second section will have landscape orientation, while the pages in the first section will still have portrait orientation. You can also adjust margin settings for pages in a section.

6 Change the Top, Bottom, Left, and Right margins to 0.5". Click OK.

The page in the second section is reformatted with landscape orientation and half-inch margins.

7 Click the Print Preview button on the Standard toolbar.

Word displays the document on the screen in preview mode, giving us a better view of the paper formatting changes you've made, as shown in Figure 4-14. Let's look at the page in the previous section.

8 Scroll up to the previous page.

Word displays the first page, in the first section, in preview mode. Notice how the page formatting—the orientation and the margins—is unchanged.

9 Close the document without saving any changes.

You probably noticed there were other break options listed in the Break dialog box, besides the Next Page Section break you used. Table 4-2 explains what these other options are.

Table 4-2. Types of Breaks

Break Type	Description
Page Break	Inserts a simple page break at the insertion point.
Column Break	Only used when working on a document with multiple newspaper-type columns. Inserts a column break at the insertion point.
Next Page Section Break	Inserts a section break at the insertion point and inserts a page break so the new section starts at the beginning of a new page.
Continuous Section Break	Inserts a section break at the insertion point and starts the section immediately, without inserting a page break.
Even Page Section Break	Inserts a section break at the insertion point and starts the next section on the next even-numbered page. If the section falls on an even-numbered page, Word leaves the next odd-numbered page blank.
Odd Page Section Break	Inserts a section break at the insertion point and starts the next section on the next odd-numbered page. If the section falls on an odd-numbered page, Word leaves the next even-numbered page blank.

QUICK REFERENCE

TO INSERT A SECTION BREAK:

1. SELECT INSERT → BREAK FROM THE MENU.

2. SELECT THE TYPE OF BREAK YOU WANT TO INSERT.

Creating and Working with Envelopes

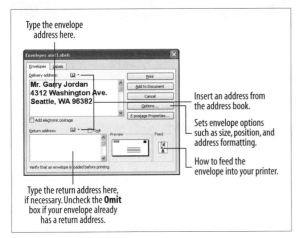

Type the envelope address here.

Insert an address from the address book.

Sets envelope options such as size, position, and address formatting.

How to feed the envelope into your printer.

Type the return address here, if necessary. Uncheck the **Omit** box if your envelope already has a return address.

Figure 4-15. The Envelopes tab of the Envelopes and Labels dialog box.

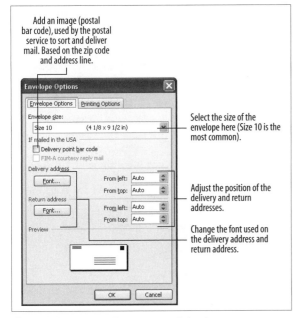

Add an image (postal bar code), used by the postal service to sort and deliver mail. Based on the zip code and address line.

Select the size of the envelope here (Size 10 is the most common).

Adjust the position of the delivery and return addresses.

Change the font used on the delivery address and return address.

Figure 4-16. The Envelope Options dialog box.

If you suffer from terrible handwriting, you can have Word address your envelopes for you. Word is great for printing envelopes *if* your printer can handle envelopes. That's a big if—many printers don't handle envelopes very well, and many others don't handle envelopes at all. The only way to really find out if you can print envelopes with your printer is by consulting the manual that came with your printer. If you've misplaced your printer manual, you can try printing several envelopes with the printer to see how they come out—just be prepared to go

through several envelopes before you find out how to feed the envelope into the printer!

1 **Open the practice file** Lesson 4C.

You want to print an envelope for this letter.

2 **Select** Tools → Letters and Mailing → Envelopes and Labels **from the menu. If the Envelope tab isn't selected, click the** Envelopes **tab.**

The Envelopes and Labels dialog box appears, as shown in Figure 4-15. Notice that Word automatically inserts the delivery address in the dialog box for you. Neat!

⸱ NOTE ⸱ *Word occasionally gets confused and either inserts a wrong portion of the document in the delivery address text box or else inserts nothing—another example of how computers still have a long way to go to catch up with even the most basic human reasoning. If Word has problems identifying the delivery address for an envelope, simply select the delivery address before opening the Envelopes and Labels dialog box. Or, just type the address into the Envelopes dialog box.*

3 **Move the insertion point to the** Return address **text box and enter your address.**

⸱ NOTE ⸱ *Word uses the User Information that is saved in the Options dialog box to fill-in the Return address box. You can change the User Information by selecting Tools → Options from the menu, clicking the User Information tab, and typing your address in the Mailing Address box.*

TIP *Clicking the "Omit" check box prints the envelope without a return address for pre-printed envelopes.*

Next, let's look at a few envelope options.

4 **Click the** Options button, **and then click the** Envelope Options **tab if it doesn't appear in front of the dialog box.**

The Envelope Options dialog box appears with the Envelope Options tab in front, as shown in Figure 4-16. Here you can specify what size of envelope you are using, font formatting and placement options for both the return and delivery addresses, and whether or not you want to include a delivery point barcode on your envelope. The Printing Options tab lets you change how you feed envelopes into your printer.

≳ NOTE ≳ *Expect to ruin a few envelopes the first time you try printing them! Make sure you look at the Feed preview area in the Envelopes and Labels dialog box to see how you're supposed to feed envelopes into your printer. Even then, chances are you won't get it right the first time. When you finally do figure out which side and direction to feed envelopes into your printer, take a blank envelope, draw an arrow on the envelope indicating the side and direction to feed envelopes, and keep it by your printer as a reference for the next time.*

The default envelope, Size 10, is the most commonly used envelope size, so leave the envelope size as it is. You do, however, want to include a delivery point barcode on your envelope.

5 Click the Delivery point barcode **check box to insert a delivery point barcode on your envelope.**

Notice a delivery point barcode is added to the envelope in the Preview area of the dialog box. You've probably seen a delivery point barcode on some of the commercial mail you've received. Delivery point bar codes help the post office sort and deliver your mail faster.

6 Click the Printing Options **tab.**

The Printing Options tab appears in front of the dialog box. Here you can specify envelope-loading options.

≳ NOTE ≳ *Before printing an envelope, verify that your printer can handle envelopes, and if so, what size.*

7 Click OK.

The Envelope Options dialog box closes and you are returned to the Envelopes and Labels dialog box.

8 Place an envelope in your printer and click Print.

You may have to refer to your printer manual to see how to properly load an envelope in your printer. Word prints the envelope.

9 Close the document without saving it.

QUICK REFERENCE

TO PRINT AN ENVELOPE:

1. SELECT THE ADDRESS IF IT APPEARS IN THE ACTIVE DOCUMENT.

2. SELECT TOOLS → LETTERS AND MAILINGS → ENVELOPES AND LABELS FROM THE MENU, AND CLICK THE ENVELOPES TAB IF NECESSARY.

3. IF NECESSARY, ENTER THE DELIVERY AND RETURN ADDRESS IN THE INDICATED AREAS.

• CLICK OPTIONS TO SPECIFY WHAT SIZE ENVELOPE YOU ARE USING, WHETHER OR NOT YOU WANT A DELIVERY POINT BARCODE INCLUDED, OR THE METHOD THE ENVELOPE IS FED INTO THE PRINTER.

Arranging Text in Multiple Columns

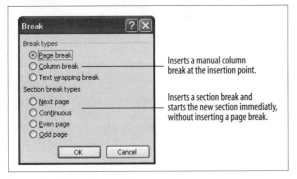

Figure 4-17. The Break dialog box.

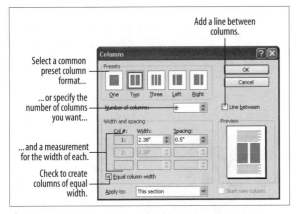

Figure 4-18. A continuous section break allows you to use different numbers of columns on the same page.

Figure 4-19. The Columns dialog box.

Up until now, you have been working with documents where the text spans the entire width of the page. Newsletters and magazines, however, often arrange text in two or more columns. This lesson explains how to arrange your document's text in multiple columns. You will also learn how to use multiple column formats together on the same page.

1 **Open the document named** Lesson 4D **and save it as** Newsletter.

This document is the rough draft of North Shore Travel's quarterly newsletter. Here's how to arrange text in columns:

2 **Click the** Columns button **on the Standard toolbar and drag to select** 2 columns.

TIP   *Another way to create multiple columns is to select* Format → Columns *from the menu.*

Word reformats the document into two columns. Notice the headline of the newsletter appears in a column instead of spanning across the page. You can format text in different columns on the same page by separating the document with section breaks. For example, a headline might appear in one column while the remainder of text on the page appears in two or more columns.

Since we want the headline to span across the page, we need to separate it from the rest of the document text by inserting a continuous section break (a section break that doesn't cause a page break). Again, here is how to insert a section break:

3 **Place the insertion point immediately in front of the heading "Two Nation Vacation" and select** Insert → Break **from the menu.**

The Break dialog box appears, as shown in Figure 4-17. You must specify that you want to insert a continuous section break (so that the section does not cause a page break).

4 **Select the** Continuous **option and click** OK.

If you're in Normal view, the continuous section break will appear as a double dotted line, as shown in Figure 4-18. If you're in Print Layout view, you won't be able to see the continuous section break—but it's there. Unless you have moved the insertion point, you should be in section two. If you're not sure which section you're in, take a look at the status bar at the bottom of the screen.

5 Place the insertion point in the first section (the newsletter headline), click the Columns button, and drag to select 1 column.

The first section is formatted as one column.

You can also create or modify multiple columns by using the Columns dialog box. Here's how:

6 Select Format → Columns from the menu.

The Columns dialog box appears, as shown in Figure 4-19. The Columns dialog box isn't as fast and easy to use as the Columns button on the Standard toolbar, but it's much more flexible and lets you take advantage of special column formatting options, such as how wide each of the columns are. You can also use the Columns dialog box to modify the column formatting for existing columns.

Look, but don't touch—the current column formatting is fine the way it is. When you've seen enough, move on to the next step.

7 Click Cancel to close the Columns dialog box without making any changes, and then save your work.

QUICK REFERENCE

TO CREATE MULTIPLE COLUMNS:

• CLICK THE COLUMNS BUTTON ON THE STANDARD TOOLBAR AND THEN DRAG TO SELECT THE NUMBER OF COLUMNS YOU WANT.

OR...

1. SELECT FORMAT → COLUMNS FROM THE MENU.

2. SPECIFY THE NUMBER OF COLUMNS YOU WANT TO INSERT FROM THE COLUMNS DIALOG BOX AND ANY ADDITIONAL FORMATTING OPTIONS, THEN CLICK OK.

TO USE DIFFERENT COLUMN FORMATTING ON THE SAME PAGE:

1. PLACE THE INSERTION POINT WHERE YOU WANT TO SEPARATE THE DIFFERENT FORMATTING OPTIONS AND SELECT INSERT → BREAK FROM THE MENU.

2. SELECT THE CONTINUOUS OPTION AND CLICK OK. YOU CAN NOW CHANGE THE COLUMN FORMATTING OPTIONS FOR EACH SECTION INDEPENDENTLY OF EACH OTHER.

TO MODIFY EXISTING COLUMNS:

• SELECT FORMAT → COLUMNS FROM THE MENU.

Chapter Four Review

Lesson Summary

Adjusting Margins

To Change a Document's Margins (Using the Menu): Select File → Page Setup from the menu, click the Margins tab, and adjust the top, bottom, left, and/or right margins as necessary.

To Change a Document's Margins (Using the Ruler): Click and drag the Left or Right margin line on the ruler.

Creating Headers and Footers

To Add or View a Document Header or Footer: Select View → Header and Footer from the menu.

To Switch Views Between the Header and Footer: Click the Switch between Header and Footer button on the Header and Footer toolbar.

To Insert a Page Number in a Header or Footer: Display the header or footer and position the insertion point where you want the page number, and then click the Insert Page Number button on the Header and Footer toolbar.

Changing the Paper Orientation and Size

To Change a Page's Orientation: Select File → Page Setup from the menu, click the Margins tab, and select Portrait or Landscape in the Orientation section.

To Change the Paper Size: Select File → Page Setup from the menu, click the Paper tab, and click the Paper Size list arrow to select from a list of common paper sizes. You can also change the paper size by entering the paper's size in the Width and Height text boxes.

Previewing a Document

To Preview Multiple Pages on the Screen: Click the Print Preview button on the Standard toolbar or select File → Print Preview from the menu. Click the Multiple Pages button and drag to select how many pages you want to preview.

To Prevent a Document from Flowing onto an Additional Printed Page (Shrink to Fit): Preview the document, then click the Shrink to Fit button while in Print Preview mode.

Shrink to Fit will work only if a small amount of text appears on the last page of a short document.

Controlling where the Page Breaks

To Insert a Manual Page Break: Place the insertion point where you want to insert the page break and press Ctrl + Enter.

To Delete a Page Break: Place the insertion point on the line that contains the page break and press the Delete key.

It's easier to delete a page if you're in Normal View. Switch to Normal view by clicking the Normal View button on the horizontal ruler at the bottom of the screen, or select View → Normal from the menu.

To Adjust the Line and/or Page Break Settings for a Paragraph: Select the paragraph, select Format → Paragraph from the menu, and click the Line and Page Break tab. Select the line and/or page break options for the selected paragraph and click OK.

Working with Section Breaks and Multiple Page Formats

By separating a document using section breaks, you can apply different page formatting to the different sections.

To Insert a Section Break: Select Insert → Break from the menu and select the type of break you want to insert.

Creating and Working with Envelopes

To Print an Envelope: Select the address if it appears in the active document, select Tools → Envelopes and Labels from the menu, and click the Envelopes tab if necessary. If necessary, enter the delivery and return address in the indicated areas. Click Options to specify what size envelope you are using, to specify whether or not you want a delivery point barcode included, or to specify the method the envelope is fed into the printer.

Arranging Text in Multiple Columns

To Create Multiple Columns (Using the Toolbar): Click the Columns button on the Standard toolbar and then drag to select the number of columns you want.

To Create Multiple Columns (Using the Menu): Select Format → Columns from the menu. Specify the number of columns you want to insert from the Columns dialog box and any additional formatting options, and then click OK.

To Use Different Column Formatting on the Same Page: Place the insertion point where you want to separate the different formatting options and select Insert → Break from the menu. Select the Continuous option and click OK. You can now change the column formatting options for each section independently of each other.

To Modify Existing Columns: Select Format → Columns from the menu.

Quiz

1. A footer is:

   A. A type of measurement used in Australia.

   B. Text that appears at the bottom of every page in a document.

   C. A tool used in reports to cite your sources and any quotations.

   D. A special type of tab stop.

2. How do you adjust a page's margins?

   A. Click and drag the edge of the page to where you want the margin set.

   B. Select Format → Page Setup from the menu, click the Margins tab, and adjust the margins.

   C. Select File → Page Setup from the menu, click the Margins tab, and adjust the margins.

   D. Click the Margins button on the Formatting toolbar.

3. How do you view a document's header or footer?

   A. Click the Header/Footer button on the Standard toolbar.

   B. Double-click the Header/Footer area of the Status bar.

   C. Select File → Page Setup from the menu and click the Header and Footers tab, and then click View.

   D. Select View → Header and Footer from the menu.

4. What type of page orientation does a document have when it is laid out so that it is wider than it is tall?

   A. Portrait.

   B. Side.

   C. Landscape.

   D. Horizontal.

5. You can use different page formatting within the same document by separating the differently formatted areas with a ___ _.

   A. Section break.

   B. Column break.

   C. Page break.

   D. Formatting break.

6. To insert a page break press:

   A. Alt + Enter.

   B. Shift + Enter.

   C. Ctrl + Enter.

   D. Shift + Ctrl + Enter.

7. You want to keep an important paragraph together on a page, but it's breaking between two pages. How can you keep the paragraph together?

   A. Select Format → Paragraph from the menu, click the Line and Page Breaks tab, and then check the Keep lines together box.

   B. Select File → Page Setup from the menu, click the Paragraph tab, and then click the Keep together box.

   C. Select Format → Paragraph from the menu, click the Line and Page Breaks tab, and then check the Keep with next box.

   D. There isn't an option to do this.

8. You're trying to print an envelope but your letter's delivery address doesn't appear in the Delivery address box. What can you do to make sure the delivery address appears?

   A. Quit fooling around with these high-tech gimmicks and address the envelope the old-fashioned way—with a pen!

B. Make sure you select the delivery address before you select Tools → Letters and Mailings → Envelopes and Labels from the menu.

C. Make sure that the Omit Delivery Address check box in the Envelopes and Labels dialog box is not checked.

D. Open the Envelopes and Labels dialog box, click Options, and make sure the AutoSelect Delivery check box is checked.

9. How could you verify that a paragraph stays on the same page as the next paragraph?

A. Press Enter repeatedly to enter a series of blank lines until the paragraph falls on the same page as the next paragraph.

B. Click the Print Preview button on the Standard toolbar and then click the Shrink to Fit button on the Print Preview toolbar.

C. Select Format → Paragraph from the menu, click the Line and Page Breaks tab, and select the Keep with next option.

D. Place the insertion point in the paragraph, and press Ctrl + N.

10. Which of the following is NOT a type of section break?

A. Next page.

B. Continuous.

C. Next column.

D. Odd page.

11. Which of the following statements is NOT true?

A. The Shrink to Fit button attempts to fit a document onto a single page.

B. You can access the Shrink to Fit button by previewing a document.

C. You can change the number of columns in a document by clicking the Columns button and selecting the desired number of columns.

D. You can change the paper size by selecting Format → Page from the menu, clicking the Paper Size tab, and specifying the paper size.

12. You're trying to create a newspaper on alien abductions. You want your newspaper to have two columns and a single heading section that spans these two columns. How can you do this?

A. You can't do this kind of fancy page formatting with Microsoft Word—that's what Microsoft Publisher is there for!

B. Insert a continuous section break between the two sections and format the bottom section with two columns.

C. Click the Column button on the toolbar and select the Two-Column Newsletter option.

D. Insert a column break between the two sections and format the bottom section with two columns.

Homework

1. Open Homework 4 and save it as "Art Letter."

2. Change the page margins: Select File → Page Setup from the menu and click the Margins tab. Change the top, bottom, left, and right margins to 1 inch.

3. View the document's footer: Select View → Header and Footer from the menu, and click the Switch Between Header and Footer button on the Header and Footer toolbar.

4. In the footer area type "Page," press Spacebar, and click the Insert Page Number button on the Header and Footer toolbar. Center the text and then return to the main document area by clicking the Close button on the Header and Footer toolbar.

5. Add a section break between the "Teletubbie" picture and the other two pictures: Place the insertion immediately after the "Teletubbie" picture and select Insert → Break from the menu. Select the "Next Page" option under the Section breaks section and click OK.

6. Change the page orientation for page 3 (the page with the picture of the young girl and woman): Go to page 3, select File → Page Setup from the menu, and

click the Paper Size tab. Select the "Landscape" option and click OK.

7. Take a look at pages 1 and 2—notice how they retain their Portrait page orientation because of the Section break that separates them from page 3.

8. Print an envelope: Select Tools → Envelopes and Labels from the menu. Click Print if you want to print the envelope. Otherwise, click Cancel.

9. Save your work and exit Microsoft Word.

Quiz Answers

1. B. A footer is a piece of text that appears at the bottom of every page in a document.

2. C. Select File → Page Setup from the menu and click the Margins tab to adjust your document's margins.

3. D. You can view the headers and footers in a document by selecting View → Header and Footer from the menu.

4. C. Landscape orientation is wider than it is tall.

5. A. A section break allows you to use different page formats in the same documents.

6. C. Press Ctrl + Enter to insert a page break.

7. A. To keep a paragraph together on a page, select Format → Paragraph from the menu, click the Line and Page Breaks tab, and then check the Keep lines together box.

8. B. Word sometimes gets confused when it selects the delivery address for an envelope. When this happens, simply make sure you select or highlight the delivery address before selecting Tools → Letters and Mailings → Envelopes and Labels from the menu.

9. C. To keep a paragraph on the same page as the next paragraph, select Format → Paragraph from the menu, click the Line and Page Breaks tab, and select the Keep with next option.

10. C. While there is a column break, it isn't a type of section break.

11. D. You can change the paper size by selecting File → Page Setup from the menu, clicking the Paper Size tab, and specifying the paper size.

12. B. You can use multiple column formats on the same page as long as they are separated by a continuous section break.

CHAPTER 5
WORKING WITH TABLES

CHAPTER OBJECTIVES:

Creating a table, Lessons 5.1–5.3 and 5.12

Adjusting row height and column width, Lessons 5.4 and 5.5

Inserting and deleting rows and columns, Lesson 5.6

Formatting a table with borders and shading, Lessons 5.7–5.7

Formatting characters and paragraphs in a table, Lesson 5.15

Splitting and merging cells in a table, Lesson 5.14

Sorting information in a table, Lesson 5.11

Performing calculations in a table, Lessons 5.10 and Lesson 5.13

Working with tables that span multiple pages, Lesson 5.16

Resizing, moving, and positioning a table, Lesson 5.17

CHAPTER TASK: CREATE A TABLE THAT TRACKS REGIONAL TICKET SALES

Prerequisites

- **How to open and save a document.**
- **How to use menus, toolbars, dialog boxes, and shortcut keystrokes.**
- **How to select text.**

Tables are great: they are ranked right up there with the spell checker as one of the neatest word processing features. In word processing, a table isn't something on which one eats; it's used to present information in an organized, attractive manner. A table neatly arranges text and data in a grid, organized by columns and rows. Once you have entered information in a table, you can do all kinds of great things with it. For example, you can sort the information alphabetically or numerically; add and delete columns and/or rows; and make your table stand out by formatting it with a dramatic border, and selecting shading and coloring options. Tables can do so many things that many veteran word processing users routinely use them instead of tab stops to organize and layout information in an attractive, organized manner.

As powerful as tables are, only a few word processor users seem to know how to use them effectively, if at all. Tables are so important that this entire chapter is devoted to them and to helping you become an expert with tables.

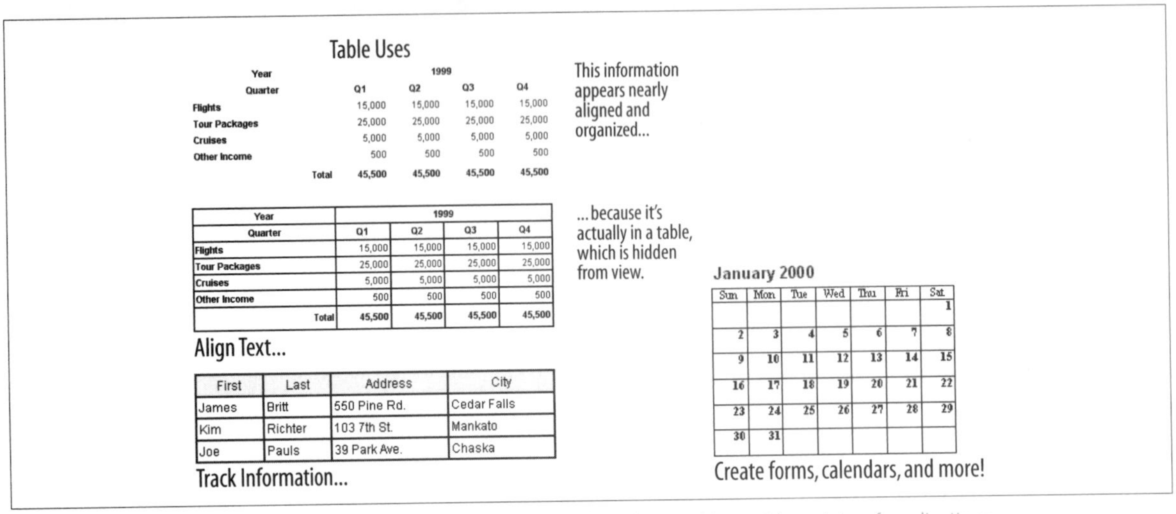

Figure 5-1. Tables are one of Word's most powerful features and can be used in a wide variety of applications.

Taking the time to learn how to use Microsoft Word's table feature is definitely worth the effort. Once you know how to create and work with tables, you will wonder how you ever managed without them. You may be surprised by the many ways in which you can use tables. For example, with a table you can:

- **Align Text, Numbers, and Graphics:** Tables make it easy to align text, numbers, and graphics in columns and rows. Many users prefer using tables to align text instead of tab stops, because text can wrap to multiple lines in a table.

- **Create a Form:** You can use tables to store lists of telephone numbers, clients, and employee rosters.

- **Track Information:** Word's mail merge feature actually stores information, such as names and addresses, in a table. You can also easily copy and paste a table's information into a Microsoft Excel worksheet.

- **Create a Publication:** Tables allow you to create calendars, brochures, business cards, and many other publications. See Figure 5-1 for examples of various tables.

Tables are such an important feature of Word that they get their very own menu, with a lot of options to choose from. Table 5-1 describes what each of the choices in the Table menu is for—you'll get a chance to try most of them throughout this chapter.

Table 5-1. The Table Menu

Command	Description
Draw Table	Uses a freehand pencil to draw a table, and add cells, columns, or rows.
Insert (Cells, Rows Columns, Table)	Depending on the location of the insertion point, inserts columns, rows, cells, or a new table.
Delete (Rows, Columns)	Deletes the selected cells or the cell that contains the insertion point, or the selected column or row.
Merge Cells	Combines several selected cells into a single larger cell.
Split Cells	Splits the selected cells into a specified number of rows and columns.
Select Row	Selects the row that contains the insertion point.
Select Column	Selects the column that contains the insertion point.
Select Table	Selects the entire table that contains the insertion point.
Table AutoFormat	Automatically applies predefined formatting to a table.

Table 5-1. The Table Menu (Continued)

Command	Description
Distribute Rows Evenly	Changes the selected rows or cells to equal row height.
Distribute Columns Evenly	Changes the selected columns or cells to equal column width.
Cell Height and Width	Adjusts the height, width, alignment, indents, and other formatting of rows and columns in a table.
Headings	Designates the selected rows to be a table heading that is repeated on subsequent pages if the table spans more than one page.
Convert Text to Table	Converts the selected text to a table, or converts the selected table to text. Text you convert into a table must include separator characters, such as tab characters or commas.
Sort	Arranges the information in selected rows or lists alphabetically, numerically, or by date.
Formula	Performs mathematical calculations on numbers.
Split Table	Divides a table into two separate tables and inserts a paragraph mark above the row that contains the insertion point.
Hide Gridlines	Displays or hides dotted gridlines to help you see which cell you're working in. Table gridlines don't print; if you want to add printable gridlines to your table, use the Borders and Shading command located in the Format menu.

Click the Insert Table button and drag to select how many columns and rows you want.

Figure 5-2. The Insert Table button on the Standard toolbar creates a table.

Figure 5-3. The Insert Table dialog box.

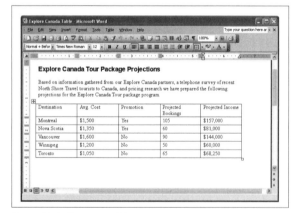

Figure 5-4. The new table.

In this lesson, you will learn how to create a table and then enter information into it. To create a table, you must first specify how many columns (which run up and down) and rows (which run left to right) you want to appear in your table. *Cells* are small, rectangular-shaped boxes where the rows and columns of a table intersect. The number of columns and rows will determine the number of cells in a table, which will determine how much information the table can contain. If you don't know how many columns and rows you want in your table, take an educated guess—you can always add or delete columns and rows later.

1 **Open Microsoft Word.**

2 **Find and open the** Lesson 5A **document and save it as** Explore Canada Table.

3 **Press** Ctrl + End **to place the insertion point at the end of the document.**

This is where you want to insert a table. Like so many other functions in Word, there are several ways to insert a table. We'll walk through the quickest and easiest method—using the Insert Table button on the Standard toolbar.

4 **Click the** Insert Table button **on the Standard toolbar, hold the mouse button down, and then drag inside the grid to select** 4 rows **and** 5 columns, **as shown in Figure 5-2. Release the mouse button when you are finished.**

> *Another way to insert a table is to select* Table → Insert → Table *from the menu, enter the number of columns and rows, and click* OK.

A blank table appears with four rows and five columns. If you have trouble using the Insert Table button, you can also insert a table with the Insert Table dialog box, shown in Figure 5-3. Just select Table → Insert → Table from the menu to open it.

Let's go ahead and enter some information into the new table.

5 Place the insertion point in the first cell (the one in the upper left-hand corner of the table) by clicking the cell.

6 Type Destination, then press Tab to move to the next cell.

The Tab key moves the insertion point to the next cell in the row. Finish adding the column headings for your table. Make sure you press Tab to move to the next cell.

7 Type Avg. Cost, press Tab, type Promotion, press Tab, type Projected Bookings, press Tab, and type Projected Income.

Table 5-2.

Ottawa	$1,500	Yes	105	$157,000
Nova Scotia	1,350	Yes	60	$81,000
Vancouver	$1,600	No	90	$14,400

Whoops, you've run out of rows! Just press Tab to enter a new row at the end of a table.

Table 5-3.

Winnipeg	$1,200	No	50	$60,000
Toronto	$1,050	No	65	$68,250

When you're finished, your table should look similar to the one in Figure 5-4.

12 Save your work.

Congratulations! You've just created your first table! Sorry for all the typing you had to do in this lesson, but now you have an idea of how easy tables make it to enter and present information. Now that you know how to create a table, you will appreciate the upcoming lessons where you learn how to add and delete columns and rows, how to format the table, and even how to perform calculations based on the information in a table. Working with a Table

Whoops, you've run out of rows! Just press Tab to enter a new row at the end of a table.

8

9 Press Tab to move the insertion point to the first cell in the second row.

Pressing Tab not only moves the insertion point to the next row, but it also inserts a new row if you are at the end of the table.

10 Type the following text in the table. Press Tab after entering the text in each cell (see Table 5-2).

11 Press Tab to create a new row. Enter the Winnipeg information and press Tab again to enter a row for the Toronto information (see Table 5-3).

QUICK REFERENCE

TO CREATE A TABLE:

- CLICK THE INSERT TABLE BUTTON ON THE STANDARD TOOLBAR, THEN DRAG INSIDE THE GRID TO SELECT THE NUMBER OF COLUMNS AND ROWS THAT YOU WANT.

OR

- SELECT TABLE → INSERT → TABLE FROM THE MENU, SPECIFY THE NUMBER OF ROWS AND COLUMNS YOU WANT, AND CLICK OK.

TO MOVE FROM CELL TO CELL IN A TABLE:

- PRESS TAB TO MOVE FORWARD ONE FIELD OR CELL, AND PRESS SHIFT + TAB TO MOVE BACK ONE FIELD OR CELL.

TO INSERT A NEW ROW:

- IN THE BOTTOM-RIGHT TABLE CELL, PRESS THE TAB KEY.

TO DELETE TEXT IN A CELL:

- SELECT THE CELL(S) AND PRESS THE DELETE KEY.

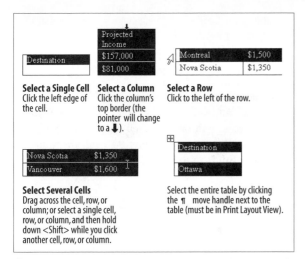

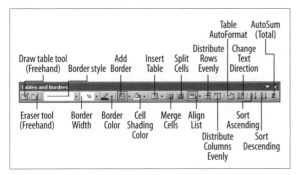

Figure 5-5. Techniques for selecting a table's cells, rows, and columns.

Figure 5-6. The Tables and Borders toolbar (your Tables and Borders toolbar may look a little different).

Working with tables can be a little bit tricky the first few times you try it. You have to be extra careful when selecting a table's cells, rows, and columns—and many users have difficulty doing so at first. You already know that once you select text in a document, you can format it, delete it, move or copy it, or replace it—just by typing. The same rules apply to tables—you have to select cells, rows, and columns if you want to format, delete, or move them. This lesson explains how to select a table's cells, rows, and columns, and how to use the Tables and Borders toolbar to help make working with tables easier. Figure 5-5 shows techniques for selecting a table's cells, rows, and columns.

Here's how to select a row in a table…

1 Select the first row in the table by moving the pointer to the far left of the table until the pointer changes directions, from ⌖ to ⟋. Click to select the first row.

> **TIP**
> *Another way to select a row or column is to place the insertion point in the row or column, and select Table → Select → Row or Column from the menu.*

If you're having problems selecting a row using the mouse, you can also select the row by placing the insertion point in the row you want to select, then selecting Table → Select Row from the menu. If you want to select more than one row, you would click and hold the mouse button, and then drag the ⟋ pointer down to select the rows.

Now that you have selected the row, you can format its text.

2 With the row still selected, click the Center button and the Bold button on the Formatting toolbar.

The text in the selected row appears in bold and is centered in each row.

3 Select the last column in the table (Projected Income) by moving the pointer over the very top of the column, until it changes to a ↓. Click to select the column.

As with selecting rows, you can also select a column by placing the insertion point in the row you want to select and then selecting Table → Select Column from the menu. You can also select more than one column by holding down the mouse button and dragging the ↓ pointer across the columns you want to select.

4 Click the Bold button twice on the Formatting toolbar.

The contents of the selected column appear in bold.

5 Select the Ottawa cell by clicking just inside the left side of the cell (the pointer should change directions, ⬈).

Remember that anything you type replaces the current selection—and the contents of a cell are no exception to this rule.

6 Type Montreal **and press the** Tab **key.**

The Tables and Borders toolbar can be a big help when you're working with tables. If the Tables and Borders toolbar doesn't automatically appear when you create or work on a table, it's easy to display it. Here's how:

7 **Click the** Tables and Borders button **on the Standard toolbar. If the Draw Table button is shaded, click it to turn off the Draw Table tool.**

TIP

Another way to disolay the Tables and Borders toolbbar is to right-click any toolbar or menu, and select Tables and Borders. Or, Select View → Toolbars → Tables and Borders from the menu.

The Tables and Borders toolbar appears, as shown in Figure 5-6.

Selecting cells, rows, and columns might seem very boring to you, but it's crucial that you get it down if you're going to work with tables. When people have problems doing something with a table, 90% of the time it's because they didn't properly select the table.

QUICK REFERENCE

TO SELECT A CELL:

• CLICK THE LEFT EDGE OF THE CELL.

TO SELECT A ROW OR COLUMN:

• ROW: CLICK TO THE LEFT OF THE ROW.

• COLUMN: CLICK THE COLUMN'S TOP BORDER (THE POINTER WILL CHANGE TO A DOWN ARROW).

OR...

• PLACE THE INSERTION POINT IN THE ROW OR COLUMN AND SELECT TABLE → SELECT → ROW OR COLUMN FROM THE MENU.

TO SELECT SEVERAL CELLS:

• DRAG ACROSS THE CELL, ROW, OR COLUMN, OR SELECT A SINGLE CELL, ROW, OR COLUMN AND HOLD DOWN SHIFT WHILE YOU CLICK ANOTHER CELL, ROW, OR COLUMN.

TO SELECT THE ENTIRE TABLE:

• CLICK THE MOVE HANDLE NEXT TO THE TABLE (MUST BE IN PRINT LAYOUT VIEW).

TO DISPLAY THE TABLES AND BORDERS TOOLBAR:

• CLICK THE TABLES AND BORDERS BUTTON ON THE STANDARD TOOLBAR.

OR...

• RIGHT-CLICK ANY TOOLBAR AND SELECT TABLES AND BORDERS.

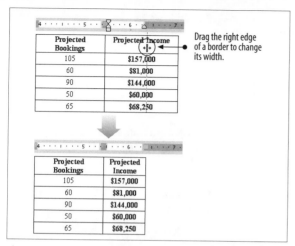

Drag the right edge
of a border to change
its width.

Figure 5-7. You can adjust column width using the mouse.

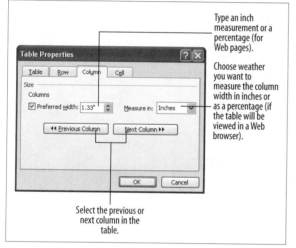

Type an inch
measurement or a
percentage (for
Web pages).

Choose weather
you want to
measure the column
width in inches or
as a percentage (if
the table will be
viewed in a Web
browser).

Select the previous or
next column in the
table.

Figure 5-8. The Column tab of the Table Properties dialog box.

When you create a table, all of the rows and columns usually appear the same size. As you enter information in a table, you will quickly discover that some of the columns are not wide enough to properly display the information they contain. This lesson explains how to change the width of a column.

If you have the Explore Canada Table document open from the previous lesson, you can skip the first step of this exercise. Otherwise, you will need to open the Lesson 5B file…

1 If necessary, find and open the Lesson 5B file and save it as Explore Canada Table.

Here's how to resize the width of a column…

2 Carefully position the pointer over the very last column border, after the heading Projected Income, until it changes to a +‖+ as shown in Figure 5-7. Click and hold the mouse button, drag the pointer to the 6 inch mark on the horizontal ruler, and then release the mouse button.

The width of the "Projected Income" column is now much smaller.

You've just learned how to adjust the width of a column using the mouse, but like many operations in Word, you can also use the menu to do the same thing.

3 Select the last column (Projected Income).

You learned how to select columns in the previous lesson. Now that the column is selected, you can adjust its width using the menu.

4 Select Table → Table Properties from the menu.

The Table Properties dialog box appears.

5 Click the Column tab to bring the column settings to the front of the dialog box.

The Column tab appears, as shown in Figure 5-8. Here you can adjust column width and the amount of spacing between columns.

6 Type 1 in the Preferred width text box.

This will change the column width to one inch. Notice the "Measure in" text box to the right of the "Preferred width" box. There are two ways you can measure the width of a column:

- **Inches:** Measures column width with a fixed measurement. Unless you are using Word to create Web pages, this is the setting you will almost always use.

- **Percent:** Choose Percent if the table will be viewed in a Web browser. In Web Layout view, the column width is measured as a percentage of the screen.

Let's close the dialog box.

7 Click OK.

The dialog box closes and Word adjusts the width of the selected column to one inch. Another fast and easy way to adjust a column's width is to use Word's *AutoFit* feature. AutoFit adjusts the width of a column automatically to fit the text of the column.

8 Select Table → AutoFit → AutoFit to Contents from the menu.

Another way to AutoFit a column is to double-click the right edge of the column.

Word automatically adjusts the column widths of the table so that the text fits inside them. Another neat trick you should know when adjusting the width of columns is that you can distribute columns evenly, which changes the selected columns or cells to equal column width.

9 Click anywhere inside the table, then click the ⊞ move handle in the upper-left corner of the table.

⋮ NOTE ⋮ *You must be in Print Layout view or the ⊞ move handle won't appear when you select the table. If you don't see the table's ⊞ move handle, select View → Print Layout and then click anywhere inside the table.*

When the entire table is selected, any height or width adjustments made will affect every column or row in the entire table. Move on to the next step to use the Distribute Columns Evenly Command, which changes the selected columns or cells to equal column width.

10 Click the Distribute Columns Evenly button on the Tables and Borders toolbar.

Another way to distribute columns evenly is to select Table → AutoFit → Distribute Columns Evenly.

Word adjusts the width of all the columns in the selected table so that they are equal.

QUICK REFERENCE

TO ADJUST THE WIDTH OF A COLUMN:

- CLICK AND DRAG THE COLUMN'S RIGHT BORDER TO THE LEFT OR RIGHT.

OR...

1. PLACE THE INSERTION POINT IN THE COLUMN.

2. SELECT TABLE → TABLE PROPERTIES FROM THE MENU AND CLICK THE COLUMN TAB.

3. SPECIFY THE COLUMN WIDTH AND CLICK OK.

TO ADJUST THE WIDTH OF A COLUMN USING AUTOFIT:

- SELECT THE COLUMN AND SELECT TABLE → AUTOFIT → AUTOFIT TO CONTENTS FROM THE MENU.

TO DISTRIBUTE COLUMNS EVENLY IN A TABLE:

- SELECT THE COLUMNS AND CLICK THE DISTRIBUTE COLUMNS EVENLY BUTTON ON THE TABLES AND BORDERS TOOLBAR.

OR...

- SELECT TABLE → AUTOFIT → DISTRIBUTE COLUMNS EVENLY FROM THE MENU.

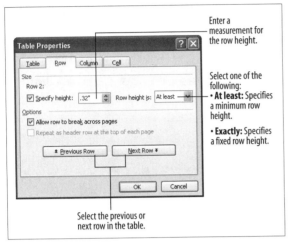

Enter a measurement for the row height.

Select one of the following:
- **At least:** Specifies a minimum row height.
- **Exactly:** Specifies a fixed row height.

Select the previous or next row in the table.

Figure 5-9. The Row tab of the Table Properties dialog box.

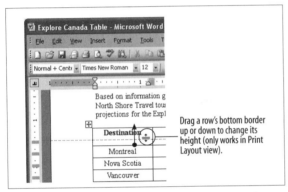

Drag a row's bottom border up or down to change its height (only works in Print Layout view).

Figure 5-10. You can adjust the height of a row using the mouse, but only if you're in Print Layout view.

In the previous lesson, you learned how to change the width of a column. In this lesson, we'll look at changing the height of a row. You will seldom need to change a row's height because, unless you specify otherwise, rows automatically expand to the tallest cell in the table—the one that contains the most lines of text.

Here's one way of adjusting the height of a row…

1 Place the insertion point anywhere in the first row.

Now you can change the height of the current row.

2 Select Table → Table Properties from the menu and click the Row tab.

The Table Properties dialog box appears with the Row tab selected, as shown in Figure 5-9. Here, you can adjust the row height, alignment of text in the cells,

and whether or not you want to allow the row to break across pages or not.

The *specify height* box is especially important:

- **Specify height box unchecked:** Automatically adjusts the row height for the tallest cell in the row (the one with the most text in it). This option makes it easy to change a row's height—just press Enter and the cell will expand to hold the new blank line(s). This is the default setting and the one you will usually want to use.

- **Specify height box checked:** Lets you manually adjust the row height by entering a value in the "Specify height" box.

Let's try manually changing the row height.

3 Check the Specify height box.

Now you can specify the height of the row.

4 Type .5 in the Specify height text box.

There are two additional options you can specify when manually adjusting the height of a row, listed in the "Row height is" box:

- **At Least:** Specifies a minimum row height (enter the minimum height in the "Specify height" text box). If cell contents cause the cell to exceed the height specified, Word will adjust the height of the row to fit the contents.

- **Exactly:** Specifies a fixed row height (enter the height in the "Specify height" text box). If cell contents exceed the fixed height, Word will print only the contents that fit in the cell.

5 Select At least from the Row Height list and click OK.

The dialog box closes and the height of the selected rows is adjusted to a half-inch. You can also adjust the width of all the columns or height of all the rows in a table at once by selecting the entire table, selecting Table → Table Properties from the menu, and clicking the Row tab, and then specifying the row height.

You can also adjust the height of the row using the mouse, but make sure you are in Print Layout view first.

6 Make sure you are in Print Layout view—if you're not, click the Print Layout View button on the Horizontal scroll bar located near the bottom of the screen.

≳ NOTE ≳ *You must be in Print Layout view in order to adjust the height of a row with the mouse.*

7 Position the pointer directly on the bottom border of the first row, until it changes to ÷. Click and hold the mouse button and drag the pointer up a smidgen, as shown in Figure 5-10. Then, release the mouse button.

8 Save your work.

As with column width, you can also change selected rows or cells to equal row height. Simply select the rows that you want to be the same height, and select Table → AutoFit → Distribute Rows Evenly from the menu. Or you can right-click the selected row(s) and select Distribute Rows Evenly from the shortcut menu.

QUICK REFERENCE

TO ADJUST THE HEIGHT OF A ROW:

1. PLACE THE INSERTION POINT IN THE ROW.

2. SELECT TABLE → TABLE PROPERTIES FROM THE MENU AND CLICK THE ROW TAB.

3. SPECIFY THE ROW HEIGHT AND CLICK OK.

OR...

• MAKE SURE YOU ARE IN PRINT LAYOUT VIEW AND DRAG THE ROW'S BOTTOM BORDER UP OR DOWN.

Inserting and Deleting Rows and Columns

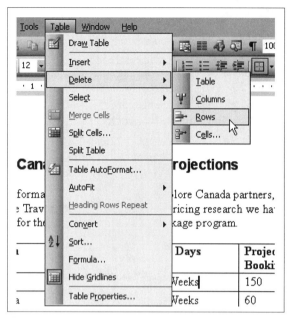

Figure 5-11. You can delete a row using the Table menu.

Destination	Avg. Cost	Avg. Days	Projected Bookings	Projected Income
Quebec	$2,000	2.5 Weeks	150	$300,000
Nova Scotia	$1,350	1.5 Weeks	60	$81,000
Vancouver	$1,600	2 Weeks	90	$144,000
Winnipeg	$1,200	1.5 Weeks	50	$60,000
Toronto	$1,050	1 Week	65	$68,250

Figure 5-12. The table with new rows and columns.

In the previous lessons, you learned how to adjust the size of rows and columns. In this lesson, you will learn how to delete entire columns and rows (and any text they contain), and how to insert new columns and rows into a table.

First you need to select the column or row you want to delete…

1 Place the insertion point anywhere in the Montreal row.

Here's how to delete the current row:

2 Select Table → Delete → Rows from the menu, as shown in Figure 5-11.

The Montreal row is deleted. Now try inserting a new row.

3 If necessary, place the insertion point in the Nova Scotia row.

Now you can insert a row before or after the current row.

4 Select Table → Insert → Rows Above from the menu.

A new row is inserted immediately above the Nova Scotia row.

5 Place the insertion point in the first cell in the new row, type Quebec, press Tab, and then type the following numbers in the cells in the new row: $2,000 Tab No Tab 150 Tab $300,000.

If you're at the last cell of a table, there is another simple way to insert rows.

6 Place the insertion point in the very last cell in the bottom right-hand corner of the table.

7 Press the Tab key.

Word adds a new row at the end of the table and moves the insertion point to the first cell in the new row. Normally, pressing the Tab key moves to the next cell in a table, but since this is the last cell in the table, Word assumes you need another row in the table and automatically adds one. Don't worry about the blank row at the end of the table—we'll be using it in an upcoming lesson.

Now that you have deleted and inserted a row, try deleting and inserting a column.

8 Place the insertion point anywhere in the Promotion column.

Here's how to delete the current column:

9 Select Table → Delete → Columns from the menu.

The Promotion column is deleted. Now try inserting a column.

10 Place the insertion point anywhere in the Avg. Cost column.

Move on to the next step to insert a new column.

11 Select Table → Insert → Columns to the Right from the menu.

A new column appears to the right of the Avg. Cost column. Go ahead and type some information in this new column:

12 Place the insertion point in the top cell of the new column and type Avg. Days.

13 Press the Down Arrow Key ↓ to move down to the next empty cell in the column.

Complete the rest of the column.

14 Type 2.5 Weeks, press the Down Arrow Key to move down to the next empty cell in the column, type 1.5 Weeks, press the Down Arrow Key, type 2 Weeks, press Down Arrow Key, type 1.5 Weeks, press Down Arrow Key, and type 1 Week.

Your table should look similar to the one in Figure 5-12.

15 Save your work.

QUICK REFERENCE

TO DELETE A COLUMN OR ROW:

- SELECT THE COLUMN OR ROW YOU WANT TO DELETE. THEN CLICK THE RIGHT MOUSE BUTTON AND SELECT DELETE CELLS FROM THE SHORTCUT MENU. SELECT WHAT YOU WANT TO DELETE FROM THE DELETE CELLS DIALOG BOX.

OR...

- SELECT THE COLUMN OR ROW YOU WANT TO DELETE, THEN SELECT TABLE → DELETE → COLUMNS OR ROWS FROM THE MENU.

TO INSERT A COLUMN:

1. SELECT THE COLUMN THAT YOU WANT THE NEW COLUMN TO BE INSERTED IN FRONT OF.

2. CLICK THE RIGHT MOUSE BUTTON AND SELECT INSERT COLUMNS FROM THE SHORTCUT MENU.

    OR...

    SELECT TABLE → INSERT → COLUMNS TO THE LEFT OR COLUMNS TO THE RIGHT.

TO INSERT A ROW:

1. SELECT THE ROW THAT YOU WANT THE NEW ROW TO BE INSERTED ABOVE.

2. CLICK THE RIGHT MOUSE BUTTON AND SELECT INSERT ROWS FROM THE SHORTCUT MENU.

    OR...

    SELECT TABLE → INSERT → ROWS ABOVE OR ROWS BELOW FROM THE MENU.

Adding Borders to a Table

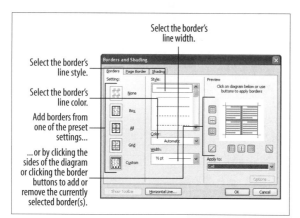

Figure 5-13. The Borders tab of the Borders and Shading dialog box.

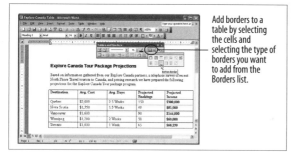

Figure 5-14. The table with the modified borders.

Borders improve a table's appearance, giving it a polished, professional look. Borders can often make it easier to read the information in a table, especially when the information is in numbers. When you create a table, Word automatically adds borders or lines around every cell in the table, but it's very easy to change, add, or remove your table's borders. The easiest way to add borders to your tables is to use the Border button on either the Formatting toolbar or the Tables and Borders toolbar.

This lesson will give you some practice working with borders. For the purpose of this exercise, we'll start by removing all the borders that Word automatically adds whenever you create a new table.

If you have the Explore Canada Table document open from the previous lesson you can skip the first step of this exercise, otherwise you will need to open the Lesson 5C file…

1 If necessary, find and open the Lesson 5C document and save it as Explore Canada Table.

First we want to remove the original borders from this table—and we will have to select the entire table in order to do that.

2 Select the entire table by clicking the ⊞ move handle in the upper-left corner of the table.

⸫ NOTE ⸫   *If you don't see the table's* ⊞ *move handle, click anywhere inside the table.*

3 Click the Border button list arrow on either the Formatting toolbar or the Tables and Borders toolbar.

A list appears with several border options.

4 Select the No Border option from the list.

Word removes all the borders from the table. The table's gridlines remain however, to help you see what cell you're working on. Unlike borders, gridlines don't print.

Now let's add a border to the table's top row.

5 Select the table's top row, click the Border button list arrow, and select the Outside Border option.

Word adds a border around the selected cells. If the Tables and Borders toolbar is displayed, you can also change the border's style, width, and color.

6 Select the Toronto's Projected Income cell—the cell that contains $68,250.

You want to add a thick, dark border to the bottom of this cell. Here's how to change the border's width:

7 Click the Line Weight list arrow on the Tables and Borders toolbar and select 2π pt from the list.

Now that you've selected the border's width (or weight), you can add the border.

8 Click the Border button list arrow and select the Bottom Border option.

Word adds a thick border to the bottom of the cell.

Now let's hide the gridlines in the table.

9 Select Table → Hide Gridlines **from the menu.**

Word hides the table gridlines, so you can easily see the borders you've added to the table. Table gridlines don't print and they help you see which cell you're working in—so it's usually best to display them.

10 Select Table → Show Gridlines **from the menu.**

The table gridlines reappear and your document should look like Figure 5-14. The Border button is the fastest and easiest method to add borders to your tables. However, if it doesn't have the border option you want, you'll have to use the Borders and Shading dialog box.

11 Select Format → Borders and Shading **from the menu. Click the** Borders **tab if necessary.**

The Borders and Shading dialog box appears, as shown in Figure 5-13. Here you can find every option imaginable for adding, removing, and configuring your table's borders.

12 Click Cancel **to close the Borders and Shading dialog box.**

The Borders and Shading dialog box closes.

QUICK REFERENCE

TO ADD A BORDER TO A TABLE:

1. SELECT THE CELLS WHERE YOU WANT TO APPLY THE BORDERS.

2. CLICK THE BORDER BUTTON LIST ARROW ON THE FORMATTING TOOLBAR OR THE TABLES AND BORDERS TOOLBAR, AND SELECT THE BORDER OPTION YOU WANT.

OR...

SELECT FORMAT → BORDERS AND SHADING FROM THE MENU, CLICK THE BORDERS TAB, AND SPECIFY THE OPTIONS YOU WANT.

Adding Shading and Patterns

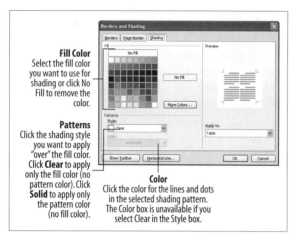

Fill Color
Select the fill color you want to use for shading or click No Fill to remove the color.

Patterns
Click the shading style you want to apply "over" the fill color. Click **Clear** to apply only the fill color (no pattern color). Click **Solid** to apply only the pattern color (no fill color).

Color
Click the color for the lines and dots in the selected shading pattern. The Color box is unavailable if you select Clear in the Style box.

Figure 5-15. The Shading tab of the Border and Shading dialog box.

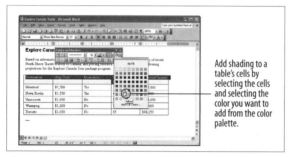

Add shading to a table's cells by selecting the cells and selecting the color you want to add from the color palette.

Figure 5-16. The table with the new shading options.

Adding shading, colors, and patterns to a table is similar to adding borders—you select the cells and then select the shading options from either the Shading Color button on the Tables and Borders toolbar, or by selecting Format → Borders and Shading from the menu and clicking the Shading tab. This lesson will give you some practice adding colors, shading, and patterns to your table.

First you need to select the column(s) or row(s) where you want to apply shading.

1 Select the top row of the table.

This is where you want to apply shading.

2 Click the Shading Color button list arrow on the Tables and Borders toolbar.

>
> *Another way to apply shading is to select Format → Borders and Shading from the menu, click the Shading tab, and specify the shading options.*

A color palette appears below the Shading Color button.

3 Select the yellow color.

The selected row is shaded with a yellow color. As with borders, you can also apply shading to a table using the Borders and Shading dialog box.

4 Select Format → Borders and Shading from the menu and click the Shading tab.

The Shading tab of the Borders and Shading dialog box appears, as shown in Figure 5-15. The Borders and Shading dialog box gives you more colors, patterns, and shading options than the Shading toolbar.

5 Click the Style list arrow, scroll all the way down to familiarize yourself with the available shading and patterns, and then scroll back up and select the 10% option. Click OK.

The Borders and Shading dialog box closes, and Word formats the selected cells with the specified 10 percent shading.

QUICK REFERENCE

TO ADD SHADING TO A TABLE:

1. SELECT THE CELLS WHERE YOU WANT TO APPLY THE SHADING.

2. CLICK THE SHADING COLOR BUTTON LIST ARROW ON THE TABLES AND BORDERS TOOLBAR AND SELECT THE SHADING COLOR YOU WANT.

OR...

SELECT FORMAT → BORDERS AND SHADING FROM THE MENU, CLICK THE SHADING TAB, AND SPECIFY THE SHADING OPTION(S).

Using AutoFormat

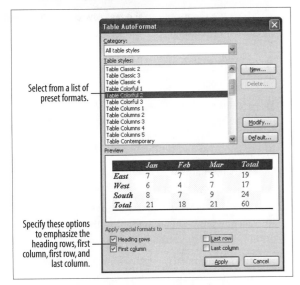

Select from a list of preset formats.

Specify these options to emphasize the heading rows, first column, first row, and last column.

Figure 5-17. The Table AutoFormat dialog box.

Destination	Avg. Cost	Promotion	Projected Bookings	Projected Income
Winnipeg	$1,200	No	50	$60,000
Vancouver	$1,600	No	90	$144,000
Toronto	$1,050	No	65	$68,250
Quebec	$2,000	Yes	105	$300,000
Nova Scotia	$1,350	Yes	60	$81,000
			370	$653,250.00

Figure 5-18. The table after being formatted with the Colorful 2 Table AutoFormat setting.

This lesson explains how Word can automatically format your tables with the Table AutoFormat command. Auto-Format is a built-in collection of formats—including font sizes, patterns, and alignments—that you can quickly apply to a table. AutoFormat lets you select from 40 different preset formats, and is a great feature if you want your table to look sharp and professional but don't have the time to format it yourself.

1 Place the insertion point anywhere in the table and select Table → Table AutoFormat from the menu.

The Table AutoFormat dialog box appears, as shown in Figure 5-17. The 40 preset formats are listed in the Table styles list. To see what a preset format looks like, select it from the Table styles list and then look at the Preview area of the dialog box.

2 Select the Table Colorful 2 option from the Table styles list.

The format is shown in the Preview area of the dialog box. You can further format the table for emphasis in the "Apply special formats to" area at the bottom of the dialog box.

3 Check the Heading rows and First column boxes and click Apply.

The dialog box closes and the table is formatted with the Table Colorful 2 formatting, and the heading row and first column are specially formatted, as shown in Figure 5-18.

QUICK REFERENCE

TO FORMAT A TABLE USING AUTOFORMAT:

1. PLACE THE INSERTION POINT ANYWHERE IN THE TABLE AND SELECT TABLE → TABLE AUTOFORMAT FROM THE MENU.

2. SELECT A PRESET FORMAT FROM THE LIST.

Totaling Numbers in a Table

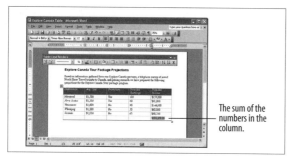

The sum of the numbers in the column.

Figure 5-19. Click the AutoSum button on the Tables and Borders toolbar to add up the numbers in a column or row.

Here's another quick and easy lesson. If your table contains numbers, you don't have to dig out your calculator to find the total of a column or row—let Word make the calculation for you! With the click of a single button, Word will add up all of the numbers in a column or row.

1 If necessary, click the Tables and Borders button to display the Tables and Borders toolbar.

To total a column or row, simply place the insertion point in the last cell in the column or row and click the AutoSum button.

2 Click the empty cell in the last row under the Projected Income column.

3 Click the Σ AutoSum button on the Tables and Borders toolbar.

Word totals the numbers in the Projected Income column—$653,250.00. Notice the total appears gray, because it's a *field*—a placeholder for information that changes.

Let's see what happens if we change some of the numbers in the table.

4 Change the 300,000 amount in the second row of the Projected Income column to 200,000.

Unlike its cousin Microsoft Excel, Word doesn't automatically recalculate any totals, until you print or reopen the document, or manually command Word to recalculate.

5 Right-click the total field in the last cell and select Update Field from the shortcut menu.

Word recalculates and displays the new column total: $553,250.00, as shown in Figure 5-19.

QUICK REFERENCE

TO TOTAL NUMBERS IN A COLUMN OR ROW:

• PLACE THE INSERTION POINT IN THE BLANK CELL BELOW OR TO THE RIGHT OF THE CELLS YOU WANT TO TOTAL, AND CLICK THE AUTOSUM BUTTON ON THE TABLES AND BORDERS TOOLBAR.

Sorting Information in a Table

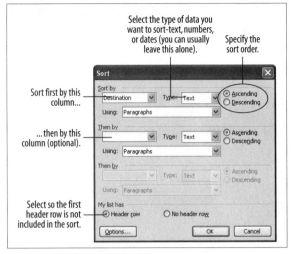

Select the type of data you want to sort—text, numbers, or dates (you can usually leave this alone).

Specify the sort order.

Sort first by this column...

...then by this column (optional).

Select so the first header row is not included in the sort.

Figure 5-20. The Sort dialog box.

Another of Word's many useful functions is its ability to sort information. Word can sort items in a list alphabetically, numerically, or chronologically (by date). In addition, Word can sort information in ascending (A to Z) or descending (Z to A) order. Table 5-4 shows sort examples. You can sort an entire table or a portion of a table by selecting what you want to sort. You can even sort information that isn't in a table at all, as long as you select it first. This lesson will show you several techniques you can use to sort information in your tables.

1 If necessary, open the Lesson 5D in your Practice folder, save it as Explore Canada Table, and click the Tables and Borders button to display the Tables and Borders toolbar.

First, you need to select the column you want to sort.

2 Click any cell in the Destination column.

You want to sort the table by this column.

3 Click the Sort Descending button on the Tables and Borders toolbar.

The table is sorted in descending alphabetical order, from Z to A, based on the values in the Destination column. The Winnipeg row should appear in the first row (after the headings row).

You can also sort information with the Sort dialog box, which offers more sorting options.

4 Click any cell in the table and select Table → Sort from the menu.

The Sort dialog box appears, as shown in Figure 5-20. The Sort dialog box lets you specify how you want to sort the information in your table. You can specify which column to sort by, specify the sort order, and specify whether or not you want to sort the table by any additional columns. For example, you could sort a table by last name, and then by first name.

5 Make sure Destination appears in the "Sort by" box and click the Ascending option.

⌇ NOTE ⌇   *To sort the table by numeric or chronological order, you must select the column's heading in the "Sort by" box. For example, to sort this table in numeric order, "Projected Bookings" or "Projected Income" would have to appear in the "Sort by" box.*

6 In the "My list has" section, make sure the Header row option is selected.

This option ensures that Word does not sort the first row of the table—the column heading row.

7 Click OK.

The dialog box closes and the table is sorted in ascending order based on the values in the Destinations column.

8 Save your work and close the Explore Canada
Table document.

Table 5-4. Sort Examples

Order	Alphabetic	Numeric	Date
Ascending	A, B, C	1, 2, 3	1/1/99, 1/15/99, 2/1/99
Descending	C, B, A	3, 2, 1	2/1/99, 1/15/99, 1/1/99

QUICK REFERENCE

TO SORT INFORMATION IN A TABLE:

1. SELECT THE CELLS OR INFORMATION YOU WANT
   TO SORT.

2. SELECT TABLE → SORT FROM THE MENU, THEN
   SPECIFY THE ORDER YOU WANT TO SORT BY
   (ASCENDING OR DESCENDING).

OR...

DEPENDING ON HOW YOU WANT TO SORT THE
INFORMATION, CLICK EITHER THE SORT ASCENDING
BUTTON OR THE SORT DESCENDING BUTTON ON
THE TABLES AND BORDERS TOOLBAR.

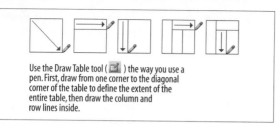

Use the Draw Table tool ( ) the way you use a pen. First, draw from one corner to the diagonal corner of the table to define the extent of the entire table, then draw the column and row lines inside.

Figure 5-21. Using the Draw Table tool.

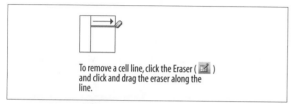

To remove a cell line, click the Eraser ( ) and click and drag the eraser along the line.

Figure 5-22. Using the Eraser tool.

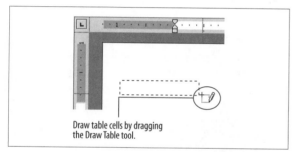

Draw table cells by dragging the Draw Table tool.

Figure 5-23. You can add a row to a table with the Draw Table tool.

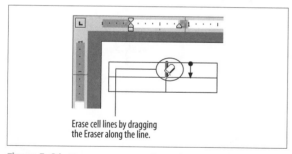

Erase cell lines by dragging the Eraser along the line.

Figure 5-24. You can erase a column from a single row using the Eraser.

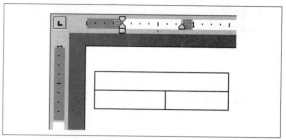

Figure 5-25. The completed table.

The Draw Table and Eraser tools on the Tables and Borders toolbar let you draw and modify tables the same way you would use a pencil to draw a table on a piece of paper. Some people prefer the Draw Table tools to Word's menus and toolbar commands, especially when creating or modifying complicated and irregular tables. Figures 5-21 and 5-22 demonstrate how to use the Draw Table tool and the Eraser tool.

This lesson will give you some practice using the Draw Table and Eraser tools.

1 Create a new blank document.

2 Click the Draw Table button **on the Tables and Borders toolbar.**

The Draw Table button on the Tables and Borders toolbar is highlighted orange, and the cursor changes to the Draw Table tool .

3 Click and drag the pointer to create a box about 4 inches wide and 2 inches tall.

This is the outside border of a new table. Next, you can use the Draw Table tool to create the smaller cells inside the table.

4 Click the middle of the left side of the table, and drag the pointer straight across to the right side of the table. Release the mouse button.

As you drag the pointer across the table, a dotted line shows where the new cell border will appear.

5 Click the top of the table in the middle and drag the ✏ pointer straight down to the bottom border of the table. Release the mouse button.

Another tool you can use to modify tables is the Eraser tool. By clicking the Eraser button and dragging across a cell line with the ✐ pointer, you remove the cell line from the table.

6 Click the 🔲 Eraser button on the Tables and Borders toolbar. Click the top of the table, at the column line that splits the table. Drag the ✐ pointer straight

down to the bottom of the first row, as shown in Figure 5-24, then release the mouse button.

Use the Draw Table tool (see Figure 5-23) to add one more row to your table and you're finished.

7 Click the Draw Table button on the Tables and Borders toolbar. Click in the middle of the left side of the table and dragging the ✏ pointer straight across to the right side of the table. Release the mouse button.

Compare your table with the one in Figure 5-25.

8 Close your document without saving any changes.

QUICK REFERENCE

TO USE THE DRAW TABLE TOOL:

- CLICK THE DRAW TABLE BUTTON ON THE TABLES AND BORDERS TOOLBAR AND DRAG TO CREATE A TABLE. REPEAT TO ADD CELLS TO THE TABLE.

TO USE THE ERASER TOOL:

- CLICK THE ERASER BUTTON ON THE TABLES AND BORDERS TOOLBAR AND ERASE TABLE LINES BY CLICKING AND DRAGGING ACROSS THEM.

Creating Table Formulas

	A	B	C
1	A1	B1	C1
2	A2	B2	C2
3	A3	B3	C3
4	A4	B4	C4

Figure 5-26. Cells are referenced as A1, A2, B1, B2, and so on, with the letter representing a column and the number representing a row.

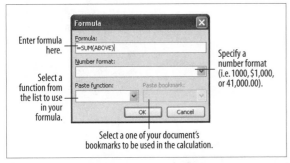

Enter formula here.

Select a function from the list to use in your formula.

Specify a number format (i.e. 1000, $1,000, or 41,000.00).

Select a one of your document's bookmarks to be used in the calculation.

Figure 5-27. Cell references for the Two-Year Cash Flow Projection table.

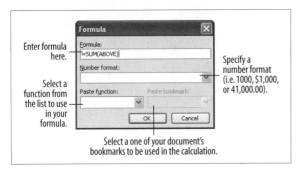

Enter formula here.

Select a function from the list to use in your formula.

Specify a number format (i.e. 1000, $1,000, or 41,000.00).

Select a one of your document's bookmarks to be used in the calculation.

Figure 5-28. The Formula dialog box.

Word can do many more calculations on the numbers in a table than simply adding them together—you can add, subtract, multiply, divide, and find averages of the data in a table. Make no mistake, Word is not a spreadsheet program—like Microsoft Excel, which is made to perform calculations and formulas—but it *can* do some rudimentary arithmetic.

To enter your own calculations, you need to use the Formula dialog box, and you must refer to the cells in a table using *cell references*. A cell reference identifies where the cell is located in a table. Every cell reference contains a letter (A, B, C and so on) to represent its column and a number (1, 2, 3 and so on) to represent its row. Look at Figure 5-26 to see how a table's cells are referenced.

1 Open the Lesson 5E document, save it as Two-Year Cash Flow, and, if necessary, click the Tables and Borders button to display the Tables and Borders toolbar.

Most of the formulas in this table have already been entered.

2 Place the insertion point in the blank cell in the last column, under the 12,000 cell (cell I18).

> **TIP** Though a grid for cell references does not appear in Word, you can still use cell references in formulas.

The reference for this particular cell would be *I18* (refer to Figure 5-27 to see why). All the other expense columns have already been totaled. It's almost always easier to total values in a table by clicking the Auto-Sum button on the Tables and Borders toolbar, but here we will manually enter the formula instead.

3 Select Table → Formula from the menu.

The Formula dialog box appears, as shown in Figure 5-28. Word suggests a formula for this cell, based on its location in the table. This is the formula we want, but before we move on, let's learn more about formulas.

A *formula* performs calculations, such as adding, subtracting, and multiplying. Formulas are actually a type of value, but, unlike values that contain only numbers, formulas contain information to perform a numerical calculation—such as adding, subtracting, multiplying, or even finding an average. A cell with the formula =5+3 would display the result: 8.

All formulas must start with an equal sign (=). The equal sign tells Word that you want to perform a calculation. Once you have entered an equal sign, you must specify two more types of information: the values you want to calculate, and the arithmetic operator(s) and function name(s) you want to use to calculate the values. Formulas can contain explicit values, such as the numbers 5 or 8, but more often they will reference the values contained in other cells. For example, the formula =A5+A6 would add together whatever values were in the cells A5 and A6. Arithmetic operators include math symbols such as the plus sign (+) to perform addition between values and the minus sign (-) to perform subtraction. *Functions*, such as the SUM function, are used to perform calculations that are more complicated. Table 5-5 at the end of this lesson gives some examples of operators and functions.

4 Click OK.

The Formula dialog box closes, and Word totals the expenses.

5 Place the insertion point in the blank cell in the last column of the Difference row (cell I20) and select Table → Formula from the menu.

Here you want to calculate the difference between the projected income and expenses for the fourth quarter of the year 2000. Move on to the next step to enter the formula.

6 In the Formula text box, type =I8-I18 and click OK.

The Formula dialog box closes, and Word subtracts the total fourth quarter income in cell I8 from the total fourth quarter expenses in cell I18.

 You should only perform a few simple calculations inside a table. If you want to perform numerous or more complex calculations, you should consider using an embedded Microsoft Excel spreadsheet instead of a table. Excel is much faster and easier to use for working with numbers and calculations.

Table 5-5. Examples of Formulas, References, and Operators in Tables

Operator or Function Name	Purpose	Example
=	All formulas must start with an equal sign.	
+	Performs addition between values.	
-	Performs subtraction between values.	
*	Performs multiplication between values.	
/	Performs division between values.	
SUM	Adds all the numbers in a range of fields.	
AVERAGE	Calculates the average of all the numbers in a range of fields.	
COUNT	Counts the number of items in a list.	

QUICK REFERENCE

TO ADD A FORMULA TO A CELL:

1. PLACE THE INSERTION POINT IN A BLANK CELL WHERE YOU WANT TO INSERT THE FORMULA AND SELECT TABLE → FORMULA FROM THE MENU.

2. ENTER THE FORMULA IN THE FORMULA BOX.

   REMEMBER: ALL FORMULAS START WITH AN EQUAL SIGN FOLLOWED BY THE NUMBERS AND CELL REFERENCES YOU WANT TO INCLUDE IN THE FORMULA.

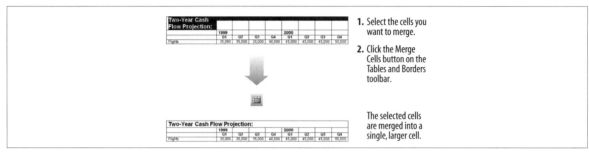

Figure 5-29. Cells merging.

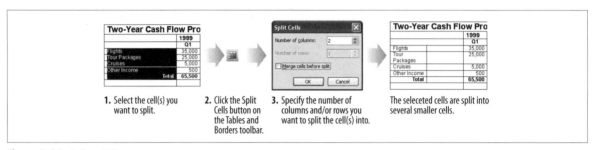

Figure 5-30. Cells splitting.

Figure 5-31. The reformatted table.

If you have been working with tables for a while, there may be times when you wish you could have a single, larger cell that spans several smaller columns. The Merge Cells command allows you to do this. This command merges or combines several smaller cells into a single larger cell that spans the space that the previous cells occupied. Merged cells and non-merged cells can also be broken-up into several smaller cells by using the Split Cells command. Merging and splitting cells sounds more confusing than it really is, so let's get started with this lesson so it will make more sense to you.

First we need to select the cells we want to merge.

1 If necessary click the Tables and Borders button to display the Tables and Borders toolbar, then select all the cells in the top row.

Once you select several cells, you can merge them or combine them into a single, larger cell.

2 Click the Merge Cells button on the Tables and Borders toolbar to merge the selected cells.

> **TIP** Another way to merge cells is to select cells you want to merge and select Table → Merge Cells from the menu, or select cells you want to merge and click the selection with the right mouse button and select Merge Cells from the shortcut menu, or use the Eraser button on the Tables and Borders toolbar to erase the lines between cells.

The selected cells are merged into a single cell that spans across the entire table, as shown in Figure 5-29. Let's try it again!

3 Select the 1999 cell and the following three cells in the second row, then click the Merge Cells button.

All four cells are merged into a single cell that spans across all four quarters.

4 Select the 2000 cell and the following three cells in the second row, then click the Merge Cells button.

All four cells are merged into a single cell that spans across all four quarters.

The procedure for splitting a single cell into several smaller cells is almost as easy as merging cells.

5 In the first column, select the five cells beginning with Flights and ending with Total, as shown in Figure 5-30.

You want to split the selected cells into several smaller cells.

6 Click the Split Cells button on the Tables and Borders toolbar.

> **TIP** *Another way to split cells is to select the cell(s) you want to split and select Table → Split Cells from the menu. Or, select the cell(s) you want to split, click the selection with the right mouse button, and select Split Cells from the shortcut menu. Or, use the Draw Table button on the Tables and Borders toolbar to draw lines to create the new cell(s).*

The Split Cells dialog box appears, as shown in Figure 5-30.

7 Verify that the number 2 appears in the Number of Columns box, and click the Merge cells before split box to uncheck it.

This will split the selected cells into two columns. You may notice that in the Split Cells dialog box there is a Number of Columns text box and a Number of Rows text box. If you wanted to split a cell into multiple rows, you would type the number of rows here.

When selected, the Merge cells before split option would merge the selected cells into a single, larger cell, before splitting them into multiple cells. Checking the "Merge cells before split" option makes it easy to quickly reconfigure a table (for example, to change a 3×3 table to a 4×4 table) if it doesn't contain any information.

You should remove the check from the "Merge cells before split" box if the cells you want to split already contain information.

8 Click OK.

The dialog box closes and the selected cells are each split into two smaller cells, as shown in Figure 5-30.

9 Using either the cut and paste method or drag and drop method, move the headings from the first column (Flights, Tour Packages, Cruises, Other Income, Total) into the newly created second column.

Now let's merge the empty cells into a single larger cell.

10 In the first column, select the five blank cells—beginning with the cell to the left of the Flights cell, ending with the cell to the left of the Total cell—and then click the Merge Cells button on the Tables and Borders toolbar.

The five empty cells become one large cell. Now let's see if you can do the same to the expense accounts.

11 Select the nine cells in the first column, starting with Advertising and ending with Total, and repeat Steps 6-10; splitting the cells, moving their contents, and creating a single larger cell.

Compare your table with Figure 5-31.

QUICK REFERENCE

TO MERGE CELLS:

- SELECT THE CELLS YOU WANT TO MERGE, THEN SELECT TABLE → MERGE CELLS FROM THE MENU.

OR...

- SELECT THE CELLS YOU WANT TO MERGE, THEN CLICK THE MERGE CELLS BUTTON ON THE TABLES AND BORDERS TOOLBAR.

TO SPLIT A CELL:

- SELECT THE CELL YOU WANT TO SPLIT, THEN SELECT TABLE → SPLIT CELLS FROM THE MENU.

OR...

- SELECT THE CELL YOU WANT TO SPLIT AND CLICK THE SPLIT CELLS BUTTON ON THE TABLES AND BORDERS TOOLBAR.

Orienting, Aligning, and Spacing Cell Contents

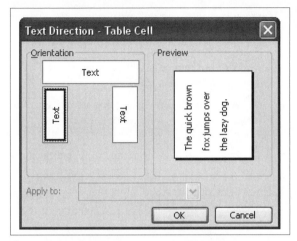

Figure 5-32. The Text Direction dialog box.

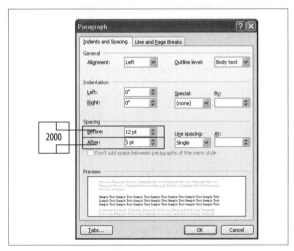

Figure 5-33. Use the Spacing Before and After boxes in the Paragraph dialog box to specify how much space should appear before and after the text in a cell.

Two-Year Cash Flow Projection:									
		1999				2000			
		Q1	Q2	Q3	Q4	Q1	Q2	Q3	Q4
Income	Flights	35,000	35,000	35,000	40,000	45,000	45,000	45,000	50,000
	Tour Packages	25,000	25,000	25,000	25,000	35,000	35,000	35,000	35,000
	Cruises	5,000	5,000	5,000	5,000	4,000	4,000	4,000	4,000
	Other Income	500	500	500	500	2,500	2,500	2,500	2,500
	Total	65,500	65,500	65,500	70,500	86,500	86,500	86,500	91,500
Expenses	Advertising	2,500	2,500	2,500	2,500	4,000	4,000	4,000	4,000
	Commission	25,000	25,000	25,000	25,000	35,000	35,000	35,000	35,000
	Legal	500	500	500	500	1,000	1,000	1,000	1,000
	Office	250	250	250	250	500	500	500	500
	Payroll	5,000	5,000	5,000	5,000	7,500	7,500	7,500	7,500
	Professional Fees	250	250	250	250	500	500	500	500
	Rent	1,250	1,250	1,250	1,250	1,250	1,250	1,250	1,250
	Taxes	8,000	8,000	8,000	8,000	12,000	12,000	12,000	12,000
	Total	42,750	42,750	42,750	42,750	61,750	61,750	61,750	
	Difference	22,750	22,750	22,750	27,750	24,750	24,750	24,750	

Figure 5-34. The completed table.

In this lesson, you will learn how to align text horizontally and vertically in a cell. You can even change the text direction in a cell. For example, you could change the text direction in a cell from horizontal orientation to vertical orientation. Like other table operations, aligning and orienting cell contents is easiest if you use the Tables and Borders toolbar.

1 Drag the left border of the table to the right 0.75 inches.

You can also change the width of a cell by placing the insertion point in the cell, selecting Table → Table Properties from the menu, clicking the Column tab, and specifying the column width.

2 Place the insertion point in the first merged cell (to the left of the income accounts).

3 Click the Change Text Direction button on the Tables and Borders toolbar twice, so the button appears like this ⬚.

Clicking the Change Text button has three different text orientations. You will choose the third one.

4 Type Income.

Notice the text appears in a vertical direction, from the bottom of the cell to the top. You may find it easier to orient text using the Text Orientation dialog box.

5 Place the insertion point in the second merged cell (to the left of the expense accounts) and select Format → Text Direction from the menu.

The Text Direction dialog box appears, as shown in Figure 5-32. The Text Direction dialog box allows you to preview and select a text orientation.

6 Select the vertical bottom-to-top text orientation and click OK.

The dialog box closes and Word will vertically orient any text in the cell from the bottom-to-top of the cell.

7 Type Expenses.

The text appears in a vertical direction, from the bottom of the cell to the top. Here's how to align the contents of a cell horizontally and vertically:

8 With the insertion point still in the second merged cell, click the Alignment button list arrow on the Tables and Borders toolbar and select the Align Center option.

The text between the top and bottom borders and the left and right borders of the cell is now center-aligned.

9 Place the insertion point in the first merged cell and repeat Step 7 to vertically and horizontally center the text within the cell.

You can also align a paragraph inside of a cell.

10 Select both of the merged cells in the second row that contain the years 1999 and 2000 and click the Center button on the Formatting toolbar.

The cell contents are centered horizontally in the cell. If you want to specify how much space appears between the cell contents and the top and bottom of the cell, select Format → Paragraph to bring up the Paragraph dialog box and then adjust the spacing Before and After the paragraph.

11 With the two cells still selected, select Format → Paragraph from the menu.

The Paragraph dialog box appears, as shown in Figure 5-33.

12 Change the Before box to 12 pt and the After box to 6 pt.

This will add a 12 pt space before the paragraph and a 6 pt space after the paragraph.

13 Click OK.

The dialog box closes, and the spacing before and after the contents of the selected paragraphs is adjusted.

14 Compare your table with the one in Figure 5-34.

QUICK REFERENCE

TO HORIZONTALLY ALIGN A CELL'S CONTENTS:

- SELECT THE CELL(S) AND CLICK THE ALIGN LEFT, CENTER, OR ALIGN RIGHT BUTTON ON THE FORMATTING TOOLBAR.

OR...

- SELECT FORMAT → PARAGRAPH FROM THE MENU AND SELECT THE ALIGNMENT.

TO VERTICALLY ALIGN A CELL'S CONTENTS:

- SELECT THE CELL(S), CLICK THE ALIGNMENT BUTTON LIST ARROW ON THE TABLES AND BORDERS TOOLBAR, THEN SELECT AN ALIGNMENT OPTION FROM THE LIST.

TO CHANGE TEXT DIRECTION:

- CLICK THE CHANGE TEXT DIRECTION BUTTON ON THE TABLES AND BORDERS TOOLBAR TO TOGGLE BETWEEN THREE DIFFERENT TEXT DIRECTIONS.

OR...

- SELECT FORMAT → TEXT DIRECTION FROM THE MENU AND SELECT THE TEXT DIRECTION.

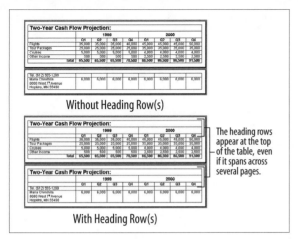

Without Heading Row(s)

With Heading Row(s)

The heading rows appear at the top of the table, even if it spans across several pages.

Figure 5-35. A table without heading rows versus a table with heading rows.

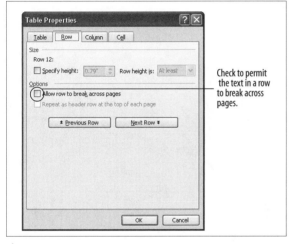

Check to permit the text in a row to break across pages.

Figure 5-36. You can allow table rows to break across pages.

If you're working with a larger table, you might have problems when it spans several pages. One problem is that the column headings appear only on the first page, which makes it difficult to read and understand the table on subsequent pages. Another problem with multiple page tables is that their rows can break across a page when you don't want them to. For example, a table can break across a page in the middle of a row, separating the row's contents onto two pages.

Fortunately, the people at Microsoft came up with solutions for these multiple page table problems. This lesson explains how to create heading rows that appear on top of each page that a table occupies and how to keep from breaking across pages.

1 Click the ☒ Next Page button on the vertical scroll bar to go to the next page of the document.

Notice the portion of the table on the second page does not have any column headers—they're on the first page, as shown at the top of Figure 5-35. This makes it somewhat difficult to read the table, doesn't it? There is a way to make sure the column headers appear on top of a table even when it spans multiple pages.

2 Go to the previous page and select the table's first three rows.

Since this table contains several merged cells, selecting its cells can be a little tricky. If you're having trouble, place your cursor in the left margin and click and drag to select the three rows.

The selected rows will be the table's heading rows. You want these heading rows to appear above the table's columns, even if the table breaks across several pages.

3 Select Table → Heading Rows Repeat from the menu.

The selected rows are set as the table's headings and will appear at the top of every page of the table, as shown at the bottom of Figure 5-35.

4 Click the Next Page button on the vertical scroll bar to go the second page of the document.

Notice the headings appear above this section of the table.

You may notice that the information from the last row on the first page spills over onto the next page. You can prevent this problem by telling Word not to let this row break onto a new page.

5 Place your insertion point in the last row on the first page.

This is the row we want to keep together.

To apply this property to more than one row at a time, select all rows.

6 Select Table → Table Properties from the menu, and click the Row tab, as shown in Figure 5-36.

You only have to change one option here to prevent the table's rows from breaking across pages.

7 **Click the** Allow row to break across pages **box to uncheck it.**

This will prevent the selected rows from breaking across pages.

8 **Click** OK.

The dialog box closes and the row adjusts.

9 Save your work and close the current document.

QUICK REFERENCE

TO ADD A HEADING TO A TABLE:

* SELECT THE TABLE'S HEADING ROW AND SELECT TABLE → HEADING ROWS REPEAT FROM THE MENU.

TO KEEP A ROW FROM BREAKING ACROSS PAGES:

1. SELECT THE ROW, SELECT TABLE → TABLE PROPERTIES FROM THE MENU, AND CLICK THE ROW TAB IF NECESSARY.

2. UNCHECK THE ALLOW ROW TO BREAK ACROSS PAGES OPTION AND CLICK OK.

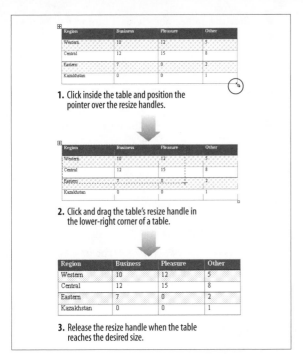

1. Click inside the table and position the pointer over the resize handles.

2. Click and drag the table's resize handle in the lower-right corner of a table.

3. Release the resize handle when the table reaches the desired size.

Figure 5-37. How to resize an entire table proportionally.

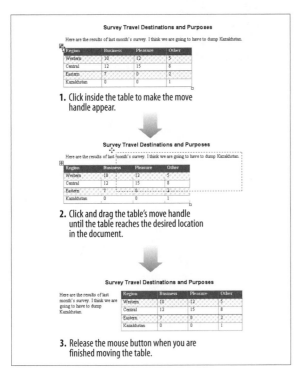

1. Click inside the table to make the move handle appear.

2. Click and drag the table's move handle until the table reaches the desired location in the document.

3. Release the mouse button when you are finished moving the table.

Figure 5-38. How to move a table.

In the past, table layout commands were very confusing. For example, if you wanted to change the overall size of a table, you needed to change the height of every row and the width of every column.

In Word 2003, you don't have to worry about confusing table layout commands—Microsoft has done everything it can to make changing the position and size of a table as easy as possible.

- To move a table, simply click inside the table and then drag it to the new position on the page using the ⊞ table move handle, located in the upper-left corner of the table.

- To resize a table, click inside the table and then resize the table by clicking and dragging the ⊞ table resize handle, located in the bottom-right corner of the table.

In this lesson, you will practice moving and resizing tables.

1 Open Lesson 5F and save it as Survey Table.

You must be in Print Layout view in order to use Word's new move and size commands for tables.

2 Verify that you are in Print Layout view.

This document contains some text and a simple table. Before you can resize or move a table, you need to click somewhere inside the table.

3 Click anywhere inside the table.

The ⊞ table move handle and table □ resize handle appear when the insertion point is located inside the table. Here's how to proportionally resize a table:

4 Click the ⊞ table resize handle in the lower-right corner of the table, and then drag it up and to the left about two inches, as shown in Step 2 of Figure 5-37.

That's all you have to do to resize a table in Word 2003.

Moving a table in Word 2003 is just as easy. Once again, the insertion point must be located somewhere in the table so that the ⊞ move and □ resize handles appear.

5 Click inside the table.

You can use the table move handle to select a table and to move a table to a new position on the page.

6 Click the ⊞ table move handle in the upper-left corner of the table, and then drag it up and to the right about two inches, as shown in Step 2 of Figure 5-38.

The table is moved to a new position on the page. Since you've finished the chapter, you can hide the Tables and Borders toolbar for the time being.

7 Click the Tables and Borders button on the Standard toolbar to hide the Tables and Borders toolbar.

You can also hide the Tables and Borders toolbar by right-clicking any toolbar and selecting Tables and Borders from the shortcut menu.

8 Exit Microsoft Word without saving your work.

QUICK REFERENCE

TO RESIZE A TABLE:

1. MAKE SURE YOU ARE IN PRINT LAYOUT VIEW.

2. CLICK ANYWHERE INSIDE THE TABLE.

3. CLICK AND DRAG THE TABLE RESIZE HANDLE UNTIL THE TABLE IS THE DESIRED SIZE.

TO MOVE A TABLE:

1. MAKE SURE YOU ARE IN PRINT LAYOUT VIEW.

2. CLICK ANYWHERE INSIDE THE TABLE.

3. CLICK AND DRAG THE TABLE MOVE HANDLE TO A NEW LOCATION ON THE PAGE.

Lesson Summary

Creating a Table

To Create a Table (Using the Toolbar): Click the Insert Table button on the Standard toolbar and drag inside the grid to select how many columns and rows you want.

To Create a Table (Using the Menu): Select Table → Insert → Table from the menu, specify the number of rows and columns you want, and click OK.

To Move from Cell to Cell in a Table: Move between cells by pressing Tab to move forward one field or cell; Shift + Tab to move back one field or cell.

To Insert a New Row: In the bottom-right table cell, press the Tab key.

To Delete Text in a Cell: Select the cell(s) and press the Delete key.

Working with a Table

To Select a Cell: Click the left edge of the cell.

To Select a Row or Column: To select a row, click to the left of the row. To select a column, click the column's top gridline or border (the pointer will change to a ⬇). Or, place the insertion point in the row or column and select Table → Select → Row or Column from the menu.

To Select Several Cells: Drag across the cell, row, or column (or select a single cell, row, or column) and then hold down Shift while you click another cell, row, or column.

To Select the Entire Table: Click the ✛ move handle next to the table.

To Display the Tables and Borders Toolbar: Click the Tables and Borders button on the Standard toolbar, or select View → Toolbars → Tables and Borders from the menu, or right-click any toolbar or menu and select Tables and Borders.

Adjusting Column Width

To Select a Column: Click the top of a column to select it. You can also select a column by placing the insertion point anywhere in the column and selecting Table → Select → Column from the menu.

To Select an Entire Table: Make sure the insertion point is located somewhere inside the table, and then select Table → Select → Table from the menu.

To Adjust the Width of a Column: Click and drag the column's right border to the left or right. You can also adjust a column's width by selecting the column, selecting Table → Table Properties from the menu, clicking the Column tab, entering the width of the column, and clicking OK.

AutoFit: You can use AutoFit to adjust a column's width to fit the column's widest entry. To use AutoFit, select the column and select Table → AutoFit → AutoFit to Contents from the menu.

To Distribute Columns Evenly in a Table: Select the columns and click the Distribute Columns Evenly button on the Tables and Borders toolbar. Or, select Table → AutoFit → Distribute Columns Evenly from the menu.

Adjusting Row Height

To Select a Row: Click to the far left of the row. You can also select a row by placing the insertion point anywhere in the row, and selecting Table → Select → Row from the menu.

To Adjust the Height of a Row: Select the row, select Table → Table Properties and click the Row tab, enter the height of the row, and click OK. You can also adjust a row's height by being in Print Layout view and dragging the row's bottom border up or down.

Inserting and Deleting Rows and Columns

To Delete a Column or Row (Using the Right Mouse Button): Select the column or row you want to delete. Then click the right mouse button and select Delete Cells from the shortcut menu. Select what you want to delete from the Delete Cells dialog box.

To Delete a Column or Row (Using the Menu): Select the column or row you want to delete, then select Table → Delete → Columns or Rows from the menu.

To Insert a Column: Select the column that you want the new column to be inserted in front of, click the right mouse button, and select Insert Columns from the shortcut menu. Or, select Table → Insert → Columns to the Left or Columns to the Right.

To Insert a Row: Select the row that you want the new row to be inserted above, click the right mouse button and select Insert Rows from the shortcut menu. Or, select Table → Insert → Rows Above or Rows Below from the menu.

Applying Borders to a Table

Adding Borders (Using the Formatting Toolbar): Select the cell(s), column(s), or row(s) where you want to apply the border(s) and click the Border Button list arrow on the Tables and Borders toolbar. Select the border(s) you want.

Adding Borders (Using the Menu): Select the cell(s), column(s), or row(s) where you want to apply the border(s), select Format → Borders and Shading from the menu, click the Borders tab, and add the border by clicking the preview area of the dialog box.

You can view the Tables and Borders toolbar by clicking the Tables and Borders button on the Standard toolbar or by selecting View → Toolbars → Tables and Borders from the menu.

Adding Shading and Patterns

Adding Shading (Using the Formatting Toolbar): Select the cell(s), column(s), or row(s) where you want to apply the shading, click the Shading Color button list arrow on the Tables and Borders toolbar, and select the shading you want.

Adding Shading (Using the Menu): Select the cell(s), column(s), or row(s) where you want to apply the border(s), select Format → Borders and Shading from the menu, click the Shading tab, and enter the shading options.

Using AutoFormat

AutoFormat lets you quickly format all elements of a table, including its fonts, borders, and shading options by selecting from 40 preset formats.

To AutoFormat a Table: Make sure the insertion point is located in the table, and then select Table → Table Auto-Format from the menu. Select a preset format from the list.

Totaling Numbers in a Table

To calculate the total of a row or column, select the last cell in the row or column and click the AutoSum button on the Tables and Borders toolbar.

Sorting Information in a Table

Using the Menu: Select the cells or information you want to sort, select Table → Sort from the menu, and specify the order you want to sort by (ascending or descending).

Using the Toolbar: Click either the Sort Ascending button or the Sort Descending button on the Tables and Borders toolbar.

Using the Draw Table and Eraser Buttons

Use the Draw Table and Eraser buttons on the Tables and Borders toolbar to create a table like you would on a piece of paper.

To Use the Draw Table Tool: Click the Draw Table button on the Tables and Borders toolbar and drag to create a table and add cells to the table.

To Use the Eraser Tool: Click the Eraser button on the Tables and Borders toolbar and erase table lines by clicking and dragging across them.

Creating Table Formulas

To Add a Formula to a Cell: Select the cell where you want to place the results of the calculation, select Table → Formula from the menu, and enter the cell formula in the Formula box.

All formulas must start with an equal sign (=), and usually contain the values or bookmark names you want to calculate and the arithmetic operator(s) or function name(s) you want to use to calculate the values (such as + or SUM).

Merging and Splitting Cells

To Merge Cells: You can merge multiple cells into a single, larger cell by selecting the cells you want to merge and selecting Table → Merge cells from the menu, or by clicking the Merge Cells button on the Tables and Borders toolbar. You can also use the Eraser button on the Tables and Borders toolbar to merge cells by erasing the lines between them.

To Split a Cell: You can split a cell into several smaller, multiple cells by selecting the cell you want to split and selecting Table → Split cells from the menu, or by clicking the Split Cells button on the Tables and Borders toolbar. You can also use the Draw Table button on the Tables and Borders toolbar to split cells by drawing lines between them.

Orienting, Aligning, and Spacing Cell Contents

To Horizontally Align a Cell's Contents: Select the cell(s) and click the Align Left, Center, or Align Right button on the Formatting toolbar, or select Format → Paragraph from the menu and select the alignment.

To Vertically Align a Cell's Contents: Select the cell(s), click the Alignment button list arrow on the Tables and Borders toolbar, then select an alignment option from the list.

To Change Text Direction: Click the Change Text Direction button on the Tables and Borders toolbar to toggle between the three different text directions, or select Format → Text Direction from the menu and select the text direction.

Working with Tables that Span Multiple Pages

To Add a Heading to a Table: Select the table's heading row, and then select Table → Heading Rows Repeat from the menu.

To Keep a Row from Breaking across Pages: Select the row, select Table → Table Properties from the menu, and click the Row tab if necessary. Uncheck the Allow row to break across pages option and click OK.

Resizing, Moving and Positioning a Table

To Resize a Table: Make sure you are in Print Layout view. Click anywhere inside the table. Click and drag the ☐ table resize handle until the table is the desired size.

To Move a Table: Make sure you are in Print Layout view. Click anywhere inside the table. Click and drag the ⊕ table move handle to a new location on the page.

Quiz

1. Which of the following is NOT a way to create a table?

   A. Select Table → Insert → Table from the menu.

   B. Click the Insert Table button on the Standard toolbar.

   C. Select Insert → Table from the menu.

   D. Select View → Toolbars → Tables and Borders to view the Tables and Borders toolbar and click the Draw Table button on the Tables and Borders menu.

2. Which of the following statements about tables is NOT true?

   A. You can format the characters and paragraphs in a table.

   B. You can sort information in a table alphabetically, numerically, or chronologically.

   C. You can split a cell into several smaller cells, or merge several smaller cells into a single, larger cell.

   D. Since Word's tables can perform mathematical calculations, you should save yourself some money and use Word's tables for all your calculation needs instead of buying a spreadsheet program.

3. Which keys can you use to enter information and navigate a table? (Select all that apply.)

   A. Tab to move to the next cell, Shift + Tab to move to the previous cell.

   B. Enter to move to the next cell, Shift + Enter to move to the previous cell.

   C. → to move to the next cell, Shift + ← to move to the previous cell.

   D. All of the above.

4. Word can sort words alphabetically in a table, but not numerically. (True or False?)

5. Which of the following statements is NOT true?

A. The AutoFit feature automatically adjusts the width of a column so that it fits its longest entry.

B. You can prevent a row from breaking across pages.

C. A table's gridlines always appear when printed.

D. You can merge several cells into a single cell and split a single cell into several smaller cells.

6. You can use the Draw Table tool to draw doodles and pictures in a table. (True or False?)

7. Which of the following procedures can you use to add borders to a table? (Select all that apply.)

A. Select the cells where you want to apply the borders and select the desired border from the Borders button on the Formatting toolbar, or on the Tables and Borders toolbar.

B. Select Tables → Table Border Wizard from the menu and follow the onscreen instructions.

C. Click the Draw Table button on the Tables and Borders toolbar and then draw the border.

D. Select the cells where you want to apply the borders, select Format → Borders and Shading from the menu, and specify the borders.

8. A table you're working with has become so large that it breaks across several pages. How can you ensure the column heads always appear at the top of the table?

A. You can't—there isn't a way to do this.

B. Select the row that contains the column headings and click the Table Headings button on the Tables and Borders toolbar.

C. Press F1 to summon the Office Assistant and type "Fix this table for me, slave!" in the Office Assistant's speech balloon.

D. Select the row that contains the column headings and select Table → Heading Rows Repeat from the menu.

9. You have four cells that you would like to combine into one. Which of the following methods can you use to combine the cells? (Select all that apply.)

A. Select the four cells and click the Merge Cells button on the Tables and Borders toolbar.

B. Select the four cells and select Table → Merge Cells from the menu.

C. Select the four cells and select Table → Combine Cells from the menu.

D. Select the four cells and press Ctrl + M.

10. You can change the text direction in a cell so that you can read it from bottom to top or from top to bottom by selecting Format → Text Direction from the menu. (True or False?)

11. How can you sort items in a table into alphabetical order?

A. Select Tools → Sort from the menu.

B. Click the Sort Ascending (A to Z) button on the Tables and Borders toolbar.

C. Click the Sort Ascending (A to Z) button on the Formatting toolbar.

D. Select Edit → Sort from the menu.

12. How can you add shading to a table?

A. Put an umbrella over the table.

B. Click the Fill Color button on the Formatting toolbar.

C. Select Tables → Shading from the menu.

D. Click the Shading button on the Tables and Borders toolbar.

13. You want to find the total of the expense column in a table. How can you do this?

A. Place the insertion point in a blank cell at the end of the column and click the AutoSum button on the Tables and Borders toolbar.

B. Word can't calculate numbers—that's what Microsoft Excel is there for!

C. Select the cells that contain the numbers you want to total and select Tools → Total from the menu.

D. Place the insertion point in a blank cell at the end of the column and type =SUM(ABOVE).

Homework

1. Start Microsoft Word.

2. Create a table with five rows and five columns.

3. Enter the following information into the table:

   Remember to use the arrow keys, Tab, Shift + Tab and Enter to move from cell to cell.

Quarter	Q1	Q2	Q3	Q4
Flights	15,000	15,000	15,000	15,000
Tours	25,000	25,000	25,000	25,000
Cruises	5,000	5,000	5,000	5,000
Scams	1,500	1,500	1,500	1,500

4. Display the Tables and Borders toolbar by clicking the Tables and Borders button on the Standard toolbar, or by selecting View → Toolbars → Tables and Borders from the menu.

5. Change the width of the first column to one inch.

6. Format the table headings: Select the table's top row and click the Center button and the Bold button on the Formatting toolbar.

7. Sort the table: Place the insertion point in the table's first column and click the Sort Ascending button.

8. Save the document as "Table Homework" and exit Microsoft Word.

Quiz Answers

1. C. You would think selecting Insert → Table would be a way to insert a table using the menu, but the actual menu command is Table → Insert → Table.

2. D. You can perform rudimentary calculations in a Word table, but you'll want to use a spreadsheet program for most computations.

3. A and C. You can use any of these keys to enter information and move around in a table.

4. False. Word can sort words, numbers, and dates in alphabetical, numerical, or chronological order.

5. C. A table's gridlines appear onscreen as a visual reference so that you know where the table's columns, rows, and cells are. You can add borders to a table so that the gridlines appear when printed, or you can remove the borders so that they don't.

6. False. The Draw Table tool is used to add columns and rows to a table.

7. A, C and D. You can use any of these methods to add borders to a table.

8. D. Select Table → Heading Rows Repeat from the menu to ensure that the table's column headings always appear at the top of the table.

9. A and B. Either of these methods will combine or merge several cells into a single cell.

10. True. Select Format → Text Direction from the menu to change the direction of text in a table.

11. B. You can sort items in a table by clicking the Sort Ascending (A to Z) button on the Tables and Borders toolbar.

12. D. Click the Shading button on the Tables and Borders toolbar to add shading to a table.

13. A. Click the AutoSum button on the Tables and Borders toolbar to total the numbers in a column or row.

CHAPTER 6

WORKING WITH TEMPLATES AND STYLES

CHAPTER OBJECTIVES:

Creating and using templates, Lesson 6.1

Creating and applying paragraph styles, Lesson 6.2

Creating and applying a character style, Lesson 6.3

Modifying an existing style, Lesson 6.4

Displaying styles in a document, Lesson 6.5

Attaching a different template to a document, Lesson 6.6

Copying styles between documents and templates, Lesson 6.7

CHAPTER TASK: USE STYLES TO QUICKLY FORMAT AN ITINERARY

Prerequisites

- **How to open and save a document.**
- **How to use menus, toolbars, and dialog boxes.**
- **How to select text.**
- **How to format characters and paragraphs.**

This chapter covers *templates and styles*. You may be unfamiliar with how to use these features, but they can save you untold amounts of time creating and formatting documents.

First, we'll examine templates. A *template* is like a mold. Once you define the properties of a template (text, macros, formatting properties, etc.) you can create new documents that have those same properties. In fact, every document you create in Word is based on a template. You will learn how to save time creating similar documents using this technique.

Second, we'll learn all about styles. A *style* is a set of character and paragraph formats stored under a name. Styles are useful because you can apply a whole group of formatting options in a single step. If you decide to change the formatting options of a style, every character or paragraph formatted with that style is automatically updated with the new formatting options, instead of having to go through the document and manually update each and every paragraph. Styles are rather abstract, so don't worry if you still don't understand them—they will make more sense to you after you work with them.

Creating and Using a Document Template

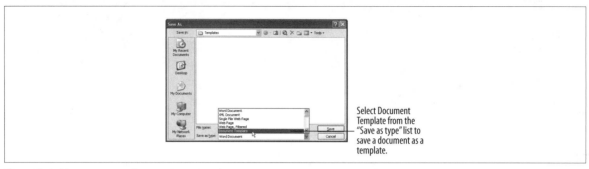

Figure 6-1. You can save a document as a template.

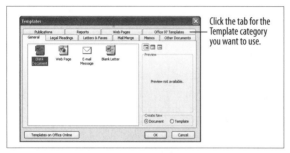

Figure 6-2. The Templates dialog box.

Click the tab for the Template category you want to use.

If you find yourself applying and creating the same properties and features each time you begin a new document, you could probably save yourself some time by using a template. A *template* is like a mold for Word documents; it contains formatting options and document properties that you can use again and again when creating new documents. In fact, every Word document is based on a template.

Templates can contain the following information:

Text	Tables and graphics	Formatting
Styles[a]	Macros[a]	AutoText[a]
Toolbars[a]	Menus	Shortcut keys

a. Can be copied between documents and/or templates.

Creating a template is actually very simple. This lesson will show you how to create your own template and how to use the template to create new documents.

 TIP

Word uses a document template file named NORMAL.DOT as its default template to create blank documents. You can make changes to the Normal template.

1 Open Word and then open the Lesson 6A document.

This document is the starting point for a letter. Since the letter doesn't contain much information yet, it can be saved as a document template so that you don't have to enter the addresses, date, and signature each time you want to create a new letter.

2 Select File → Save As from the menu.

The Save As dialog box appears. We want to save the letter as a template instead of as a Word document. Word templates are stored with a .DOT extension instead of the normal .DOC extension for Word documents.

3 Click the Save as type list arrow and select Document Template, as shown in Figure 6-1.

⋮ NOTE ⋮ *To manually find out where Word templates are saved on your computer, select Tools → Options from the menu. Click the File Locations tab and note the location for user template files.*

4 In the File Name **box, type** Blank Letter **and then click** Save.

Word saves the document as a Blank Letter document template.

5 Close all open documents.

Now that you have created a template, you can use the template to create a new document. Try it!

6 Select File → New **from the menu. Click the** On my computer **link in the Templates area of the New Document task pane.**

The Templates dialog box appears, as shown in Figure 6-2. Word organizes the templates into different categories, and any templates you create will usually appear in the General tab.

7 If necessary, click the General **tab. Select the** Blank Letter template **and click** OK.

A new document based on the Blank Letter template appears in the document window.

8 Select the line Type your text here. **Replace the text by typing:**

Joe, I got your information on the senior citizens excursion; however, I was unable to find any pricing in your letter. Could you please either mail me this pricing data or fax it to me at (612) 555-2200?

Now that you have finished typing your letter, save it as a normal document file.

9 Select File → Save As **from the menu.**

The Save As dialog box appears.

10 Select Word Document **from the "Save as type" list and save the file as** Letter to Joe. **Click** Save **and close the document.**

The document is saved as a normal Word document. You don't want to leave the Blank Letter template on this computer, so let's delete it.

11 Select File → New **from the menu. Click the** On my computer **link in the Templates area of the New Document task pane. Right-click the** Blank Letter **tem-**

plate, **and select** Delete **from the shortcut menu. Then click** Yes **to confirm the deletion.**

QUICK REFERENCE

TO CREATE A DOCUMENT TEMPLATE:

1. EITHER CREATE OR OPEN A DOCUMENT THAT YOU WANT TO USE FOR THE TEMPLATE.

2. SELECT FILE → SAVE AS FROM THE MENU.

3. SELECT DOCUMENT TEMPLATE FROM THE SAVE AS TYPE LIST, GIVE THE TEMPLATE A NAME, AND CLICK SAVE TO SAVE THE TEMPLATE.

TO CREATE A DOCUMENT BASED ON A TEMPLATE:

1. SELECT FILE → NEW FROM THE MENU.

2. CLICK THE ON MY COMPUTER LINK IN THE TEMPLATES AREA OF THE NEW DOCUMENT TASK PANE.

3. SELECT THE TEMPLATE YOU WANT TO USE AND CLICK OK.

TO DELETE A DOCUMENT TEMPLATE:

1. SELECT FILE → NEW FROM THE MENU.

2. CLICK THE ON MY COMPUTER LINK IN THE TEMPLATES AREA OF THE NEW DOCUMENT TASK PANE.

3. RIGHT-CLICK THE TEMPLATE YOU WANT TO DELETE AND SELECT DELETE FROM THE SHORTCUT MENU. CLICK YES TO CONFIRM THE DELETION.

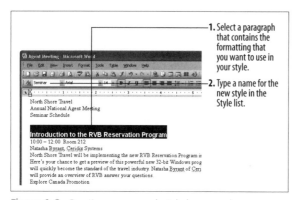

Figure 6-3. Creating a paragraph style by example.

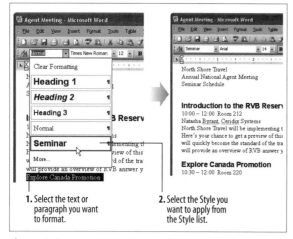

Figure 6-4. Selecting a style from the Style list on the Formatting toolbar.

A *style* is a group of character and paragraph format settings stored under a single name. Styles save a lot of time and ensure that your documents are formatted in a consistent manner. For example, you want to format all the headings in a document using 14 pt Arial boldfaced font. Instead of formatting each heading one at a time, you could format them all at once using a style. Then, if you make changes to a style, every character or paragraph formatted with that style is automatically updated to reflect the changes. For example, if the headings of your document use a 14 pt Arial, boldfaced font, and you decide you want to change your headings to a 16 pt font, you don't have to reformat every heading in the document.

There are four different types of styles:

- **Character styles:** A combination of any of the character formats in the Font dialog box.

- **Paragraph styles:** A combination of character, paragraph, tab, border, and bullets and numbering formats. Paragraph styles are identified by a ¶ symbol to the left of the style name.

- **Table styles:** Provides a consistent style for all borders, shading, alignment and fonts in tables.

- **List styles:** Applies similar alignment, numbering, or bullet characters and fonts to lists.

There are two ways to create and/or modify a style:

- **By example:** The quickest and easiest way to create a new style or modify an existing style is to find and select the text or paragraph with the formatting you want to use, then create a new style based on the formatting of the selected characters or paragraph.

- **From scratch:** You can create and/or modify both character and paragraph styles by opening the Style task pane (click the Styles and Formatting button on the Formatting toolbar) and then specifying the style's formatting options.

In this lesson, you'll learn how to create a paragraph style by example, and how to apply it to other paragraphs.

1 Open the Lesson 6B document and save it as Agent Meeting.

This document contains several different types of headings. You could format each heading individually, but we'll save a lot of time and effort by using a style instead.

2 Select the line Introduction to the RVB Reservation Program.

First, we have to format this paragraph with the settings we want to include in the style.

3 With the text still selected, click the Bold button on the Formatting toolbar, select Arial from the Font list, and select 14 from the Font Size list.

The selected text is formatted with boldfaced Arial 14 pt Font, as shown in Figure 6-3. These are really character style formats, but a paragraph style can include both character and paragraph formatting.

Next, let's format the paragraph.

4 With the text still selected, select Format → Paragraph from the menu.

The Paragraph dialog box appears.

5 Click the Spacing Before up arrow twice so it displays 12 pt.

This will add a 12 pt space—the equivalent of a blank line—above the paragraph.

6 Click OK.

The Paragraph is formatted with 12 pt spacing above it. In Steps 2–5, you applied several different font and paragraph formatting options to the line "Introduction to the RVB Reservation Program." Instead of repeating each of the these steps to apply the same character and paragraph formatting options to the other headings, you could create a style based on the "Introduction to the RVB Reservation Program" line and then apply the style to all the headings at once.

Here's how to create a style by example:

7 Make sure the paragraph you want to base the style on (the "Introduction to the RVB Reservation Program" line) is selected. Then click the Style list arrow on the Formatting toolbar.

To create a style based on the selected paragraph, all you have to do is type a name for the new style in the Style list.

8 Type Seminar in the Style list and press Enter to create the name for the new style.

Another way to create a style by example is to select the paragraph that contains the formatting you want to use for your style. Open the Style dialog box by selecting Format → Styles and Formatting from the menu. Click the New Style button in the Styles and Formatting task pane, type a new name for the style and click OK.

You've just created a new style named "Seminar" that has boldfaced Arial 14 pt font and 12 pt paragraph spacing before.

Now you can use the Seminar style to format the remaining headings.

9 Select the line Explore Canada Promotion.

Actually, since the style we are applying has paragraph formatting, you don't have to select the text. Just make sure the insertion point is located somewhere within the paragraph.

Here's how to apply an existing style to a paragraph:

10 Click the Style list arrow on the Formatting toolbar and select Seminar.

The selected paragraph is formatted with the Seminar paragraph style formatting options. Wasn't that a lot faster and easier than all that pointing and clicking you did in Steps 2–6?

11 Repeat Steps 9 and 10 and apply the Seminar style to the remaining Seminar headings: Better Team Communication, Exploring Childcare, and The Internet and Travel.

QUICK REFERENCE

TO CREATE A PARAGRAPH STYLE BY EXAMPLE:

1. SELECT A PARAGRAPH THAT CONTAINS THE FORMATTING YOU WANT TO USE IN YOUR STYLE.

2. TYPE A NAME FOR THE STYLE IN THE STYLE BOX ON THE FORMATTING TOOLBAR AND PRESS ENTER.

TO APPLY A PARAGRAPH STYLE:

1. SELECT THE PARAGRAPH YOU WANT TO FORMAT WITH THE STYLE.

2. CLICK THE STYLE LIST ARROW ON THE FORMATTING TOOLBAR AND SELECT THE STYLE YOU WANT TO APPLY TO THE SELECTED PARAGRAPH.

Creating and Applying a Character Style

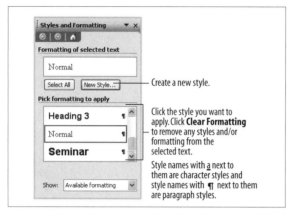

Create a new style.

Click the style you want to apply. Click **Clear Formatting** to remove any styles and/or formatting from the selected text.

Style names with a next to them are character styles and style names with ¶ next to them are paragraph styles.

Figure 6-5. The Styles and Formatting task pane.

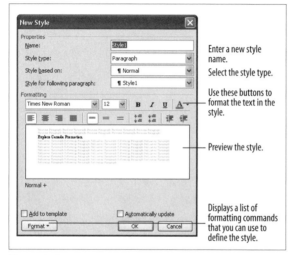

Enter a new style name.

Select the style type.

Use these buttons to format the text in the style.

Preview the style.

Displays a list of formatting commands that you can use to define the style.

Figure 6-6. The New Style dialog box.

While paragraph styles can contain paragraph and character formatting, character styles only include the formatting options found in the Font dialog box. Character styles are identified by the a symbol to the left of the style name.

In this lesson, you'll learn how to create and apply character styles. You'll also get a chance to work with the Styles and Formatting task pane, which can be opened by selecting Format → Styles and Formatting.

1 Select the entire line Natasha Byrant, Ceridix Systems.

The easiest way to create a new character style is by example, which is to find and select some text that contains the character formatting you want to base your new character style on. If such formatted text

doesn't exist in your document, you'll have to format something first so that you have an example to base your style on. Move on to the next step to do this.

2 Click the Bold button and then the Italics button on the Formatting toolbar.

Boldface and italic formatting is applied to the selected characters.

> ⋮ NOTE ⋮ *You can't create a character style by typing a new name in the Style list as you can with paragraph styles—you have to open the Styles and Formatting task pane.*

3 With the same text still selected, click the Styles and Formatting button on the Formatting toolbar.

> TIP *Another way to view the Styles and Formatting task pane is to select Format → Styles and Formatting from the menu.*

The Styles and Formatting task pane appears, as shown in Figure 6-5. Here you can easily view, apply, modify, and create new styles. You want to create a new character style based on the selected text.

4 Click the New Style button in the Styles and Formatting task pane.

The New Style dialog box opens, as shown in Figure 6-6. This is where you can create new character and paragraph styles. First you need to give your new style a name and specify the type of style—paragraph or character.

5 In the Name box, type Speaker and select Character from the Style type list.

This will save the formatting options in a character style named "Speaker." You can also change or specify additional formatting options, or create a new style from scratch, in the New Style dialog box—just select the formatting using the Format button.

6 Click the Format button and select Font.

> TIP *You can also change a style's font formatting using the Formatting buttons in the New Style dialog box.*

The Font dialog box appears.

7 Click the Font color list arrow, select Dark Blue and click OK.

The Font dialog box closes.

Let's save the "Speaker" style and exit the New Style dialog box.

8 Click OK to close the New Style dialog box.

The New Style dialog box closes. Now that you've created the Speaker character style, you can apply it to the speaker lines.

9 Click the Speaker style in the Styles and Formatting task pane.

Word applies the Speaker style to the selected text.

10 Select the entire line Brian Nordet, North Shore Travel.

You can also apply the style by selecting it from the Style list on the Formatting toolbar. Here's how…

11 Click the Style list arrow on the Formatting toolbar and select Speaker.

The text is formatted with the Speaker character style formatting options. Move on to the next step to apply the Speaker character style to the remaining speaker headings.

12 Repeat the procedure in Steps 10-11 and apply the Speaker style to the remaining speaker headings:

Susan Flint, Synergy Inc.
Jack Lake, North Shore Travel
John Barrons, High Energy Computer Corp

The characters in the selected lines are formatted using the Speaker character style.

13 Save your work.

Besides making it faster to format characters, styles ensure that you use consistent formatting throughout your documents.

QUICK REFERENCE

TO CREATE A CHARACTER STYLE BY EXAMPLE:

1. SELECT THE CHARACTERS THAT CONTAIN THE FORMATTING ON WHICH YOU WANT TO BASE YOUR NEW STYLE.

2. CLICK THE STYLES AND FORMATTING BUTTON ON THE FORMATTING TOOLBAR.

3. CLICK THE NEW STYLE BUTTON.

4. GIVE THE STYLE A NAME, SELECT CHARACTER FROM THE STYLE TYPE LIST, AND CLICK OK.

TO APPLY A CHARACTER STYLE:

1. SELECT THE TEXT YOU WANT TO FORMAT.

2. CLICK THE STYLE LIST ARROW ON THE FORMATTING TOOLBAR AND SELECT THE STYLE YOU WANT TO APPLY TO THE SELECTED TEXT.

OR...

CLICK THE STYLE IN THE STYLES AND FORMATTING TASK PANE.

You can modify a style by example by clicking the style's ▼ arrow and selecting **Update to Match Selection.**

Figure 6-7. It's easy to modify and update styles and formatting.

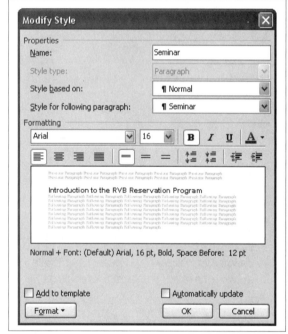

Figure 6-8. The Modify Style dialog box.

Now that you know how to create and apply styles, you can move on to what's really cool about styles—modifying them. You can modify the formatting options for a style similar to the way you can modify the formatting options for a paragraph. However, when you modify the formatting options for a style, every character or paragraph that is based on that style is updated to reflect the formatting changes. So, if your boss tells you to change the font in the 50+ headings in a 300-page report before lunch, you won't have to frantically go through the entire document, finding and reformatting each and every heading. All you have to do is modify the style the head-

ing is formatted with, and viola—all the headings are reformatted with only a few clicks of the mouse.

There are two ways to modify an existing style:

- **By example:** The quickest and easiest way to modify an existing style is to find and select the text or paragraph that contains the formatting you want to use in your modified style.

- **Using the Modify Style dialog box:** You can modify a style by opening the Modify Style dialog box and then specifying the style's formatting options.

First, we'll learn how to modify a style by example (the fast and easy way).

1 Select the Introduction to the RVB Reservation Program line.

To modify a style, you need to apply new formatting to a paragraph that uses the style you want to change.

2 With the same text still selected, click the Font Size list arrow on the Formatting toolbar, then scroll to and click 16.

The font size of the selected text changes from 14 to 16. Here's how you can modify the Seminar style based on the currently selected text:

3 If necessary, click the Styles and Formatting button on the Formatting toolbar. Move the pointer over the Seminar style in the Styles and Formatting task pane and click the Seminar style ▼ arrow.

A list of actions that you can perform on the selected style appears, as shown in Figure 6-7. To modify a style by example, select the "Update to Match Selection" option.

4 Select the Update to Match Selection option from the list.

Every paragraph based on the Seminar style is automatically updated to reflect the 16-point font size. What a timesaver! If you hadn't used a style, you would have had to reformat each heading individually, leaving the chance that you might miss reformatting one of the headings.

Modifying an existing style with the Style dialog box takes a little bit longer than modifying a style by example, but it allows you to format the style with greater precision.

5 Move the pointer over the Seminar style **in the task pane, click the** Seminar style ▾ arrow, **and select** Modify.

The Modify Style dialog box appears, as shown in Figure 6-8. This is where you can modify a style's formatting options or specify additional formatting options.

6 Click the Format button **and select** Border **from the list.**

The Borders and Shading dialog box appears.

Let's add a border beneath the Seminar style to make it stand out.

7 Add a border to the bottom of the paragraph by clicking the bottom of the paragraph in the preview diagram.

A line appears under the model paragraph, allowing you to see how the paragraph will look once it has a border below it.

8 Click OK **to close the Borders and Shading dialog box.**

A border is added to the Seminar style, and the Borders and Shading dialog box closes.

9 Click OK **to close the Modify Style dialog box.**

The Modify Style dialog box closes. Notice that all the headings formatted with the Seminar style are updated with borders underneath them.

You can close the Styles and Formatting task pane since you're finished using it.

10 Close the Styles and Formatting task pane and save your work.

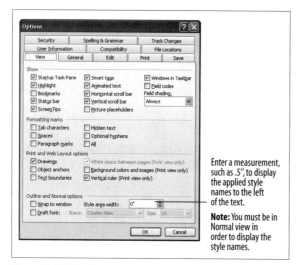

Figure 6-9. The View tab in the Options dialog box.

Enter a measurement, such as .5", to display the applied style names to the left of the text.

Note: You must be in Normal view in order to display the style names.

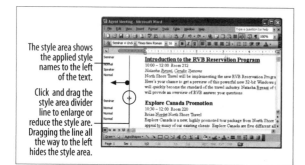

The style area shows the applied style names to the left of the text.

Click and drag the style area divider line to enlarge or reduce the style are. Dragging the line all the way to the left hides the style area.

Figure 6-10. The Style area in a document.

If you're working on a document that uses styles created by someone else, or that uses styles you created a long time ago, it is useful to display the style names. That way you can see which styles are being used.

1 If necessary, navigate to your Practice folder and open Lesson 6C. **Save the file as** Agent Meeting.

2 Click the ≡ Normal View button **on the horizontal scroll bar, located near the bottom of the screen.**

The document window changes to Normal view. You must be in Normal view to display the style area.

3 Select Tools → Options **from the menu, and then click the** View **tab.**

The Options dialog box appears with the View tab in front, as shown in Figure 6-9.

4 Click the Style area width **up arrow until it displays** 1" **and then click** OK.

The Options dialog box closes.

You can also modify a style by double-clicking the style name in the Style area.

The style names appear in the left side of the document window, as shown in Figure 6-10. You can adjust the width of the Style area by dragging the vertical line between the document and the Style area.

5 Position the pointer over the vertical line between the Style area and the document until it changes to a ◄‖►. Click and drag the line until the Style area is no wider than the longest Style name, and then release the mouse button.

The Style area is resized. Now let's hide the Style area.

6 Position the pointer over the vertical line between the Style area and the document until it changes to a ◄‖►, click and drag the line to the far left until the Style area disappears, then release the mouse button.

The Style area disappears from the document window.

7 Click the ▣ Print Layout View button **on the horizontal scroll bar.**

The document window appears in Print Layout view.

QUICK REFERENCE

TO DISPLAY THE STYLES USED IN A DOCUMENT:

1. CLICK THE NORMAL VIEW BUTTON ON THE HORIZONTAL SCROLL BAR.

2. SELECT TOOLS → OPTIONS FROM THE MENU AND CLICK THE VIEW TAB.

3. CLICK THE STYLE AREA WIDTH UP ARROW UNTIL THE STYLE AREA IS THE SIZE YOU WANT (AROUND 1 INCH IS FINE), AND CLICK OK.

TO CHANGE THE SIZE OF THE STYLE AREA:

• DRAG THE LINE THAT SEPARATES THE STYLE AREA AND THE DOCUMENT TO THE RIGHT OR THE LEFT UNTIL THE STYLE AREA IS THE SIZE YOU WANT.

TO STOP DISPLAYING THE STYLE AREA:

• DRAG THE LINE THAT SEPARATES THE STYLE AREA AND THE DOCUMENT TO THE LEFT UNTIL THE STYLE AREA DISAPPEARS.

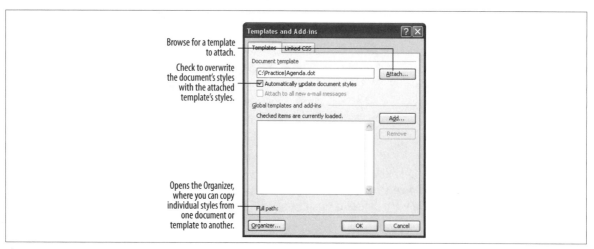

Browse for a template to attach.

Check to overwrite the document's styles with the attached template's styles.

Opens the Organizer, where you can copy individual styles from one document or template to another.

Figure 6-11. The Templates and Add-ins dialog box.

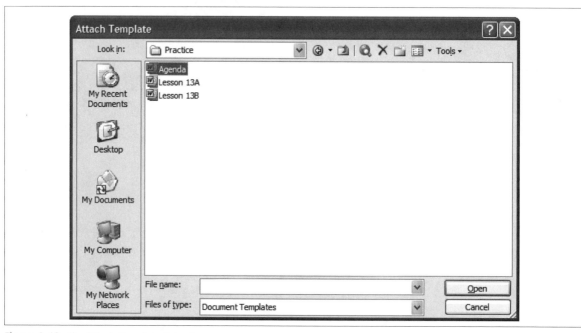

Figure 6-12. The Attach Template dialog box.

Unfortunately, styles are only available in the document or template they were created in, so they're not available in other documents. But you can work around this by attaching a template to a document. When you attach a template to a document, you use that template's styles, as well as its macros, AutoText entries, menus, toolbars, and shortcut keys.

This lesson explains how to attach a different template to a document, and how to update the current document's styles with the styles from the attached template.

1 **Select** Tools → Templates and Add-ins **from the menu.**

The Templates and Add-ins dialog box appears, as shown in Figure 6-11.

2 **Click the** Attach button **to browse for the template you want to attach to the Agent Meeting document.**

All your templates are normally stored in a special folder called Templates, located in the Microsoft

Office folder. Word automatically opens this folder and displays only document templates when you click the Attach button. For this exercise, however, the template you're going to attach is in your practice folder.

3 Navigate to your Practice folder.

Now attach the template named Agenda to the current Agent Meeting document.

4 Select the Agenda document template, as shown in Figure 6-12, and click Open.

Because you want to use the styles in the attached Agenda template instead of the styles in the current Agent Meeting document, you'll want to select the "Automatically update document styles" option.

5 Click the Automatically update document styles box to select it and click OK.

Word attaches the Agenda template to the Agent Meeting document.

Since the "Automatically update document styles" check box was checked, Word overwrites the document's styles with the styles from the Agenda template.

⁞ NOTE ⁞ *Be careful when you select the "Automatically update document styles" check box. Use this option only when you're sure you want to override all of the current document's styles.*

We don't really want to use these styles, so let's undo the style changes.

6 Select Edit → Undo from the menu.

Now, the document styles return to their original formatting.

QUICK REFERENCE

TO ATTACH A DIFFERENT TEMPLATE TO A DOCUMENT:

1. SELECT TOOLS → TEMPLATES AND ADD-INS FROM THE MENU.

2. CLICK ATTACH AND FIND AND SELECT THE TEMPLATE YOU WANT TO ATTACH TO THE CURRENT DOCUMENT.

3. CLICK THE AUTOMATICALLY UPDATE DOCUMENT STYLES CHECK BOX TO SELECT IT AND CLICK OK.

Copying Styles Between Documents and Templates

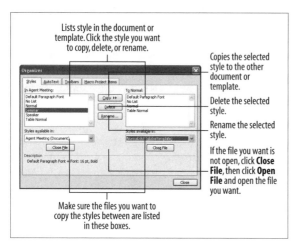

Lists style in the document or template. Click the style you want to copy, delete, or rename.

Copies the selected style to the other document or template.

Delete the selected style.

Rename the selected style.

If the file you want is not open, click **Close File**, then click **Open File** and open the file you want.

Make sure the files you want to copy the styles between are listed in these boxes.

Figure 6-13. The Styles tab of the Organizer dialog box.

In the previous lesson, you learned how to attach a different template to a document, allowing you to use all the template's styles, macros, AutoText entries, menus, and shortcut keys. Sometimes, however, you may own want to use only a few styles from a template, and attaching a different template may be overkill.

This lesson explains how you can use the Organizer to copy styles between documents and templates.

1 Select Tools → Templates and Add-ins **from the menu.**

2 Click the Organizer button **and click the** Styles **tab if necessary.**

The Styles tab of the Organizer dialog box appears, as shown in Figure 6-13.

The left side of the dialog box displays the name and styles of the current document: the Agent Meeting document. The right side of the dialog box displays the name and styles of the currently attached template: the Normal template. You must close the NOR-MAL.DOT template before you can open another template.

3 Click the Close File button **on the right side of the dialog box to close the Normal template.**

Now you can open the template that contains the style you want to copy.

4 Click the Open File button **on the right side of the dialog box.**

Now you need to find the document or template that contains the style you want to copy.

5 If necessary, navigate to your Practice folder.

Open the Agenda template so you can copy one of its styles.

6 Select the Agenda template **and click** Open.

The styles in the Agenda template appear in the "To Agenda" list on the right side of the Organizer dialog box.

Now copy the Seminar style from the Agenda template to the Agent Meeting document.

7 Select the Seminar style **from the** To Agenda **list (the style list on the right side of the dialog box).**

Notice that the arrows on the Copy button point to the other list.

8 Click Copy **to copy the Seminar style from the Agenda template to the Agent Meeting document.**

Since the Seminar style name exists in both files, Word asks you if you're sure you want to overwrite the existing Seminar style in the Agent Meeting document.

9 Click Yes **to overwrite the existing Seminar style.**

Word copies the Seminar style from the Agenda template to the Agent Meeting document.

Before you close the Organizer dialog box, let's take a look at the other tabs. You've probably already noticed there are several other tabs besides the Style tab. The organizer can copy the following items between two documents or templates:

- **Styles:** You should already know this one—a style is a set of character and paragraph formats stored under a style name.

- **AutoText:** AutoText allows you to save frequently used text or graphics so that you can use them again and again.

- **Toolbars:** Templates can contain custom toolbars with buttons for the commands you use the most.

• **Macro Project Items:** A macro is a set of commands and instructions you can use to automate a routine task.

You don't need to worry about what an AutoText entry, toolbar, or macro is for now (we'll discuss them more in the last chapter). What's important is that you use the Organizer dialog box to copy items between two templates, the procedure exercised in this lesson.

10 Click the Close button to close the Organizer dialog box.

Notice that the Seminar style changes from black to dark red.

11 Exit Word without saving changes to the document.

QUICK REFERENCE

TO COPY A STYLE BETWEEN TWO DOCUMENTS OR TEMPLATES:

1. SELECT TOOLS → TEMPLATES AND ADD-INS FROM THE MENU.

2. CLICK THE ORGANIZER BUTTON IN THE TEMPLATES AND ADD-INS DIALOG BOX.

3. NAVIGATE TO AND OPEN THE TEMPLATE WITH THE STYLE YOU WANT TO COPY.

4. CLICK THE CLOSE FILE BUTTON ON THE RIGHT SIDE OF THE DIALOG BOX.

5. CLICK THE OPEN FILE BUTTON AND OPEN THE DOCUMENT OR TEMPLATE THAT CONTAINS THE STYLE(S) YOU WANT TO COPY.

6. SELECT THE STYLE(S) YOU WANT TO COPY AND CLICK THE COPY BUTTON.

7. CLICK THE CLOSE BUTTON WHEN YOU'RE FINISHED.

Lesson Summary

Creating and Using a Document Template

A template is a document that contains the text and formatting options that you can use again and again when creating new documents.

To Create a Document Template: Either create or open a document that you want to use for the template and edit as necessary. When you're finished, select File → Save As from the menu, select Document Template from the Save as type list, give the template a name, and click Save to save the template.

To Create a Document Based on a Template: Select File → New from the menu and click the On my computer link in the Templates area of the New Document task pane. Select the template you want to use from the dialog box and click OK.

To Delete a Document Template: Select File → New from the menu and click the On my computer link in the Templates area of the New Document task pane. Right-click the template you want to delete and select Delete from the shortcut menu. Click Yes to confirm the deletion.

Creating and Applying Paragraph Styles

A style is a group of character and paragraph formatting settings that are stored under a single name that can be applied all at once.

There are two types of styles: character and paragraph. (Paragraph styles can include formatting both for characters and paragraphs.)

To Create a Paragraph Style by Example: Select a paragraph that contains the formatting you want to use in your style, type a name for the style in the Style box on the Formatting toolbar, and press Enter.

To Apply a Paragraph Style: Select the paragraph you want to format with the style, click the Style list arrow on the Formatting toolbar, and select the style you want to apply to the selected paragraph.

Creating and Applying a Character Style

To Create a Character Style by Example: Select the characters that contain the formatting you want to base your new style on. Click the Styles and Formatting button on the Formatting toolbar. Click New Style button to create a new style based on the selected text, give the style a name, select Character from the style type list and click OK.

To Apply a Character Style: Select the text you want to format. Click the Style list arrow on the Formatting toolbar and select the style you want to apply to the selected text, or click the style in the Styles and Formatting task pane.

Modifying a Style

When you modify a style's formatting options, every paragraph and/or character formatted with that style in the document is updated to reflect the changes.

To Modify an Existing Style by Example: Click the Styles and Formatting button on the Formatting toolbar. Select the text or paragraph that contains the formatting you want to copy to an existing style. Click the style ▾ arrow and select Update to Match Selection.

To Modify an Existing Style using the Modify Style Dialog Box: Click the Styles and Formatting button on the Formatting toolbar. In the Styles and Formatting task pane, click the ▾ arrow of the style you want to modify and select Modify. Click the Format button and select the element you want to change. Change the formatting options for the selected element. Click OK, OK to close the dialog boxes.

To Delete a Style: Select Format → Styles and Formatting from the menu. In the Styles and Formatting task pane, click the ▾ arrow of the style you want to delete and select Delete. Click Yes to confirm the deletion.

Displaying Styles in a Document

To Display the Styles in a Document: Click the Normal View button on the horizontal scroll bar near the bottom of the screen. Select Tools → Options from the menu, click the View tab, click the Style area width up arrow until the style area is the size you want (around 1 inch is fine), and click OK.

To Change the Size of the Style Area: Drag the line that separates the Style area and the document to the right or left until the Style area is the size you want.

To Stop Displaying the Style Area: Drag the line that separates the Style area and the document to the left until the Style area disappears.

Attaching a Different Template to a Document

Styles, macros, custom toolbars, and AutoText entries are stored in template files. By attaching a template to a document, you give it access to these items.

To Attach a Different Template to a Document: Select Tools → Templates and Add-Ins from the menu, click Attach, and find and select the template you want to attach to the current document. Click the the Automatically update document styles check box to select it and click OK.

Copying Styles Between Documents and Templates

You can copy styles, macros, toolbars, and AutoText entries between documents and templates.

To Copy a Style between Two Documents or Templates: Select Tools → Templates and Add-Ins from the menu, and click the Organizer button. Make sure the files between which you want to copy the styles are listed in the "Styles available in" list boxes. If not, click one of the Close File buttons (usually the right one), and then click the Open File button and open the document or template that contains the style(s) you want to copy. Select the style(s) you want to copy and click the Copy button. Click the Close button when you're finished.

Quiz

1. What is a template?

   A. A Word document that can be read by other word processing programs.

   B. A special type of document that can contain boilerplate text, macros, and styles, and is used to create new documents.

   C. Another name for the main document in a mail merge.

   D. A Word document that contains only graphical images instead of text.

2. You write a lot of complaint letters. You have created a generic complaint letter that you want to use as a template. How can you do this?

   A. Select File → Save As Template from the menu.

   B. Select Tools → Templates and Add-Ins form the menu, and click the Organizer tab.

   C. Select File → Save As from the menu, and select Document Template from the Save as Type list.

   D. You have to purchase Microsoft's Template Builder, sold separately, to do this.

3. In Microsoft Word, a style is:

   A. The same as it is in the world of fashion.

   B. A set of character and/or paragraph formatting settings that are stored under a name, and can be quickly applied in a single step.

   C. A special type of document.

   D. A formatting element that is only used in Web pages.

4. Which of these procedures is a way to create a new style? (Select all that apply.)

   A. Select the characters or paragraphs that contain the formatting you want to use in the style, and then type the style name in the Style box on the Formatting toolbar.

   B. Click the New Style button on the Formatting toolbar.

   C. Select Format → Styles and Formatting from the menu, click the New Style button, give the style a name, and specify its formatting options.

   D. Select File → Style from the menu, click New, give the style a name, and specify its formatting options.

5. The two types of styles in Word are:

   A. Page Styles and Paragraph Styles.

   B. Template Styles and Document Styles.

   C. Page Styles and Font Styles.

   D. Paragraph Styles and Character Styles.

6. When you modify a style's formatting options, every character or paragraph formatted in a document based on that Style is updated to reflect the Style change. (True or False?)

7. You want to create a FAX cover page. How do you display and use Word's templates?

   A. Click the Styles and Templates button on the Formatting toolbar.

   B. Select File → New Template from the menu and click New Document in the New Document task pane.

   C. Select File → New from the menu and click the "On my computer" link in the Templates area of the New Document task pane.

   D. Select Tools → Templates and Add-Ins from the menu.

8. What is the name of the default template that Word uses to create blank documents?

   A. Blank.DOT.

   B. Default.DOT.

   C. Word doesn't use a template to create blank documents.

   D. Normal.DOT.

Homework

1. Select File → New, click the "On my computer" link in the Templates area of the New Document task pane, select any template that intrigues you, and click OK. Word creates a new document based on the template you selected.

2. Close the new document without saving any changes when you've finished looking at it.

3. How would you save an existing Word document as a template?

4. Open the Homework 6 document and save it as "Deadly Animals."

5. Select the "Venus Fly Trap" line of text and format it with Arial, Bold, 14 pt font.

6. With the "Venus Fly Trap" paragraph selected, select Format → Paragraph from the menu, click the Line and Page Break tab, check the "Keep with next" option, and click OK.

7. Create a paragraph style based on the selected paragraph: With the "Venus Fly Trap" paragraph selected, click the Style list on the Formatting toolbar, type "Animal," and press Enter.

8. Apply the new Animal style to the remaining animal paragraph. Select each paragraph and select "Animal" from the Style list on the Formatting toolbar.

9. Modify an existing style by example: Select any Price paragraph and click the Increase Indent button on the Formatting toolbar. With the price paragraph still selected, click the Price style arrow in the Styles and Formatting task bar and select Update to Match Selection. Notice that all the "Price" paragraphs are updated with indented paragraph formatting.

10. Modify a style using the Modify Style dialog box: Click the Styles and Formatting button on the Formatting toolbar. In the Styles and Formatting task pane, click the style arrow of the style you want to modify and select Modify Style. Click the Format button, select Font from the list, and select a dark blue color from the Color list. Confirm the modification. Notice that all the "Animal" paragraphs are updated with indented paragraph formatting.

11. **Extra Credit:** Copy a style from another template to the current document: Select Tools → Templates and Add-Ins from the menu and click Organizer. Click the Close File button on the *right side* of the dialog box, then click Open File and select the Agenda template located in your Practice folder. Copy the "Speaker" style from the Agenda template into the "Deadly Animals" folder you're working on.

Quiz Answers

1. B. A template is a special type of document that can contain boilerplate text, macros, and styles and is used to create new documents.

2. C. To save a document as a template, select File → Save As from the menu and select Document Template from the Save as Type list.

3. B. A style is a set of character and/or paragraph formatting settings that are stored under a name and can be quickly applied in a single step.

4. A and C. Both of these are methods to create a style.

5. D. Paragraph and Character are the two types of styles in Word.

6. True. When you modify a style's formatting options, every character or paragraph formatted in a document based on that Style is updated to reflect the Style change.

7. C. Select File → New from the menu and click the "On my computer" link in the Templates area of the New Document task pane to view Word's available templates.

8. D. The Normal.DOT template is used to create blank documents.

CHAPTER 7
DRAWING AND WORKING WITH GRAPHICS

CHAPTER OBJECTIVES:

Drawing on your documents, Lesson 7.1

Adding, arranging, and formatting text boxes, Lesson 7.2

Selecting, resizing, formatting, and deleting objects, Lessons 7.3 and 7.4

Inserting clip art and pictures, Lessons 7.5 and 7.6

Specifying how text wraps around pictures and text, Lesson 7.7

Aligning and grouping objects, Lesson 7.10

Drawing AutoShapes, Lesson 7.9

Flipping and rotating objects, Lesson 7.10

Layering objects, Lesson 7.11

Applying shadows and 3-D effects, Lesson 7.12

CHAPTER TASKS: ADD DRAWINGS AND GRAPHICS TO A DOCUMENT

Prerequisites

• **How to open and save a document.**

• **How to use menus, toolbars, and dialog boxes.**

• **Be proficient at clicking and dragging and dropping with the mouse.**

Documents that include pictures, drawings, and graphics can be much more compelling and effective than documents that contain only boring text. Once you know how to work with pictures and graphics, you can make all kinds of neat documents, such as newsletters, greeting cards, and pamphlets. Even if you don't think you have any artistic ability, it's easy to add pictures and drawings to your Word documents, making them appear as though they were designed on a desktop publisher.

This chapter explains how to use Word's drawing tools to add lines, shapes, and text boxes in your documents; how to insert pictures and clip art; and how to make a "picture worth a thousand words" by creating charts that clearly illustrate your data.

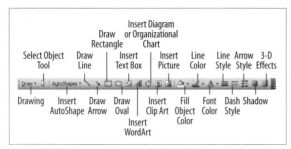

Figure 7-1. The Drawing toolbar.

1. Click the line or shape you want to draw on the Drawing toolbar.

2. Move the + pointer to the starting point of the line pr shape and click and hold the mouse button.

3. Drag the + pointer to the ending point of the shape or line and release the mouse button.

Figure 7-2. The procedure for drawing a line or shape on a document.

Figure 7-3. The updated document with lines added from the text labels to their destinations on the map.

Most of Word's drawing tools can be found on the *Drawing toolbar*. The Drawing toolbar is the electronic equivalent of the crayons, paint brushes, and scissors you used in elementary school. The toolbar's tools can be used for multiple purposes, such as drawing lines, shapes, and

arrows, and for formatting graphic objects with different coloring, shadow effects, and 3-D effects. To display the Drawing toolbar, click the Drawing button on the Standard toolbar, or select View → Toolbars → Drawing from the menu.

The shapes, lines, and text boxes you can add to your documents are called *drawing objects*. Here are some tips about drawing objects:

- By default, most drawing objects "anchor" or attach themselves to the nearest paragraph. If you move the paragraph, the drawing object will move along with it.
- You can delete drawing objects from your documents by clicking them to select them and then pressing the Delete key.
- You can change the size and shape of drawing objects by clicking them and dragging their sizing handles.
- You can move text boxes by clicking and dragging them.
- You can format drawing objects and change their fill (inside) and line (border) color.

We'll cover most of these topics in more detail later on in this chapter.

1 Start Word, open the document named Lesson 7A, and save it as American History.

To draw on your document, you first have to summon the *Drawing toolbar*.

2 Click the Drawing button on the Standard toolbar.

> **TIP** *Another way to display the Drawing toolbar is to select* View → Toolbars → Drawing *from the menu.*

The Drawing toolbar appears, as shown in Figure 7-1.

This document is supposed to show the destinations of a tour package, but several things are missing from it, such as some of the lines that connect text labels to points on the map. Let's fix this problem.

3 Click the Line button on the Drawing toolbar.

The pointer changes to a +, and a drawing canvas appears on the document.

The drawing canvas is a tool that helps you manage your drawing objects. The drawing canvas keeps everything on it together, so when the canvas is moved or resized, the objects on it work as a single unit. You can use this tool in your own drawings, but for these lessons we'll turn the canvas off.

4 Select Tools → Options **from the menu.**

The Options dialog box appears.

5 Click the General **tab. Uncheck the** Automatically create drawing canvas when inserting AutoShapes **check box. Click** OK.

Now that annoying drawing canvas won't appear when you want to draw something.

Let's get back to our original task: fixing the destinations map of the tour package.

6 Click the Line button **on the Drawing toolbar. Place the pointer below the** Black Hills, S.D. **text label above the map. Click and drag the pointer to the South Dakota marker on the map and release the mouse button, as shown in Figure 7-2.**

That's all there is to drawing a line. Try drawing another one.

7 Following the same procedure as Step 4, **draw a line between the** Philadelphia **text label and the Philadelphia marker on the map.**

You can also draw an arrow to point to an item of interest. Actually, you can format any line and change it into an arrow or vice versa—but we'll cover how to format drawing objects in another lesson. Move on to the next step and try drawing an arrow.

8 Click the Arrow button **on the Drawing toolbar.**

The pointer again changes to a $+$, indicating that you can draw an arrow.

9 Draw a line between the New Orleans **text label below the map and the New Orleans marker on the map.**

Arrows point at whatever you drag the destination line to, not where you first click. Remembering where to click and where to drag can be a bit confusing. If your arrow points in the wrong direction, you can always format it and change which end has an arrow.

See Lesson 7-4 for more information on how to do this.

Let's try drawing a rectangle next.

10 Click the Rectangle button **on the Drawing toolbar.**

TIP
You can create perfect circles and squares and straight lines by holding down the Shift key while you drag with a drawing tool.

The pointer changes to a $+$. Drawing shapes is similar to drawing lines—you click on the document where you want to draw the shape, and then drag until the shape reaches the desired size. To draw a perfect circle, rectangle, straight line, or other shape, hold down the Shift key as you drag.

11 Click in the blank area near the bottom-left corner **of the map. Hold down the** Shift **key as you drag a square like the one shown in Figure 7-3.**

QUICK REFERENCE

TO DISPLAY THE DRAWING TOOLBAR:

- CLICK THE DRAWING BUTTON ON THE STANDARD TOOLBAR.

OR...

- SELECT VIEW → TOOLBARS → DRAWING FROM THE MENU.

TO DRAW AN OBJECT:

1. CLICK THE OBJECT ON THE DRAWING TOOLBAR (SUCH AS A LINE OR CIRCLE).

2. DRAW YOUR SHAPE BY CLICKING WHERE YOU WANT TO ADD THE SHAPE AND DRAGGING UNTIL THE SHAPE REACHES THE DESIRED SIZE.

TO RESIZE AN OBJECT:

1. CLICK THE OBJECT TO SELECT IT.

2. DRAG THE OBJECT'S SIZING HANDLES TO RESIZE IT.

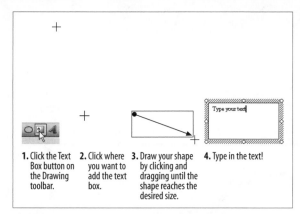

Figure 7-4. The procedure for adding a text box to a document.

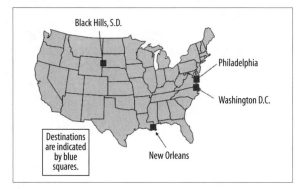

Figure 7-5. The updated document with text boxes added.

Another important drawing object you can create is the *text box*. Text boxes are containers for text that you can position anywhere on the page. This lesson will show you how to add these useful shapes to your document.

1 Click the 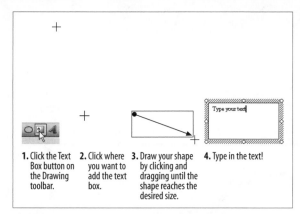 Text Box button on the Drawing toolbar.

The pointer changes to a +, indicating that you can add a text box just like you would add a rectangle drawing object—by clicking and dragging. First, we need to add a "Washington D.C." text label to the document.

2 Click near the end of the line pointing to Washington D.C. (located below the Philadelphia label) with the + pointer, and then click and drag a small, long, rectangular box.

All you have to do now is add the text! First, though, we need to change the font formatting so that it matches the other text labels in the document.

3 Select Arial from the Font List on the Formatting toolbar.

Any text we type now will appear in the Arial font type. We still need to change the font size.

4 Select 14 from the Font Size List on the Formatting toolbar.

Okay! We're ready to enter text in our text box.

5 Type Washington D.C.

That's all there is to adding a text box to a document. Figure 7-4 illustrates the procedure for adding a text box to a document. We changed the font formatting used in the text box before we entered any text, but you can also change the formatting after it's been typed by selecting the text and then formatting it. Now let's remove the border around that text box so that it matches the rest of the text boxes.

6 Click the Line Color list arrow on the drawing toolbar and select No Line from the list.

The border around the text box vanishes.

You can also add text to an AutoShape. Let's add a legend for the map.

7 Right-click anywhere on the square in the lower-left corner, and select Add Text from the shortcut menu.

The rectangle isn't a text box, but you can still enter text into it. Before you begin entering the text, let's change the formatting, so it matches the other text.

8 Repeat Steps 3 and 4 to change the text box's font formatting.

9 **Type** Destinations are indicated by blue squares.

The text automatically wraps within the box.

10 Compare your document to the one in Figure 7-5 and then save your work.

QUICK REFERENCE

TO ADD A TEXT BOX TO A DOCUMENT:

1. CLICK THE TEXT BOX BUTTON ON THE DRAWING TOOLBAR.

2. DRAW THE TEXT BOX BY CLICKING WHERE YOU WANT TO ADD THE TEXT BOX AND DRAGGING UNTIL THE SHAPE IS THE DESIRED SIZE.

3. ENTER THE TEXT.

TO RESIZE A TEXT BOX:

- CLICK THE TEXT BOX TO SELECT IT, DRAG THE OBJECT'S SIZING HANDLES UNTIL THE BOX REACHES THE DESIRED SIZE, THEN RELEASE THE MOUSE BUTTON.

NOTES ABOUT TEXT BOXES:

- A TEXT BOX'S TEXT AND PARAGRAPHS CAN BE FORMATTED JUST LIKE TEXT ANYWHERE ELSE IN THE DOCUMENT.

- TEXT BOXES ARE RARELY THE CORRECT SIZE WHEN YOU FIRST CREATE THEM AND MUST BE RESIZED PROPERLY TO FIT THE TEXT THEY CONTAIN.

Selecting, Resizing, Moving, and Deleting Objects

Click and drag the **Free Rotate handle** to rotate the picture.

Sizing Handles
Click and drag to change the size of an object.

Figure 7-6. Sizing handles and a Free Rotate handle appear around the edges of selected objects.

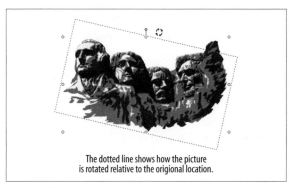

The dotted line shows how the picture is rotated relative to the origional location.

Figure 7-7. Rotating the object.

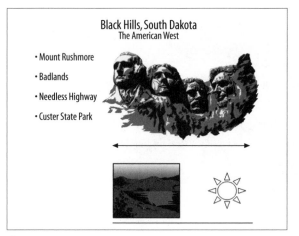

Black Hills, South Dakota
The American West

• Mount Rushmore
• Badlands
• Needless Highway
• Custer State Park

Figure 7-8. The updated document.

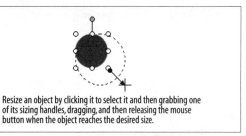

Resize an object by clicking it to select it and then grabbing one of its sizing handles, dragging, and then releasing the mouse button when the object reaches the desired size.

Figure 7-9. The procedure for resizing an object.

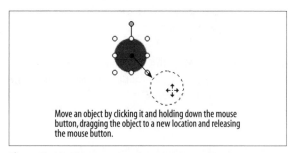

Move an object by clicking it and holding down the mouse button, dragging the object to a new location and releasing the mouse button.

Figure 7-10. The procedure for moving an object.

Selecting, resizing, rotating, moving, and deleting objects—we've got a lot of ground to cover in this lesson! Before you can edit, format, resize, move, or delete anything in a document, you have to first select the object. Ninety-nine percent of the time this won't be a problem, but if you have trouble selecting objects, try clicking the Arrow button on the Drawing toolbar.

1 Press Page Down until you reach Page 2.

This page contains the drawing objects we'll be formatting.

2 Click the Mt. Rushmore picture to select it.

When you select an object, *sizing handles* and one *free rotate handle* appear around the edge of the object, as shown in Figure 7-6. You can use sizing handles to change the size and proportions of the selected object, and the free rotate handle to tilt or turn the object.

3 Position the pointer over the bottom-left sizing handle until it changes to a ⤢. Click and hold down the mouse button and drag up and to the right until the picture is the same width as the double-arrowhead line below it. Then release the mouse button.

As you drag an object's sizing handle, a dotted outline appears to help you resize it, as shown in Figure 7-7.

4 Click the bottom, shorter horizontal line to select it.

Sizing handles appear at both ends of the line, indicating that it's selected. Figure Figure 7-9 demonstrates the procedure for resizing an object.

⟩ NOTE ⟩ *Hold down the Shift key while you drag an object's sizing handles to retain the object's proportions. If you're resizing a line, holding down the Shift key while you resize the line is great for keeping your lines straight.*

5 Hold down the Shift key and drag the line's left sizing handle to the left until the line is the same length as the line above it.

Let's move on to the next task—moving an object.

6 Click the sun object to select it.

Sizing handles appear around the sun object, indicating that it is selected. Here's how to move an object:

7 Click and hold down the mouse button anywhere inside the sun object. Drag the sun object to the right of the scenery picture and between the two horizontal lines, as shown in Figure 7-8. Release the mouse button.

By simply dragging and dropping with the mouse, you can move any object in a document—shapes, lines, pictures, or text boxes, as shown in Figure 7-10.

Sometimes after moving an object, you'll find you want to move the object just a smidgen more. Use the keyboard to move or nudge objects with greater precision.

8 With the sun object still selected, press the left arrow key.

You can also hold down the Ctrl key by pressing any of the arrow keys to nudge the selected object by a single pixel—the smallest possible increment.

We have one final topic in this lesson—how to delete an object. Deleting an object is very easy; simply select the object and press the Delete key.

9 Click the green circle to select it, and then delete it by pressing the Delete key.

10 Compare your document to the one in Figure 7-8 and save your work.

See Table 7-1 for various keystroke/mouse combinations to use in resizing, moving, and copying objects in a document.

Table 7-1. Keystroke/Mouse Combinations

Hold Down This Key	While Dragging This	To Do This
Nothing	An object's sizing handles	Resize the object
Shift	An object's sizing handles	Maintain the objects proportions while resizing it
Ctrl	An object's sizing handles	Keep the object centered while resizing it
Nothing	An object	Move the object
Shift	An object	Move the object along a straight horizontal or vertical line
Ctrl	An object	Copy the object

QUICK REFERENCE

TO RESIZE AN OBJECT:

- CLICK THE OBJECT TO SELECT IT, GRAB ONE OF ITS SIZING HANDLES, AND THEN DRAG AND RELEASE THE MOUSE BUTTON WHEN THE OBJECT REACHES THE DESIRED SIZE.

- HOLD DOWN THE SHIFT KEY WHILE DRAGGING TO MAINTAIN THE OBJECT'S PROPORTIONS WHILE RESIZING IT.

TO MOVE AN OBJECT:

- CLICK THE OBJECT AND HOLD DOWN THE MOUSE BUTTON, DRAG THE OBJECT TO A NEW LOCATION, AND THEN RELEASE THE MOUSE BUTTON TO DROP THE OBJECT.

TO DELETE AN OBJECT:

- SELECT THE OBJECT AND PRESS THE DELETE KEY.

TO COPY AN OBJECT USING DRAG AND DROP:

- FOLLOW THE SAME PROCEDURES FOR MOVING AN OBJECT, ONLY HOLD DOWN THE CTRL KEY WHILE DRAGGING TO COPY THE OBJECT.

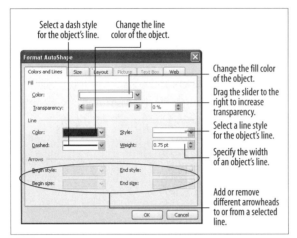

Select a dash style
for the object's line.

Change the line
color of the object.

Change the fill color
of the object.

Drag the slider to the
right to increase
transparency.

Select a line style
for the object's line.

Specify the width
of an object's line.

Add or remove
different arrowheads
to or from a selected
line.

Figure 7-11. The Colors and Lines tab of the Format AutoShape dialog box.

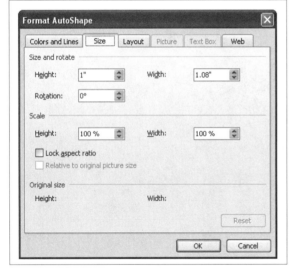

Figure 7-12. The Size tab of the Format AutoShape dialog box.

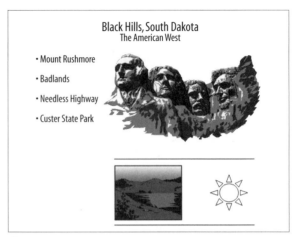

Figure 7-13. The updated document.

In this lesson, you'll learn how to format document objects. Although there are many types of shapes in Word, the procedure for formatting all of them is pretty much the same.

1 If necessary, navigate to your Practice folder, open Lesson 7B, and save the file as American History.

2 Click the sun object to select it.

Here's how to change the fill color (the color used to fill the inside) of an object.

3 Click the Fill Color button list arrow on the Drawing toolbar and select the yellow color.

> *TIP* Another way to change fill colors is to select Format → Borders and Shading from the menu.

The sun object is filled with the selected yellow color. You can also change an object's line color—or remove the line that surrounds the object altogether.

4 Click the Line Color button list arrow on the Drawing toolbar and select No Line to remove the line.

> *TIP* Another way to change an object's line color is to select Format → Borders and Shading from the menu.

The black line surrounding the sun disappears. Now let's remove the arrowheads from the line on the document.

5 Click the upper double-arrowhead line to select it, then click the Arrow Style button on the Drawing toolbar and select Arrow Style 1 (the line without any arrowheads) from the list.

Now let's change the color of the selected line.

6 Click the ✏️ ▾ Line Color button list arrow on the Drawing toolbar and select the dark blue color.

We have one more change to make to the selected line—the line style.

7 With the top line still selected, click the Line Style button on the Drawing toolbar and select the 3 pt double line.

So far, we've been using the mouse and the Drawing toolbar to change the size and format of the objects in our document. You can also use the Format AutoShape dialog box to resize and/or format a selected object. The Format AutoShape dialog box isn't quite as quick and convenient as the Drawing toolbar, but it contains more formatting options. Some people actually prefer formatting objects with the Format AutoShape dialog box, because it allows them to format and resize objects with a greater degree of precision.

We'll use the Format AutoShape dialog box to format the bottom line on the document—then you can decide for yourself which method you like better.

8 Click the bottom line and select Format → AutoShape from the menu.

The Format AutoShape dialog box appears with the Colors and Lines tab selected, as shown in Figure 7-11. You can also open the Format AutoShape dialog box by right-clicking any object and selecting Format AutoShape from the menu.

9 Click the Line Color button list arrow and select the dark blue color.

We still have to change the line style.

10 Click the Line Style button and select the 3 pt double line.

We've finished formatting the bottom line, but let's take a look at one more thing before we close the Format AutoShapes dialog box.

11 Click the Size tab.

The Size tab of the Format AutoShape dialog box appears, as shown in Figure 7-12. Here you can resize an object with greater precision than you ever could with the mouse. You can enter an exact height and width for the selected object or you can adjust its size by specifying a percentage of the original size.

If the "Lock aspect ratio" check box is selected, the Height and Width settings change in relation to one another.

12 Click OK to close the dialog box. Compare your document to the one in Figure 7-13.

QUICK REFERENCE

TO FILL A SHAPE WITH A COLOR:

- SELECT THE SHAPE, CLICK THE FILL COLOR BUTTON LIST ARROW ON THE DRAWING TOOLBAR, AND SELECT THE COLOR YOU WANT.

TO CHANGE LINE COLOR OR REMOVE A LINE:

- SELECT THE SHAPE, CLICK THE LINE COLOR BUTTON LIST ARROW ON THE DRAWING TOOLBAR, AND SELECT THE COLOR OR NO LINE.

TO CHANGE THE LINE STYLE:

- SELECT THE LINE, CLICK THE LINE STYLE BUTTON ON THE DRAWING TOOLBAR, AND SELECT THE LINE STYLE.

TO CHANGE THE DASH STYLE:

- SELECT THE LINE, CLICK THE DASH STYLE BUTTON ON THE DRAWING TOOLBAR, AND SELECT THE DASH STYLE.

TO ADD OR REMOVE ARROW HEADS:

- SELECT THE LINE, CLICK THE ARROW STYLE BUTTON ON THE DRAWING TOOLBAR, AND SELECT THE ARROW STYLE.

TO USE THE FORMAT AUTOSHAPE DIALOG BOX:

- SELECT THE OBJECT AND SELECT FORMAT → AUTOSHAPE FROM THE MENU.

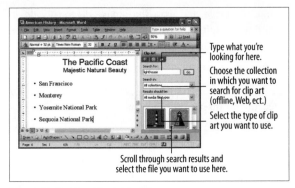

Figure 7-14. The Clip Art task pane.

Type what you're looking for here.

Choose the collection in which you want to search for clip art (offline, Web, ect.)

Select the type of clip art you want to use.

Scroll through search results and select the file you want to use here.

Figure 7-15. The updated document with a clip art picture added.

The Pacific Coast
Majestic Natural Beauty

• San Francisco

• Monterey

• Yosemite National Park

• Sequoia Natural Park

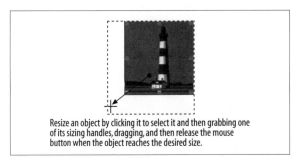

Resize an object by clicking it to select it and then grabbing one of its sizing handles, dragging, and then release the mouse button when the object reaches the desired size.

Figure 7-16. The procedure for resizing a picture.

Microsoft Office comes with thousands of graphics, called clip art, that you can use to make your documents more visually attractive. Clip art is stored and managed by a program called the Microsoft Clip Art Gallery. The Clip Art Gallery program categorizes its pictures by topic, such as holidays, business, or sports, making it easier to find the clip art graphic you need.

1 First, press Ctrl + End to move to the end of the document.

This is where we want to add a clip art picture.

2 Select Insert → Picture → Clip Art from the menu.

The Clip Art task pane appears, as shown in Figure 7-14.

‡ NOTE ‡ *Depending on how Word is installed and configured on your computer system, you may get a "The file is not available..." error message. This means Word cannot locate the Clip Art pictures. You may need to either insert the Office 2003 or Word 2003 CD-ROM into your computer.*

3 Type lighthouse in the Search for box and click the Go button.

Word searches your hard disk for lighthouse-related clip art.

4 Browse through the clip art pictures until you find a picture of a lighthouse similar to the one shown in Figure 7-15.

Depending on your computer's setup, there may be several pictures of lighthouses, or maybe only one. Now that you've found an appropriate graphic, you will need to insert it into the document.

5 Click the lighthouse picture.

Word inserts the picture of the lighthouse into the document.

6 Close the Clip Art task pane.

The pictures you insert will often be either too large or too small, or they may not fit in the document the way you want. When this happens, you will have to resize the picture or change the picture's formatting. In this example, the image was inserted in line with text, but we want it to float above text.

7 Right-click the image and select Format Picture from the shortcut menu. Click the Layout tab, select the In front of text option, and click OK.

Now the picture is "floating" and can be moved anywhere in the document.

8 Click and drag the image so the top is level with the San Francisco **text.**

Make sure there is enough room to increase the size of the image.

9 Click the picture to select it. Position the pointer over the clip art picture's lower-left sizing handle, until the pointer changes to a ↗, then click and hold the left mouse button and drag the mouse diagonally down and to the left until the picture is roughly 50% larger, as shown in Figure 7-16. Release the mouse button.

Compare your document to Figure 7-15.

You probably noticed there were several other options listed in the Insert → Picture menu. Table 7-2 shows what they are and what they do:

Table 7-2. The Insert Picture Menu

Insert	Description
	Opens the Clip Gallery where you can select a clip art image to insert.
	Inserts a graphic file created in another program.
	Scans an image and inserts it at the insertion point.
	Inserts a Microsoft Organization Chart object into the document.
	Inserts a drawing created with the Microsoft Draw program.
	Inserts a ready-made shape, such as a circle, rectangle, star, arrow, etc.
	Creates spectacular text effects.
	Creates a chart by inserting a Microsoft Graph object.

QUICK REFERENCE

TO INSERT A CLIP ART GRAPHIC:

1. SELECT INSERT → PICTURE → CLIP ART FROM THE MENU.

2. IN THE CLIP ART TASK PANE, TYPE THE NAME OF WHAT YOU'RE LOOKING FOR IN THE SEARCH FOR BOX.

3. SELECT WHICH COLLECTIONS YOU WANT TO SEARCH IN AND CLICK THE GO BUTTON.

4. SCROLL THROUGH THE CLIP ART PICTURES UNTIL YOU FIND AN APPROPRIATE GRAPHIC.

5. CLICK THE GRAPHIC YOU WANT TO INSERT.

6. CLOSE THE TASK PANE.

Inserting and Formatting Pictures

Figure 7-17. The Insert Picture dialog box.

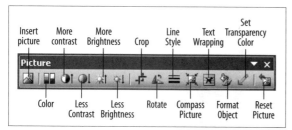

Figure 7-18. The Picture toolbar.

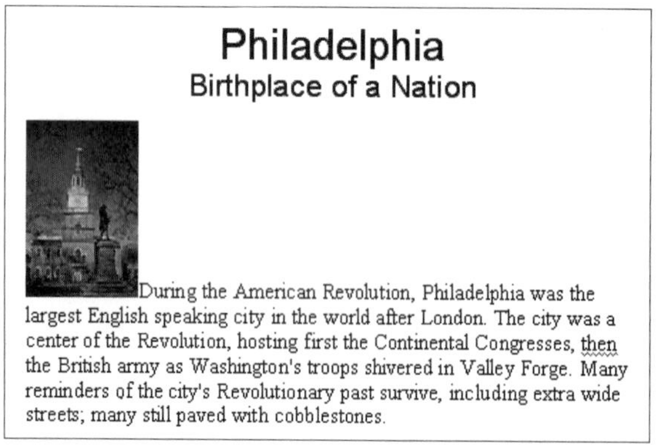

Philadelphia
Birthplace of a Nation

During the American Revolution, Philadelphia was the largest English speaking city in the world after London. The city was a center of the Revolution, hosting first the Continental Congresses, then the British army as Washington's troops shivered in Valley Forge. Many reminders of the city's Revolutionary past survive, including extra wide streets; many still paved with cobblestones.

Figure 7-19. The updated document with an external picture file inserted.

Click the crop button on the Picture toolbar and then drag the picture's sizing handles to crop a picture.

Figure 7-20. How to crop a picture.

If the Microsoft Clip Gallery doesn't have the graphic you're looking for, you can insert graphics created with other programs. There are many other clip art collections available that are much larger than the Microsoft Clip Gallery. Additionally, you can use graphics and pictures created with graphics programs such as Microsoft Paint, which comes with Windows. In this lesson, you will learn how to insert a picture into a document.

1 Make sure you're on Page 3 and place the insertion point at the beginning of the first paragraph, right before the word During.

This is where you want to insert a picture.

2 Select Insert → Picture → From File from the menu.

The Insert Picture dialog box appears, as shown in Figure 7-17. This is where you need to specify the name and location of the graphic file to be inserted into your document.

3 Click the Look in list arrow and navigate to your Practice folder.

All the graphic files located in your Practice folder appear in the file window.

4 Select the Philadelphia file.

Word displays a preview of the graphic in the right side of the Insert Picture dialog box. Let's insert this picture into the document.

5 Click the Insert button.

Word inserts the Philadelphia picture into the current document. The picture appears in line with the paragraph and Word will treat the picture just like a text character, as shown in Figure 7-19.

Sometimes an inserted picture may need some "tweaking"—perhaps it is too dark, too light, or uses the wrong colors. Here is where the Picture toolbar comes in. The Picture toolbar is like your very own photo studio and contains a variety of tools for adjusting and formatting any pictures you insert.

The Picture toolbar, as shown in Figure 7-18, should appear whenever you select a picture—if it doesn't, move on to the next step. If the Picture toolbar does appear for you, skip ahead to Step 7.

6 If the Picture toolbar does not appear, summon it by selecting View → Toolbars → Picture from the menu.

Let's change the colors in the Philadelphia picture.

7 With the Philadelphia picture still selected, click the Color button and select Grayscale.

≥ NOTE ≤   *The Picture toolbar should appear whenever a picture is selected. If the Picture toolbar doesn't appear when you select a picture, you can still display it by selecting View → Toolbars → Picture from the menu.*

Another useful tool on the Picture toolbar is the Crop button. When you crop a picture, you trim its horizontal and vertical sides. Cropping is useful if you only want to include a specific portion of a picture or when a picture contains something you want to cut out, like an ex-boyfriend.

8 Click the Crop button on the Picture toolbar. The pointer changes to a indicating that you can crop the picture.

9 Position the pointer over the right-middle sizing handle, click and hold the left mouse button, and drag the mouse to the left about a quarter-inch, as shown in Figure 7-20.

The area you cropped will no longer appear in the picture.

10 Click the Crop button on the Picture toolbar to exit cropping mode.

This isn't really how we want the picture to appear however, so undo the two changes you just made.

11 Click the Undo button on the Standard toolbar twice to undo the cropping and grayscale formatting you applied to the picture.

QUICK REFERENCE

TO INSERT A GRAPHIC CREATED IN ANOTHER PROGRAM:

1. SELECT INSERT → PICTURE → FROM FILE FROM THE MENU.
2. SELECT THE FILE LOCATION AND NAME AND CLICK INSERT.

TO CHANGE A PICTURE'S COLOR OPTIONS:

• SELECT THE PICTURE, CLICK THE COLOR BUTTON ON THE PICTURE TOOLBAR, AND SELECT A COLORING OPTION.

TO CROP A PICTURE:

1. SELECT THE PICTURE AND CLICK THE CROP BUTTON ON THE PICTURE TOOLBAR.
2. CLICK AND DRAG THE EDGE OF THE PICTURE UNTIL YOU'VE TRIMMED OFF WHAT YOU DON'T WANT.

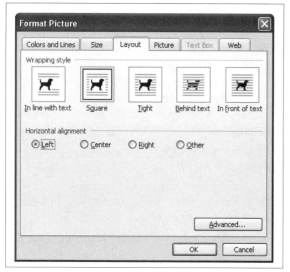

Figure 7-21. The Layout tab of the Format Picture dialog box.

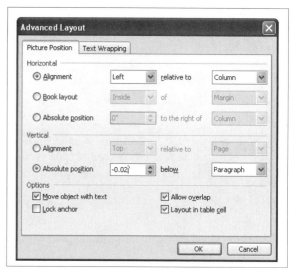

Figure 7-22. The Picture Position tab of the Advanced Layout dialog box.

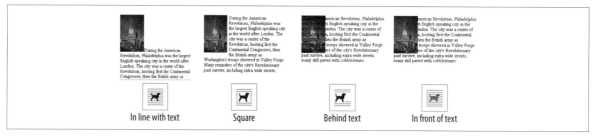

| In line with text | Square | Behind text | In front of text |

Figure 7-23. Several examples of how text wraps around a picture or graphic.

In the previous lessons you learned how to insert pictures into a document. In this lesson you will learn how to position pictures and objects. When you *position* an object, you are telling Word how you want the text near the object to appear—if the text should wrap around the graphic, whether or not the graphic should float over the text, and how much space there should be between the graphic and the text.

1 If necessary, navigate to your Practice folder, open Lesson 7C, and save the file as American History.

2 Click the building picture to select it and select Format → Picture from the menu, and then click the Layout tab.

 Another way to format a picture or object is to right-click the picture or object and select Format Picture from the shortcut menu.

The Format Picture dialog box appears with the Layout tab in front, as shown in Figure 7-21. You can specify how text wraps around pictures and graphics in the Wrapping style section. Table 7-3 describes each of the wrapping options.

If the wrapping options displayed in the Layout tab are not sufficient, you can find more options by clicking the Advanced button.

3 Click the Advanced button and click the Picture Position tab.

The Advanced Layout dialog box appears with the Picture Position tab in front, as shown in Figure 7-22. The Picture Position tab gives you various positioning options for your picture. Normally it is much faster to just drag and drop the picture where you want it, but if you need more precision, the Picture Position tab is the place to go.

We don't need to use any of the positioning options at this time, so let's look at the Text Wrapping tab.

4 Click the Text Wrapping **tab.**

 Another way to adjust text wrapping is to select the picture and click the Draw button *on the Drawing toolbar. Select the* Text Wrapping *option and select an option from the submenu.*

The Text Wrapping tab appears, where you can select from several more advanced wrapping options.

5 Select Square **in the Wrapping style section.**

If you select either the "Square" or "Tight" options, you also have to specify where you want the text to wrap around the object—to the left side, right side, both sides, or whichever side is larger. Figure 7-23 shows examples of how text can wrap around an image.

6 Select Right only **in the Wrap text section.**

This will wrap the text tightly around the right side of the picture.

7 Click OK, OK.

The dialog boxes close and the text wraps neatly around the left side of the picture.

If you're still finding this text wrapping business a little confusing, take a look at Table 7-3 for descriptions of all the wrapping options.

Table 7-3. Wrapping Options

Option	Description
	This places the object at the insertion point in a line of text in the document. The object remains on the same layer as the text
	Wraps text around all sides of a box surrounding the object. (This is called a bounding box.)
	Wraps text tightly around the edges of the actual image (instead of wrapping around the object's bounding box)
	This removes text wrapping and puts the object behind text in the document. The object floats on its own layer. You can move the object in front of or behind text or other objects by using the Order commands on the Draw menu.
	This removes text wrapping and places the object in front of text in the document. The object floats on its own layer. You can move the object in front of or behind text or other objects by using the Order commands on the Draw menu.

QUICK REFERENCE

TO CHANGE HOW TEXT WRAPS AROUND AN OBJECT:

1. SELECT THE PICTURE, SELECT FORMAT → PICTURE FROM THE MENU, AND CLICK THE LAYOUT TAB.

2. SELECT A WRAPPING STYLE AND/OR HORIZONTAL ALIGNMENT OPTION AND CLICK OK.

   OR...

   SELECT THE PICTURE AND CLICK THE DRAW BUTTON ON THE DRAWING TOOLBAR. SELECT THE TEXT WRAPPING OPTION AND SELECT AN OPTION FROM THE SUBMENU.

TO USE ADVANCED TEXT WRAPPING AND PLACEMENT OPTIONS:

1. SELECT THE PICTURE AND SELECT FORMAT → PICTURE FROM THE MENU, CLICK THE LAYOUT TAB, AND CLICK THE ADVANCED BUTTON.

2. SELECT A TEXT WRAPPING OPTION FROM THE TEXT WRAPPING TAB AND/OR A POSITION OPTION FROM THE PICTURE POSITION TAB, AND CLICK OK.

Aligning and Grouping Objects

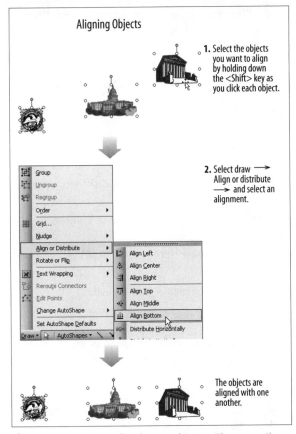

Figure 7-24. The steps for aligning objects with one another.

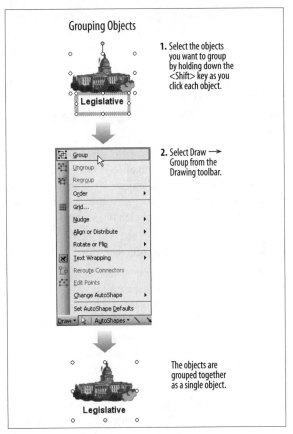

Figure 7-25. The steps for grouping objects.

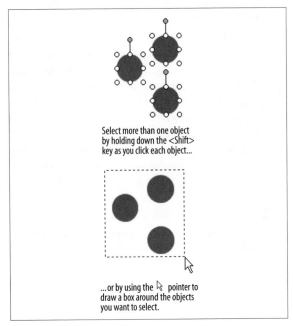

Figure 7-26. Procedures for selecting multiple objects.

Documents that have lots of pictures and drawings scattered randomly about them look terrible. The Align command, located under the Draw button on the Drawing toolbar, prevents this from happening. You can align objects so that they are lined up with one another or so they are spaced equally apart. This lesson will give you some practice aligning objects with Word's alignment commands.

This lesson also explains how to *group* and *ungroup* objects. A *group* is a collection of objects that Word treats as though it were a single object. By grouping several objects together, you can move or resize the entire group instead of moving or resizing each object one by one.

1 Go to Page 4 of the document.

Someone sure was sloppy when they created this page—the pictures and text are all over the place! You could manually move the objects and align the objects with one another by using the mouse and eyeballing it, but that would require a lot of time, and unless you have eyes like a hawk, it would be difficult to align the objects perfectly. Instead, we'll align the objects using Word's alignment commands.

First, you need to select the objects you want to align with one another. There are two ways to select more than one object, as shown in Figure 7-26:

• Hold down the Shift key as you click each object that you want to select.

• Click the ⟐ Select Objects button on the Drawing toolbar and use the arrow pointer (⟐) to draw a box around the objects that you want to select. Point to a location above and to the left of the objects that you want to select, and click and drag the mouse down and to the right until the box surrounds all the objects. When you release the mouse button, all the objects in the box will be selected. The disadvantage of this method is that it's not as selective as using the Shift + click method.

2 Hold down the Shift key as you select the Executive, Legislative, and Judicial pictures, as shown in Figure 7-24.

Now you can align the selected objects with one another.

3 Click the Draw ▾ Draw button on the Drawing toolbar and select Align or Distribute → Align Bottom.

The selected objects are aligned with the bottom-most object, the Executive branch picture. Next, we need to center align the Judicial text box with the Judicial branch picture.

4 Click in a blank area on the screen to deselect the objects. Click on the Judicial branch picture to select it. Then hold down the Shift key and click the Judicial text box.

Now let's center align the two selected objects.

5 Click the Draw button on the Drawing toolbar and select Align or Distribute → Align Center.

Word centers the picture and text label.

The procedure for grouping several objects into a single object is very similar to aligning several objects—first select the objects you want to group, then select the Group command from the Draw button on the Drawing toolbar.

6 Click the Legislative branch picture, then hold down the Shift key, and click the Legislative text box.

Since these two objects should always remain together, it makes sense to group them together to work with a single object rather than two.

7 Click the Draw button on the Drawing toolbar and select Group.

Word groups the selected picture and text box into a single object, as shown in Figure 7-25. You can break a group back into its original components at any time by selecting the grouped object, clicking the Draw button, and selecting Ungroup.

8 Following the procedure you just learned, group the Judicial branch picture and the Judicial text box together, and then group the Executive branch picture and the Executive text box together.

You can also use the Align and Distribute command to distribute selected objects so there is equal horizontal or vertical distance between all the objects. Move on to the next step to try distributing the selected object horizontally.

9 Select the Executive, Legislative, and Judicial objects, click the Draw button on the Drawing toolbar, and select Align or Distribute → Distribute Horizontally.

Word evenly distributes the selected objects.

QUICK REFERENCE

TO SELECT MULTIPLE OBJECTS:

- PRESS AND HOLD DOWN THE SHIFT KEY AS YOU CLICK EACH OBJECT THAT YOU WANT TO SELECT.

OR...

- USE THE ARROW POINTER TO DRAW A BOX AROUND THE OBJECTS THAT YOU WANT TO SELECT.

TO ALIGN OBJECTS WITH ONE ANOTHER:

1. FOLLOW THE ABOVE STEPS TO SELECT THE OBJECTS YOU WANT TO ALIGN.

2. CLICK THE DRAW BUTTON ON THE DRAWING TOOLBAR, SELECT ALIGN OR DISTRIBUTE, AND SELECT HOW YOU WANT TO ALIGN OR DISTRIBUTE THE SELECTED OBJECTS.

TO GROUP SEVERAL OBJECTS:

1. SELECT THE OBJECTS YOU WANT TO GROUP TOGETHER.

2. CLICK THE DRAW BUTTON ON THE DRAWING TOOLBAR AND SELECT GROUP.

TO UNGROUP A GROUPED OBJECT:

- SELECT THE GROUPED OBJECT, CLICK THE DRAW BUTTON ON THE DRAWING TOOLBAR, AND SELECT UNGROUP.

Drawing AutoShapes

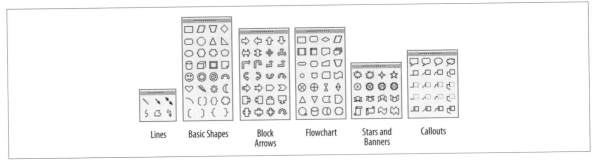

Figure 7-27. These shapes are available under the AutoShapes button on the Drawing toolbar.

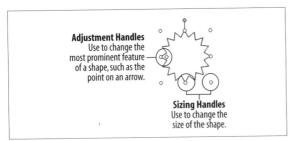

Adjustment Handles
Use to change the most prominent feature of a shape, such as the point on an arrow.

Sizing Handles
Use to change the size of the shape.

Figure 7-28. Many AutoShapes have an Adjustment handle in addition to sizing handles.

Washington D.C.
The Branches of Government

Meet your local Representative

Executive   Legislative   Judicial

Figure 7-29. AutoShapes enhance the look of a document.

You're not limited to drawing simple rectangles, ovals, and lines with Word. The *AutoShapes* button on the Drawing toolbar contains over a hundred common shapes and lines, such as arrows, stars, and pentagons. Figure 7-27 shows all the AutoShapes that are available. As you can see from the illustration, the AutoShapes menu is organized into several categories:

- **Lines:** Straight lines, curved lines, scribbly lines, arrows, and free form drawing shapes.
- **Basic Shapes:** Squares, rectangles, triangles, circles, pentagons, and more.

- **Block Arrows:** Arrows that point up, down, left, and right.
- **Flowchart:** Basic shapes used to create flowcharts.
- **Stars and Banners:** Shapes that boldly announce something.
- **Callouts:** Text box shapes that point to and describe something.
- **More Autoshapes:** Allows you to insert an object from the Clip Gallery.

1 Click the I AutoShapes button on the Drawing toolbar.

A menu listing all of the various AutoShape categories appears. Figure 7-27 lists the AutoShapes that are available under each category.

2 Select the Stars and Banners category and select the 16-Point Star shape.

The pointer changes to a I indicating you can draw the selected shape. Drawing an AutoShape is no different from drawing an ordinary shape—just click and drag until the shape is the size you want.

3 Place the + pointer just below the middle of the word Government in the Document title. Click and drag the I pointer down and to the right until the right edge of the shape is about 1 inch from the right edge of the document. Release the mouse button. Compare the size and position of your AutoShape with the one in Figure 7-29.

If your AutoShape is still selected, you'll notice a yellow diamond ¨on the left side. This is an *adjustment handle*. By grabbing and dragging an adjustment handle, you can adjust the most prominent feature of an AutoShape, such as the point on an arrow or the spikes on a star. Adjustment handles are not used to resize an object—you still need to click and drag one of the object's sizing handles to do that.

4 **Click and drag the 16-Point Star's yellow** adjustment handle (♦) **to the left just a smidgen.**

By dragging the star's adjustment handle you've changed the size of the star's spikes. You can move, resize, and format an AutoShape just like any other shape. Move on to the next step to change the color of your star shape.

5 **With the 16-Point Star still selected, click the** Fill Color button **list arrow on the Drawing toolbar and select a** yellow **color.**

Here's another shape trick: you can add text to any shape by right-clicking the shape, selecting Add Text from the shortcut menu, and typing the text.

6 **Right-click the 16-Point Star and select** Add Text **from the shortcut menu.**

A blinking insertion point (|) appears inside the star, indicating that the shape is ready to accept any text that you type. We have to change the font size and type first so that it will fit into the AutoShape.

7 **Select** Arial **from the** Font List **and** 18 **from the** Font Size List **on the Formatting toolbar.**

Any text we type now will appear in Arial 18 pt font type. We are ready to enter text in our object.

8 **Type** Meet your local Representative! **Your star should look like the one shown in Figure 7-29.**

QUICK REFERENCE

TO INSERT AN AUTOSHAPE:

1. CLICK THE AUTOSHAPES BUTTON ON THE DRAWING TOOLBAR.

2. SELECT THE CATEGORY AND AUTOSHAPE YOU WANT TO INSERT.

3. DRAG THE CROSSHAIR POINTER TO DRAW THE AUTOSHAPE.

TO ADJUST AN AUTOSHAPE:

1. SELECT THE AUTOSHAPE AND DRAG ITS ADJUSTMENT HANDLE TO ADJUST THE MOST PROMINENT FEATURE OF THE SHAPE.

TO ADD TEXT TO A SHAPE:

1. RIGHT-CLICK THE SHAPE AND SELECT ADD TEXT FROM THE SHORTCUT MENU.

2. TYPE THE TEXT.

1. Select the object you want to rotate.   2. Click and drag the objecy's rotate handle.   3. The rotated object.

Figure 7-30. How to rotate an object with the Free Rotate tool.

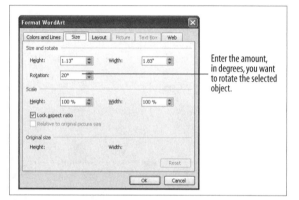

Figure 7-31. The Size tab in the Format WordArt dialog box.

Figure 7-32. The updated document with the arrows and Mardi Gras text flipped or rotated.

In this lesson, you'll learn how to flip and rotate drawing objects on your documents. When you *flip* an object, you create a mirror image of it. Word's flip commands allow you to flip an object vertically or horizontally to create a mirror image of the object.

When you *rotate* an object, you turn it around its center. You can rotate objects in 90-degree increments, or you can use the *rotate tool* to rotate an object to any angle.

1 If necessary, navigate to your Practice folder and open Lesson 7D. Save the file as American History.

2 Go to Page 5.

This document contains several objects that need to be flipped and rotated. The first object we'll fix is the arrow located between the "French Rule" and "Spanish Rule" boxes, which should be pointing in the opposite direction.

3 Click the upward-pointing arrow, click the Draw button on the Drawing toolbar, and select Rotate or Flip → Flip Vertical.

Word vertically flips the upward-pointing arrow, changing it to a downward-pointing arrow.

Now we must flip the second arrow located between the "Spanish Rule" and "American Rule" boxes.

4 Click the right-pointing arrow, click the Draw button on the Drawing toolbar, and select Rotate or Flip → Rotate Right 90˚.

TIP

Another way to rotate an object is to select the object, select Format → AutoShape from the menu, click the Size tab, and enter the amount in degrees you want to rotate the object in the Rotation box.

⁞ NOTE ⁞

The Flip and Rotate commands can sometimes be a little tricky, especially if you're directionally challenged. If you accidentally flip or rotate an object in the wrong direction, simply use the Undo command to return the object to its original state.

The rotate command has one limitation—it can only rotate objects in 90-degree increments. To rotate objects by other degree intervals, you need to use either the Free Rotate handle or the Format AutoShape dialog box. Move on to the next step and we'll see how the Free Rotate handle works.

5 Select the Mardi Gras **text object.**

A green rotate handle (•) appears above the Mardi Gras object.

6 Place the ⬧ pointer over the Mardi Gras object's rotate handle **(•) and then click and hold the mouse button and drag the object around until it's at a 45 degree angle, as shown in Figure 7-30. Release the mouse button.**

Dragging an object's rotate handle is the fastest and easiest way to rotate an object, but you can also rotate an object with the Format AutoShape dialog box.

7 With the Mardi Gras object still selected, select **Format** → **WordArt from the menu and click the** Size **tab.**

The Format WordArt dialog box appears, as shown in Figure 7-31. You can rotate a selected object by entering the amount in degrees that you want to rotate the object in the Rotation box.

8 Type 15 **in the** Rotation **box and click** OK.

Word rotates the Mardi Gras object by 15 degrees.

9 Compare your document to the one in Figure 7-32 **and save your work.**

If you're still having trouble knowing how each rotate command rotates an object, look at Table 7-4 for a visual reference.

Table 7-4. Flip and Rotate Commands

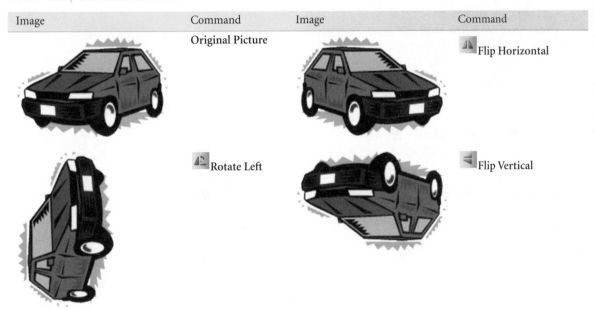

Image	Command	Image	Command
	Original Picture		Flip Horizontal
	Rotate Left		Flip Vertical

Table 7-4. Flip and Rotate Commands

Image	Command	Image	Command
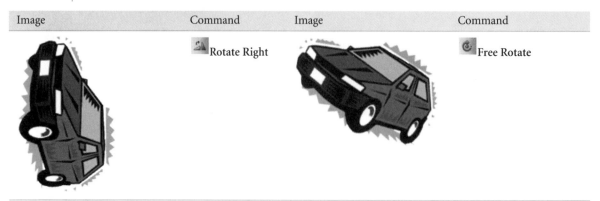	Rotate Right		Free Rotate

QUICK REFERENCE

TO ROTATE AN OBJECT BY 90 DEGREES:

- SELECT THE OBJECT, CLICK THE DRAW BUTTON ON THE DRAWING TOOLBAR, SELECT ROTATE OR FLIP FROM THE MENU, AND SELECT ROTATE RIGHT OR ROTATE LEFT.

TO FLIP AN OBJECT:

- SELECT THE OBJECT, CLICK THE DRAW BUTTON ON THE DRAWING TOOLBAR, SELECT ROTATE OR FLIP FROM THE MENU, AND SELECT FLIP HORIZONTAL OR FLIP VERTICAL.

TO FREE ROTATE AN OBJECT:

1. SELECT THE OBJECT.
2. CLICK AND DRAG THE OBJECT'S ROTATE HANDLE.

   OR...

   SELECT THE OBJECT, SELECT FORMAT → AUTOSHAPE FROM THE MENU, CLICK THE SIZE TAB, AND ENTER THE AMOUNT IN DEGREES YOU WANT TO ROTATE THE OBJECT IN THE ROTATION BOX.

Layering Objects

Figure 7-33. The Mardi Gras text object appears before the mask.

Figure 7-34. The procedure for layering an object.

The order in which you select and send objects to the front or back is very important, as shown here.

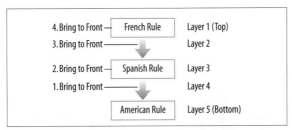

Figure 7-35. The updated document with the objects properly layered.

Whenever you have more than one object on a page, it's possible for one or more objects to overlap one another. This presents a problem: how can you make sure one object appears in front of, or in back of, another object? Word (and most other drawing programs) solves this problem by *layering* objects, similar to a stack of papers. The first object is on the bottom layer, and the last object is on the top layer. Of course, you can change the order in which objects appear, and that's the topic of this lesson.

There are four layering commands:

- **Bring to Front:** This places the selected object to the very top layer of the document. All other objects will appear behind the selected object.
- **Send to Back:** This places the selected object to the very back layer of the document. All other objects will appear in front of the selected object.
- **Bring Forward:** Brings the selected object one layer up on the document.
- **Send Backward:** Sends the selected object one layer down on the document.

Ready to get some layering practice? Let's get started.

1 Click the Mardi Gras **text object to select it.**

We want to send the Mardi Gras object to the back layer, so that it appears in the back of the document.

2 Click the Draw button **on the Drawing toolbar and select** Order → Send Backward.

The selected Mardi Gras text object is sent one layer backward so that it appears behind the mask graphic, as shown in Figure 7-33.

When you want to layer several objects in a particular sequence, the order in which you select the object and then send it to the front or back is very important. For example, if you bring object A to the front (or on top), and then bring object B to the front (or on top), object A moves down one layer, so that it would appear behind object B if the two objects overlapped each other.

Confused? Let's try layering the objects in the document's flowchart so you'll better understand why the order in which you select and layer objects is so important.

3 Select the arrow between Spanish Rule and American Rule, click the Draw button **on the Drawing toolbar, and select** Order → Bring to Front.

Word brings the selected arrow to the front layer, in front of both the Spanish Rule and American Rule boxes. We want the arrow to appear in front of the American Rule box, but not in front of the Spanish Rule box. Move on to the next step to bring the Spanish Rule box in front.

4 Select the Spanish Rule object, click the Draw button on the Drawing toolbar, and select Order → Bring to Front.

Word brings the Spanish Rule object to the front layer, in front of the arrow that had previously been on the top layer. Notice that the bottom arrow still appears on top of the American Rule box, however.

Go to the next step and finish layering the object in the flowchart.

5 Follow the sequence shown in Figure 7-34 (you're on Step 3 in the diagram) and layer the remaining arrow and French Rule box.

When you're finished, your document should look like the one in Figure 7-35. Had you selected the objects and brought them to the front in any other sequence, the objects wouldn't appear in the correct order.

QUICK REFERENCE

TO CHANGE THE ORDER IN WHICH OBJECTS APPEAR IN A DOCUMENT:

1. SELECT THE OBJECT.

2. CLICK THE DRAW BUTTON ON THE DRAWING TOOLBAR, SELECT ORDER, AND SELECT ONE OF THE FOLLOWING LAYERING COMMANDS:

- BRING TO FRONT: THIS PLACES THE SELECTED OBJECT ON THE VERY TOP LAYER OF THE DOCUMENT. ALL OTHER OBJECTS WILL APPEAR BEHIND THE SELECTED OBJECT.

- SEND TO BACK: THIS PLACES THE SELECTED OBJECT TO THE VERY BACK LAYER OF THE DOCUMENT. ALL OTHER OBJECTS WILL APPEAR IN FRONT OF THE SELECTED OBJECT.

- BRING FORWARD: BRINGS THE SELECTED OBJECT ONE LAYER UP ON THE DOCUMENT.

- SEND BACKWARD: SENDS THE SELECTED OBJECT ONE LAYER DOWN ON THE DOCUMENT.

- THE ORDER IN WHICH YOU SELECT AND LAYER OBJECTS WILL DETERMINE THE ORDER IN WHICH THEY APPEAR ON THE DOCUMENT. FOR EXAMPLE, THE LAST OBJECT YOU BRING TO THE FRONT WILL ALWAYS APPEAR ON THE TOP LAYER.

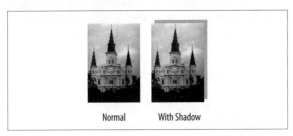

Figure 7-36. A photograph with and without a shadow effect.

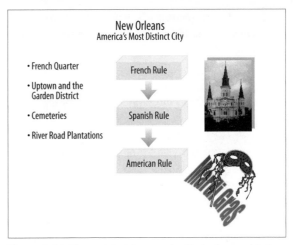

Figure 7-40. The updated document with shadow and 3-D effects added to its objects.

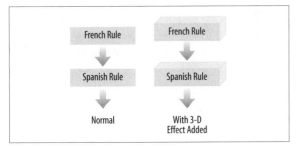

Figure 7-37. Graphic objects with and without 3-D effects.

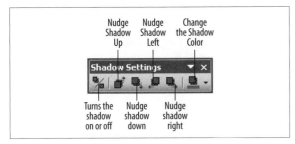

Figure 7-38. The Shadow Settings toolbar.

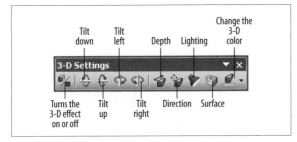

Figure 7-39. The 3-D Settings toolbar.

Breathe new life into the flat and boring objects in your documents! Adding shadows and 3-D effects to your shapes makes them stand out and look exciting. In this lesson we'll learn how to apply both shadow and 3-D effects to your document objects.

Adding a shadow to an object gives it a sense of depth by making it appear as if the object is casting a shadow, as shown in Figure 7-36. Not only can you add a shadow to an object, but you can also change the length of the shadow and where it falls.

The 3-D button on the drawing toolbar turns a lifeless object into a dramatic three-dimensional object without having to put on any red and blue 3-D glasses. As with shadowing, you can change the perspective and depth of any 3-D object, as shown in Figure 7-37.

1 Click the photograph object to select it and click the Shadow Style button on the Drawing toolbar.

A list of different shadow angles and effects appears above the Shadow button—all you have to do is select the type of shadow you want.

2 Select the Shadow Style 2 option (the second option in the top row) from the shadow list.

If the selected shadow still isn't exactly what you're looking for, you can change the position and color of the shadow.

3 With the photograph still selected, click the Shadow Style button on the Drawing toolbar and select Shadow Settings.

The Shadow Settings toolbar appears, as shown in Figure 7-38. By clicking the Shadow Settings toolbar's buttons, you can adjust the shadow's position and change the shadow's color. Let's try it!

4 Click the Nudge Shadow Left button on the Shadow Settings toolbar twice, then click the Nudge Shadow Down button twice.

Clicking any of the Shadow Settings toolbar's Nudge buttons moves the shadow a smidgen in the specified direction.

5 Close the Shadow Settings toolbar by clicking its Close button.

The 3-D button is probably the coolest button on the Drawing toolbar. It turns ordinary two-dimensional objects into dazzling three-dimensional objects that look like professionally designed graphics.

6 Click the Mardi Gras word object to select it.

It may be difficult to click the Mardi Gras object since most of it is covered by the mask graphic—try clicking the far-right side of the Mardi Gras object.

7 Click the 3-D Style button on the Drawing toolbar.

A list of different 3-D effects appears above the 3-D button. Just like the Shadow Style button, you simply need to select the 3-D effect you want from the list.

8 Select the 3-D Style 1 option from the 3-D list.

Word applies the 3-D effect to the Mardi Gras object, transforming it into a 3-D object. You can fine-tune the appearance of any 3-D object by adjusting its angle, depth, and lighting effects.

9 With the Mardi Gras object still selected, click the 3-D Style button on the Drawing toolbar and select 3-D Settings.

The 3-D Settings toolbar appears, as shown in Figure 7-39. The 3-D Settings toolbar contains buttons that adjust the depth and direction of the 3-D object and change the object's color and light effects.

10 Click the Depth button on the 3-D Settings toolbar, select the Custom option, type 24, and press Enter.

The Mardi Gras 3-D object now only extends 24 points instead of 36 points.

11 Close the 3-D Settings toolbar by clicking its Close button.

Move on to the next step to add 3-D effects to the flow chart boxes on the document.

12 Use the procedure you learned in Steps 6-8 to add the 3-D Style 1 effect to the three text boxes in the flow chart (Spanish, French and American Rule).

Compare your document with the one in Figure 7-40.

13 Save your work and exit the Word program.

QUICK REFERENCE

TO ADD A SHADOW TO AN OBJECT:

- SELECT THE OBJECT, CLICK THE SHADOW STYLE BUTTON ON THE DRAWING TOOLBAR, AND SELECT THE SHADOW EFFECT YOU WANT TO USE.

TO MODIFY A SHADOW:

- SELECT THE OBJECT, CLICK THE SHADOW STYLE BUTTON ON THE DRAWING TOOLBAR, SELECT SHADOW SETTINGS, AND MODIFY THE SHADOW BY CLICKING THE APPROPRIATE BUTTON(S) ON THE SHADOW SETTINGS TOOLBAR.

TO ADD A 3-D EFFECT TO AN OBJECT:

- SELECT THE OBJECT, CLICK THE 3-D STYLE BUTTON ON THE DRAWING TOOLBAR, AND SELECT THE 3-D EFFECT YOU WANT TO USE.

TO MODIFY A 3-D EFFECT:

- SELECT THE OBJECT, CLICK THE 3-D STYLE BUTTON ON THE DRAWING TOOLBAR, SELECT 3-D SETTINGS, AND MODIFY THE 3-D OBJECT BY CLICKING THE APPROPRIATE BUTTON(S) ON THE 3-D SETTINGS TOOLBAR.

Chapter Seven Review

Lesson Summary

Drawing on Your Documents

To Display the Drawing Toolbar: Click the Drawing button on the Standard toolbar or select View → Toolbars → Drawing from the menu.

To Draw an Object: Click the object you want to draw on the drawing toolbar (such as a line or circle) and draw your shape by clicking on the document with the pointer and dragging until the shape reaches the desired size.

To Resize an Object: Click the object to select it, drag the object's sizing handles until the shape reaches the desired size, and then release the mouse button.

Adding, Arranging, and Formatting Text Boxes

To Add a Text Box to a Document: Click the Text Box button on the Drawing toolbar, click where you want to insert the text with the insertion point, and then type the text in the box.

To Resize a Text Box: Click the text box to select it, drag the object's sizing handles until the box reaches the desired size, and release the mouse button.

Notes about Text Boxes: A text box's text and paragraphs can be formatted just like text anywhere else in the document. Text boxes are rarely the correct size when you first create them and must be resized properly to fit their text.

Selecting, Resizing, Moving, and Deleting Objects

To Resize an Object: Click the object to select it, drag the object's sizing handles until the shape reaches the desired size, and release the mouse button.

To Resize an Object Proportionally: Follow the above procedures, only hold down the Shift key while dragging to maintain the object's proportions while resizing it.

To Move an Object: Click the object and hold down the mouse button, drag the object to a new location, and release the mouse button to drop the object.

To Delete an Object: Select the object and press the Delete key.

To Copy an Object using Drag and Drop: Follow the above procedures, only hold down the Ctrl key while dragging to copy the object.

Formatting Objects

To Fill a Shape with a Color: Select the shape, then click the Fill Color button list arrow on the Drawing toolbar and select the color you want.

To Change Line Color or Remove a Line: Select the shape, then click the Line Color button list arrow on the Drawing toolbar and select the color you want or select No Line.

To Change the Line Style: Select the line, then click the Line Style button on the Drawing toolbar and select the line style you want.

To Change the Dash Style: Select the line, then click the Dash Style button on the Drawing toolbar and select the dash you want.

To Add or Remove Arrow Heads: Select the line, then click the Arrow Style button on the Drawing toolbar and select the arrow style you want.

To Use the Format AutoShape Dialog Box: Select the object and select Format → AutoShape from the menu, or right-click the object you want to format and select Format AutoShape from the menu.

Inserting Clip Art

To Insert a Clip Art Graphic: Select Insert → Picture → Clip Art from the menu. In the Clip Art task pane, type the name of what you're looking for in the Search for box. Select which collections you want to search in and click the Go button. Scroll through the clip art pictures until you find an appropriate graphic and click the graphic you want to insert. Close the task pane.

Inserting and Formatting Pictures

To Insert a Graphic Created in Another Program: Select Insert → Picture → From File from the menu, then select the file location and name and click Insert.

Use the Picture toolbar to change the brightness and contrast of a selected picture.

To Change a Picture's Color Options: Use the Color button on the Picture toolbar to modify a picture's colors, making it appear in black and white, grayscales, or washout.

To Crop a Picture: Click the picture to select it, click the Crop button on the Picture toolbar, and drag the cropping handle bars around the area of the picture you want to keep.

Positioning Objects

To Change How Text Wraps around an Object: Make sure that the picture is floating over the text in the document, select the picture or object, select Format → Picture from the menu, click the Layout tab, select a wrapping option, and click OK. Or, select the picture and click the Draw button on the Drawing toolbar. Select Text Wrapping from the menu and select the desired wrapping option from the submenu.

To Use Advanced Text Wrapping and Placement Options: Select the picture and select Format → Picture from the menu, click the Layout tab, and click the Advanced button. Select a text wrapping option from the Text Wrapping tab and/or a position option from the Picture Position tab and click OK.

Aligning and Grouping Objects

To Select Multiple Objects: Press and hold down the Shift key as you click each object that you want to select, or use the arrow pointer to draw a box around the objects that you want to select.

To Align Objects with Each Other: Follow the above steps to select the objects you want to align, click the Draw button on the Drawing toolbar, select Align or Distribute, and select how you want to align or distribute the selected objects.

To Group Several Objects: Select the objects you want to group together, click the Draw button on the Drawing toolbar, and select Group.

To Ungroup a Grouped Object: Select the grouped object, click the Draw button on the Drawing toolbar, and select Ungroup.

Drawing AutoShapes

To Insert an AutoShape: Click the AutoShapes button on the Drawing toolbar and select the category and AutoShape that you want to insert. Drag the crosshair pointer to draw the AutoShape.

To Adjust an AutoShape: Select the AutoShape and drag its adjustment handle (♦) to adjust the most prominent feature of the shape.

To Add Text to a Shape: Right-click the shape, select Add Text from the shortcut menu, and type the text.

Flipping and Rotating Objects

To Rotate an Object by 90 Degrees: Select the object, click the Draw button on the Drawing toolbar, select Rotate or Flip from the menu, and select Rotate Right or Rotate Left.

To Flip an Object: Select the object, click the Draw button on the Drawing toolbar, select Rotate or Flip from the menu, and select Flip Horizontal or Flip Vertical.

To Free Rotate an Object: Select the object, then click and drag the object's rotate handle (●) with the arrow pointer. You can also rotate an object by selecting the object, selecting Format → AutoShape from the menu, clicking the Size tab, and entering the amount in degrees you want to rotate the object in the Rotation box.

Layering Objects

To Change the Order in Which Objects Appear in a Document: Select the object, click the Draw button on the Drawing toolbar, select Order, and select one of the following layering commands:

Bring to Front: Places the selected object to the very top layer of the document. All other objects will appear behind the selected object.

Send to Back: Places the selected object to the very back layer of the document. All other objects will appear in front of the selected object.

Bring Forward: Brings the selected object one layer up on the document.

Send Backward: Sends the selected object one layer down on the document.

The order in which you select and layer objects will determine the order in which they appear on the document. For example, the last object you bring to the front will always appear on the top layer.

Applying Shadows and 3-D Effects

To Add a Shadow to an Object: Select the object, click the Shadow Style button on the Drawing toolbar, and select the shadow effect you want to use.

To Modify a Shadow: Select the object, click the Shadow Style button on the Drawing toolbar, select Shadow Settings, and modify the shadow by clicking the appropriate button(s) on the Shadow Settings toolbar.

To Add a 3-D Effect to an Object: Select the object, click the 3-D Style button on the Drawing toolbar, and select the 3-D effect you want to use.

To Modify a 3-D Effect: Select the object, click the 3-D Style button on the Drawing toolbar, select 3-D Settings, and modify the 3-D object by clicking the appropriate button(s) on the 3-D Settings toolbar.

Quiz

1. Which of the following statements is NOT true?

   A. Holding down the Shift key while you draw an object creates perfect squares, circles and straight lines.

   B. The Drawing toolbar contains tools for drawing shapes, lines, arrows and more.

   C. The text in a text box can't be formatted.

   D. You can change the size of a text box by selecting it and dragging its sizing handles.

2. Which of the following are methods to select multiple objects on a document? (Select all that apply.)

   A. Click the Select Object button on the Standard toolbar, click the objects you want to select, and press Enter when you're finished.

   B. Hold down the Shift as you select each object.

   C. You can only select one object at a time in Word.

   D. Click the Select Object button on the Drawing toolbar and drag a rectangle around the objects you want to select.

3. You can format drawing objects by: (Select all that apply.)

   A. Selecting the object and formatting it with the Drawing toolbar.

   B. Selecting the object, selecting Format → AutoShape from the menu, and specifying your formatting options from the Format AutoShape dialog box.

   C. Right-clicking the object, selecting Format AutoShape from the shortcut menu, and specifying your formatting options from the Format AutoShape dialog box.

   D. Selecting the object, pressing Ctrl + F, and specifying your formatting options from the Format AutoShape dialog box.

4. You can change the brightness and contrast of a picture and crop it using the buttons on the Drawing toolbar. (True or False?)

5. Block Arrows, Stars and Banners, and Callouts are all examples of:

   A. Different types of children's building blocks.

   B. Clip art categories located in the Microsoft Clip Gallery.

   C. AutoShape categories.

   D. Yet several more technical terms that I don't understand.

6. You need to wear special glasses in order to see and appreciate 3-D effects created by the 3-D Effects button on the Drawing toolbar. (True or False?)

7. You are creating a document about the life of Harvester ants and have inserted several-dozen ant pictures onto your document. Now you're having problems moving and keeping track of all of those pictures. What can you do to make working with these pictures easier?

   A. Delete the ants, insert a picture of an anteater, and write a note to your audience explaining what happened.

   B. Group the ants together: Select all the ants by holding down the Shift key as you click each ant, or by drawing a box around them with the Select Objects pointer. Once you have selected all the ants, group them together by clicking the Draw button on the Drawing toolbar and selecting Group.

C. Select Edit → Select Ants from the menu whenever you want to move or work with all the ants at once.

D. Do a project on something else.

8. Some AutoShapes have a yellow diamond ♦ on them. What is this yellow diamond and what is it used for?

A. It's a *sizing* handle and it is used to make AutoShapes larger or smaller.

B. It's *moving* handle—click and drag it to move the AutoShape to a different location on the screen.

C. It's an *adjustment* handle and is used to change an AutoShape's most prominent feature, such as the point on an arrow or the spikes on a star.

D. It's the *confusion* handle—it doesn't have any function and is there only to perplex you.

Homework

1. Start Microsoft Word, open the Homework 7 document and save it as "Paper Games."

2. Go to Page 2. Click the Oval button on the Drawing toolbar. Position the pointer in the upper-left corner of the middle box, press and hold the Shift, and then drag down and to the right to create a circle that is the same size as the circle below it.

3. Click the Fill Color list arrow on the Drawing toolbar and select No Fill.

4. Go to Page 3. Select the yellowish rectangle, click the 3-D button on the Drawing toolbar, and select the first option.

5. Select all of the hangman objects (hold down the Shift key as you click each object or click or drag a rectangle around the objects). Click the Draw menu button on the Drawing toolbar and select Group.

6. Select Insert → Picture → Clip Art from the menu. Search for a person for the hangman, and insert it in the document. Then close the Clip Art task pane.

7. Click the clip art picture to select it. Select Format → Picture from the menu. From the Layout tab, select Behind text and click OK.

8. Drag any of the cartoon's sizing handles until the figure is small enough to fit under the gallows.

9. Click and drag the cartoon figure under the gallows.

10. Save your work and exit Microsoft Word.

Quiz Answers

1. C. Of course you can format a text box's text!

2. B and D. Either of these methods will select multiple objects.

3. A, B, and C. You can format drawing objects using any of these methods.

4. False. You will have to summon the Picture toolbar to accomplish these tasks.

5. C. AutoShape categories.

6. False. Of course not! What a silly question!

7. B. Grouping all those ants will make them easier to work with.

8. C. That yellow diamond is the adjustment handle and is used to change an AutoShape's most promi-

CHAPTER 8
PERFORMING A MAIL MERGE

CHAPTER OBJECTIVES:

Creating and working with a mail merged main document, Lesson 8.1–8.3, 8.7 and 8.8

Creating a data source for the mail merge, Lesson 8.4

Entering records into the data source, Lesson 8.5

Inserting merge fields into the main document, Lesson 8.6

Inserting IF...THEN...ELSE fields, Lesson 8.10

Creating and working with labels, Lesson 8.9

Using an existing database as the data source, Lesson 8.11

CHAPTER TASK: CREATE A MAIL MERGE FORM LETTER

Prerequisites

- **How to open and save a document.**
- **How to use menus, toolbars, and dialog boxes.**
- **How to work with tables.**

Here's a secret for you: your dentist probably didn't have someone manually type that check-up reminder you received this month. And no one manually typed your weekly Publisher's Clearing House sweepstakes letter either. A process known as *mail merge* has created these "personalized" letters.

Mail merge letters are used to send the same or similar documents to many different people at once. Since they contain the recipient's name, address, and other information, mail merge letters feel more personal—just like Publisher's Clearing House: *Bob Boyarksi, if you have the winning number, you are the winner of $10 Million Dollars!*

Performing a mail merge isn't a very difficult process, but it is a rather lengthy one. This chapter will take you step by step through the mail merge process. When you've completed this chapter, you will be able to send "personal" mail merge letters to all your friends and relatives during the holidays in one-tenth the time, and no one will know the difference!

An Overview of the Mail Merge Process

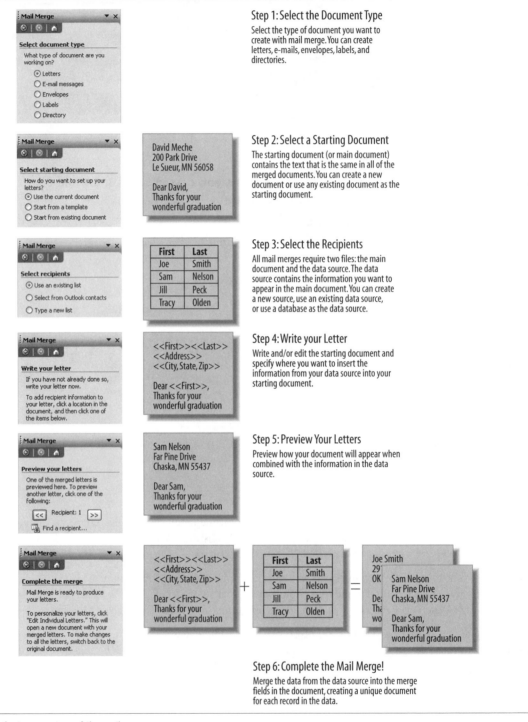

Step 1: Select the Document Type

Select the type of document you want to create with mail merge. You can create letters, e-mails, envelopes, labels, and directories.

Step 2: Select a Starting Document

The starting document (or main document) contains the text that is the same in all of the merged documents. You can create a new document or use any existing document as the starting document.

Step 3: Select the Recipients

All mail merges require two files: the main document and the data source. The data source contains the information you want to appear in the main document. You can create a new source, use an existing data source, or use a database as the data source.

Step 4: Write your Letter

Write and/or edit the starting document and specify where you want to insert the information from your data source into your starting document.

Step 5: Preview Your Letters

Preview how your document will appear when combined with the information in the data source.

Step 6: Complete the Mail Merge!

Merge the data from the data source into the merge fields in the document, creating a unique document for each record in the data.

Figure 8-1. An overview of the mail merge process.

There's no getting around it—performing a mail merge is a long and complicated process. In fact, it's so long that we'll be spending the rest of the lessons in this chapter on it! This lesson is an overview of what needs to happen during a mail merge, as shown in Figure 8-1. If you become confused during one of the next lessons, come back here to see where and how the step you're on fits into the mail merge process.

Microsoft has done just about everything they can to make performing mail merges in Word user-friendly.

Word's Mail Merge task pane helps you through each step in the mail merge, and is very easy to understand, as shown in Figure 8-1.

Since you're going to be working on mail merges this entire chapter, you may want to take a look at Table 8-1 for the definitions of the mail merge terms. You will be seeing these terms frequently in the upcoming lessons, so it would be a good idea to become familiar with them.

Table 8-1. Mail Merge Definitions

Term	Definition
Starting Document (Main Document)	A document that contains the information that is the same for each merged document. The starting document contains the field names for the variable information, like the names and addresses that will be inserted.
Data Source or Address List	A file that contains the information to be inserted into the main document during a mail merge. For example, it has records containing the names and addresses of the people who will receive the letter.
Data Field	A field that stores a specific piece of information. For example, the field LastName would only contain people's last names.
Record	A record is an entire set of data fields that relate to a single thing or person. For example, a single record might include information in various fields about a person's first and last names, address, phone number, and date of birth.
Merge Field	A merge field is where you want to insert the information from a data source into a main document. Merge fields appear with chevrons (« ») around them. An example would be: Dear «FirstName».
Address Block	A group of merge fields that make up the address block in a mail merge document. Word can automatically insert all the appropriate address fields at once, so that you don't have to insert the five or six merge fields yourself.
Greeting Line	A group of merge fields that make up the greeting line of a mail merge document, such as "Dear Mr. McDonald." Word can automatically insert all the appropriate greeting text and fields at once, so that you don't have to insert the text and required merge fields yourself.
Header Row	Data source information is stored in a table. The first row of the table is the header row and contains the field names for the data source. For example, FirstName, LastName, Address.

QUICK REFERENCE

TO PERFORM A MAIL MERGE YOU NEED TWO FILES:

1. A STARTING DOCUMENT (OR MAIN DOCUMENT), WHICH CONTAINS THE TEXT THAT APPEARS IN ALL OF THE MERGED DOCUMENTS.

2. A DATA SOURCE FILE OR ADDRESS LIST, WHICH CONTAINS THE INFORMATION YOU WANT TO INSERT INTO THE MERGED DOCUMENTS.

Selecting the Document Type

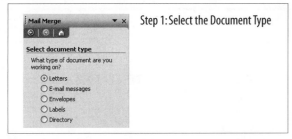

Step 1: Select the Document Type

Figure 8-2. The Mail Merge task pane assists you through each step in creating a mail merge.

All mail merges in Word require two files: a *main document* and a *data source*. The *main document* contains the text that is the same in all of the merged documents. This text that never changes in a mail merge is sometimes called *boilerplate text*.

The first step in the mail merge process is specifying which type of mail merge document you want to create—and this lesson will walk you through it. Let's get started!

1 Start a new blank document in Microsoft Word.

Let's send a letter to all of North Shore Travel's clients that have visited Canada in the past two years.

2 Select Tools → Letters and Mailings → Mail Merge from the menu.

The Mail Merge task pane appears, as shown in Figure 8-2. The Mail Merge walks you through the mail merge process and provides helpful instructions on performing a mail merge.

First, specify which type of mail merge document you want to create. You have five choices: Letters, E-mail messages, Envelopes, Labels, or Directory. See Table 8-2 for more information on each of these document types.

3 Ensure that the Letters option is selected in the Mail Merge task pane.

Letters are a common type of mail merge document and the default document type for a mail merge.

4 Click Next: Select starting document at the bottom of the Mail Merge task pane.

The next step of the Mail Merge wizard appears in the task pane.

That's all there is to specifying the document type for a mail merge. If it seems like this lesson is ending in midstream, you're right—move on to the next lesson to learn how to select the main document for your mail merge.

Table 8-2. Mail Merge Document Types

Document Type	Description
Letters	Each record is printed on a separate document.
E-mail messages	Each e-mail is personalized for each record.
Envelopes	Each record is printed on a single envelope.
Labels	Each record is printed on a single label. Use labels when you want to create mailing labels, nametags, or filing labels.
Directory	All the records in the data source are printed on a single merged catalog document. Any standard text you add to the main document is repeated for each set of data. Use directories as your main document when you want to create a membership directory, parts list, or similar document.

QUICK REFERENCE

TO SPECIFY A MAIL MERGE DOCUMENT TYPE:

1. SELECT TOOLS → LETTERS AND MAILINGS → MAIL MERGE FROM THE MENU.

2. SELECT THE DOCUMENT TYPE IN THE MAIL MERGE TASK PANE.

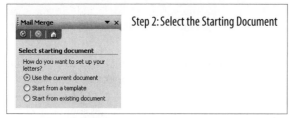

Figure 8-3. Word asks if you want to use the active document as the mail merge starting document, or if you want to create a new document from scratch.

Once you have determined the type of document you want to use, the next step in the mail merge process is specifying the starting document (or main document). You have several options:

- **Use the current document:** Use the document you currently have open on your screen as the starting document, as shown in Figure 8-3.

- You can use any of your Word documents as a starting document. For example, you could open a letter and delete specific information, such as the client's name and address. If the starting document is a new blank document, you could create the starting document from scratch as you would any other document.

- **Start from a template:** Create a starting document by using a ready-to-use mail merge template that you can edit and customize to meet your needs.

- **Start from existing document:** Open an existing mail merge document and make changes to the content and recipients as needed.

For this exercise, we will open an existing document and use it as the starting document.

1 Select the Start from existing document **option from the Mail Merge task pane and click the** Open button **on the Standard toolbar.**

The Open dialog box appears.

Navigate to the file you want to use as your starting document.

2 Navigate to your Practice folder and open Lesson 8. **Save the file as** Mail Merge Letter.

You want to send this letter to all of North Shore Travel's clients that have visited Canada in the past two years.

Notice that the "Use the current document" option is now selected in the Mail Merge task pane. You're ready to go on to the next step.

3 Click Next: Select recipients **in the Mail Merge task pane.**

So much for Step 2 of the mail merge process. Move on to the next lesson and we'll start Step 3.

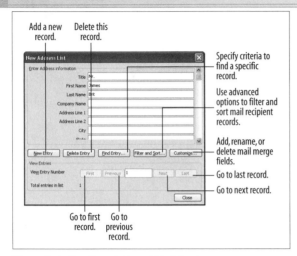

Add a new record. · Delete this record. · Specify criteria to find a specific record. · Use advanced options to filter and sort mail recipient records. · Add, rename, or delete mail merge fields. · Go to last record. · Go to next record. · Go to first record. · Go to previous record.

Figure 8-4. The New Address List dialog box.

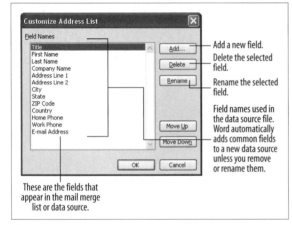

Add a new field. · Delete the selected field. · Rename the selected field. · Field names used in the data source file. Word automatically adds common fields to a new data source unless you remove or rename them. · These are the fields that appear in the mail merge list or data source.

Figure 8-5. The Customize Address List dialog box.

You probably know by now that when you perform a mail merge, you are really just combining two separate files: a document and a data source. If you've gotten this far, you've already established the contents of the document. Now you need to establish the data source and its contents, or the "recipients" of the mail merge document.

You have several options for selecting the recipients of a mail merge. You can:

- **Use an existing list:** If you've already created and saved a data source file for another mail merge, you can use that. You can also use a list saved in a Microsoft Access database, Excel worksheet, or a comma-delimited text file. Once you've specified the data file you want to use, you

select the records you want to include in the mail merge and you're ready to begin Step 4: write your letter.

- **Select from Outlook contacts:** If you use Microsoft Outlook, you can select the names and addresses from your Contacts List, and use them as the data source for your mail merge. When you select this option, you can select which records you want to include in the mail merge and go on to Step 4: write your letter.

- **Type a new list:** If the other two options don't apply, you can create a new data source list in Word. There are two steps in this process. The first step is deciding what information you want to include in each record by creating *field names* for each piece of information. For example, a field called LastName would be used to store last names, and a field called Address would store addresses.

Once you've entered the field names, you're ready for the next step: entering the record information, such as name and address. This is covered in the next lesson.

For this exercise, complete the first step in typing a new list, and decide the information to include in the mail merge by creating field names.

1 Click the Type a new list **option, and click** Create **in the Mail Merge task pane.**

The New Address List dialog box appears, as shown in Figure 8-4. The New Address List dialog box already has several common field names, such as First Name, Last Name, and Address. You can create your own field names as well.

Click the Customize button to add, edit, or change a field name.

2 Click the Customize **button.**

The Customize Address List dialog box appears, as shown in Figure 8-5. Here you can add your own fields to the list, edit a field name, or delete a field.

3 In the Field Names list, select Company Name, click Delete, and click Yes to confirm the deletion.

The Company Name field is removed from the list and will not be used in the data source. Now remove the other fields you don't need.

4 Repeat Step 3 to remove the following field names: Address Line 2, Country, Home Phone, Work Phone, and E-mail Address.

Now that you have removed all the unnecessary fields, try adding a field of your own.

5 Click the Add button, type Travel Date, then click OK.

The field "Travel Date" is added to the Field Names list. You're done creating the Field Names list, so you can close the Customize Address List dialog box.

6 Click OK.

Now that you've customized the data source or address list, it's time to enter the individual records. We'll cover that topic in the next lesson.

QUICK REFERENCE

TO SELECT THE RECIPIENTS OF A MAIL MERGE:

SELECT FROM ONE OF THE FOLLOWING OPTIONS IN THE MAIL MERGE TASK PANE:

- USE AN EXISTING LIST
- SELECT FROM OUTLOOK CONTACTS
- TYPE A NEW LIST

...THEN CONTINUE BY FOLLOWING THE STEPS LISTED IN THE MAIL MERGE TASK PANE.

TO CREATE FIELD NAMES FOR A NEW LIST:

1. IN THE MAIL MERGE TASK PANE, SELECT TYPE A NEW LIST AND CLICK CREATE.

2. CLICK CUSTOMIZE TO ADD, DELETE, AND/OR EDIT THE DEFAULT FIELDS.

3. SELECT A FIELD IN THE FIELD NAME LIST AND CLICK DELETE TO DELETE A FIELD.

4. CLICK ADD AND ENTER THE NEW FIELD. REPEAT AS NECESSARY, UNTIL YOU HAVE ENTERED ALL THE FIELDS YOU NEED IN THE FIELD NAME LIST.

Adding Records to the Data Source

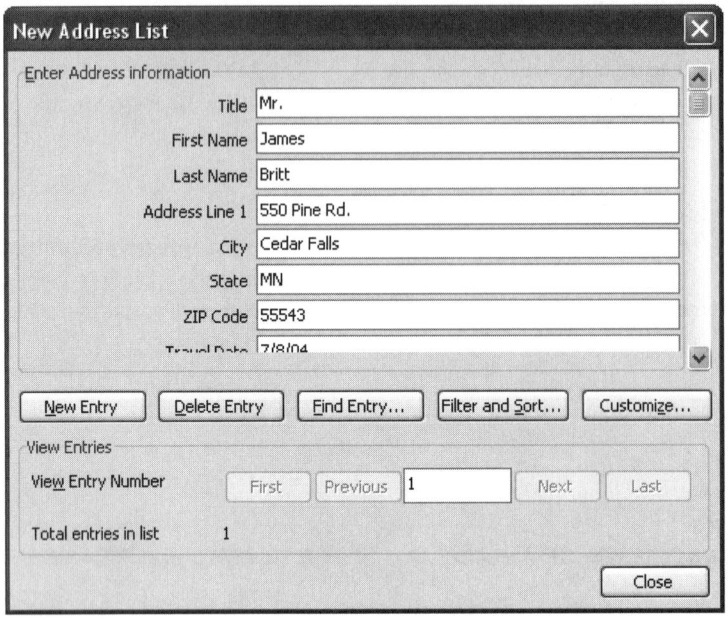

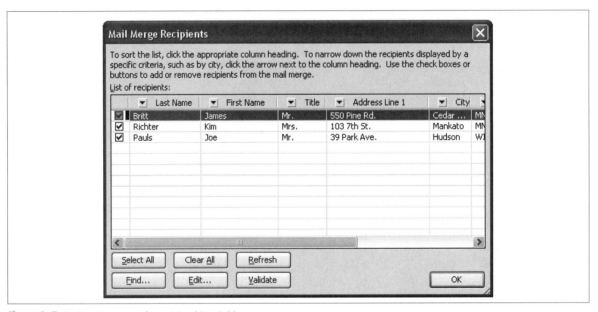

Figure 8-6. The New Address List dialog box.

Figure 8-7. Data source records contained in a table.

After creating the fields, you must enter the information, or records, into the data source. The information for each person you are sending a mail merge letter to is stored in a *record*. The Data Form dialog box makes it easy to add, edit, and delete records from the data source file.

Before starting this lesson, the New Address List dialog box (shown in Figure 8-6) should still be open from the previous lesson so you can add records to the data source.

1 Make sure the insertion point is in the Title field and type `Mr.`, then press `Tab`.

Press the `Tab` key to move to the next field, and `Shift` + `Tab` to move to the previous field.

The text "Mr." appears in the Title field and the insertion point moves to the next field, First Name.

2 Type `James` in the First Name field and press `Tab`.

Go ahead and add the rest of the record.

3 Finish entering the following information in the record:

Remember to press Tab after each entry to move to the next field.

Add a few more records to the data source.

Title	First Name	Last Name	Address Line 1	City	State	Zip Code	Travel Date
Mr.	James	Britt	550 Pine Rd.	Cedar Falls	MN	55543	7/8/04
Mrs.	Kim	Richter	103 7th St.	Mankato	MN	56001	4/5/04
Mr.	Joe	Pauls	39 Parl Ave.	Hudson	WI	55318	6/9/04

4 Click the New Entry button and enter the next record. When you are finished entering the first record, click the New Entry button to add the next record.

When you're working with a database, you don't have to save your work. The information is automatically saved for you.

5 Click Close after you've completed entering the records.

The Save Address List dialog box appears. You must give your data source a name and save it.

6 Type `Mail Merge Letter Data` in the File name box and click Save.

⸱ NOTE ⸱ *If you use an existing data source file or Outlook contacts for your data source, you will also use the Mail Merge Recipients dialog box to sort and deselect records from the mail merge.*

7 Click the Last Name column heading to sort the list by Last Name.

You can also include or exclude recipients from a mail merge by checking or unchecking the box next to their names.

8 Uncheck the box next to the Joe Pauls recipient.

Although Joe Pauls still appears in the address list, he no longer will be included in the mail merge.

9 Click OK.

The Mail Merge Recipients dialog box closes.

10 Click Next: Write your letter in the Mail Merge task pane.

QUICK REFERENCE

TO ADD RECORDS TO THE DATA SOURCE WITH THE DATA FORM:

1. IN THE MAIL MERGE TASK PANE, SELECT TYPE A NEW LIST AND CLICK CREATE.

   PRESS TAB TO MOVE TO THE NEXT FIELD AND SHIFT + TAB TO MOVE TO THE PREVIOUS FIELD.

   CLICK NEW ENTRY TO ADD A NEW RECORD.

   CLICK DELETE ENTRY TO DELETE A RECORD.

2. CLICK CLOSE WHEN YOU'RE FINISHED ENTERING AND/OR MODIFYING RECORDS.

3. CLICK THE COLUMN HEADING YOU WANT TO SORT THE ADDRESS LIST BY (OPTIONAL).

4. CHECK OR UNCHECK THE CHECK BOXES TO THE LEFT OF RECIPIENTS TO ADD OR REMOVE A RECIPIENT FROM THE MAIL MERGE (OPTIONAL).

5. CLICK OK.

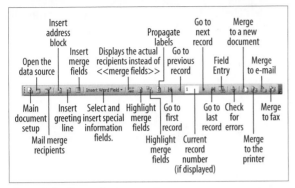

Figure 8-8. The Mail Merge toolbar.

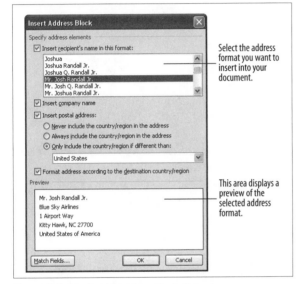

Figure 8-9. The Insert Address Block dialog box.

Figure 8-10. The Insert Merge Field dialog box.

Okay! The mail merge document and the data source are ready to go. Now you have to specify where you want the information from the data source to appear in the document. You do this by inserting *merge fields*.

In this lesson we will cover how to specify which fields from the data source you want to include, and make changes to your mail merge letter.

1 In the mail merge document, place the insertion point at the end of the May 1, 2004 date line and press Enter twice.

This is where you will place the address block.

2 Click the Address block link in the Mail Merge task pane.

The Insert Address Block dialog box appears, as shown in Figure 8-9. Here you can select which elements you want to include in the address block and how the address block is formatted.

⁑ NOTE ⁑ *You can also use the buttons on the Mail Merge toolbar (see Figure 8-8) to insert fields into the document.*

3 Select several of the address formats from the list and see how they appear in the preview area at the bottom of the dialog box. When you're finished, select the Mr. Josh Randell Jr. format and click OK.

The address block field is inserted into the document. You may have noticed that chevrons (« ») surround the address block text. The chevrons indicate that the text is a merge field.

4 Press Enter twice.

Next, we need to insert a greeting…

5 Click the Greeting line link in the Mail Merge task pane.

The Greeting Line dialog box appears, where you can specify the type of greeting to insert. For this lesson, we will accept the default settings.

6 Click OK to accept and insert the default greeting option.

Word inserts a greeting line into the document.

Only one more merge field to go. Give your letter a more personal touch by adding the Travel Date in the letter.

7 Place the insertion point immediately before the X in the first body paragraph, in the sentence Since you used North Shore Travel on X.

This is where we will insert the travel date.

8 Click the More Items option on the Mail Merge task pane.

The Insert Merge Field dialog box appears, similar to the one shown in Figure 8-10. You simply have to

select the field you want to add to your mail merge document, and click Insert.

9 Select Travel Date from the field list, click Insert, and click Close.

The Travel Date field is inserted into the document.

10 Delete the X in the sentence and save your work.

11 Click Next: Preview your letters in the Mail Merge task pane.

QUICK REFERENCE

TO INSERT AN ADDRESS:

1. PLACE THE INSERTION POINT WHERE YOU WANT TO INSERT THE ADDRESS BLOCK.

2. CLICK ADDRESS BLOCK IN THE MAIL MERGE TASK PANE.

3. SPECIFY THE FORMAT AND ELEMENTS YOU WANT TO APPEAR IN THE ADDRESS BLOCK AND CLICK OK.

TO INSERT A GREETING LINE:

1. PLACE THE INSERTION POINT WHERE YOU WANT TO INSERT THE GREETING LINE.

2. CLICK GREETING LINE IN THE MAIL MERGE TASK PANE.

3. SPECIFY WHAT YOU WANT TO APPEAR IN THE GREETING LINE AND CLICK OK.

TO INSERT MERGE FIELDS INTO THE DOCUMENT:

1. PLACE THE INSERTION POINT WHERE YOU WANT TO INSERT A MERGE FIELD.

2. CLICK MORE ITEMS ON THE MAIL MERGE TASK PANE, SELECT THE FIELD YOU WANT TO INSERT, AND CLICK INSERT.

Previewing a Mail Merge

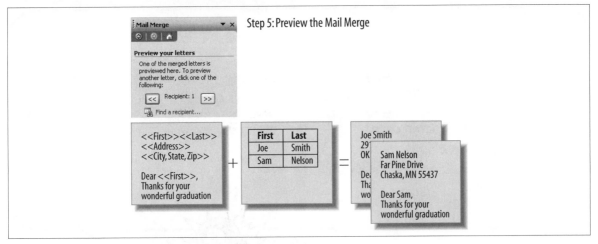

Figure 8-11. An example of how the record is converted into the letter.

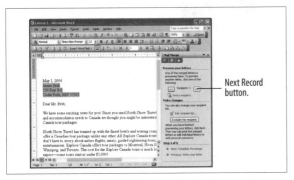

Figure 8-12. A preview of the merged main document.

Sometimes it is helpful to see what the data will look like once it has been inserted into a document, instead of only viewing the obscure merge field names. Figure 8-11 shows an example of how a record is merged into a letter.

Notice that the main document already shows a preview of the first record.

1 Click the >> Next Record button in the Mail Merge task pane, as shown in Figure 8-12, to display the next record.

The next record, Kim Richter, is displayed.

Notice that the recipient number skips from one to three, because you excluded the second record in the data source from the mail merge.

You can use the << >> buttons to scroll through and preview all the recipients or records in your data source.

If you see a recipient who you don't want to include in the mail merge, simply click the "Exclude this recipient" button in the task pane.

Likewise, if the list is missing a recipient, click the "Edit recipient list" option in the task pane, and the Mail Merge Recipients dialog box appears.

In a way, this is the point of no return; this is the last time you can make changes to the mail merge before completing it. So, make sure you preview the records, and make sure the main document includes all the fields you need.

2 Click Next: Complete the merge in the Mail Merge task pane.

The next lesson covers what you've been waiting for—performing an actual mail merge.

QUICK REFERENCE

TO VIEW MERGED DATA IN THE MAIN DOCUMENT'S MERGE FIELDS:

• CLICK THE RECORD BUTTONS IN THE MAIL MERGE TASK PANE TO PREVIEW THE RECORDS.

TO EDIT THE RECIPIENT LIST:

• CLICK THE EXCLUDE RECIPIENT BUTTON IN THE MAIL MERGE TASK PANE.

OR...

CLICK THE EDIT RECIPIENT LIST OPTION IN THE MAIL MERGE TASK PANE AND SELECT THE CHECK BOX OF THE RECORD YOU WISH TO ADD TO THE LIST.

Completing the Merge

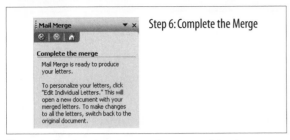

Step 6: Complete the Merge

Figure 8-13. The Merge to New Document dialog box.

Figure 8-14. The new, merged document.

You've made it! After all your sweat and toil, this is the lesson where you finally get to merge the information you entered from a data source into the main document. For all the work that goes into preparing a mail merge, performing the actual mail merge takes only a second.

Depending on the type of main document you chose in the first step, the final step—completing the merge—will offer different options. Since we chose to create a letter mail merge, the final pane of the Mail Merge task pane offers two options:

- **Print:** You can print out a merged main document for every record in the recipient list.

- **Edit individual letters:** Word creates a merged main document for every record in the recipient list so you can edit the letter even more.

For this lesson, we'll edit individual letters.

1 Click the Edit individual letters option in the Mail Merge task pane.

The Merge to New Document dialog box appears, as shown in Figure 8-13.

You can tell Word to merge all the selected records in your data source, to merge only the current record, or to merge the record numbers that you specify. For example, you could merge only records 5 to 10.

2 Select All and click OK.

Word merges the main document "Mail Merge Letter" and the information from the first record of the data source "Mail Merge Letter Data" into a new document called "Letters1," as shown in Figure 8-14.

The new merged document contains two letters—one letter for each recipient—that are separated with a page break.

3 Move to the next page of the document to view the second letter.

Notice that this letter uses data from the second record in the data source. If you want, go ahead and print the merged letter.

Let's save the merged document.

4 Select File → Save As from the menu.

The Save As dialog box appears.

5 In the File name box, type Merged Letter and click Save.

NOTE **You can edit the merged letters if you want.**

Congratulations! You've performed your first mail merge—a task many people consider to be the most difficult procedure in word processing.

QUICK REFERENCE

TO MERGE A DOCUMENT:

• CLICK ON THE OPTION IN THE MAIL MERGE TASK
  PANE THAT IS MOST SUITABLE FOR THE PURPOSES
  OF YOUR MAIL MERGE.

Creating and Working with Labels

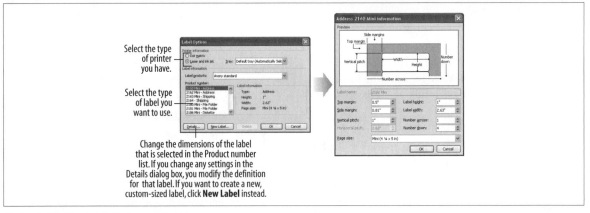

Figure 8-15. The Label Options dialog box.

Figure 8-16. The merged label document.

So far we've been using the mail merge feature to create formal letters, but you can also use it to create professional-looking mail labels or envelopes. Word can print on a variety of brand-name mailing labels—just make sure you know the product label (such as Avery 5150).

1 If you don't have the Mail Merge Letter document open, find and open Lesson 8B, and save it as Mailing Labels.

≥ NOTE ≥ *If a dialog box appears asking to run an SQL command when you open Lesson 8B, click Yes.*

2 If necessary, select Tools → Letters and Mailings → Mail Merge from the menu to display the Mail Merge task pane.

First of all, we need to change the type of mail merge document to labels—we have to start from the beginning of the mail merge process in order to do this.

3 If necessary, click Previous at the bottom of the Mail Merge task pane until you reach Step 1: Select document type.

Next, we have to tell Word that we want to use labels as the main mail merge document.

4 Select the Labels option. Click Next: Starting document in the Mail Merge task pane.

Now we need to set up the mailing labels.

5 Select the Change document layout option and click Label options.

The Label Options dialog box appears, as shown in Figure 8-15. Here you need to tell Word the exact type of label you are using. The default label, Avery standard, appears in the "Label Product" box. Select the product number for the label.

6 In the Product number box, scroll to and click 5160 – Address, then click OK.

A dialog box informs you that in order to change document types, Word must delete the contents of the current document.

7 Click OK. Click Next: Select recipients in the Mail Merge task pane.

Word deletes the contents of the original mail merge document and changes the mail merge document type to mailing labels.

Now select the data source.

8 Click the Use an existing list option. Click Next: Arrange your labels.

⋮ NOTE ⋮ *If the Select Data Source dialog box appears, select Mail Merge Letter Data and click Open. Make changes in the Mail Merge Recipients dialog box if necessary, and click OK.*

9 Ensure that the insertion point appears in the first mailing label and click the Address block link in the Mail Merge task pane.

The Insert Address Block dialog box appears. Here you can select which elements you want to include in the address block and how the address block is formatted. We will use the default address block format for this lesson.

10 Click OK to insert the selected address block.

Word inserts an address block in the first label. You can copy the layout of the first label by clicking the "Update all labels" button.

11 Click the Update all labels button on the Mail Merge task pane.

Word copies the address block field from the first label to the remaining labels on the page.

12 Click Next: Preview your labels on the Mail Merge task pane.

The records from the data source appear as labels on the screen.

13 Click Next: Complete the merge, and click the Edit individual labels link on the Mail Merge task pane. Click All, and click OK.

⋮ NOTE ⋮ *If you have one less record on your sheet, or if the labels are in a different order from Figure 8-16, that's okay.*

14 Close the merged document and the source document without saving them.

Using IF...THEN...ELSE Fields

Figure 8-17. The Insert Word Field: IF dialog box.

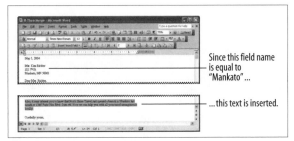

Figure 8-18. You can use the If...Then...Else Word field in a mail merge.

In addition to merge fields, you can insert *fields* into the main document to customize your mail merge documents even more. In this lesson, you'll learn how to insert one of the most common fields: the IF...THEN...ELSE field. An IF...THEN...ELSE field compares the information in the data source to a specific value. It then inserts one piece of text if the comparison is true, and another piece of text if the comparison is false.

You'll probably want to skip this lesson unless you're really into mail merges; most people will never really need to use it.

1 Find and open Lesson 8B, and save it as If-Then Merge.

If a dialog box appears asking to run an SQL command when you open Lesson 8B, click Yes.

2 Select Tools → Letters and Mailings → Mail Merge from the menu.

Now let's try inserting an If...Then...Else field in this document.

3 Place the insertion point on the blank line immediately below the last body paragraph in the letter and press Enter.

This is where you want to insert the If...Then...Else... field.

4 Click the Insert Word Field button on the Mail Merge toolbar and select the If...Then...Else... option from the list.

The Insert Word Field: IF dialog box appears, as shown in Figure 8-17. This is where Word will enter the text that meets the specific criteria.

5 Select City in the Field Name box, verify that the Comparison text box says Equal to, and type Mankato in the Compare to box.

Next, you need to type the text that will be inserted if a record's city equals Mankato.

6 In the "Insert this text" box, type:

Also, it may interest you to know that North Shore Travel just opened a branch in Mankato last month at 1345 Park Glen Blvd. Suite #4. Now we can help you with all your travel arrangements locally.

If the specified condition isn't met, you can insert a different block of text by typing it in the "Otherwise insert this text" box. If you leave the "Otherwise insert this text" box blank, Word won't insert anything when the specified condition isn't met.

7 In the "Otherwise insert this text" box, type Thank you for your business.

This message will appear on records that are not from Mankato.

8 Click OK and press Enter to add a blank paragraph beneath the Word field.

Word inserts the If...Then...Else field. Now let's see how Word inserts the conditional text if a client is from Mankato.

9 Click the View Merged Data button on the Mail Merge toolbar so that it is shaded. Click the Next Record button on the Mail Merge toolbar several times to view the different records in the data source.

Notice how the message changes if the client is from the city of Mankoto, as shown in Figure 8-18.

⦂ NOTE ⦂ *To preview all the mail merge fields, click Next at the bottom of the Mail Merge task pane until you get to Step 5: Preview your letters.*

10 Close the document without saving changes

Table 8-3 gives a brief description of some other Word Fields you might use when performing a mail merge.

Table 8-3. Commonly Used Word Field Descriptions

Term	Definition
Ask...	Prompts for information from the user as Word merges each data record with the main document. The response is printed in the specific form letter.
If...Then...Else...	Prints information only if a specified condition is met.
Merge Record #	Prints the number of the merged data record in the merged document.
Merge Sequence #	Counts the number of data records that were successfully merged with the main document.
Next Record	Instructs Word to merge the next data record into the current merged document, rather than starting a new merged document. Often used with labels and catalogs.
Next Record If...	Compares two expressions. If the comparison is true, Word merges the next data record into the current merge document.

QUICK REFERENCE

- FIELDS ARE USED AS PLACEHOLDERS FOR DATA THAT MIGHT CHANGE IN A DOCUMENT OR MAIL MERGE.

TO INSERT A FIELD:

- SELECT THE FIELD FROM THE INSERT WORD FIELD BUTTON ON THE MAIL MERGE TOOLBAR.

TO INSERT AN IF... THEN...ELSE FIELD:

1. CLICK THE INSERT WORD FIELD BUTTON ON THE MAIL MERGE TOOLBAR AND SELECT THE IF...THEN...ELSE... OPTION.

2. SELECT THE FIELD NAME YOU WANT TO USE AND ENTER THE LOGICAL TEST USING THE COMPARISON AND COMPARE TO LISTS.

3. ENTER THE TEXT IF THE LOGICAL TEST IS TRUE IN THE FIRST TEXT BOX AND THE TEXT IF THE LOGICAL TEXT IS FALSE IN THE SECOND TEXT BOX.

4. CLICK OK.

Figure 8-19. A Microsoft Access database in the Select Data Source dialog box.

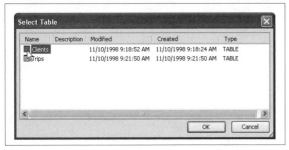

Figure 8-20. The Select Table dialog box.

If you have a database that contains the information that you want to use for a mail merge document, you don't have to retype all that existing information into a new data source. Word can use many different types of databases as data sources for a mail merge main document, such as Microsoft Access, dBase, FoxPro, Excel, and text file databases as data sources. Using a database created with an external program may sound complicated, but it's actually almost as easy as working with the data sources you've already created.

1 If you don't have the Mail Merge Letter document open, find and open Lesson 8B.

If the Mail Merge task pane isn't already displayed, you will have to summon it by following the next step.

2 Select Tools → Letters and Mailings → Mail Merge from the menu to display the Mail Merge task pane.

First of all, we need to select the recipients—we have to go to Step 3 of the mail merge process in order to do this.

3 If necessary, navigate through the Mail Merge task pane until you reach Step 3: Select recipients.

Now you need to open the existing data source, a Microsoft Access database.

4 In the Mail Merge task pane, select the Use an existing list option and click Select a different list.

The Select Data Source dialog box appears.

5 Click the Files of type list arrow, and then select Access Databases.

Only Microsoft Access database files now appear in the Select Data Source dialog box.

6 Navigate to your Practice folder, find and select the Canada tourists file, and click Open, as shown in Figure 8-19.

The Select Table dialog box appears that shows the names of the tables in the database, as shown in Figure 8-20.

Information is stored in tables within a database. You need to specify what table contains the data you want to use. If you're not sure of which table contains the information you want, speak to someone who is knowledgeable about the database.

7 Since the table you want, Clients, is selected, you can click OK.

A dialog box appears, asking if you want to replace an invalid field.

8 Click OK. Click OK again to close the Mail Merge Recipients dialog box.

You may notice that the fields in the document have already changed.

Move on for a closer look at the changed mail merge.

9 Click Next in the Mail Merge task pane until you reach Step 6: Complete the merge.

The Microsoft Access Canada tourists database is attached to the main document.

10 Click the Edit individual letters link in the Mail Merge task pane.

The Merge to New Document dialog box appears.

11 Ensure that All is selected and click OK.

Word merges the main document and the Microsoft Access database information into a new document.

12 Close the merged document and the source document without saving them.

That's all there is to using an existing database as a data source for a mail merge—it's not much different from working with a data source created in Word. Word can import information from the types of files (in Table 8-4), as long as you have the right conversion files installed:

Table 8-4. Types of Data Sources

Data File	Notes

Spreadsheet Files
   Microsoft Excel
   Lotus 1-2-3
	You will need to specify the cell range or the entire file.

Database Files
   dBase
   Fox Pro
   Microsoft Access
   Microsoft Outlook
	If the database contains more than one table, you will have to select the table you want to use.

Word Processing Files
   Microsoft Word
   WordPerfect
	Records must be stored in a table or in a tab-delimited list.

Text Files	Must be a tab or comma delimited text file.

QUICK REFERENCE

TO USE AN EXISTING DATA SOURCE:

1. DISPLAY THE MAIL MERGE TASK PANE BY SELECTING TOOLS → LETTERS AND MAILINGS → MAIL MERGE FROM THE MENU.

2. GO TO STEP 3: SELECT RECIPIENTS IN THE MAIL MERGE TASK PANE.

3. IN THE MAIL MERGE TASK PANE, CLICK THE USE AN EXISTING LIST OPTION AND CLICK SELECT A DIFFERENT LIST.

4. IN THE OPEN DATA SOURCE DIALOG BOX, CLICK THE FILES OF TYPE LIST ARROW, AND SELECT THE DATABASE YOU WANT TO USE. CLICK OK.

5. CLICK NEXT AT THE BOTTOM OF THE MAIL MERGE TASK PANE UNTIL YOU REACH STEP 6: COMPLETE THE MERGE, AND CHOOSE THE OPTION THAT IS MOST APPROPRIATE FOR YOUR NEEDS.

Chapter Eight Review

Lesson Summary

An Overview of the Mail Merge Process

Performing a Mail Merge is a six step process:

Step 1: Select the Document Type: Select the type of document you want to create. You can create letters, e-mails, envelopes, labels, and directories.

Step 2: Select a Starting Document: The starting document (or main document) contains the text that is the same in all of the merged documents. You can create a new main document or use any existing document as the main document.

Step 3: Select the Recipients: All mail merges require two files: the main document and the data source. The data source contains the information you want to appear on the main document. You can create a new data source, use an existing data source, or use a database as the data source.

Step 4: Write Your Letter: Write and/or edit the starting document and specify where you want to insert the information from your data source into your starting document.

Step 5: Preview Your Letters: Preview how your document will appear when combined with the information in the data source.

Step 6: Complete the Merge: Merge the data from the data source into the merge fields in the starting document, creating a unique document for each record in the data source.

Step 1: Select the Document Type

Select Tools → Letters and Mailings → Mail Merge from the menu. Mail merges can be created in five different document types: Letters, E-mail messages, Envelopes, Labels, and Directories. Select the type that is best suited for your needs.

Step 2: Select a Starting Document

To Select the Starting Document: Specify the starting document you want to use in your mail merge. Depending on your selection, you can do one of several things for the starting document:

- **Use the current document:** You will need to either create a new, blank document from scratch or open an existing document and edit it as needed.

- **Start from a template:** You will need to specify the template you want to use for your main document and edit it as needed.

- **Start from an existing document:** You will need to open the existing mail merge document and edit it as needed.

Step 3: Select the Recipients

To Select the Recipients of a Mail Merge: Select from one of the following options in the Mail Merge task pane:

- Use an existing list
- Select from Outlook contacts
- Type a new list

…then continue by following the steps listed in the Mail Merge task pane.

To Create Field Names for a New List: In the Mail Merge task pane, select Type a new list and click Create. Click Customize to add, delete, and/or edit the default fields. Select a field in the Field Name list and click Delete to delete a field. Click Add and enter the new field. Repeat as necessary, until you have entered all the fields you need in the Field Name list.

To Add Records to the Data Source with the Data Form: In the Mail Merge task pane, select Type a new list and click Create. (Press Tab to move to the next field and Shift + Tab to move to the previous field. Click New Entry to add a new record. Click Delete Entry to delete a record.) Click Close when you're finished entering and/or modifying records. Click the column heading you want to sort the address list by (optional). Check or uncheck the check boxes to the left of recipients to add or remove a recipient from the mail merge (optional). Click OK.

Step 4: Write Your Letter

To Insert an Address: Place the insertion point where you want to insert the address block. Click Address block in the Mail Merge task pane. Specify the format and elements you want to appear in the address block and click OK.

To Insert a Greeting Line: Place the insertion point where you want to insert the greeting line. Click Greeting line in the Mail Merge task pane. Specify what you want to appear in the greeting line and click OK.

To Insert Merge Fields into the Document: Place the insertion point where you want to insert a merge field. Click More items in the Mail Merge task pane, select the field you want to insert, and click Insert.

Step 5: Preview Your Document

To View Merged Data in the Main Document's Merge Fields: Click the buttons to preview the records.

To Edit the Recipient List: Click the Exclude Recipient button in the Mail Merge task pane. Or, click the Edit recipient list option in the Mail Merge task pane and select the check box of the record you wish to add to the list.

Step 6: Complete the Merge

To Merge a Document: Click on the option in the Mail Merge task pane that is most suitable for the purposes of your mail merge.

You can merge information directly to the printer or to a new document.

Printer: Click Printer in the Mail Merge task pane.

Edit individual document: Click the Edit individual document link in the Mail Merge task pane.

Creating and Working with Labels

To Create Mailing Labels from a Mail Merge: Display the Mail Merge task pane by selecting Tools → Letters and Mailings → Mail Merge Wizard from the menu. Click Labels in the Mail Merge task pane and click Next: Starting document. Select the type of label you want to use and click OK. Click Next: Select recipients and locate the source of your records. Click Next: Arrange your labels and enter the text and/or merge fields you want to appear in your labels. Usually you will want to click the Address Block option in the Mail Merge task pane. Click the Update all labels button to copy the first label to the

remaining labels. Click Next: Preview your labels and preview the labels to make sure they are correct. Click Next: Complete the merge. Finally, either print the labels, or edit them individually.

Using IF... THEN... ELSE Fields

To Insert a Field: Select the field from the Insert Word Field button on the Mail Merge toolbar. Fields are used as placeholders for data that might change in a document or mail merge.

An IF field prints information only if a specified condition is met. For example, adding a company line if a record contains a company field, and skipping the company line if a record does not contain a company field.

To Insert an IF... THEN...ELSE Field: Click the Insert Word Field button on the Mail Merge toolbar and select the If...Then...Else... option. Select the Field name you want to use and enter the logical test using the Comparison and Compare to lists. Enter the text if the logical test is true in the first text box and the text if the logical text is false in the second text box and click OK.

Using an Existing Data Source

You can use Word documents, Microsoft Access databases, Excel worksheets, and other database files as the mail merge data source.

To Use an Existing Data Source in a Mail Merge: Display the Mail Merge task pane by selecting Tools → Letters and Mailings → Mail Merge from the menu. Go to Step 3: Select recipients in the Mail Merge task pane. In the Mail Merge task pane, click the Use an existing list option and click Select a different list. In the Open Data Source dialog box, click the Files of type list arrow, and select the type of database you want to use. Click OK. Click Next at the bottom of the Mail Merge task pane until you reach Step 6: Complete the merge, and choose the option that is most appropriate for your needs.

If the data source is a relational database, you will need to select the table that contains the data you want to use.

Quiz

1. To perform a mail merge you need to either create or open these two files:

   A. A starting document and a data source.

   B. A starting document and a merge document.

   C. A mail merge form and a merge document.

   D. A data source and a merge field source.

2. You can use an existing document as a starting document for mail merge. (True or False?)

3. What file contains the information, or records, to be inserted in a mail merge?

   A. The main document.

   B. The data source.

   C. The merge document.

   D. The data field.

4. You can open the Mail Merge task pane by:

   A. Selecting Table → Mail Merge Helper from the menu.

   B. Clicking the Mail Merge Helper button on the Standard toolbar.

   C. Selecting Tools → Letters and Mailings → Mail Merge from the menu.

   D. Clicking the Mail Merge Helper button on the Mail Merge toolbar.

5. Which of the following is NOT a type of document that you can create using mail merge?

   A. Form letters.

   B. Envelopes.

   C. Web pages.

   D. Directories.

6. You can specify which records you want to include in a mail merge by clicking the Query Options button in the Mail Merge task pane. (True or False?)

7. Word saves the records for a data source file in:

   A. A comma-delimited text format.

   B. A tab-delimited text format.

   C. A rich text file format.

   D. A table.

8. You want to add several more addresses to a data source. To do this:

   A. Click the Add Record button on the Mail Merge toolbar.

   B. Select Tools → Letters and Mailings → Edit Data Source from the menu.

   C. Select Tools → Mail Merge → Add Records from the menu.

   D. Open the data source document and add the record.

9. Instead of confusing merge fields, you want to see the actual records that will appear in the main document. How can you do this?

   A. You can't.

   B. Select Tools → Mail Merge from the menu and click View Records.

   C. Select Tools → Mail Merge → View Records from the menu.

   D. Click the View Merged Data button on the Mail Merge toolbar.

10. When you perform a mail merge, you can directly send the results to: (Select all that apply.)

    A. A printer.

    B. A Microsoft Access database.

    C. A Microsoft Excel spreadsheet.

    D. A new document.

11. Which of the following files can you use as the data source for a mail merge? (Select all that apply.)

    A. A Microsoft Access database.

    B. A Microsoft Excel spreadsheet.

    C. A Microsoft Word document.

    D. A comma-delimited text file.

Homework

1. Open the document "Homework 8" and save it as "Cover Letter."

2. Select Tools → Letters and Mailings → Mail Merge from the menu.

3. Select Letters and click Next: Starting document.

4. Select "Use the current document" and click Next: Select recipients.

5. Select "Type a new list" and click the Create link.

6. Click the Customize button to edit the data source so it includes the following fields: Title, Last Name, Company Name, Address Line 1, City, State, ZIP Code, Product.

Quiz Answers

1. A. You need a main document and a data source to perform a mail merge.

2. True. You can use any existing document as a starting document.

3. B. The data source contains the records used in a mail merge.

4. C. Open the Mail Merge task pane by selecting Tools → Letters and Mailings → Mail Merge from the menu.

5. C. You cannot create Web pages with a mail merge.

6. False. You cannot run a query when using a mail merge, although you can select which records you want to include in the mail merge after you have selected the data source.

7. D. Word saves the records for a data source file in a table.

8. D. Open the data source document and add the record. If you created your data source in Word, click the Edit Recipient List link in the "Select the recipients" step of the Mail Merge task pane.

9. D. Click the View Merged Data button on the Mail Merge toolbar to view the actual records that will be included in the mail merge.

10. A and D. You can send mail merge results to a printer or to a new document.

11. A, B, C, and D. You can use any of these files as the data source for a mail merge.

CHAPTER 9

DOCUMENT COLLABORATION

CHAPTER OBJECTIVES:

Adding revisions to a document, Lessons 9.1

Accepting and rejecting revisions, Lesson 9.2

Inserting comments, Lesson 9.3

Saving versions of a document, Lesson 9.4

Comparing documents, Lessons 9.5 and 9.6

Collaborating with document workspace, Lesson 9.7

Protecting and password-protecting a document, Lessons 9.8 and 9.9

CHAPTER TASK: REVISE A RESPONSE TO A COMPLAINT LETTER

Prerequisites

- **How to open and save a document.**
- **How to use menus, toolbars, and dialog boxes.**
- **How to select, edit, and delete text.**

Like it or not, it's likely that someday you will have to create a document with a team of individuals. For example, you might write a draft of a letter, have your manager review it, make changes to it, and return it to you. Then you go back to the document, make the changes, and then send the document to its final destination.

The folks at Microsoft realized that people often need to work together when creating documents, so they included a whole slew of features that enable several people to work together to create and update a document. Revisions, comments and versions are just a few of these features. Some of the updated and new features in Word 2003, such as comparing side by side and a more expansive document workspace, are huge assets in the collaboration process. And, if you decide you're tired of having other people work on your documents, you can always password-protect them so that only you have access to them—something else this chapter covers.

Whew! That's a lot of ground to cover! We'd better get started…

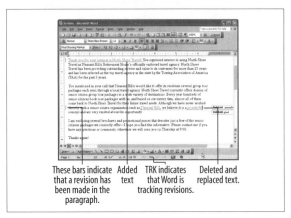

These bars indicate
that a revision has
been made in the
paragraph.
Added
text
TRK indicates
that Word is
tracking revisions.
Deleted and
replaced text.

Figure 9-1. Tracked and Highlighted changes in a document.

If you have a supervisor who makes changes to your document, and he uses Microsoft Word, you should seriously consider photocopying this lesson for him. Revising a document in Word works just like revising a document with a printed copy and a red pen; you can easily see the original text and any additions, deletions, or changes made to the document. Using Word to make revisions differs from the traditional method, in that when the revisions are made, you can review them and then decide if you want to accept or reject the revisions. That way, you don't have to manually retype all of the changes yourself.

1 Start Word, open the Lesson 9A document, and save it under the name Seniors.

2 Select Tools → Track Changes from the menu.

Another way to track changes is to double-click the TRK *indicator in the Word status bar, or press* Ctrl + Shift + E.

Now any changes, additions, or deletions you make to the document will be tracked and highlighted on the screen. Notice that the TRK indicator appears on the status bar, indicating that you are currently tracking revisions.

3 Place the insertion point at the beginning of the first body paragraph. Type Thank you for your interest in North Shore Travel!

Notice that the new text is colored and italicized or underlined, indicating that it has been added to the document.

4 Find and select the word yourselves in the last sentence of the second body paragraph. Press the Delete key to delete the selected text.

The word "yourselves" is deleted from the document, however Word marks the deletion by adding a balloon in the right margin.

5 Type Pleasant Hills.

The text appears with different formatting, indicating it has been inserted.

6 Select the word great in the last sentence of the second body paragraph, and replace it by typing wonderful.

The word "great" is deleted and appears in a balloon in the margin to mark the deletion. The word "wonderful" is added, appearing colored and italicized or underlined and your document looks like Figure 9-1.

You're done making revisions, so you can stop tracking your changes.

7 Select Tools → Track Changes from the menu.

Any changes, additions, or deletions you make to the document will no longer be tracked and highlighted on the screen. Notice that the TRK, the revision indicator, on the status bar no longer appears in black.

8 Replace the number 3 with the number 4 in the last sentence of the first body paragraph.

Notice that your changes are no longer being tracked and highlighted.

Now that you've revised your document, turn the page to learn how to accept or reject the changes you've made.

QUICK REFERENCE

TO TRACK REVISIONS:

1. SELECT TOOLS → TRACK CHANGES FROM THE MENU.

    OR...

    DOUBLE-CLICK THE TRK INDICATOR IN THE STATUS BAR.

    OR...

    PRESS CTRL + SHIFT + E.

2. EDIT THE DOCUMENT—YOUR REVISIONS WILL BE HIGHLIGHTED.

    USE THE SAME PROCEDURE TO STOP TRACKING REVISIONS.

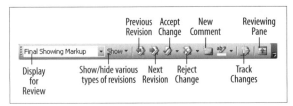

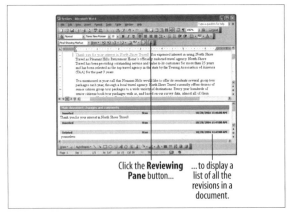

Figure 9-2. The Reviewing toolbar.

Figure 9-3. The Reviewing pane.

Once a document has been revised using Word's revisions feature, you can review the changes and decide if you want to accept the changes and make them part of the document, or reject the changes. Revising documents using Word's revision features can save a lot of time, because the changes are already typed in your document—you merely have to accept the changes to incorporate them into your document.

The Reviewing toolbar contains useful reviewing and group collaboration commands, as shown in Figure 9-2. The first command on the Reviewing toolbar that we'll look at is the Reviewing Pane button, which displays a complete list of text revisions in a document.

1 Click the 📷 Reviewing Pane button on the Reviewing toolbar.

The Reviewing Pane appears at the bottom of the screen and displays all the revisions in the document, as shown in Figure 9-3.

2 Click the Reviewing Pane button on the Reviewing toolbar once again to hide the Reviewing pane.

Word hides the Reviewing pane from view.

If you are working on a document with several users, you can hide and display revisions according to who reviewed the document.

3 Click the Show button on the Reviewing toolbar and select Reviewers.

Here you can select whose revisions you want displayed. Since you're the only reviewer who has made any changes to the current document, only your name (or the default user for your version of Microsoft Word) will appear in the list.

4 Click anywhere outside the Show menu to close the list without selecting any options.

Now let's decide if we want to accept or reject the revisions we have made to this document.

5 Press Ctrl + Home to go to the beginning of the document.

Now you can begin reviewing the changes that have been made to the document.

6 Click the 📎 Next button on the Reviewing toolbar.

Word selects the first change in the document, the inserted "Thank you for you interest in North Shore Travel!" sentence. Let's accept this change.

7 Click the 📝 Accept Change button on the Reviewing toolbar.

 Another way to accept or reject a revision is to right-click the revision and select the appropriate option from the shortcut menu.

Word accepts the change and removes the underlining and color from the inserted sentence. Now let's find the next document change.

8 Click the Next button on the Reviewing toolbar, and then click the Accept Change button.

Word finds and accepts the deleted "yourselves" text.

9 Click the Next button on the Reviewing toolbar, and then click the Accept Change button.

Word finds and accepts the inserted "Pleasant Hills" text. Now let's try rejecting a change that was made to the document.

10 Click the Next button on the Reviewing toolbar.

Word finds the deleted word "great." Reject this change and keep the original text.

11 Click the  Reject Change/Delete Comment button on the Reviewing toolbar.

Word rejects the deleted "great" text and restores the word, removing its color and strikethrough. Now reject the inserted "wonderful" text change.

12 Click the Next button on the Reviewing toolbar, then click the Reject Change/Delete Comment button.

Word rejects the "wonderful" text insertion and removes it from the document.

13 Save your work.

See how much time you can save using Word's revisions feature? Imagine how much longer it would have taken if you had to manually type all the previous changes instead of merely accepting them.

QUICK REFERENCE

TO ACCEPT OR REJECT REVISIONS:

1. SELECT TOOLS → TRACK CHANGES FROM THE MENU.

2. CLICK THE NEXT BUTTON TO MOVE THROUGH THE REVISIONS IN YOUR DOCUMENT.

3. CLICK EITHER THE ACCEPT CHANGE BUTTON OR THE REJECT CHANGE/DELETE COMMENT BUTTON ON THE REVIEWING TOOLBAR.

OR...

RIGHT-CLICK THE REVISION AND SELECT THE DESIRED ACTION FROM THE SHORTCUT MENU.

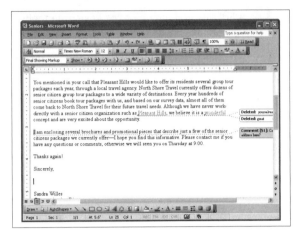

Figure 9-4. Comments appear in the margins of the document.

This lesson explains how to add comments to a document. Adding a comment to a document is like a sticking a Post-It note to it. You can use Word's comments feature to add suggestions, notes, or reminders to your documents. You can add a comment virtually anywhere in a document. Comments appear in the document in bold colors and are almost impossible to miss. Comments are easy to read, too—you simply position the pointer over the comment and a window appears, displaying the comment's text.

1 Move the insertion point to the very beginning of the third body paragraph (the one that begins with I am enclosing).

This is where you want to insert a comment.

2 Click the  Insert Comment button on the Reviewing toolbar.

> **TIP** Another way to insert a comment is to select Insert → Comment from the menu.

A Comment balloon appears in the right margin, as shown in Figure 9-4. This is where you can enter comments or notes about a document to yourself or to other users.

3 Type Can we add our web address here? in the comment balloon.

Word adds the comment at the insertion point. You can easily hide a document's comments and revisions if you find them distracting. Here's how:

4 Click the Show ▾ Show button on the Reviewing toolbar and select Comments.

Word hides all the comments in the document.

5 Click the Show button on the Reviewing toolbar and select Comments.

Word displays all the comments in the document.

You can easily make changes to a comment simply by typing in any comment balloon.

6 Click near the end of the text in the comment balloon and type It's www.northshoretravel.com.

You can also delete a comment when it is no longer needed.

7 Right-click the comment balloon and select the Delete Comment from the shortcut menu.

The selected comment is deleted.

8 Save your work.

QUICK REFERENCE

TO INSERT A COMMENT:

1. PLACE THE INSERTION POINT OR SELECT THE TEXT WHERE YOU WANT TO INSERT THE COMMENT.

2. CLICK THE INSERT COMMENT BUTTON ON THE REVIEWING TOOLBAR.

    OR...

    SELECT INSERT → COMMENT FROM THE MENU.

TO HIDE OR DISPLAY COMMENTS IN A DOCUMENT:

*   CLICK THE SHOW BUTTON ON THE REVIEWING TOOLBAR AND SELECT COMMENTS.

TO EDIT A COMMENT:

*   CLICK IN THE COMMENT BALLOON AND EDIT THE TEXT AS NEEDED.

TO DELETE A COMMENT:

*   RIGHT-CLICK THE COMMENT BALLOON AND SELECT DELETE FROM THE SHORTCUT MENU.

OR...

*   CLICK THE REJECT CHANGE/DELETE COMMENT BUTTON ON THE REVIEWING TOOLBAR.

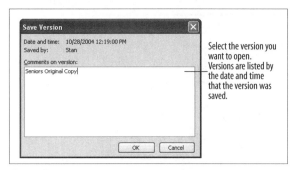

Figure 9-5. The Versions in Seniors dialog box.

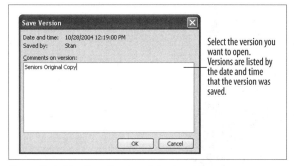

Figure 9-6. The Save Version dialog box.

If you make changes to an existing document but want to keep a copy of the original, unchanged document, you can use Word's Versions feature instead of saving several copies of the same document. You can save multiple versions of a document in a single document file, which is easier to manage and track than multiple document files. Using versions instead of several saved document files saves hard disk space as well.

1 If necessary, navigate to your Practice folder and open Lesson 9B. Save the file as Seniors.

2 Select File → Versions from the menu.

The Versions in Seniors dialog box appears, as shown in Figure 9-5. Here you can save several versions of a document in the same file.

3 Click Save Now.

The Save Version dialog box appears, as shown in Figure 9-6. Here you can add a description to help you identify each document version.

4 Type Seniors Original Copy, then click OK.

Both the Save Version and the Versions in Seniors dialog boxes close. The current document is saved in the *Seniors Original Copy* version. Any further changes you make to the document will be saved in a new version.

Now let's make some changes to the document and save them in a new version.

5 In the last body paragraph, move the insertion point immediately before the sentence beginning with Please contact me and type: You can also visit us on the Web at www.northshoretravel.com.

Next, add an address to the letter.

6 Press Ctrl + Home to move to the beginning of the document, then type the letter's address:
William Pratt
Pleasant Hills Retirement Home
455 Lake View Road
Two Harbors, MN 54039

7 Press Enter twice.

After adding the address, you can save a new version of the document.

8 Select File → Versions on the menu.

The Versions in Seniors dialog box appears. You need to give this new version a meaningful description.

9 Click Save Now, type Added Web Address, and click OK.

You can easily open and view a previously saved version of a document.

10 Select File → Versions from the menu.

The Versions in Seniors dialog box appears, with both versions listed in the Existing versions list.

11 Select the Seniors Original Copy version and click Open.

The earlier version of the document appears in a new, separate document window. Notice that the comment, date, and time appear in the title.

12 Compare the two versions of the document, and then close the Seniors Original Copy document.

The window closes and you are left with the newer version of the document open.

13 Click the Maximize button of the "Added Web Address" document window and then click the Save button.

QUICK REFERENCE

TO SAVE A DOCUMENT VERSION:

1. SELECT FILE → VERSIONS FROM THE MENU AND CLICK SAVE NOW.

2. ENTER A NAME FOR THE VERSION AND CLICK OK.

TO OPEN A VERSION:

1. SELECT FILE → VERSIONS FROM THE MENU.

2. SELECT THE VERSION YOU WANT TO OPEN AND CLICK OPEN.

Comparing and Merging Documents

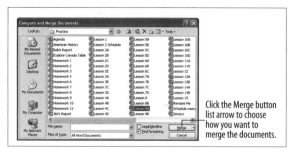

Figure 9-7. *The Compare and Merge Documents dialog box.*

Click the Merge button list arrow to choose how you want to merge the documents.

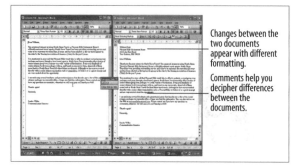

Changes between the two documents appear with different formatting.

Comments help you decipher differences between the documents.

Figure 9-8. *The new merged document.*

Comparing and merging documents lets you integrate the content from two documents into one document. For example, if you and a co-worker have made changes to the same document in separate files, you can merge them together and Word will highlight all the differences between the two documents for you, saving you time and increasing accuracy.

Here's how to merge and compare documents:

1 Select Tools → Compare and Merge Documents from the menu.

The Compare and Merge Documents dialog box appears, as shown in Figure 9-7. This is where you will select the document against which you will compare the open document.

For this lesson, we're going to compare and merge the open Seniors document to Lesson 9A.

Don't try to compare and merge documents that don't have similar content. The results will be very difficult to sort through.

2 Navigate to your Practice folder and then select Lesson 9A.

You can merge the documents three different ways:

- **Merge:** This option merges the results in the selected document. In this example, the Lesson 9A document would open and display all the differences between the documents.

- **Merge into current document:** This option merges the results in the open document. In this example, the Seniors document would display all the differences between the documents.

- **Merge into new document:** This option merges the results in a brand new document. This is a good option, because neither of the original documents are changed.

Let's merge the results into a new document.

3 Click the Merge button list arrow. Select Merge into new document from the list.

Word compares the two documents and the results appear in a new document, as shown in Figure 9-8. Notice the formatted text in the document, indicating changes.

Once the documents are merged, you can go through and accept or reject changes with the Reviewing toolbar. Since you already know how to do this, close the documents without saving changes.

4 Close the new document without saving changes.

The merged document closes but the Seniors document is still open on your screen.

QUICK REFERENCE

TO COMPARE AND MERGE DOCUMENTS:

1. OPEN ONE OF THE DOCUMENTS YOU WANT TO COMPARE AND MERGE.

2. SELECT TOOLS → COMPARE AND MERGE DOCUMENTS FROM THE MENU.

3. SELECT THE DOCUMENT AGAINST WHICH YOU WILL COMPARE THE OPEN DOCUMENT.

4. CLICK THE MERGE BUTTON LIST ARROW AND SELECT HOW YOU WANT TO VIEW THE RESULTS.

5. ACCEPT OR REJECT CHANGES IN THE MERGED DOCUMENT.

Compare Side by Side toolbar.

Figure 9-9. Two documents compared side by side.

Word's compare and merge feature is great when you're integrating the contents of two documents into one document. The only problem is that you can only compare the documents after they're merged; you can't compare them at the same time. In Word 2003, Microsoft solves this problem with a new feature: Compare Side by Side. This feature opens the document windows side by side so that you can view and scroll through them at the same time, yet still make changes to each document individually.

First, open the two documents that you want to compare side by side.

1 Navigate to your Practice folder and open Lesson 9A.

The two documents you want to compare, Seniors and Lesson 9A, are open.

2 Select Window → Compare Side by Side with Seniors from the menu.

The two document windows appear side by side, as shown in Figure 9-9. You can easily see the differences between the two documents.

The Compare Side by Side toolbar has two buttons. The Synchronous Scrolling button is automatically selected and allows you to scroll through the documents at the same time. The Reset Window Position button resizes the windows for the best view.

3 Scroll down in the Lesson 9A document.

Notice that the Seniors document scrolls down at the same time.

4 Click the Close Side by Side button on the Compare Side by Side toolbar.

The windows are stacked on top of each other once again.

5 Close the Lesson 9A document.

QUICK REFERENCE

TO COMPARE DOCUMENTS SIDE BY SIDE:

1. OPEN THE TWO DOCUMENTS YOU WANT TO COMPARE.

2. SELECT WINDOW → COMPARE SIDE BY SIDE FROM THE MENU.

3. CLICK THE CLOSE SIDE BY SIDE BUTTON ON THE COMPARE SIDE BY SIDE TOOLBAR WHEN YOU'RE FINISHED.

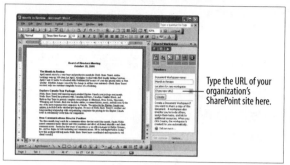

Type the URL of your organization's SharePoint site here.

Figure 9-10. The Shared Workspace task pane enables you to work with and access the shared document.

Document collaboration is redefined in Word 2003 with the Document Workspace. This new tool allows you and your team to share a workspace through the Internet so you can all work together on a document at the same time. By giving team members access to a single document, they can work directly on the document in the shared workspace, or work on their own copy that they can regularly synchronize with the shared workspace.

There are two ways to create a shared workspace: by sending an e-mail with a shared attachment (the document to be shared) or setting up a document workspace through the Shared Workspace task pane in Word. In both cases you will have to work with your network administrator to get permission to create a shared workspace on your organization's SharePoint Services Web site, but this lesson will show you how to get started.

1 Open the document you want to upload to the shared workspace.

2 Select Tools → Shared Workspace from the menu.

The Shared Workspace task pane appears, similar to that shown in Figure 9-10.

3 Type the Web address (URL) of the SharePoint Web site where the document will be located.

You will have to get this information and permission from your network administrator.

4 Click the Create button in the Shared Workspace task pane.

When the URL is accepted, you can add who you want to have access to the document.

5 Click Add New Members and type the e-mail addresses or user names for individuals you want to add to the shared workspace.

Make sure you separate each e-mail address or user name with a semicolon.

You can also set different permissions for group members here.

Password-Protecting a Document

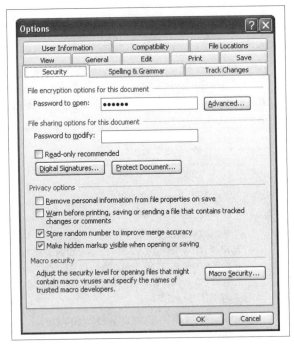

Figure 9-11. You can password-protect a document in the Options dialog box.

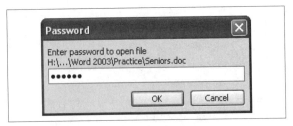

Figure 9-12. The Password dialog box.

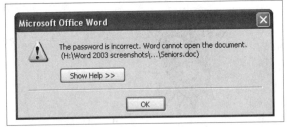

Figure 9-13. When you enter an incorrect password, the Microsoft Office Word dialog box appears.

If you have a document you don't want anyone else to see or modify, such as a love letter or a Christmas list, you can password-protect the document, restricting access only to yourself or people who know the password. You can assign security settings that require users to enter a

password to either open a document and/or modify a document. This lesson will show you how to add a password to a document, how to open a password-protected document, and how to remove a password.

1 **If necessary, open the** Lesson 9B **document and save it as** Seniors.

Here's how to password-protect a document.

2 **Select** Tools → Options **from the menu and click the** Security **tab.**

The Options dialog box appears, as shown in Figure 9-11. Here you can assign passwords to your document, requiring users to enter a password to either open or modify the document. Notice there are two text boxes where you can enter a password:

- **Password to open:** Adding a password here will require that a user enter the assigned password in order to open the document.
- **Password to modify:** Adding a password here will require that a user enter the assigned password in order to modify the document.

3 **In the** Password to open **text box, type** flower.

Notice the text you type appears as a string of • bullets. This is done so that no one can look over your shoulder and see your password.

4 **Click** OK.

The Confirm Password dialog box appears. You must reenter your password once more, just in case you mistyped it the first time.

5 **Type** flower, **then click** OK.

Now you need to save your document.

6 **Click the** Save button **on the Standard toolbar.**

Word saves the Seniors document.

7 **Close the document.**

Now let's try out the new password.

8 Select File → 1 Seniors **from the recent files list on the menu.**

The Password dialog box appears, as shown in Figure 9-12. You or anyone else trying to open the document must enter the document's password here. Try entering an incorrect password just to see what happens.

9 Type pencil **and click** OK.

The Microsoft Office Word dialog appears, as shown in Figure 9-13, informing you that you have entered an incorrect password. You cannot open a password-protected document without entering the correct password.

10 Click OK **to close the Microsoft Office Word dialog box.**

11 Select File → 1 Seniors **from the menu.**

The Password dialog box appears. This time enter the correct password.

12 Type flower **and click** OK.

The document opens. Removing password protection from a document is just as easy as adding it.

13 Select Tools → Options **from the menu and click the** Security **tab.**

The options dialog box appears.

14 Delete the ● ● ● ● ● ● **in the "Password to open" text box, and click** OK.

15 Click the Save button **on the Standard toolbar.**

Word saves the document without any password protection.

QUICK REFERENCE

TO PASSWORD-PROTECT A DOCUMENT:

1. SELECT TOOLS → OPTIONS FROM THE MENU AND CLICK THE SECURITY TAB.

2. TYPE A PASSWORD IN EITHER THE PASSWORD TO OPEN OR PASSWORD TO MODIFY TEXT BOX AND CLICK OK.

TO REMOVE PASSWORD PROTECTION FROM A DOCUMENT:

- REPEAT THE ABOVE STEPS, ONLY DELETE THE PASSWORD FROM EITHER THE PASSWORD TO OPEN OR PASSWORD TO MODIFY TEXT BOX AND CLICK OK.

Protecting a Document

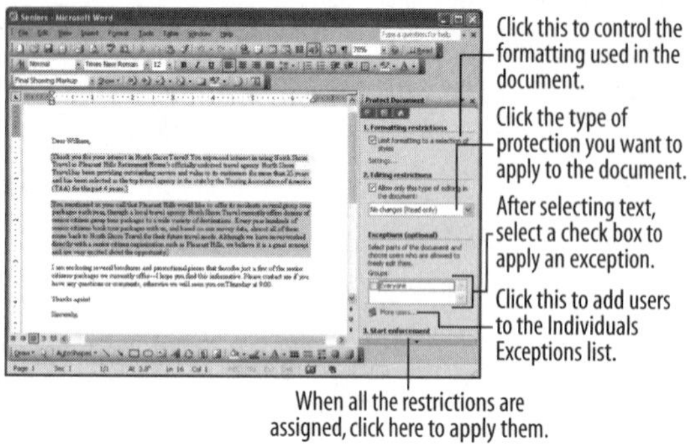

Click this to control the formatting used in the document.

Click the type of protection you want to apply to the document.

After selecting text, select a check box to apply an exception.

Click this to add users to the Individuals Exceptions list.

When all the restrictions are assigned, click here to apply them.

Figure 9-14. Set the document's restrictions in the Protect Document task pane. A different shaded color is applied for different types of exceptions.

In previous versions, document protection was only possible three ways: 1) password-protect the entire document, 2) track any changes made to the document by other reviewers, or 3) protect the document's content so that reviewers could only insert comments into the document.

Document protection has taken some big advances in Word 2003. You protect a document the same way as before, but now you can protect the document's formatting, control which sections of the document are protected, and you can even grant permissions for different users to modify specific parts of the document. Sound confusing? Don't worry—once you finish this lesson, everything will make a lot more sense.

1 Select Tools → Protect Document **from the menu.**

The Protect Document task pane appears, where you set and control the document's protection, as shown in Figure 9-14.

2 Check the Limit formatting to a selection of styles **check box in the Formatting restrictions area of the task pane.**

Activating this protection will restrict the formatting in the document to specific styles. It will also prevent users from the ability to apply formatting directly to the document. For example, another user couldn't apply bold formatting to a heading.

3 Click the Settings **link.**

The Formatting Restrictions dialog box appears.

To restrict the formatting in the document to the use of specific styles, select the check boxes of the styles you want to use. We don't need to do that right now though, so close the dialog box.

4 Click Cancel.

Controlling the content of the document is another valuable restriction. This kind of document protection hasn't changed from earlier versions, but what *has* changed is the ability to apply exceptions to the document protection. For example, the entire document is "Read only" protected *except* certain areas that you designate.

5 Select the Allow only this type of editing in the document **check box.**

Notice that the drop-down menu below the check box is now activated and the Exceptions area of the Protect Document task pane appears.

First, choose the type of protection you want to use. There are four options available in the drop-down menu:

- **No changes (Read only):** No editing or modifying is allowed.
- **Tracked changes:** Any change or modification made by the user is tracked and highlighted. (You cannot use exceptions with this type of protection.)
- **Comments:** Users cannot change or modify the document text, but they can insert comments.
- **Filling in forms:** This option is applicable only in documents where forms are used.

6 Make sure No changes (Read only) **appears in the drop-down menu.**

When you use the "No changes (Read only)" and "Comments" types of protection, you can apply exceptions to the document. This means that users can change and modify the document wherever you apply an exception.

Make an exception so that everyone who views the document can change or modify the first paragraph of the document.

7 Select the first body paragraph of the document. Click the Everyone check box in the Exceptions area of the task pane.

The exception is applied to the selected paragraph.

NOTE
You can also grant exceptions to individual users by adding them in the Exceptions area. Just click the Add Users link and enter their user names or e-mail addresses, separated by semicolons. Then select the document content and click the check box next to their name in the Individuals list.

When you have finally entered all the restrictions and exceptions in the task pane, you're ready to apply them to the document.

8 Click the Yes, Start Enforcing Protection button in the Protect Document task pane.

You can also apply a password to the protection. This means that if you want to stop applying the protection to the document, you have to know the password. Click OK to skip the password.

9 Click OK.

The Start Enforcing Protection dialog box disappears and the new protection is applied to the document.

QUICK REFERENCE

TO PROTECT DOCUMENT FORMATTING:

1. SELECT TOOLS → PROTECT DOCUMENT FROM THE MENU.

2. SELECT THE LIMIT FORMATTING TO A SELECTION OF STYLES CHECK BOX.

3. CLICK THE SETTINGS LINK TO SELECT THE STYLES YOU WANT TO USE IN THE DOCUMENT.

TO PROTECT DOCUMENT CONTENTS:

1. SELECT TOOLS → PROTECT DOCUMENT FROM THE MENU.

2. SELECT THE ALLOW ONLY THIS TYPE OF EDITING IN THE DOCUMENT CHECK BOX.

3. SELECT A TYPE OF PROTECTION FROM THE DROP-DOWN MENU.

TO ADD AN EXCEPTION:

1. SELECT THE TEXT YOU WANT TO EXEMPT FROM PROTECTION IN THE DOCUMENT.

2. CLICK THE CHECK BOX OF THE GROUP OR INDIVIDUAL YOU WANT TO GRANT THE EXCEPTION TO.

TO ADD INDIVIDUAL EXCEPTIONS:

1. CLICK THE ADD USERS LINK.

2. TYPE THE USER NAMES OR E-MAIL ADDRESSES SEPARATED BY SEMICOLONS, AND CLICK OK.

Chapter Nine Review

Lesson Summary

Using Revisions

To Track Revisions: Select Tools → Track Changes from the menu, or double-click the indicator in the status bar, or press Ctrl + Shift + E. When you edit the document, your revisions will be highlighted.

To Stop Tracking Revisions: Select Tools → Track Changes from the menu.

Accepting and Rejecting Revisions

To Accept or Reject Revisions: Select Tools → Track Changes from the menu. Click the Next button to move through the revisions in your document. Click either the Accept Change button or the Reject Change/Delete Comment button on the Reviewing toolbar. Or, right-click the revision and select the desired action from the shortcut menu.

Inserting Comments

To Insert a Comment: Place the insertion point where you want to insert the comment and click the Insert Comment button on the Reviewing toolbar, or select Insert → Comment from the menu.

To Hide or Display Comments in a Document: Click the Show button on the Reviewing toolbar and select Comments.

To Edit a Comment: Click in the comment balloon and edit the text as needed.

To Delete a Comment: Right-click the comment balloon and select Delete from the shortcut menu. Or, click the Reject Change/Delete Comment button on the Reviewing toolbar.

Saving Versions of a Document

Versions allow you to save several different copies, or revisions, of a document in the same file.

To Save a Document Version: Select File → Versions from the menu and click Save Now, enter a name for the version, and click OK.

To Open a Version: Select File → Versions from the menu, select the version you want to open, and click Open.

Comparing and Merging Documents

Open one of the documents you want to compare and merge and select Tools → Compare and Merge Documents from the menu. Select the document against which you will compare the open document. Click the Merge button list arrow and select how you want to view the results. Then accept or reject changes in the merged document.

Comparing Documents Side by Side

Open the two documents you want to compare and select Window → Compare Side by Side from the menu. Click the Close Side by Side button on the Compare Side by Side toolbar when you're finished.

About the Document Workspace

With the **Document Workspace**, you and your team can share a workspace over the Internet, allowing all of you to work together on a document at the same time.

To Create a Shared Workspace: Open the document you want to upload to the shared workspace. Select Tools → Shared Workspace from the menu. Type the Web address of the SharePoint Web site. Click the Create button on the Shared Workspace task pane. Click Add New Members and type the e-mail addresses or user names of the individuals to be added to the shared workspace.

Password-Protecting a Document

You can password-protect a document so that users must enter a password to open and/or modify the document.

To Password-protect a Document: Select Tools → Options from the menu and click the Security tab. Type a password in either the Password to open or Password to modify text box, and click OK.

To Remove Password Protection from a Document: Repeat the above steps, only delete the password from either the Password to open or Password to modify text box, and click OK.

Protecting a Document

To Protect Document Formatting: Select Tools → Protect Document from the menu and select the Limit formatting to a selection of styles check box. Click the Settings link to select the styles you want to use in the document.

To Protect Document Contents: Select Tools → Protect Document from the menu and select the Allow only this type of editing in the document check box. Select a type of protection from the drop-down menu.

To Add an Exception: Select the text you want to exempt from protection in the document. Click the check box of the group or individual you want to grant the exception to.

To Add Individual Exceptions: Click the Add Users link. Type the user names or e-mail addresses separated by semicolons and click OK.

Quiz

1. What is the purpose of Word's track changes feature?

   A. It gives you the ability to save multiple versions of a document in the same file.

   B. It lets others make changes to your document which you can later review and then accept and incorporate into the document, or reject.

   C. It allows you to see how many times you have opened and/or modified a document.

   D. It keeps track of any changes you make to Word's default settings.

2. How do you track changes in a document? (Select all that apply.)

   A. Select Tools → Track Changes from the menu.

   B. Select File → Track Changes → On from the menu.

   C. Click the Track Changes button on the Reviewing toolbar.

   D. Double-click the Track Changes indicator (TRK) on the Status bar.

3. To view a comment, position your cursor over the comment marker. (True or False?)

4. Saving a version of a document lets you:

   A. Make changes to the document which you or other users can later review and then accept and incorporate into the document, or reject.

   B. Distribute the document to other users by email.

   C. Save multiple revisions or copies of the document in the same file, saving hard drive space and making it easier to track and manage the different versions.

   D. See how many times you have opened, modified, and/or printed the document.

5. You can password-protect and restrict access to which two areas of a document?

   A. Opening and/or modifying a document.

   B. Opening and/or printing a document.

   C. Modifying and/or printing a document.

   D. Opening and/or viewing protected areas of a document.

6. Your boss copies one of your Word documents onto a floppy disk, makes some changes, saves the document, and then returns the floppy to you. What is the fastest, easiest way to compare the original document with the modified document?

   A. Select File → Versions, Compare from the menu.

   B. Select Tools → Track Changes → Highlight Changes from the menu.

   C. Select Tools → Compare and Merge Documents from the menu.

   D. There is no simple way to compare documents—you will have to do it manually.

7. The Protect Document task pane can do which of the following? (Select all that apply.)

 A. Protect your document from viruses.

 B. Protect the formatting in a document.

 C. Apply exceptions to the protection in specific areas of the document.

 D. Protect document content.

8. Individuals can access and modify the same document in a shared workspace. (True or False?)

9. The letters TRK appear on Word's status bar. What does this mean?

 A. TRK indicates that several versions of this document have been saved in the same file.

 B. TRK stands for "Try Remedial Komputing," because Word has noticed you have been making a lot of stupid mistakes lately.

 C. TRK indicates that Word is tracking changes or revisions made to the document.

 D. TRK indicates that the macro recorder is tracking what you are doing.

10. What happens when you merge and compare two documents?

 A. The two original document files are deleted and the contents of the documents are merged into a new file.

 B. The two documents are deleted and they go back to the source.

 C. A mail merge is performed.

 D. Word compares their contents and the differences between the two documents are tracked and highlighted.

11. When documents are compared side by side, the differences between the two are tracked and highlighted. (True or False?)

Homework

1. Open the document "Homework 9," and save it as "Conoco Letter."

2. Insert a comment: Place insertion point at the end of the "Customer Service" line in the delivery address, select Insert → Comment from the menu, type "Is this the right address?"

3. Delete the comment: Right-click the comment marker and select "Delete Comment" from the shortcut menu.

4. Track changes made to the document: Select Tools → Track Changes from the menu.

5. In the first paragraph of the letter, delete the phrase "(6'8", 550 pounds)".

6. In the first paragraph of the letter, replace the word "fluid" with the word "beverages."

7. Display the Reviewing toolbar: Select View → Toolbars → Reviewing from the menu.

8. Review your revisions: Press Ctrl + Home to move to the beginning of the document, and click the Next Change button on the Reviewing toolbar to find the first revision. Accept this revision.

9. Click the Next Change button on the Reviewing toolbar to find the next revision. Reject this revision.

10. Save your changes in a version: Select File → Versions from the menu and click Save Now.

11. Exit Microsoft Word.

Quiz Answers

1. B. When you use Word's track changes feature, you or other users can make changes to a document and then review those changes and accept or reject them.

2. A and D. Both of these methods will track any changes you make to a document.

3. False. Comments appear automatically in the margins of a document.

4. C. When you save a version, you are storing multiple copies and revisions of the document in the same file.

5. A. You can assign a password to restrict users from opening a document and/or editing a document.

6. C. You can compare two documents by selecting Tools → Compare and Merge Documents from the menu.

7. B, C and D. You cannot protect a document from viruses in the Protect Document task pane.

8. True. Individuals can access and modify the same document in a shared workspace.

9. C. The TRK indicator means that Word is tracking any changes or revisions you are making to a document.

10. D. When you merge and compare two documents, Word compares their contents and the differences between the two documents are tracked and then highlighted.

11. False. When documents are compared side by side, they are aligned vertically to one another. The differences between them are not highlighted or tracked.

CHAPTER 10

WORKING WITH OUTLINES AND LONG DOCUMENTS

CHAPTER OBJECTIVES:

Using Outline View to create an outline, Lesson 10.1

Viewing an outline—expanding and collapsing headings, Lesson 10.2

Organizing an outline, Lessons 10.3 and 10.4

Adding cross-references, Lesson 10.7

Adding bookmarks, Lesson 10.5

Adding footnotes, Lesson 10.6

Creating a table of contents, Lessons 10.8 and 10.9

Creating an index, Lesson 10.10

Creating a master document, Lesson 10.11 and 10.12

CHAPTER TASK: WORK ON A LONG PROPOSAL DOCUMENT

Prerequisites

- **How to open and save a document.**
- **How to use menus, toolbars, and dialog boxes.**
- **How to Apply and modify paragraph styles.**

If you're considering writing a long report, thesis, or book, then this is the chapter for you. In this chapter we'll take a look at how Word can help you work with outlines and long documents. If you still remember your English classes from days gone by, you may remember that creating an outline is the first step when making a report, which is where this chapter starts.

Once you have created a long document, you will learn how to add cross-references, bookmarks, footnotes, a table of contents, and an index—things you probably weren't even aware you could do with a word processor.

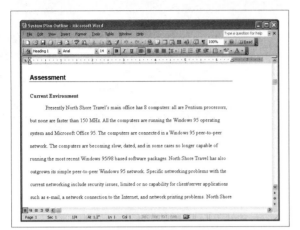

Figure 10-1. Normal view and Print Layout view are great for editing the text in a document, but not for working with the document's overall structure.

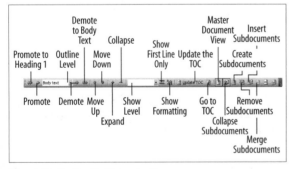

—Outline View button

Figure 10-2. The same document displayed in Outline view.

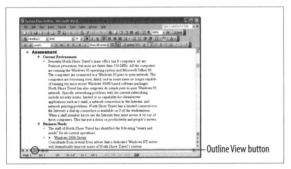

Figure 10-3. The Outlining toolbar.

Word's Outline view is a valuable tool that helps you to organize your ideas and topics when you create a long document. You can also use Outline view to view longer documents, separating the "forest from the trees" by *collapsing*, or hiding, the text in the document so that only the document's headings appear.

This lesson shows you how to use Outline view to outline several topics and subtopics for a longer document.

1 Start Word.

2 Click the Outline View button **located on the horizontal scroll bar at the bottom of the document window.**

> **TIP** *Another way to switch to Outline view is to select View → Outline from the menu.*

The main document window changes from Normal view, as shown in Figure 10-1, to Outline view, as shown in Figure 10-2. Outline view makes it much easier to create, view, and organize an outline.

3 Type Executive Summary.

Look at the Outline Level box on the Outlining toolbar (Figure 10-3). Notice that the line is given a Level 1 style, which is the highest level in an outline. The Level 2 style is the next highest level, and so on, all the way down to Level 9. The minus symbol (⊐) located to the left of the line you just typed indicates that the current heading does not contain any subordinate items, such as body text or subheadings.

4 Press Enter and type Assessment.

This line is also assigned to the Level 1 style.

5 Press Enter and type Current Environment.

In Outline view, it's easy to change heading styles. For example, you could change (or demote) a Level 1 to a Level 2 style, or change (or promote) a Level 2 style to a Level 1 style. There are three ways to promote headings:

- **Using the keyboard:** Press the Tab key to demote the current heading and press Shift + Tab to promote the current heading. This is probably the fastest and easiest method.

- **Using the Outlining toolbar buttons:** Click either the Promote button or Demote button on the Outlining toolbar.

- **Using the Outlining toolbar:** Select the level from the Outline Level list on the Outlining toolbar. This is the fastest way to skip between outline levels.

Here's how to demote a heading using the keyboard method:

6 With the insertion point at the end of the Current Environment line, press Tab.

The selected line is demoted and formatted with the Level 2 style. Notice the line is indented and italicized, showing that it is subordinate to the "Assessment" heading above it. Also, notice that the minus outline symbol (━) located to the left of the "Assessment" heading changes to a plus (✛), indicating that the heading contains subheadings or subordinate text.

7 Press Enter and type Business Needs.

> **NOTE** *If you want to add a blank line, click the Demote to Body Text button on the Outlining toolbar and then press Enter. If you don't, the resulting line will be formatted as a heading level and will cause problems with any automatic numbering or table of contents in your document.*

8 Press Enter and type System Strategies.

This line needs to be a Level 1 heading instead of a Level 2 heading. Here's how to promote a heading to the next highest level.

9 Press Shift + Tab.

The selected line is formatted with the Level 1 style. Notice that the line is no longer indented.

10 Press Enter, then Tab to demote the heading, type Hardware, press Enter, type Software, and press Enter.

The selected lines are indented, indicating that they are subheadings under the "System Strategies" heading.

Here's how to add body text under a heading.

11 Click the ➡ Demote to Body Text button on the Outlining toolbar.

The current paragraph is demoted to ordinary body text.

12 Type The proposed operating system of North Shore Travel is Windows XP.

Super! You've just created your first outline in Word.

13 Save the file as Outline, then close it.

QUICK REFERENCE

TO VIEW A DOCUMENT IN OUTLINE VIEW:

- CLICK THE OUTLINE VIEW BUTTON ON THE HORIZONTAL SCROLL BAR AT THE BOTTOM OF THE DOCUMENT WINDOW.

OR...

- SELECT VIEW → OUTLINE FROM THE MENU.

TO DEMOTE THE CURRENT HEADING:

- PRESS TAB.

OR...

- CLICK THE DEMOTE BUTTON ON THE OUTLINING TOOLBAR.

OR...

- SELECT THE OUTLINE LEVEL FROM THE OUTLINE LEVEL LIST ON THE OUTLINING TOOLBAR.

TO PROMOTE THE CURRENT HEADING:

- PRESS SHIFT + TAB.

OR...

- CLICK THE PROMOTE BUTTON ON THE OUTLINING TOOLBAR.

OR...

- SELECT THE OUTLINE LEVEL FROM THE OUTLINE LEVEL LIST ON THE OUTLINING TOOLBAR.

TO DEMOTE A HEADING TO BODY TEXT:

- CLICK THE DEMOTE TO BODY TEXT BUTTON ON THE OUTLINING TOOLBAR.

Viewing an Outline

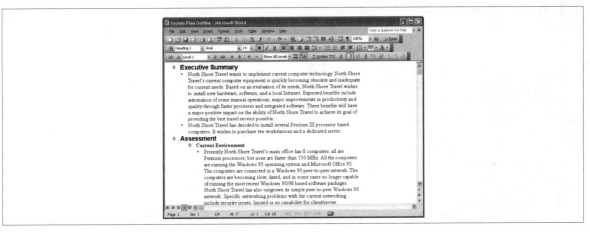

Figure 10-4. A document displayed in Outline view.

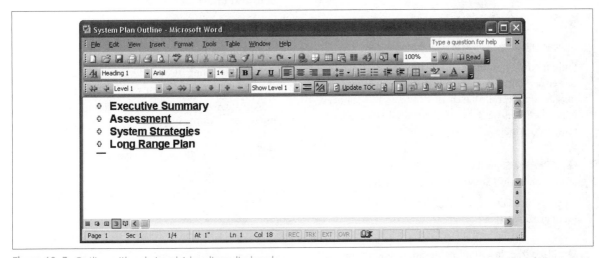

Figure 10-5. Outline with only Level 1 headings displayed.

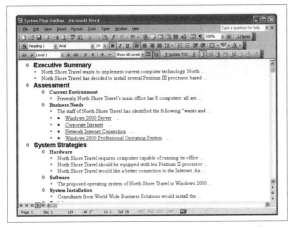

Figure 10-6. Outline with only first lines displayed.

As a document grows longer and longer, it can be become increasingly difficult to see its overall structure. Outline view can tame even the longest, wildest documents and let you separate "the forest from the trees." Outline view lets you decide how much of your document's structure you want to see. You can *collapse* a heading and hide its subheadings and text, and *expand* a collapsed heading to display its subheadings and text. The symbol to the left of the text indicates whether it is collapsed (▬), expanded (✛), or ordinary body text (▫). This lesson will give you some practice expanding and collapsing headings in Outline view.

1 Open the file named Lesson 10A and save it as System Plan Outline.

The document "System Plan Outline" appears in the main document window in Print Layout view. This document contains several headings and subheadings, and will be easier to view and work with in Outline view.

2 Click the Outline View button located on the horizontal scroll bar at the bottom of the document window.

The document appears in Outline view, as shown in Figure 10-4. Text that is not formatted as a heading is called *body text* and is identified by a small square (⬚) to the left of the text.

3 Click the Show Level list arrow on the Outlining toolbar and select Show Level 1 from the list.

Only the first heading levels of the document are displayed, as shown in Figure 10-5. It is sometimes useful to view only certain levels of headings and subheadings when you want to see the overall structure of a longer document.

4 Click the Show Level list arrow on the Outlining toolbar and select Show Level 2 from the list.

Only the first and second heading levels of the document are displayed.

5 Place the insertion point anywhere in the last heading, Long Range Plan.

The ⬚ symbol indicates this heading contains several subheadings and body text. Expand this heading to display anything under it.

6 Click the ⊞ Expand button on the Outlining toolbar.

 Another way to expand or collapse a heading is to double-click the headings or ⬚ *symbol.*

The subordinate text under the "Long Range Plan" heading appears. You can also collapse the heading to hide any subheadings and text under it.

7 Click the ⊟ Collapse button on the Outlining toolbar.

The "Long Range Plan" heading collapses, hiding subordinate text and subheadings.

8 Click the Show Level list arrow on the Outlining toolbar and select Show All Levels from the list.

All of the text levels are now displayed. Instead of viewing all of the subordinate text in a document, sometimes it is useful to view only the first line of the body text under each heading.

9 Click the ☰ Show First Line Only button on the Outlining toolbar.

Only the first line of body text under each heading is shown, as shown in Figure 10-6. This gives you an idea of the content under each heading, without having to see all of the body text.

10 Click the Show First Line Only button on the Outlining toolbar again.

All the text in the document is visible once again.

QUICK REFERENCE

TO EXPAND A HEADING:

- MAKE SURE THE INSERTION POINT IS IN THE HEADING AND CLICK THE EXPAND BUTTON ON THE OUTLINING TOOLBAR.

OR...

- DOUBLE-CLICK THE HEADING'S + SYMBOL.

TO COLLAPSE A HEADING:

- MAKE SURE THE INSERTION POINT IS IN THE HEADING AND CLICK THE COLLAPSE BUTTON ON THE OUTLINING TOOLBAR.

OR...

- DOUBLE-CLICK THE HEADING'S ▭ SYMBOL.

TO DISPLAY ALL THE HEADINGS IN A DOCUMENT:

- CLICK THE SHOW LEVELS LIST ARROW ON THE OUTLINING TOOLBAR AND SELECT SHOW ALL LEVELS.

TO DISPLAY ONLY THE FIRST LINE OF BODY TEXT:

- CLICK THE SHOW FIRST LINE ONLY BUTTON ON THE OUTLINING TOOLBAR.

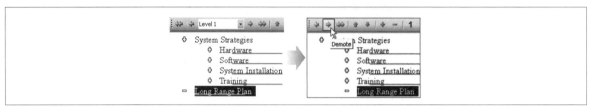

Figure 10-7. You can demote a heading in an outline.

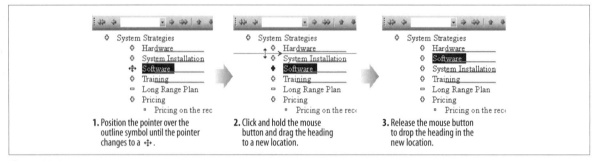

1. Position the pointer over the outline symbol until the pointer changes to a ✛.

2. Click and hold the mouse button and drag the heading to a new location.

3. Release the mouse button to drop the heading in the new location.

Figure 10-8. You can rearrange an outline by using drag and drop.

Another benefit of working in Outline view is that you can modify an outline. You can easily rearrange the topics in an outline by moving the headings and subheadings to different positions and locations in the document. You can also change the levels of the headings in an outline, promoting a Level 2 subheading to a Level 1 heading, and so on.

1 Click the Show Level list arrow on the Outlining toolbar and select Show Level 2 from the list.

Only the first and second heading levels of the document are displayed.

2 Select the heading Long Range Plan then click the Demote button on the Outlining toolbar.

TIP

Another way to demote a heading is to press the Tab *key, or drag the heading's plus (✛) or minus (–) symbol to the left.*

The heading "Long Range Plan" is demoted to a Level 2 subheading under the previous Level 1 heading, "System Strategies," as shown in Figure 10-7.

3 Select the subheading Software then click the Move Down button on the Outlining toolbar.

TIP

Another way to rearrange outline headings is to click and drag the headings to a new location.

NOTE

When you move a heading in an outline, any subordinate text and/or subheadings it contains are moved with it.

You can also move headings using the mouse instead of the toolbar.

4 Position the pointer over the plus outline symbol (✛) for the subheading Software, until the pointer changes to a ✛, then click and hold the mouse button. Drag the subheading directly under the Hardware subheading, then release the mouse button.

The selected "Software" subheading is moved under the "Hardware" subheading, as shown in Figure 10-8.

5 Now press Ctrl + End to move to the end of the document.

6 Press Enter, then type Pricing, and then press Enter again.

Notice the text is assigned a Level 2 style. Next, add the body text under the "Pricing" heading.

7 Click the Demote to Body Text button on the Outlining toolbar.

The current line is indented and a body text symbol (▫) appears.

8 Type Pricing on the recommended computer network system has not been established.

9 If there is a printer connected to your computer, click the Print button on the Standard toolbar.

The printed copy will be in Outline view, showing only the levels and text you see on your screen. When you've finished working on the structure of a document, you'll want to switch back to Normal view or Print Layout view.

10 Click the Print Layout View button on the Horizontal scroll bar near the bottom of the screen.

The document appears in Print Layout view.

11 Save the document.

QUICK REFERENCE

TO REARRANGE AN OUTLINE:

- PLACE THE INSERTION POINT IN THE HEADING YOU WANT TO MOVE, AND PRESS EITHER THE MOVE UP BUTTON OR MOVE DOWN BUTTON ON THE OUTLINING TOOLBAR.

OR...

- DRAG THE HEADING'S OUTLINE SYMBOL TO A NEW LOCATION IN THE OUTLINE.

TO DEMOTE THE CURRENT HEADING:

- PRESS TAB.

OR...

- CLICK THE DEMOTE BUTTON ON THE OUTLINING TOOLBAR.

OR...

- SELECT THE OUTLINE LEVEL FROM THE OUTLINE LEVEL LIST ON THE OUTLINING TOOLBAR.

TO PROMOTE THE CURRENT HEADING:

- PRESS SHIFT + TAB.

OR...

- CLICK THE PROMOTE BUTTON ON THE OUTLINING TOOLBAR.

OR...

- SELECT THE OUTLINE LEVEL FROM THE OUTLINE LEVEL LIST ON THE OUTLINING TOOLBAR.

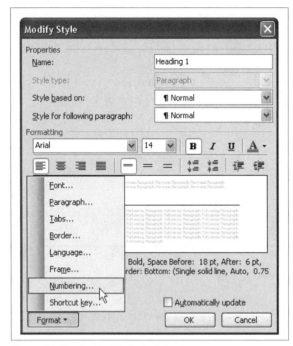

Figure 10-9. The Modify Style dialog box.

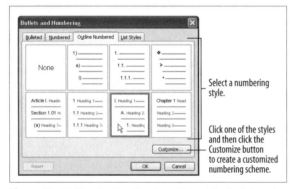

Figure 10-10. The Outline Numbered tab of the Bullets and Numbering dialog box.

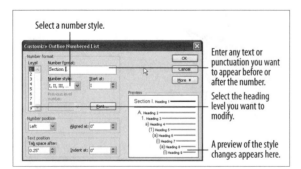

Figure 10-11. The Customize Outline Numbered List dialog box.

What would an outline be without the numbers? Actually you will probably choose *not* to apply numbering to the headings in most of your documents. If you do decide that you want the heading levels in your document to be numbered, however, this lesson explains how to do it.

Each of the nine heading levels that you can use in an outline are based on built-in styles, named Level 1, Level 2, Level 3, and so on. The easiest way to automatically number headings in a document is to modify the Level Style you want numbered. This is a little easier to demonstrate than explain, so let's start the lesson…

1 If necessary, navigate to your Practice folder and open Lesson 10B. Save the file as System Plan Outline.

2 Select View → Outline from the menu.

Now you're ready to work on the document in Outline view.

3 Place the insertion point anywhere in the first heading, Executive Summary.

Notice the Style List on the Formatting toolbar displays the Style name the heading is based on—"Heading 1." To number the outline, we need to change the Heading 1 style so that it includes numbering.

4 Click the Styles and Formatting button on the Formatting toolbar.

> **TIP**
> *Another way to view the Styles and Formatting task pane is to select* Format → Styles and Formatting *from the menu.*

The Styles and Formatting task pane appears. Since the insertion point was in a paragraph formatted with the Heading 1 style, the Heading 1 style is already selected. We want to modify the Heading 1 style so that it is automatically numbered.

5 Hold the pointer over the Heading 1 style in the task pane, click the Heading 1 ˅ arrow, and select Modify.

The Modify Style dialog box appears, as shown in Figure 10-9. Next, you have to select which of the Style formatting options you want to modify.

6 Click the Format button, select Numbering, and click the Outline Numbered tab.

The Bullets and Numbering dialog box appears with the Outline Numbered tab selected, as shown in Figure 10-10. All you have to do is click the numbered list style you want to apply to the heading style. If none of the numbering schemes are what you're looking for, you can modify the numbering schemes by selecting the scheme you want to change and clicking the Customize button.

7 Click the third numbering option in the bottom row and click the Customize button.

The Customize Outline Numbered List dialog box appears, as shown in Figure 10-11. This busy-looking dialog box lets you customize how Word numbers your headings. One way to change numbering is to add text and/or punctuation that appears before or after every number, such as a period, so that "1" will appear as "1."

8 Place the insertion point BEFORE the number in the Number format box and type Section, followed by a Space. Next, replace the . (period) following the number with a : (colon).

Be careful and don't accidentally delete the number!

The new style formatting will number all the Heading 1 paragraphs in your document with Section I: Section II: and so on.

9 Click OK, OK, OK to close the dialog boxes and apply the outline numbering.

Word numbers your outline according to the number scheme you selected.

10 Close the Styles and Formatting task pane and save your work.

QUICK REFERENCE

TO NUMBER AN OUTLINE:

1. SELECT THE HEADING STYLE THAT YOU WANT TO MODIFY AND CLICK THE STYLES AND FORMATTING BUTTON ON THE FORMATTING TOOLBAR.

2. CLICK THE HEADING STYLE'S ARROW IN THE TASK PANE, AND SELECT MODIFY FROM THE DROP-DOWN MENU.

3. CLICK THE FORMAT BUTTON, SELECT NUMBERING, AND SELECT THE OUTLINE NUMBERED TAB.

4. SELECT THE NUMBER SCHEME YOU WANT TO USE TO NUMBER YOUR OUTLINE.

   YOU CAN CUSTOMIZE ANY NUMBER SCHEME BY SELECTING IT AND CLICKING THE CUSTOMIZE BUTTON.

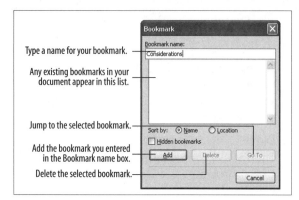

Type a name for your bookmark.

Any existing bookmarks in your document appear in this list.

Jump to the selected bookmark.

Add the bookmark you entered in the Bookmark name box.

Delete the selected bookmark.

Figure 10-12. The Bookmark dialog box.

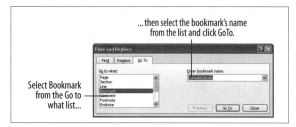

...then select the bookmark's name from the list and click GoTo.

Select Bookmark from the Go to what list...

Figure 10-13. The Go To tab of the Find and Replace dialog box.

A *bookmark* in Word is just like a bookmark you would use to mark your place in a novel. You use *bookmarks* in Word to mark a location in a document so that you can quickly find and jump back to that location. Bookmarks can also be used to create cross-references. For example, you could bookmark a paragraph about the life of armadillos and then create a cross-reference to that bookmark.

Bookmarks can be from 1 to 40 characters in length, must begin with a letter, and can only contain numbers, letters, or the underscore character—no spaces! This lesson explains how to insert a bookmark.

1 Click the Print Layout View button located on the horizontal scroll bar at the bottom of the document window.

The document appears in Print Layout view.

2 Go to Page 4 of the document and place the insertion point in the Long Range Plan heading.

This is where you want to insert a bookmark.

3 Select Insert → Bookmark from the menu.

The Bookmark dialog box appears, as shown in Figure 10-12. Here you can create, delete, or jump to other bookmarks in your document.

4 In the Bookmark name box, type Considerations, then click Add.

⋮ NOTE ⋮ *Bookmark names can be up to 40 characters long, cannot contain any spaces, and must begin with a letter.*

The dialog box closes. Nothing appears to have happened, but Word has inserted a bookmark at your current position in the document.

5 Press Ctrl + Home to go to the beginning of the document.

Here's how to quickly jump to a bookmark:

6 Select Edit → Go To from the menu.

TIP *Another way to go to a location in a document is to double-click the Page number area (Page 3   Sec 1) of the Status bar, or press F5, or press Ctrl + G.*

The Find and Replace dialog box appears with the Go To tab in front, as shown in Figure 10-13. Here you can quickly jump to a specified location in a document, such as a specific page, heading, or bookmark.

7 In the "Go to what" list, click Bookmark.

The text box to the right changes to a list box to display all the bookmarks in the document. Since you only have one bookmark in this document, the bookmark "Considerations" is selected.

8 Click Go To, then Close.

Word jumps to the "Considerations" bookmark.

9 Save your work.

QUICK REFERENCE

TO INSERT A BOOKMARK:

1. PLACE THE INSERTION POINT WHERE YOU WANT TO INSERT THE BOOKMARK.

2. SELECT INSERT → BOOKMARK FROM THE MENU.

3. ENTER A NAME FOR THE BOOKMARK.

TO JUMP TO A BOOKMARK:

1. SELECT EDIT → GO TO FROM THE MENU.

   OR...

   DOUBLE-CLICK THE PAGE NUMBER AREA OF THE STATUS BAR.

OR...

PRESS F5, OR CTRL + G.

2. SELECT BOOKMARK FROM THE GO TO WHAT LIST, SELECT THE BOOKMARK NAME FROM THE DROP-DOWN LIST, AND CLICK GO TO.

Figure 10-14. The Footnote and Endnote dialog box.

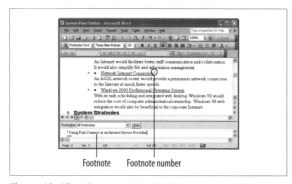

Footnote   Footnote number

Figure 10-15. A footnote is inserted into a document.

You're probably already familiar with footnotes and/or endnotes if you have ever had to write a paper for an English class. Footnotes and endnotes explain, comment on, or provide references for text in a document. Footnotes appear at the bottom, or the foot, of each page in a document, while endnotes appear at the end of a document. Other than that, they work the same way.

Footnotes and endnotes have two linked parts: the note reference mark (usually a number) and the corresponding footnote or endnote. Word automatically numbers footnote and endnote marks for you, so when you add, delete, or move notes, they are automatically renumbered.

1 Click the Outline View button located on the horizontal scroll bar at the bottom of the document window.

The document appears in Outline view.

2 Click the Show Level list arrow and select Show All Levels from the list. Scroll down to Page 2, and place the insertion point at the end of the Network Internet Connection text.

Insert a footnote here.

3 Select Insert → Reference → Footnote from the menu.

The Footnote and Endnote dialog box appears, as shown in Figure 10-14. This is where you can insert a footnote or endnote. Here's the difference between the two:

- **Footnote:** Appears on the same page as the text it explains.
- **Endnote:** Appears at the end of the section or document.

We want to insert a footnote for this exercise, and since that's the default option, we don't need to change anything in the dialog box.

4 Click the Insert button.

Word inserts a footnote number at the insertion point and moves the insertion point to the bottom of the page, where you can type the footnote.

⁂ NOTE ⁂   *In Normal and Outline view, a separate area appears where you can edit your footnote, like the one shown in Figure 10-15. In Print Layout view, you can edit the footnote right on the bottom of the page.*

5 Type Using Fast-Connect as an Internet Service Provider. in the footnote area.

Let's preview your document onscreen so that you can see how the footnote looks.

6 Click the Print Preview button on the Standard toolbar.

Word displays a preview of how the document will look when it's printed. Notice the footnote at the bottom of the page.

7 Click the 🔍 pointer near the bottom of the page to magnify it.

Word zooms in so you can view the footnote a little better.

8 Click Close to return to the document.

You can easily read a footnote without Print Preview as well.

9 Position the pointer over the footnote number until it changes to a 🖳, and leave it there for a few moments.

The contents of the footnote appear in a small pop-up window.

To edit an existing footnote, double-click the footnote number.

10 Double-click the footnote number to edit it.

Word jumps to the footnote text.

11 Edit the footnote so it reads Using Quick-Connect **instead of** Using Fast-Connect.

You can return to the rest of your document once you've finished editing the footnote.

12 Click Close to return to the document.

There's just one more thing you should know about footnotes and endnotes: how to delete them.

13 Select the footnote number 1. you just inserted and press Delete.

The footnote number and reference at the bottom of the page are deleted.

14 Save your work.

QUICK REFERENCE

TO INSERT A FOOTNOTE OR ENDNOTE:

1. PLACE THE INSERTION POINT WHERE YOU WANT THE FOOTNOTE OR ENDNOTE TO BE INSERTED, AND SELECT INSERT → REFERENCE → FOOTNOTE FROM THE MENU.

2. SPECIFY WHETHER YOU WANT TO INSERT A FOOTNOTE OR ENDNOTE AND CLICK INSERT.

3. TYPE THE FOOTNOTE OR ENDNOTE.

TO VIEW A FOOTNOTE OR ENDNOTE:

• POSITION THE POINTER OVER THE FOOTNOTE OR ENDNOTE NUMBER FOR SEVERAL MOMENTS.

TO EDIT A FOOTNOTE OR ENDNOTE:

• DOUBLE-CLICK THE FOOTNOTE OR ENDNOTE NUMBER.

TO DELETE A FOOTNOTE OR ENDNOTE:

• SELECT THE FOOTNOTE OR ENDNOTE NUMBER AND PRESS THE DELETE KEY.

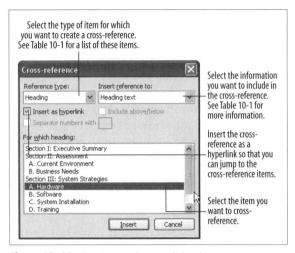

Select the type of item for which you want to create a cross-reference. See Table 10-1 for a list of these items.

Select the information you want to include in the cross-reference. See Table 10-1 for more information.

Insert the cross-reference as a hyperlink so that you can jump to the cross-reference items.

Select the item you want to cross-reference.

Figure 10-16. The Cross-reference dialog box.

A cross-reference points the reader to another part of the document where they can find more information about something. An example of a cross-reference would be "See Penguin Feeding Behaviors on page 17 for more information." You might be wondering why you would need to use a cross-reference when you can just type the information in yourself, but what happens if you add or delete several pages in the document? Page 17 could all of a sudden be page 14, thus causing any references to page 17 to be incorrect. A cross-reference inserted by Word, however, is automatically updated if the item it references is moved.

1 If necessary, navigate to your Practice folder and open Lesson 10C. **Save the file as** System Plan Outline.

2 Select View → Print Layout from the menu.

This view is easier to work in when adding cross-references.

3 Go to Page 2 of the document and place the insertion point at the end of the Windows 2000 Server paragraph, immediately after the word limitations, and then press Spacebar.

This is where we'll insert a cross-reference.

4 Select Insert → Reference → Cross-reference from the menu.

The Cross-reference dialog box appears, as shown in Figure 10-16. You can cross-reference many types of items such as bookmarks, headings, and more. The first thing you have to do is specify which type of item you want to cross-reference.

5 Click the Reference type list arrow and select Heading.

A list of all the headings in the document appears in the "For which heading" list box. You want to insert a cross-reference to the Hardware heading.

6 Select Hardware in the For which heading list box.

The final step is to specify the information you want to include in the cross-reference. For example, you could include a page number in the cross-reference, such as "See Page 3," or the heading text "See Mating Patterns."

7 Click the Insert reference to list arrow and select Heading text if it is not already selected.

This will insert the heading text in the cross-reference.

8 Make sure the Insert as hyperlink check box is checked.

The Insert as hyperlink check box attaches a hyperlink, like those you use on the Internet, so that you can click the cross-reference and jump to the cross-referenced item when working in the document.

9 Click Insert and then Close.

The Hardware heading appears as a cross-reference at the insertion point. Let's use the cross-reference feature again—this time to insert a cross-reference to the page that the "Hardware" heading is on.

10 Press Spacebar, type on page, and then press Spacebar again.

Make sure you add a space after the word "page."

11 **Select** Insert → Reference → Cross-reference **from the menu.**

The Cross-reference dialog box appears.

12 **Click the** Reference type **list arrow and select** Heading.

A list of all the headings in the document appears in the "For which heading" list box. You want to insert a cross-reference to the Hardware page.

13 **Select** Hardware **in the** For which heading **list box, click the** Insert reference to **list arrow, and select** Page number.

This will insert the page number of the cross-reference. If the document is modified and the page that the cross-referenced item is on changes, the cross-referenced page number will be updated to reflect the change.

14 **Click** Insert **and then** Close.

The Hardware page number appears as a cross-reference at the insertion point.

If the formatting for the cross-references is different from the other text in the paragraph, use the Format Painter to apply the paragraph formatting to the references.

15 **Save your work.**

≳ NOTE ≲ *Cross-references need to be updated if the item they reference is moved. You can manually update a cross-reference by clicking the cross-reference and pressing F9—but updating each and every cross-reference would be a pain. Instead, have Word update your document's fields for you. Select Tools → Options from the menu, click the Print tab, make sure the Update fields box is checked and click OK. Now Word will update the cross-references in your document every time you print or preview it.*

Table 10-1 below shows the kind of items that can be cross-referenced.

Table 10-1. What Can Be Included in a Cross-Reference

You can cross-reference these items:	Cross-references can include this information:
Numbered Items	Entire captionExample: See **Figure 3-2: Rainfall.**
Headings	
Bookmarks	Only label and numberExample: See **Figure 3-2.**
Footnotes	
Endnotes	Page numberExample: See Page **10.**
Equations	
Figures	Only caption textExample: See **Rainfall.**
Tables	

QUICK REFERENCE

TO INSERT A CROSS-REFERENCE:

1. PLACE THE INSERTION POINT WHERE YOU WANT TO INSERT THE CROSS-REFERENCE AND SELECT INSERT → REFERENCE → CROSS-REFERENCE FROM THE MENU.

2. SELECT THE TYPE OF ITEM YOU WANT TO REFERENCE (SUCH AS HEADINGS OR BOOKMARKS) FROM THE REFERENCE TYPE LIST.

3. SELECT THE ITEM YOU WANT TO CROSS-REFERENCE FROM THE FOR WHICH HEADING LIST.

4. SELECT THE INFORMATION TO INCLUDE IN THE CROSS-REFERENCE (SUCH AS THE HEADING TEXT OR PAGE NUMBER) FROM THE INSERT REFERENCE TO LIST.

5. SPECIFY WHETHER OR NOT YOU WANT TO INSERT THE CROSS-REFERENCED ITEM AS A HYPERLINK.

6. CLICK THE INSERT BUTTON.

CLICK THE CLOSE BUTTON. **TO AUTOMATICALLY UPDATE CROSS-REFERENCE FIELDS WHEN WORD PRINTS:**

*   SELECT TOOLS → OPTIONS FROM THE MENU, CLICK THE PRINT TAB, MAKE SURE THE UPDATE FIELDS BOX IS CHECKED, AND CLICK OK.

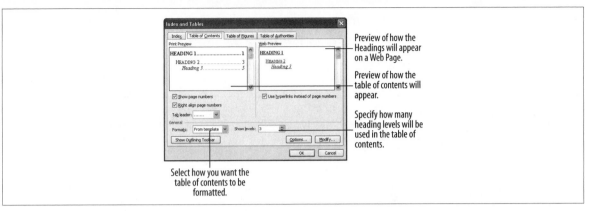

Preview of how the Headings will appear on a Web Page.

Preview of how the table of contents will appear.

Specify how many heading levels will be used in the table of contents.

Select how you want the table of contents to be formatted.

Figure 10-17. The Table of Contents tab of the Index and Tables dialog box.

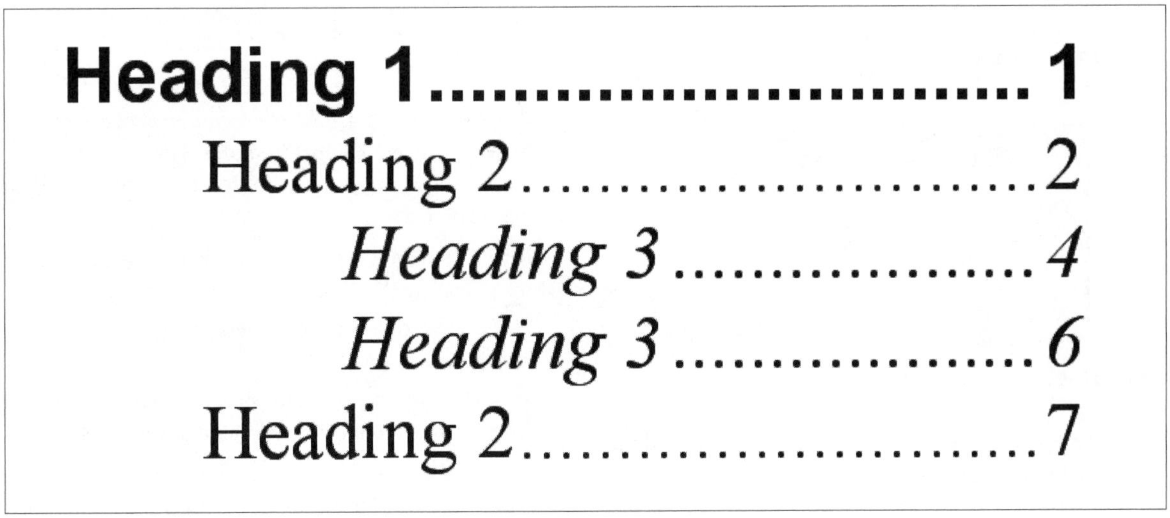

Heading 1.............................1
Heading 2..........................2
Heading 3 4
Heading 3 6
Heading 2..........................7

Figure 10-18. You can create a Table of Contents using the document's heading styles.

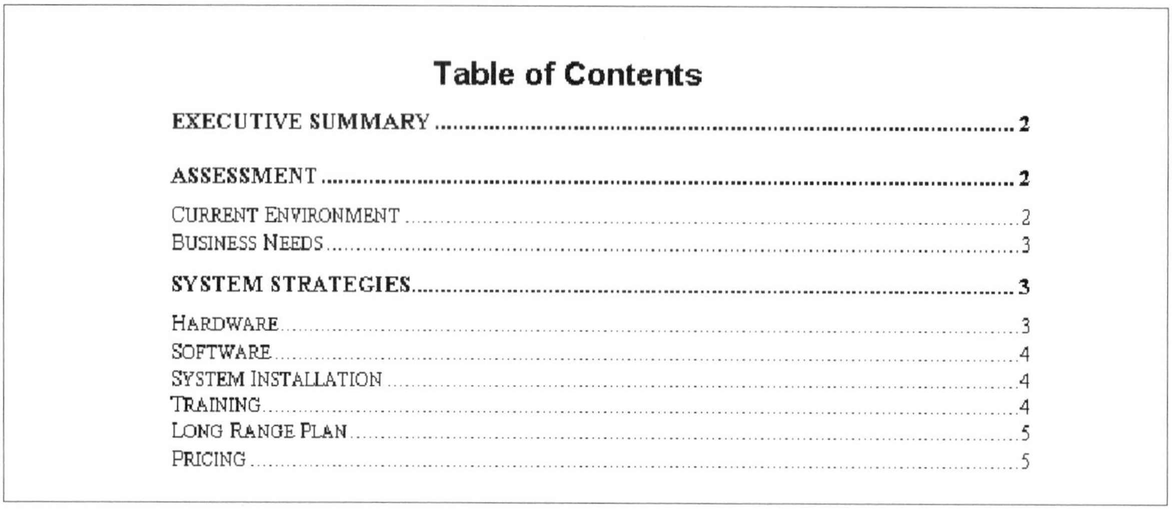

Table of Contents

EXECUTIVE SUMMARY 2

ASSESSMENT 2

CURRENT ENVIRONMENT 2
BUSINESS NEEDS 3

SYSTEM STRATEGIES 3

HARDWARE 3
SOFTWARE 4
SYSTEM INSTALLATION 4
TRAINING 4
LONG RANGE PLAN 5
PRICING 5

Figure 10-19. The newly created table of contents.

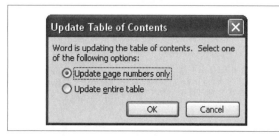

Figure 10-20. The Update Table of Contents dialog box.

Word can easily create a table of contents for longer documents with several headings. There are two ways to create a table of contents. The first method is to use the document's heading styles for the different headings in the table of contents, as shown in Figure 10-18. For example, paragraphs formatted with the Heading 1 style would be main headings in the table of contents, paragraphs formatted with the Heading 2 style would be subheadings, and so on. This is the easiest, fastest, and most common method of creating a table of contents—and that's what we'll discuss in this lesson.

1 Press Ctrl + Home to move to the beginning of the document, and press Enter.

2 Press the up arrow key and press Ctrl + Enter to enter a page break at the insertion point.

Word inserts a page break at the insertion point.

3 Press the up arrow key to move above the page break and select Normal from the Style list box on the Formatting toolbar. Type `Table of Contents`, then press Enter.

If you want, you can apply any formatting (bold, centered, etc.) to the Table of Contents heading.

Here's how to insert a table of contents:

4 Select Insert → Reference → Index and Tables from the menu then click the Table of Contents tab.

The Index and Tables dialog box appears with the Table of Contents tab in front, as shown in Figure 10-17.

5 Verify that the Show page numbers check box is checked and that 3 heading levels appear in the Show levels box.

You can select several different formats for your table of contents in the Formats box.

6 In the Formats box, select Formal and then click OK.

The Index and Tables dialog box closes, and the Table of Contents is inserted at the insertion point, as shown in Figure 10-19. If you add or delete several pages or headings, the table of contents won't automatically display the changes—you will need to update the table of contents.

7 Click anywhere in the table of contents, click the right mouse button, and select Update Field from the shortcut menu.

 Another way to update a table of contents is to click anywhere in the table of contents and press F9.

The Update Table of Contents dialog box appears, as shown in Figure 10-20:

- Select the **Update Page Numbers Only** option only if the document's page numbers have changed.
- Select the **Update entire table** option if you have added new headings to your document.

Actually, you should always play it safe and select the Update entire table option, just to make sure everything is updated.

8 Select the Update entire table option and click OK.

Nothing happens! But had you made changes to your document, the table of contents would have been updated to reflect the changes.

NOTE *Nothing's worse than forgetting to update a document's table of contents before you print it and then handing in a document with an incorrect table of contents. Updating a document's table of contents every time you make a change can be a pain—so have Word do it for you. Select Tools → Options from the menu, click the Print tab, make sure the Update fields box is checked, and click OK. Now Word will update the fields in your documents, such as the table of contents, the index, and any cross-references, every time you print or preview it.*

QUICK REFERENCE

TO INSERT A TABLE OF CONTENTS:

1. PLACE THE INSERTION POINT WHERE YOU WANT TO INSERT THE TABLE OF CONTENTS AND SELECT INSERT → REFERENCE → INDEX AND TABLES FROM THE MENU. CLICK THE TABLE OF CONTENTS TAB.

2. SPECIFY A FORMAT FOR THE TABLE OF CONTENTS AND WHICH HEADING LEVELS TO INCLUDE.

3. CLICK OK.

TO UPDATE A TABLE OF CONTENTS:

- RIGHT-CLICK THE TABLE OF CONTENTS AND SELECT UPDATE FIELD.

TO AUTOMATICALLY UPDATE THE TABLE OF CONTENTS WHEN WORD PRINTS:

- SELECT TOOLS → OPTIONS FROM THE MENU, CLICK THE PRINT TAB, MAKE SURE THE UPDATE FIELDS BOX IS CHECKED, AND CLICK OK.

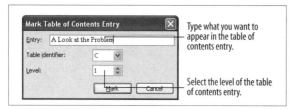

Type what you want to appear in the table of contents entry.

Select the level of the table of contents entry.

Figure 10-21. The Mark Table of Contents Entry dialog box.

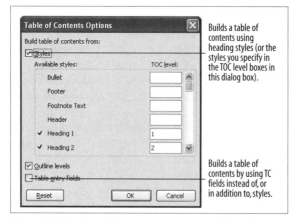

Builds a table of contents using heading styles (or the styles you specify in the TOC level boxes in this dialog box).

Builds a table of contents by using TC fields instead of, or in addition to, styles.

Figure 10-22. The Table of Contents Options dialog box.

In the previous lesson, you learned how to create a table of contents the fast and easy way—by using heading styles. Most of the time you will want to create a table of contents using the heading style method, but there may be a time when you will need to use the other method—using TC (table of contents) fields.

Inserting TC fields to indicate table of contents entries isn't nearly as fast as the heading style method, but it provides more flexibility. For example, if your document doesn't contain any heading styles—but you still want a table of contents—use TC fields. Or, if you want to use text other than your document's heading styles in a table of contents, you would use TC fields to create a table of contents to your specifications.

1 Go to Page 2 and place the insertion point in front of the heading Executive Summary.

You want to add a TC field here so that it will appear in the table of contents.

Here's how to insert a TC field.

2 Press Alt + Shift + O (the letter O, not the number 0) to mark the selected text as a table of contents entry.

The Mark Table of Contents Entry dialog box appears, as shown in Figure 10-21. Now you need to enter what you want to appear in the table of contents entry.

3 Type A Look at the Problem in the Entry box.

Next, you need to specify the level of the table of contents entry by clicking the Level list. Since you want this table of contents entry to appear at the top level of the table of contents, you don't need to change the Level list.

4 Click Mark and then Close.

You've just created a Level 1 table of contents entry. Let's add one more…

5 Go to Page 3.

You want to add another TC field here. If you spot the text you want to appear in the TC field, you can highlight it before pressing Alt + Shift + O.

6 Select the text Corporate Intranet and press Alt + Shift + O.

The Mark Table of Contents Entry dialog box reappears. Since you selected "Corporate Intranet" before pressing Alt + Shift + O, you don't have to type a table of contents entry, but you still need to specify the table of contents level.

7 Type 3 in the Level box and click Mark, and then Close.

You've just created a Level 3 table of contents entry. Now you have to create a table of contents based on the Table of Contents Entries that you've made.

8 Press Ctrl + Home to go to the beginning of the document.

You have to delete the old table of contents before you can insert the new one. Here's how to delete a table of contents:

9 Select the table of contents. Right-click the table of contents and select Toggle Field Codes from the short-cut menu.

TIP **Another way to display field codes is to press** Shift + F9.

Yikes! A strange string of characters "{TOC \O"1-3" \H\Z\U}" appears. This is the *field code* that tells Word to create a table of contents. By displaying the field code, you can easily delete the table of contents.

10 Delete the table of contents field code by selecting it and pressing the Delete key.

Okay, let's insert the new table of contents.

11 Select Insert → Reference → Index and Tables from the menu and click the Table of Contents tab if necessary.

The Index and Tables dialog box appears with the Table of Contents tab in front. By default, Word builds the table of contents using any heading styles it finds in a document, so you have to specify that you want to build the table of contents using TC fields. To do this, you need to click the Options button first.

12 Click the Options button.

The Table of Contents Options dialog box appears, as shown in Figure 10-22. Here you can specify how you want to build your table of contents. You can build your table of contents from:

- **Styles:** This option builds a table of contents based on the heading styles in your document.
- **Outline levels:** This option builds a table of contents based on text marked with outline levels in your document, instead of, or in addition to, styles.
- **Table entry fields:** This option builds a table of contents based on any table of contents entries you've defined.
- **Both:** By checking more than one check box, you can build a table of contents that includes both options in your document.

13 Uncheck the Styles and Outline levels options. Check the Table entry fields check box, click OK, and click OK again.

Word builds a new table of contents based on the TC fields you inserted in the document. Since you only inserted two TC fields, the resulting table of contents is rather short.

QUICK REFERENCE

TO CREATE A TABLE OF CONTENTS ENTRY:

- SELECT THE TEXT YOU WANT TO INCLUDE IN THE TABLE OF CONTENTS, PRESS ALT + SHIFT + O, CHANGE THE LEVEL IF NEEDED, AND CLICK OK.

TO INSERT A TABLE OF CONTENTS FROM TC FIELDS:

1. PLACE THE INSERTION POINT WHERE YOU WANT THE TABLE OF CONTENTS AND SELECT INSERT → REFERENCE → INDEX AND TABLES FROM THE MENU AND CLICK THE TABLE OF CONTENTS TAB.

2. SPECIFY A FORMAT FOR THE TABLE OF CONTENTS.

3. CLICK OPTIONS AND CLICK THE TABLE ENTRY FIELDS CHECK BOX.

4. CLICK OK, OK.

TO DELETE A TABLE OF CONTENTS:

1. SELECT THE TABLE OF CONTENTS. RIGHT-CLICK THE TABLE OF CONTENTS AND SELECT TOGGLE FIELD CODES FROM THE SHORTCUT MENU.

2. SELECT THE TABLE OF CONTENTS FIELD CODE AND PRESS DELETE.

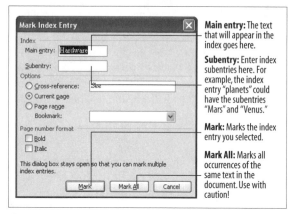

Figure 10-23. The Mark Index Entry dialog box.

Callouts from Figure 10-23:

Main entry: The text that will appear in the index goes here.

Subentry: Enter index subentries here. For example, the index entry "planets" could have the subentries "Mars" and "Venus."

Mark: Marks the index entry you selected.

Mark All: Marks all occurrences of the same text in the document. Use with caution!

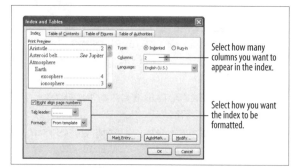

Figure 10-24. The Index tab of the Index and Tables dialog box.

Callouts from Figure 10-24:

Select how many columns you want to appear in the index.

Select how you want the index to be formatted.

Figure 10-25. A completed index.

So far, this chapter has covered such topics as outlines, footnotes and endnotes, and tables of contents. This lesson explains how to create an index. An *index* can usually be found at the end of a document, and lists the words and phrases in a document, along with the page numbers they appear on. There are two basic steps involved in creating an index: defining which word(s) you want to appear in the index, and then creating the index itself.

1 Go to Page 3 of the document and select the heading Hardware.

This is the text you want to be included and referenced in the index.

2 With the text still selected, press Alt + Shift + X.

TIP

Another way to define an index entry is to select the text you want to define and select Insert → Index and Tables from the menu, click the Index tab, and click Mark Entry or Mark All.

The Mark Index Entry dialog box appears, as shown in Figure 10-23. You have several options for the type of index entry you want to create, which include:

- **Cross-reference:** Adds a cross-reference as an index entry instead of a page number. For example, you could create an index entry that reads *See Hardware*.

- **Current page:** Lists the current page number for the selected index entry. This is the default option.

- **Page range:** Lists a range of pages that are included in the bookmark that you click in the Bookmark list. Obviously, you must first mark the range of pages with a bookmark before you can select the range of pages.

Ninety-five percent of the time, you'll use the Current page option.

3 Verify that the Current page option is selected in the Options area, click Mark, then click Close.

Word creates an index entry that will appear in the index.

NOTE

You're probably wondering what all those weird symbols that appear on the screen are. Word automatically displays all nonprinting characters such as tab characters, paragraph marks, and field codes any time you insert an index entry so that you can see what you inserted. You can hide all these confusing symbols by clicking the Show/Hide button on the Standard toolbar.

4 Go to Page 2 of the document and select the text Pentium III processor in the second paragraph under the Executive Summary heading, and press Alt + Shift + X.

The Mark Index Entry dialog box appears.

5 Click Mark All.

Mark All marks all the occurrences of the selected "Pentium III" text in the document as index entries.

6 Click Close, go to Page 3 of the document, and select the bulleted item Windows 2000 Server.

7 With the text still selected, press Alt + Shift + X and then click Mark All. Click the Close button.

"Windows 2000 Server" is added as an index entry. If you were creating an index, you would certainly have more than three entries, but that is all we need to create a simple, very short index.

⋮ NOTE ⋮ *Be careful when you use Mark All—you may end up with a lot of meaningless index entries that you really didn't want.*

8 Press Ctrl + End to move to the end of the document, then press Ctrl + Enter to insert a page break.

A page break is inserted into the document. Add a heading for the index.

9 Type Index and press Enter.

If you want, you can apply additional font and paragraph formatting (bold, centered, etc.) to the Index heading. Now you can add the index.

10 Select Insert → Reference → Index and Tables from the menu and click the Index tab.

The Index and Tables dialog box appears with the Index tab in front, as shown in Figure 10-24.

11 Select Formal in the Formats list, and then click OK.

Word creates a very small index based on the entries you specified, as shown in Figure 10-25. Because you only made three index entries, the index you created doesn't look anything like the huge indexes you find at the back of a text book. But, it's good enough to give you an idea how an index works and how to go about creating one.

12 Close the document without saving changes.

QUICK REFERENCE

TO CREATE AN INDEX ENTRY:

1. SELECT THE TEXT YOU WANT TO INCLUDE IN THE INDEX AND PRESS ALT + SHIFT + X.

2. SELECT THE TYPE OF INDEX ENTRY, IF NECESSARY, (CURRENT PAGE IS THE DEFAULT SETTING) AND CLICK MARK OR MARK ALL.

OR...

1. SELECT THE TEXT YOU WANT TO DEFINE AND SELECT INSERT → REFERENCE → INDEX AND TABLES FROM THE MENU.

2. CLICK THE INDEX TAB, AND CLICK MARK ENTRY OR MARK ALL.

TO CREATE AN INDEX:

1. FIRST, MAKE SURE YOU HAVE DEFINED YOUR INDEX ENTRIES.

2. SELECT INSERT → REFERENCE → INDEX AND TABLES FROM THE MENU AND CLICK THE INDEX TAB.

3. SELECT THE FORMAT YOU WANT TO USE FOR YOUR INDEX FROM THE FORMATS LIST, SPECIFY ANY ADDITIONAL FORMATTING OPTIONS, AND CLICK OK.

Working with Master Documents

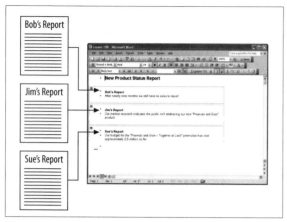

Figure 10-26. A master document combines one or more individual subdocuments.

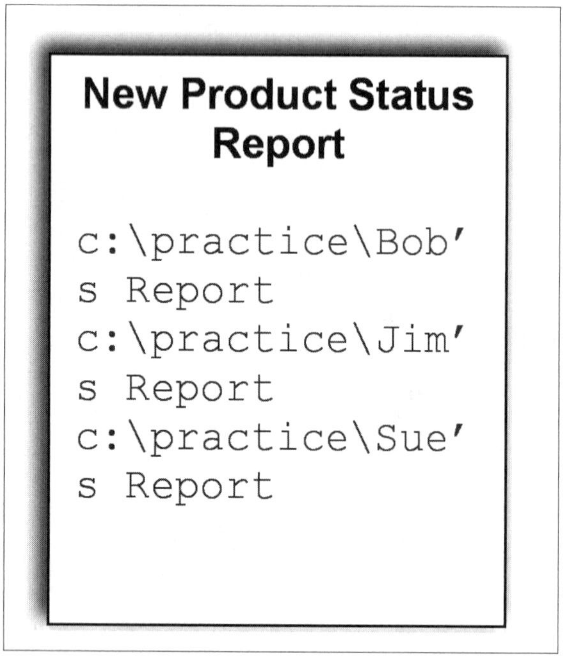

New Product Status Report

```
c:\practice\Bob'
s Report
c:\practice\Jim'
s Report
c:\practice\Sue'
s Report
```

Figure 10-27. When you open a master document, its subdocuments are closed by default.

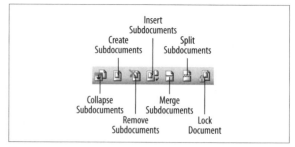

Figure 10-28. The Master Document buttons on the Outlining toolbar.

Sometimes you may want to combine several small documents to produce a single, larger document. For example, perhaps you are working on a group project and each member of your group must contribute an article to be used in a much larger report. You can incorporate several smaller, individual documents, or *subdocuments*, into a single *master document*. A master document is similar to an outline and contains several smaller, individual documents called *subdocuments*. Whenever you open a master document, all of the subdocuments open and are displayed in outline view, enabling you to work on all the documents at once, as shown in Figure 10-26.

You need to be in Outline view in order to create a master document. Once you're in Outline view, you can easily add and delete subdocuments to and from the master document and move the subdocuments to change their order. You can also open, modify, and print any subdocument from within its master document.

It's important to realize that a subdocument is not actually saved inside of its master document. Instead, a master document contains information on where to find the subdocument file. When you open a master document, all of its subdocuments are closed, or collapsed, by default. You can open a subdocument by clicking its text if the subdocuments are collapsed, or by double-clicking its ▣ subdocument icon when the subdocuments are expanded. You can open all the subdocuments in a master document by print previewing the master document.

In this lesson, you will get some experience working with a master document.

1 Open the Lesson 10D document.

The Lesson 10D document is a master document that contains three subdocuments: Bob's Report, Jim's Report, and Sue's Report. When you open a master document, all its subdocuments are closed by default with a hyperlink indicating where the subdocuments are located, as shown in Figure 10-27.

Master documents are easiest to work with in Master Document view. You can get to Master Document view by first switching to Outline view.

2 Click the Outline View button on the horizontal scroll bar.

Word displays the document in Outline view. Word usually automatically selects the Master Document view button by default, but it doesn't hurt to make sure.

3 If necessary, click the Master Document View button on the Outlining toolbar.

Word displays the Lesson 10D document in Master Document view and displays the Master Document buttons on the Outlining toolbar, as shown in Figure 10-28. Each subdocument has its own ▤ subdocument icon. You can select a subdocument by clicking its ▤ icon.

Notice the subdocuments also have a ▤ icon. This means the subdocuments are locked and cannot be modified. Usually, subdocuments are locked because they aren't opened. Here's how to open, or expand, the subdocuments in a master document.

4 Click the 🔒 Expand Subdocuments button on the Outlining toolbar.

> *TIP* Another way to expand subdocuments is to click the Print Preview button on the Standard toolbar. Click Yes when prompted to open any subdocuments.

Word expands the three subdocuments, unlocking them and displaying their contents. Let's look at the document in Print Preview.

5 Click the Print Preview button on the Standard toolbar.

Word displays the master document in Print Preview.

6 Press Page Down several times to view the subdocuments. Click Close when you're finished.

Notice that each subdocument falls on a separate page. Let's find out why.

7 Click the Normal View button on the horizontal scroll bar.

Word displays the Lesson 10D document in Normal view. Notice that the three subdocuments are separated by section breaks. These section breaks allow the subdocuments to keep their own page formatting.

Since we're finished working with the Lesson 10D master document, move on to the next step and close it.

8 Close the Lesson 10D document.

Still finding this master document/subdocument concept a little confusing? Don't worry—in the next lesson you'll get a chance to create your own master document.

QUICK REFERENCE

TO SWITCH TO MASTER DOCUMENT VIEW:

1. SWITCH TO OUTLINE VIEW BY CLICKING THE OUTLINE VIEW BUTTON ON THE HORIZONTAL SCROLL BAR OR BY SELECTING VIEW → OUTLINE FROM THE MENU.

2. CLICK THE MASTER DOCUMENT VIEW BUTTON ON THE OUTLINING TOOLBAR.

TO EXPAND SUBDOCUMENTS:

• CLICK THE EXPAND SUBDOCUMENTS BUTTON ON THE OUTLINING TOOLBAR.

OR...

• CLICK THE PRINT PREVIEW BUTTON ON THE STANDARD TOOLBAR. CLICK YES WHEN PROMPTED TO OPEN ANY SUBDOCUMENTS.

Creating a Master Document

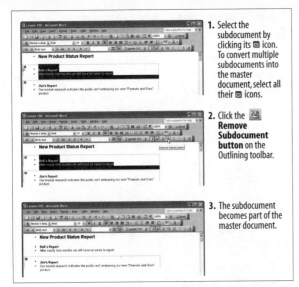

1. Select the subdocument by clicking its 🔲 icon. To convert multiple subdocuments into the master document, select all their 🔲 icons.

2. Click the Remove **Subdocument button** on the Outlining toolbar.

3. The subdocument becomes part of the master document.

Figure 10-29. The procedure for converting a subdocument into part of the master document.

All you have to do to create a master document is insert one or more subdocuments into any document.

Once you have created a master document and its subdocuments, you can start working on it. If the master document is stored on a network, several users can open and work on their own subdocuments at the same time. You can modify, rearrange, and delete the subdocuments in a master document. You can even convert a subdocument into the master document, so that it is actually part of the master document, instead of saved in a separate subdocument.

In this lesson, you will learn how to create a master document, how to delete a subdocument, and how to convert a subdocument into the master document. Figure 10-29 shows the procedure for converting a subdocument into part of the master document.

1 Create a new document by clicking the New Blank Document button **on the Standard toolbar.**

Let's give our new document a heading.

2 Click the Bold button **and the** Center button **on the Formatting toolbar, and type** New Product Status Report.

OK! You're ready to add a subdocument to the current document. You need to be in Master Document view in order to do this.

3 Click the Outline View button **on the horizontal scroll bar, and then click the** Master Document View button **on the Outlining toolbar.**

Word displays the document in Master Document view. Here's how to insert a subdocument:

4 Click the 🔲 Insert Subdocument button **on the Outlining toolbar.**

The Insert Subdocument dialog box appears. You need to specify the document you want to insert as a subdocument. You will insert the "Bob's Report" file from your Practice folder.

5 Navigate to your Practice folder, select Bob's Report and click Open.

Your document becomes a master document after you insert the "Bob's Report" document. Each subdocument is inserted as a different section, with section breaks appearing before and after the subdocument. If your master document and subdocuments contain page numbering, they would be correctly numbered, even though they are in two different document files.

Let's insert a few more subdocuments into the master document.

6 Following the procedure in Step 5, insert the Jim's Report and Sue's Report documents into the current document.

It's just as easy to remove a subdocument from a master document.

7 Select the Sue's Report subdocument by clicking its 🔲 icon, then remove it from the master document by pressing Delete.

The Sue's Report subdocument is removed from the master document.

Often, you will want to convert or combine one or more subdocuments into the master document so that they are no longer saved in a separate file. Here's how to convert a subdocument into part of the master document:

8 Select the Bob's Report subdocument by clicking its 🔲 icon.

Here's how to convert the Bob's Report subdocument into part of the master document:

9 Click the  Remove Subdocument button on the Outlining toolbar.

Word converts the Bob's Report subdocument into the master document. When you convert a subdocument into part of the master document, the subdocument file remains unchanged, in its original location.

10 Close the files without saving changes.

That's it—you've finished another chapter! Now that you know how to work with long documents, you don't have any more excuses for not starting that book you've always thought about writing.

QUICK REFERENCE

TO INSERT A SUBDOCUMENT:

1. SWITCH TO MASTER DOCUMENT VIEW.

2. CLICK THE INSERT SUBDOCUMENT BUTTON ON THE OUTLINING TOOLBAR AND SELECT THE FILE YOU WANT TO INSERT.

TO REMOVE A SUBDOCUMENT:

* CLICK THE SUBDOCUMENT'S ICON AND PRESS DELETE.

TO MAKE A SUBDOCUMENT PART OF THE MASTER DOCUMENT:

* CLICK THE SUBDOCUMENT'S ICON AND CLICK THE REMOVE SUBDOCUMENT BUTTON ON THE MASTER DOCUMENT TOOLBAR.

Lesson Summary

Creating a Document in Outline View

Outline view helps you to organize your ideas and topics and see the overall structure of a long document.

A ✚ symbol by a heading indicates the heading contains subordinate text that is currently collapsed, or hidden. A ▭ symbol by a heading indicates the heading's subordinate text is expanded, or displayed.

To View a Document in Outline View: Click the Outline View button located on the horizontal scrollbar near the bottom of the screen, or select View → Outline from the menu.

To Demote the Current Heading: Complete any of the following:

- Press Tab
- Click the Demote button on the Outlining toolbar
- Select the Heading level from the Style List on the Formatting toolbar

To Promote the Current Heading: Complete any of the following:

- Press Shift + Tab
- Click the Promote button on the Outlining toolbar
- Select the Heading level from the Style List on the Formatting toolbar

To Demote a Heading to Body Text: Click the Demote to Body Text button on the Outlining toolbar.

Viewing an Outline

To Expand a Heading: Make sure the insertion point is in the heading and click the Expand button on the Outlining toolbar, or double-click the heading's ✚ symbol.

To Collapse a Heading: Make sure the insertion point is in the heading and click the Collapse button on the Outlining toolbar, or double-click the heading's ▭ symbol.

To Display all the Headings in a Document: Click the Show Levels list arrow on the Outlining toolbar and select Show All Levels.

To Display only the First Line of Text: Click the Show First Line Only button on the Outlining toolbar.

Modifying an Outline

To Rearrange an Outline: Either place the insertion point in the heading you want to move and press the Move Up button or Move Down button on the Outlining toolbar, or drag the heading's outline symbol to a new location in the outline.

To Demote the Current Heading: Complete any of the following:

- Press Tab
- Click the Demote button on the Outlining toolbar
- Select the Heading level from the Style List on the Formatting toolbar

To Promote the Current Heading: Complete any of the following:

- Press Shift + Tab
- Click the Promote button on the Outlining toolbar
- Select the Heading level from the Style List on the Formatting toolbar

Numbering an Outline

To Number an Outline: Select the heading style you want to modify and click the Styles and Formatting button on the Formatting toolbar. Click the heading style's ▾ arrow in the task pane, and select Modify from the drop-down menu. Click the Format button, select Numbering, and click the Outline Numbered tab. Select the number scheme you want to use to number your outline.

You can customize any number scheme by selecting it and clicking the Customize button.

Adding Bookmarks

Just like a bookmark keeps track of your place in a novel, a bookmark in Word marks your location in a document so that you can quickly find and jump back to that location.

To Insert a Bookmark: Place the insertion point where you want to insert the bookmark, select Insert → Bookmark from the menu, and enter a name for the bookmark.

To Jump to a Bookmark: Select Edit → Go To from the menu; double-click the Page number area of the Status bar; or press F5 or Ctrl + G. Select Bookmark from the Go to what list, select the bookmark name from the drop-down list, and click Go To.

Adding Footnotes and Endnotes

To Insert a Footnote or Endnote: Place the insertion point where you want the footnote or endnote inserted and select Insert → Reference → Footnote from the menu. Specify if you want to insert a footnote or endnote, click Insert, and type the footnote or endnote.

To View a Footnote or Endnote: Position the pointer over the footnote or endnote number for several seconds.

To Edit a Footnote or Endnote: Double-click the footnote or endnote number.

To Delete a Footnote or Endnote: Select the footnote or endnote number, and press the Delete key.

Adding Cross-References

To Insert a Cross-Referenced: Place the insertion point where you want to insert the cross-reference, select Insert → Reference → Cross-Reference from the menu, and select the type of item you want to reference (such as headings and bookmarks) from the Reference type list. Select the item you want to cross-reference from the For which heading list, then select the information to include in the cross-reference (such as the entire caption or page number) from the Insert reference to list. Specify whether or not you want to insert the cross-referenced item as a hyperlink, click Insert, then click Close.

To Automatically Update Cross-Reference Fields when Word Prints: Select Tools → Options from the menu, click the Print tab, make sure the Update fields box is checked, and click OK.

Creating a Table of Contents using Level Styles

You can create a table of contents based on a document's heading styles. For example, paragraphs formatted with the Heading 1 style would be main headings in the table of contents, paragraphs formatted with the Heading 2 style would be subheadings, and so on.

To Insert a Table of Contents: Place the insertion point where you want the table of contents, select Insert → Reference → Index and Tables from the menu, and click the Table of Contents tab. Specify a format for the table of contents and which heading levels to include, and click OK.

To Update a Table of Contents: Right-click the table of contents and select Update field.

To Automatically Update the Table of Contents when Word Prints: Select Tools → Options from the menu, click the Print tab, make sure the Update fields box is checked, and click OK.

Creating a Table of Contents using TC Fields

You can create a table of contents based on TC (table of content) fields, which you must manually insert in the document.

To Create a Table of Contents Entry: Select the text you want to include in the Table of Contents, press Alt + Shift + O, change the level if needed, and click OK.

To Insert a Table of Contents from TC Fields: Place the insertion point where you want the table of contents, select Insert → Reference → Index and Tables from the menu, click the Table of Contents tab, and specify a format for the table of contents. Click Options, click the Table entry fields check box, then click OK, OK.

To Delete a Table of Contents: Select the table of contents. Right-click the table of contents and select Toggle Field Codes from the shortcut menu, select the table of contents field code, and press Delete.

Creating an Index

To Create an Index Entry (Using the Keyboard): Select the text you want included in the index and press Alt + Shift + X. Select the type of index entry, if necessary (current page is the default setting), and click Mark or Mark All.

To Create an Index Entry (Using the Menu): Select the text you want to define and select Insert → Reference → Index and Tables from the menu. Click the Index tab and click Mark Entry or Mark All.

To Create an Index: First, make sure you have defined your index entries. Select Insert → Reference → Index and Tables from the menu and click the Index tab. Select the format you want to use for your index from the Formats list, specify any additional formatting options, and click OK.

Working with Master Documents

A master document is similar to an outline and contains several individual documents, called subdocuments.

To Switch to Master Document View: Switch to Outline view by clicking the Outline View button on the horizontal scroll bar or by selecting View → Outline from the menu. Click the Master Document View button on the Outlining toolbar.

To Expand Subdocuments: Click the Expand Subdocuments button on the Outlining toolbar, or click the Print Preview button on the Standard toolbar and click Yes when prompted to open any subdocuments.

Creating a Master Document

To Insert a Subdocument: Click the Insert Subdocument button on the Master Document toolbar and select the file you want to insert.

To Remove a Subdocument: Click the subdocument's ▤ icon and press Delete.

To Make a Subdocument Part of the Master Document: Click the subdocument's ▤ icon and click the Remove Subdocument button on the Master Document toolbar.

Quiz

1. What are the advantages of working in Outline view?

   A. You can see the overall structure of longer documents by viewing only particular heading levels.

   B. You can easily rearrange the order of the document's headings and contents.

   C. You can promote and demote heading levels in the document.

   D. All of the above.

2. In Outline view, a ✚ symbol by a heading indicates that:

   A. The heading has been added since the document was first opened.

   B. The heading is a Level 1 heading.

   C. The heading contains hidden subheadings and/or subordinate text.

   D. The heading is the first one in the document.

3. What is the procedure for switching to Outline view? (Select all that apply.)

   A. Click the Outline View button on the horizontal scroll bar located near the bottom of the screen.

   B. Click the Outline View button on the Standard toolbar.

   C. Select View → Outline from the menu.

   D. Select Tools → Outline from the menu.

4. Which of the following is NOT a way to demote a heading?

   A. Select a heading style from the Style list on the Formatting toolbar.

   B. Click the Show Level 2 button on the Outlining toolbar.

   C. Press the Tab key.

   D. Click the Demote button on the Outlining toolbar.

5. Each of the nine heading levels Word uses for outlining are based on a style named Heading 1 the highest level, Heading 2 for the next highest level, and so on. (True or False?)

6. What is a Bookmark and how do you insert one into a document?

   A. A Bookmark is another name for a cross-reference. You can insert a Bookmark by selecting Insert → Cross-reference from the menu.

   B. A Bookmark is a location or selection of text that you name for reference purposes and to mark a location in a document. You can insert a Bookmark by selecting Insert → Bookmark from the menu.

C. A Bookmark is a TC entry. You can insert a Book-mark by selecting Insert → Bookmark from the menu.

D. A Bookmark is an index entry. You can insert a Bookmark by selecting Insert → Index Entry from the menu.

7. You want to combine several smaller documents into a single, larger document. The best way to do this would be to:

A. Change the page numbering in each document so that the page numbers are ordered sequentially between the documents, print the documents individually, then staple all the documents together into a larger report.

B. Create a master document and insert the smaller documents as subdocuments.

C. Create a new document and then individually open and copy the contents of each of the smaller documents, and then paste them into the new document.

D. Print each of the smaller documents, use whiteout to remove the incorrect page numbers, then staple all the documents together into a larger report.

8. You're working on a school report and need to cite a source. How can you add a footnote to your document?

A. Select View → Header and Footer from the menu.

B. Select Tools → Footnote from the menu.

C. Select Insert → Reference → Footnote from the menu.

D. Click the Foot button on the Standard toolbar.

9. When you open a master document, Word automatically opens the subdocuments it contains as well. (True or False?)

10. What is the procedure for inserting a cross-reference?

A. Select Insert → Reference → Cross-reference from the menu.

B. Click the Cross Reference toolbar on the Long Documents toolbar.

C. Select Tools → Cross-reference from the menu.

D. Press Insert + C + R.

11. Which of the following statements is NOT true?

A. A cross-reference is automatically updated if the item it references is moved. For example, "See Page 5" might become "See Page 8."

B. Word can build a table of contents by looking at a document's heading styles and TC fields.

C. To ensure that Word automatically updates a document's table of contents and index when you print it, select Tools → Options from the menu, click the Print tab, and make sure the Update fields box is checked.

D. To insert an Index entry, select Tools → Index Entry from the menu.

12. You're writing a reference book on pick-up lines. How can you add a table of contents to the book?

A. Select Tools → Index and Tables from the menu and click the Table of Contents tab.

B. Select Insert → Reference → Index and Tables from the menu, and click the Table of Contents tab.

C. Select Table → Of Contents from the menu.

D. Word can supposedly create a table of contents for you, however this feature is filled with bugs and should not be used.

Homework

1. Open the Homework 10 document and save it as "Dave's Catalog."

2. Click the Outline View button located on the horizontal scroll bar, near the bottom of the screen.

3. Click the Show Level 2 button on the Outlining toolbar.

4. Under the "Mean Mammals" section, move the "Long-Tailed Shrew" heading above the "Rhinoceros" heading.

5. Demote the "Black Widow Spider" level 1 heading to a level 2 heading.

6. Switch back to Print Layout View by clicking the Print Layout View button located on the horizontal scroll bar, near the bottom of the screen.

7. Insert a Table of Contents.

8. Create a cross-reference: Find the "Long-Tailed Shrew" item. Place the insertion point at the very end of the descriptive paragraph, type "Also see," press the Spacebar, then select Insert → Reference → Cross-reference from the menu, select "Heading" from the reference type list, and make sure "Heading Text" appears in the Insert Reference to list. Select the "Venus Fly Trap" heading, click Insert, then Close.

9. Finish the cross-reference by adding a reference to the "Venus Fly Trap" page number: Type "on page," press the Spacebar, select Insert → Reference → Cross-reference from the menu, select "Heading" from the reference type list, and select "Page number" from the Insert Reference to list. Select the "Venus Fly Trap" heading, click Insert, then Close.

10. Create an Index entry: Select the heading text "Long-Tailed Shrew" and press Ctrl + Shift + X and click Mark.

11. Create index entries for all the remaining animals.

12. Create an index at the end of the document: Press Ctrl + End to move to the end of the document and insert a manual page break by pressing Ctrl + Enter. Select Insert → Reference → Index and Tables from the menu, click the Index tab, and click OK.

13. Save your work and exit Microsoft Word.

Quiz Answers

1. D. All of these are advantages of Outline view.

2. C. A ✚ symbol next to a heading indicates that it contains hidden subheadings and/or subordinate text.

3. A and C. Both of these methods will let you view your documents in Outline view.

4. B. You cannot demote a heading by clicking the Show Level 2 button.

5. True. All the heading levels are based on styles.

6. B.

7. B. Create a master document and insert the smaller documents as subdocuments.

8. C. Select Insert → Reference → Footnote from the menu to insert a footnote or endnote.

9. False. When you open a master document, its subdocuments are closed by default. You can open, or expand the subdocuments by clicking the Expand Subdocuments button on the Master Document toolbar.

10. A. To insert a cross-reference, select Insert → Reference → Cross-reference from the menu.

11. D. To insert an Index entry, either press Alt + Shift + X or select Insert → Reference → Index and Tables from the menu, click the Index tab, and click Mark Entry.

12. B. To insert a table of contents, select Insert → Reference → Index and Tables from the menu and click the Table of Contents tab.

WORKING WITH WORDART AND CHARTS

CHAPTER OBJECTIVES:

Inserting a WordArt Object, Lesson 11.1

Formatting and Editing a WordArt Object, Lesson 11.2

Creating a Chart and Modifying a Chart, Lesson 11.3 and 11.4

Selecting a Chart Type, Lesson 11.5

CHAPTER OBJECTIVES: CREATE A NEWSLETTER HEADING

Prerequisites

- **Windows basics: how to use menus, toolbars, dialog boxes, and shortcut keystrokes**
- **How to select objects**
- **How to drag and resize objects**
- **How to create and work with tables**

Word processors have come a long, long way since their introduction more than twenty years ago. Older word processors were just a little better than typewriters and could only create simple letters, reports, and memos. Today, people routinely use the advanced text and graphic capabilities of modern word processors to create beautiful newsletters, brochures, and catalogs—tasks that would have seemed impossible fifteen years ago. This chapter explains how you can incorporate two types of objects into your documents to give them pizzazz and present information in an organized manner.

First, you will learn how to use Microsoft's *WordArt* program. WordArt is a program that turns ordinary text into dazzling 3-D headlines—great for emphasizing simple messages, such as "Limited Offer!"

Next, you will learn how to create and insert a chart into your documents. The person who coined the phrase "A picture is worth a thousand words" might have had a chart in mind when making the statement. One of the best ways to present numbers is with a chart—and the Microsoft Graph program makes adding charts to your documents easy. This chapter explains just about everything you need to know about charts—how to create dynamic-looking charts, how to edit and format charts, and how to work with different types of charts.

Inserting a WordArt Object

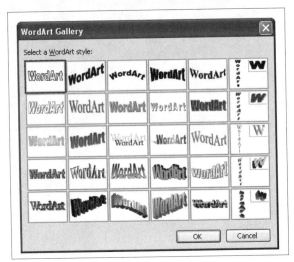

Figure 11-1. The WordArt Gallery dialog box.

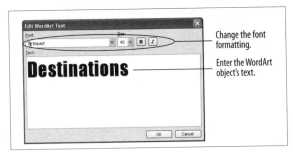

Change the font formatting.

Enter the WordArt object's text.

Figure 11-2. Type what you want your WordArt object to say in the Edit WordArt Text dialog box.

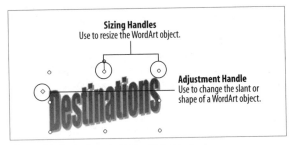

Sizing Handles
Use to resize the WordArt object.

Adjustment Handle
Use to change the slant or shape of a WordArt object.

Figure 11-3. An Inserted WordArt object.

Figure 11-4. The updated document with an inserted WordArt object.

WordArt is definitely the coolest "bonus program" that comes with Microsoft Office. With WordArt, you can create dramatic, colorful text effects that are great for using in any announcements or headlines in your documents. In this lesson, you will use WordArt to create a more visually appealing headline for the newsletter.

1 Open the Lesson 11A document and save it as Updated Newsletter.

First, delete the newsletter's boring headline.

2 Select the text Destinations! and press Delete. Click the Center button on the Formatting toolbar.

Now you will add a visually exciting Microsoft WordArt object for the headline of the newsletter.

3 Select Insert → Picture → WordArt from the menu.

The WordArt Gallery dialog box appears, as shown in Figure 11-1. The WordArt Gallery displays the various formats you can apply to your text.

4 Select the second option in the third row—the **WordArt** option—then click OK.

The Edit WordArt Text dialog box appears, as shown in Figure 11-2. Here, you enter the text you want to use in your WordArt object.

5 Type Destinations.

You can also change the font type and size in the Edit WordArt text dialog box.

6 Click the Size list arrow to select 40, and click OK.

 Another way to format WordArt is to right-click the WordArt and select Format WordArt from the shortcut menu. Change the properties in the Format WordArt dialog box and click OK.

The WordArt object is inserted into the document, as shown in Figure 11-3.

The WordArt toolbar contains buttons that modify WordArt objects, and it only appears when a WordArt object is selected. You can move, resize, and position a WordArt object just like any other object.

7 Click the Destination word art. Click the  Text Wrapping button on the WordArt toolbar. Select Top and Bottom from the list.

The WordArt's text wrapping changes so the text appears above and below the image.

8 Click the WordArt Alignment button on the WordArt toolbar. Select Center from the list.

Next, we want to change the slant of the WordArt.

If your WordArt is still selected, you'll notice a yellow diamond (♦) on its side. This is an *adjustment handle*—some WordArt objects sneak them in along with the object's sizing handles. By grabbing and dragging an adjustment handle, you can change the angle at which some WordArt objects slant or loop. Adjustment handles are not used to resize a WordArt object—you still need to click and drag one of the sizing handles to do that.

9 Click and drag the WordArt object's yellow adjustment handle (♦) up an inch.

Compare your document to the one in Figure 11-4, then…

10 Save your work.

One more important note: WordArt is actually an external program, so you can use it with all of your Microsoft Office—perhaps to add a dramatic title to an Excel chart or a headline to a PowerPoint presentation.

Go on to the next lesson to find out more about formatting WordArt.

QUICK REFERENCE

TO INSERT A WORDART OBJECT:

1. SELECT INSERT → PICTURE → WORDART FROM THE MENU.
2. SELECT A TEXT STYLE.
3. TYPE THE TEXT FOR THE WORDART OBJECT, CHANGE THE FONT TYPE AND SIZE, AND CLICK OK.

TO FORMAT A WORDART OBJECT:

- RIGHT-CLICK THE OBJECT AND SELECT FORMAT WORDART FROM THE SHORTCUT MENU.

OR...

- USE THE WORDART TOOLBAR.

TO RESIZE A WORDART OBJECT:

- CLICK THE WORDART OBJECT TO SELECT IT AND DRAG THE WORDART OBJECT'S SIZING HANDLES UNTIL THE WORDART OBJECT IS THE SIZE YOU WANT.

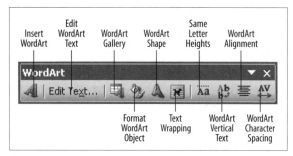

Insert WordArt
Edit WordArt Text
WordArt Gallery
WordArt Shape
Same Letter Heights
WordArt Alignment

Format WordArt Object
Text Wrapping
WordArt Vertical Text
WordArt Character Spacing

Figure 11-5. The WordArt toolbar.

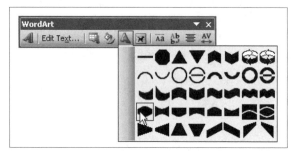

Figure 11-6. Change the shape of a WordArt object by clicking the WordArt Shape button and selecting the desired shape.

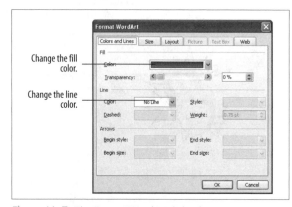

Change the fill color.

Change the line color.

Figure 11-7. The Format WordArt dialog box.

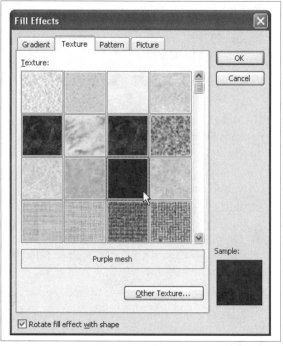

Figure 11-8. The Texture tab of the Fill Effects dialog box.

Figure 11-9. The updated WordArt object

Once you have created a WordArt object, you can change its appearance in many ways. You can change the style or shape of the WordArt object, adjust the amount of space between letters, or even rotate the WordArt object. What's more, you can format a WordArt object just like another object, changing its fill and line color, size and shape, and even add a shadow or 3-D effect. In this lesson, you will experiment with several different WordArt formatting options.

1 Click the WordArt object if it's not already selected.

The WordArt toolbar appears, as shown in Figure 11-5. You can use the WordArt toolbar to modify the selected WordArt object.

2 Click the 🖼 WordArt Gallery button on the WordArt toolbar.

The WordArt Gallery dialog box appears where you can select a different style for the selected WordArt object.

3 Select the fifth option in the second row, the **WordArt** option, and click OK.

The WordArt object is formatted with the selected style. You can also easily change the shape of the WordArt object.

4 Click the **WordArt** WordArt Shape button on the WordArt toolbar. Then select Inflate (the first option in the fourth row), as shown in Figure 11-6.

The WordArt text appears in the selected inflated style.

5 Click the ⇕AV WordArt Character Spacing button on the WordArt toolbar, then select Tight.

The letters in the WordArt object appear closer together. You can also go back and edit the WordArt object's text—even after you've formatted it.

6 Click the Edit Text... Edit Text button on the WordArt toolbar.

The Edit WordArt Text dialog box appears. Now you can change the text, font style, or font size.

7 Add an exclamation point (!) to the text, then click OK.

The Edit WordArt Text dialog box closes and the text of the WordArt object is changed. Next let's change the WordArt object's fill color.

8 Click the ⊿ Format WordArt button on the WordArt toolbar and click the Colors and Lines tab.

The Format WordArt dialog box appears, as shown in Figure 11-7.

9 Click the Line Color list arrow and select No Line.

This will remove the line that appears around the WordArt object.

We'll finish this lesson by changing the WordArt object's fill color. You can fill WordArt objects with solid colors or you can use the Fill Effect command to create more dramatic effects such as a gradient, texture, pattern, or picture.

10 Click the Fill Color list arrow, select Fill Effects from the list and click the Texture tab.

The Texture tab of the Fill Effect dialog box appears, as shown in Figure 11-8.

11 Click the Purple Mesh texture, click OK and OK again.

The Format WordArt dialog box closes and the WordArt object is colored with the purple mesh fill effect.

12 Compare your object to the one in Figure 11-9, then save your work and close the document.

QUICK REFERENCE

TO CHANGE THE STYLE OF A WORDART OBJECT:

1. CLICK THE WORDART OBJECT TO SELECT IT, AND CLICK THE WORDART GALLERY BUTTON ON THE WORDART TOOLBAR.

2. SELECT A STYLE FROM THE WORDART GALLERY.

TO CHANGE THE SHAPE OF A WORDART OBJECT:

• SELECT THE WORDART OBJECT, CLICK THE WORDART SHAPE BUTTON ON THE WORDART TOOLBAR, AND SELECT A SHAPE.

TO CHANGE THE TEXT SPACING OF A WORDART OBJECT:

• SELECT THE WORDART OBJECT, CLICK THE WORDART CHARACTER SPACING BUTTON ON THE WORDART TOOLBAR, AND SELECT A SPACING OPTION.

TO EDIT A WORDART OBJECT'S TEXT:

• SELECT THE WORDART OBJECT, CLICK THE EDIT TEXT BUTTON ON THE WORDART TOOLBAR, AND EDIT THE TEXT.

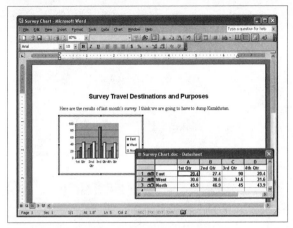

Figure 11-10. The Microsoft Graph program contains sample chart data.

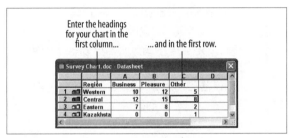

Figure 11-11. Enter what you want the chart to plot in the datasheet.

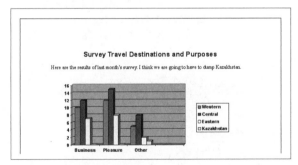

Figure 11-12. The completed chart in a Word document.

Charts graphically illustrate data, relationships, or trends. Like the idiom "a picture is worth a thousand words," charts are often much better at presenting information than hard-to-read numbers in a table. Word comes with a great built-in program for creating charts in Word called Microsoft Graph, as illustrated in Figure 11-10. This lesson introduces charts and explains how to create and insert a chart into a Word document.

1 Open the document named Lesson 11B and save it as Survey Chart.

First, you need to place the insertion point where you want to insert the chart.

2 Place the insertion point on the blank line at the bottom of the document.

Now let's insert the chart.

3 Select Insert → Picture → Chart from the menu.

The Microsoft Graph program window appears and creates a sample chart from make-believe data. To create a chart, you have to replace the sample data in the datasheet with your own information. The datasheet is made up of columns and rows and works like a simple spreadsheet program. There are several ways that you can enter information and move between the cells in the datasheet:

- Use the mouse to click the cell that you want to select or edit with the ⊕ pointer.
- Use the arrow keys to move the active cell.
- Press Enter to move down.
- Press the Tab key to move to the next cell or to the right, press Shift + Tab to move to the previous cell or to the left.

4 Click the D to select the entire D column. Then press Delete.

The data in the D column vanishes. Now let's enter data into the cells.

5 Click the first cell in the datasheet, type Region, and press Enter.

Pressing Enter confirms the cell entry and moves down one cell. Finish entering the column labels.

6 Type Western, press Enter, type Central, press Enter, type Eastern, press Enter, type Kazakhstan, and press Enter.

Notice anything you type replaces the cell's previous contents.

7 Complete the datasheet by entering the following information:

Region	Business	Pleasure	Other
Western	10	12	5
Central	12	15	8
Eastern	7	8	2
Kazakhstan	0	0	1

Remember to use the arrow keys, the Enter key, Tab, Shift + Tab to confirm your cell entries and move around the datasheet. When done, your datasheet should look like Figure 11-11.

8 **Click anywhere outside the Microsoft Graph window when you're finished entering the information in the datasheet.**

The Microsoft Graph window closes and a chart based on the information you entered in the datasheet appears in the document.

Your inserted chart will rarely be the right size, so you'll have to do some resizing. Like any other object, you resize a chart by clicking it, and then clicking and dragging one of its six sizing handles until the chart reaches the desired size.

9 **Click the chart to select it.**

Sizing handles appear around the chart.

10 **Click and drag the lower-right sizing handle down and to the right until the chart is similar to Figure 11-12.**

11 **Save your work.**

Super! You've created your first chart. The next several lessons explain how to modify a chart and work with different types of charts.

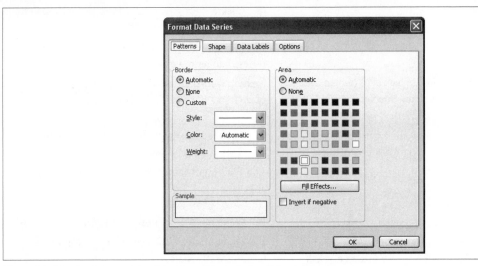

Figure 11-13. The Patterns tab of the Format Data Series dialog box.

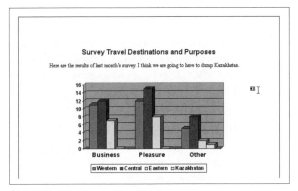

Figure 11-14. The modified chart.

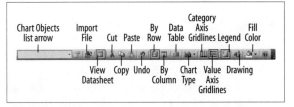

Figure 11-15. Chart buttons on the Standard toolbar.

You can select, format, and edit every object in a chart. For example, you can change the style, size, and color of any of the fonts used in a chart, or the background color of the chart. Some items that can be formatted and edited in a chart include:

Chart Title	Chart Background Area
Any Data Series	Chart Plot Area
Chart Gridlines	Data tables
Chart Legend	Category Axis

There are two methods you can use to select a chart object:

- **Click the object you want to select.** This is the fastest, most straightforward method to select an object.

- **Select the object from the Chart Object list on the Chart toolbar.** This method is useful when you're not sure where to click on the chart. (For example, what would you click to select the chart's plot area?)

After you've completed this lesson, you'll be a pro at formatting anything and everything in a chart.

1 Double-click the chart to edit it.

The first thing we want to do is change one of the numbers in the chart.

2 Click the cell that contains the value 10 (where the Business column and Western row intersect), type 11, and press Enter.

The chart is updated and plots the new value. Next let's try formatting the chart. Before you can format the chart, you need to select it.

3 Click the chart to select it.

Sizing handles appear around the selected chart.

The first object you want to format on the chart is the Pleasure Data series. Of course, you must first select the Pleasure Data series from the Chart Object list on the Chart toolbar.

⸱NOTE⸱ *When the chart is selected, the chart buttons are really an extension of the Standard toolbar.*

4 Click the Chart Objects list arrow on the Standard toolbar (see Figure 11-15) and select Series "Eastern" from the list.

Selection boxes appear on the three columns of the Eastern data series in the chart. Now that you've selected the Eastern series, you can format it.

5 Click the Format Data Series button on the Chart toolbar and click the Patterns tab, if necessary.

 Another way to format a data series is to double-click the object, or right-click the object and select Format Data Series from the shortcut menu, or click the object to select it and select Format → Selected Data Series from the menu.

The Format Data Series dialog box appears, as shown in Figure 11-13. You are presented with a variety of different formatting options that you can apply to the selected data series. We'll take a closer look at how to format a data series in an upcoming lesson—for now, just change the color of the data series.

6 Click a light green color from the color palette in the Area section and click OK.

The dialog box closes and the color of the Eastern data series changes to light green.

Next, try formatting the chart's legend so you can place it in a better location on the chart.

7 Double-click the chart's legend to format it and select the Placement tab.

The Placement tab of the Format Legend dialog box appears.

8 Select the Bottom option and click OK.

The dialog box closes and the legend appears at the bottom of the chart.

The last thing to format in this lesson is the chart's title.

9 Double-click the Category Axis (the horizontal line at the bottom of the chart where the labels "Business," "Pleasure," and "Other" appear) to format it and click the Font tab.

The Format Axis dialog box appears. Change the font of the chart's category axis labels as follows:

10 Select Arial from the Font Style list, select 16 from the Size list, and click OK.

The dialog box closes and the category axis is formatted with the font options you selected.

11 Compare your chart to the one in Figure 11-14 and save your work.

There are so many different types of chart objects, each with their own individual formatting options, that it would take days to go through all of them. Instead, this lesson has given you a general guideline to follow to select and format any type of chart object you encounter.

QUICK REFERENCE

TO SELECT A CHART OBJECT:

- CLICK THE CHART OBJECTS LIST ARROW ON THE CHART TOOLBAR AND SELECT THE OBJECT.

OR...

- CLICK THE OBJECT.

TO FORMAT A CHART OBJECT:

1. DOUBLE-CLICK THE OBJECT.

   OR...

   SELECT THE OBJECT AND CLICK THE FORMAT CHART OBJECT BUTTON ON THE STANDARD TOOLBAR.

OR...

RIGHT-CLICK THE OBJECT AND SELECT FORMAT CHART OBJECT FROM THE SHORTCUT MENU.

OR...

SELECT THE OBJECT AND SELECT FORMAT → SELECTED CHART OBJECT FROM THE MENU.

2. CLICK THE TAB THAT CONTAINS THE ITEMS YOU WANT TO FORMAT AND SPECIFY YOUR FORMATTING OPTIONS.

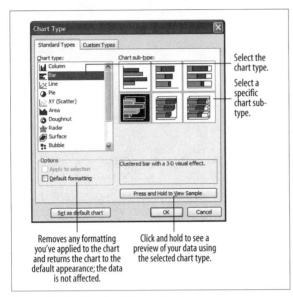

Select the chart type.

Select a specific chart sub-type.

Removes any formatting you've applied to the chart and returns the chart to the default appearance; the data is not affected.

Click and hold to see a preview of your data using the selected chart type.

Figure 11-16. The Chart Type dialog box.

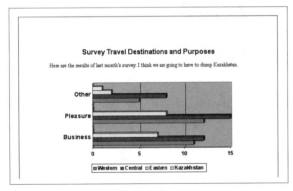

Figure 11-17. The modified bar chart.

Just as some lures are better than others for catching certain types of fish, some charts are better than others for presenting different types of information. So far, you have been working on a *column chart*, which is great for comparing values for different items, but not so great for illustrating trends or relationships. In this lesson, you will learn how and when to use different types of charts available in Microsoft Graph.

1 If the Datasheet is not open, double-click the chart.

2 Select Chart → Chart Type from the menu.

The Chart Type dialog box appears. Here you can specify the type of chart or graph you want to use to display your data. Note that some charts are better than others at displaying certain types of information (see Table 11-1). You want to change your chart from a column chart to a 3-D bar chart.

3 In the Chart type list click Bar, then in the Chart sub-type section, click the Clustered bar with a 3-D visual effect option, as shown in Figure 11-16, and then click OK.

The Chart Type dialog box closes and the column chart is changed to a bar chart, which really doesn't display the data very well. You can also quickly change chart types by clicking the Chart Type button on the Graph toolbar.

4 Click the [Chart Type button] Chart Type button list arrow on the Standard toolbar.

A list of various chart types appears below the Chart Type button.

5 Select the 3-D Area Chart from the list.

The chart becomes a 3-D area chart, as shown in Figure 11-17.

6 Save your work.

Because Microsoft Graph offers so many different types of charts and graphs, you should have a general idea which charts are best suited for your needs. Table 11-1 shows some of the more common charts and graphs and gives an explanation about how and when they are used.

Table 11-1. Types of Charts and Graphs

Chart or Graph Type	Description
	Column charts are used when you want to compare different values vertically side-by-side. Each value is represented in the chart by a vertical bar. If there are several values in an item, each value is represented by a different color.
	Bar charts are just like column charts, except they display information in horizontal bars rather than in vertical columns.
	Line charts are used to illustrate trends. Each value is plotted as a point on the chart and is connected to other values by a line. Multiple items are plotted using different lines.
	Pie charts are useful for showing values as a percentage of a whole. The values for each item are represented by different colors.
	XY or Scatter charts are used to plot clusters of values using single points. Multiple items can be plotted by using different colored points or different point symbols.
	Area charts are the same as line charts, except the area beneath the lines is filled with color.

QUICK REFERENCE

TO CHANGE THE CHART TYPE:

- SELECT CHART → CHART TYPE FROM THE MENU.

OR...

- CLICK THE CHART TYPE BUTTON LIST ARROW ON THE STANDARD TOOLBAR.

OR...

- RIGHT-CLICK ON THE CHART AND SELECT CHART TYPE FROM THE SHORTCUT MENU.

Chapter Eleven Review

Lesson Summary

Inserting a WordArt Object

To Insert a WordArt Object: Select Insert → Picture → WordArt from the menu, select a text style, type the text for the WordArt object, change the font type and size if necessary, and click OK.

To Format a WordArt Object: Right-click the object and select Format WordArt from the shortcut menu. Or, use the WordArt toolbar.

To Resize a WordArt Object: Click the WordArt object to select it and drag the WordArt object's sizing handles until the WordArt object is the size you want.

Formatting a WordArt Object

To Change the Style of a WordArt Object: Click the WordArt object to select it, and click the WordArt Gallery button on the WordArt toolbar. Select a style from the WordArt Gallery.

To Change the Shape of a WordArt Object: Select the WordArt Object, click the WordArt Shape button on the WordArt toolbar, and select a shape.

To Change the Text Spacing of a WordArt Object: Select the WordArt Object, click the WordArt Character Spacing button on the WordArt toolbar, and select a spacing option.

To Edit a WordArt Object's Text: Select the WordArt Object, click the Edit Text button on the WordArt toolbar, and edit the text.

Creating a Chart

To Insert a Chart: Select Insert → Picture → Chart from the menu. Enter your own data into the datasheet.

To Move Around in the Datasheet:

- Use the mouse to click the cell that you want to select or edit with the ⊕ pointer.
- Use the arrow keys to move the active cell.
- Press Enter to move down.
- Press the Tab key to move to the next cell or to the right, press Shift + Tab to move to the previous cell or to the left.

Modifying a Chart

To Select a Chart Object: Click the Chart Objects list arrow on the Chart toolbar and select the object, or simply click the object if you can find it.

To Format a Chart Object: Use any of these methods:

Double-click the object:

- Select the object and click the ▥ Format Chart Object button on the Chart toolbar.
- Right-click the object and select Format Chart Object from the shortcut menu.
- Select the object and select Format → Selected Chart Object from the menu.
- Then click the tab that contains the items you want to format, and specify the formatting options

Selecting a Chart Type

To Change the Chart Type: Select Chart → Chart Type from the menu or click the Chart Type button list arrow on the Standard toolbar. Or, right-click on the chart and select Chart Type from the shortcut menu.

Quiz

1. You can change the angle at which some WordArt objects slant or loop by dragging their ♦ adjustment handles. (True or False?)

2. Which of the following statements is NOT True?
   A. WordArt is an independent program and can be used by any Microsoft Office program, such as Word or Excel.
   B. WordArt has its own toolbar that features buttons to change the shape, angle, and color of a Word-Art object.
   C. You can change the color or texture of a WordArt object by clicking the Format WordArt object on the WordArt toolbar, clicking the Colors and Lines tab, and selecting a color from the Fill Color list.
   D. You can animate WordArt objects so that they shimmer, spin, dance, or flash on the screen.

3. You can edit or format a chart object using any of the following methods, except…
   A. Double-clicking the object.
   B. Right-clicking the object and selecting Format Chart Object from the shortcut menu.
   C. Selecting the object from the Chart Object list on the Standard toolbar and clicking the Format Chart Object button.
   D. Selecting Chart → Format from the menu, selecting the object from the Object list, and clicking Format.

4. The datasheet for a new chart contains sample information that you must replace with the actual information you want to plot in the chart. (True or False?)

5. You want to track the progress of the stock market on a daily basis. Which type of chart should you use?
   A. A line chart.
   B. A column chart.
   C. A row chart.
   D. A pie chart.

6. How do you insert a WordArt object in a document?
   A. Select Insert → Picture → WordArt from the menu.
   B. Select Tools → WordArt from the menu.
   C. Click the WordArt button on the Formatting toolbar.
   D. Select Edit → WordArt from the menu.

7. How do you insert a chart in a document?
   A. Click the Excel button on the Standard toolbar and select the Chart option.
   B. Select Tools → Chart from the menu.
   C. Select Insert → Picture → Chart from the menu.
   D. Select Edit → Chart from the menu.

Homework

1. Start Microsoft Word.

2. Add a WordArt object for the document's heading. Select Insert → Picture → WordArt from the menu, select the **WordArt** option, and click OK.

3. Type "Canadian Tours" and click OK. Click and drag the WordArt object's sizing handles, and resize the WordArt object so that it is about half as long the document.

4. Click and drag the WordArt object so that is appears centered and on top of the page.

5. Add a chart to the page: Select Insert → Picture → Chart from the menu

6. Enter the following information into the data table

	Qtr 1	Qtr 2	Qtr 3	Qtr 4
Vancouver	42,000	28,000	38,000	35,000
Prince Edward Island	20,000	9,000	14,000	14,000
Nova Scotia	49,000	38,000	54,000	45,000
Montreal	65,000	45,000	63,000	5,000

7. Change the font of the chart legend to Arial 12 pt. Click the legend to select it, select Arial from the Font list on the Formatting toolbar and 12 from Font Size list on the Formatting toolbar.

8. Change the chart type to a 3-D Bar chart. Click the Chart Type list arrow and select the option.

9. Give the chart the title "Package Sales." Select Chart → Chart Options from the menu, type "Package Sales" in the Chart title box, and click OK.

10. Change the color of the Montreal color series to dark red. Double-click any of the Montreal bars, select a dark red color, and click OK.

11. Click anywhere outside the chart.

12. Save your document as "Canadian Tours Chart" and exit Microsoft Word.

Quiz Answers

1. True.

2. D. The current version of WordArt does not have these features.

3. D. This is not a method for formatting a chart object (This question was really difficult – sorry!)

4. True.

5. A. Line charts are great for illustrating trends or changes that occur over time.

6. A. To insert a WordArt object, select Insert → Picture → WordArt from the menu.

7. C. To insert a chart, select Insert → Picture → Chart from the menu.

CHAPTER 12

WORKING WITH OTHER PROGRAMS

CHAPTER OBJECTIVES:

Inserting an Excel worksheet file into a Word document, Lesson 12.1

Modifying an embedded Excel worksheet, Lesson 12.2

Inserting a linked Excel chart in a Word document, Lesson 12.3

Opening and saving files in different formats, Lesson 12.4

CHAPTER TASKS: INSERT AN EXCEL WORKSHEET IN A WORD DOCUMENT

Prerequisites

- **How to open and save files.**
- **How to start and operate Microsoft Excel.**
- **How to edit and work with Excel worksheets and charts.**

One of the great benefits of Windows-based programs is that they can share information with each other. In this chapter, you'll learn how to insert a Microsoft Excel worksheet and a Microsoft Excel chart into a Word document. You'll also learn the subtle differences between *embedding* an object created in another program and *linking* a file created in another document. Finally, you will learn how Word can open and save files in different file formats.

Inserting an Excel Worksheet into a Word Document

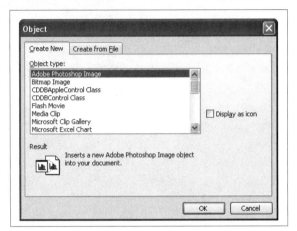

Figure 12-1. The Create New tab of the Object dialog box.

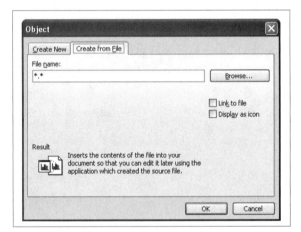

Figure 12-2. The Create from File tab of the Object dialog box.

Figure 12-3. A Microsoft Excel worksheet inserted in a Word document.

Microsoft Excel is a worksheet program that can calculate numbers and information, create charts and graphs, and perform many other useful functions. In this lesson, you will learn how to *embed* an Excel worksheet into a Word document.

1 Start Word.

2 Open the document named Lesson 12 and then save it as Trade Show Expenses.

The Lesson 12 document, an interoffice memo, appears in the main document window.

3 Place the insertion point at the very end of the document in the last blank line.

Here's how to insert an Excel worksheet into a Word document:

4 Select Insert → Object from the menu.

> **TIP** *Another way to insert an Excel worksheet is to click the Insert Microsoft Excel Worksheet button and drag inside the grid until the worksheet contains the number of columns and rows you want.*

The Object dialog box appears with the Create New tab in front, as shown in Figure 12-1. You can create and then insert new objects in the Create New tab, or you can insert an existing file, using the Create from File tab. You have already created and saved a worksheet in Excel, so you need to insert the worksheet from an existing file.

5 Click the Create from File tab.

The Create from File tab appears in front, as shown in Figure 12-2. Here, you must specify the name and location of the file you want to insert into your document.

6 Click the Browse button.

The Browse dialog box appears, allowing you to find and locate the file you want to insert into your document.

7 If necessary, navigate to your Practice folder.

The file list box is updated to show all the files on the Practice folder.

8 Select the Trade Show Expenses file.

Notice that the icon for the Trade Show Expenses file indicates that it is a Microsoft Excel file.

9 Click Insert.

The Browse dialog box closes and you return to the Create from File tab of the Object dialog box. Notice the "Trade Show Expenses" file name and location now appear in the File name text box.

There are several other options on this page you should know about:

- **Link to file:** Inserted objects are normally embedded, or saved in the documents they are inserted in. If you select the Link to file option, the object will still be inserted in the document, but Word will create a link to the original file instead of saving a copy of it in the document. The Link to file option should be used when you want to ensure that any changes made in the original file are updated and reflected in the Word file.

- **Display as icon:** Inserted objects are normally viewable directly from the Word document window. Checking the "Display as icon" option causes the inserted objects to appear only as an icon in Word. You must double-click the object in order to view it.

10 Click OK.

Word accesses the Excel file and then inserts it into the document at the insertion point.

11 Compare your document with the one in Figure 12-3, then save it.

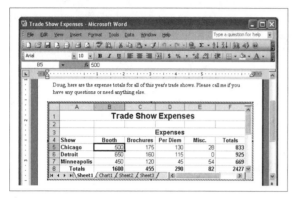

Figure 12-4. An Excel Worksheet object can be modified.

After you insert an Excel worksheet, you can make changes to the worksheet simply by double-clicking it. Double-clicking any embedded or linked object in Word opens the source program the object was created in, in this case, Microsoft Excel. If the program the object was created with isn't installed on your computer, you can still view and print the object in Word, you just can't make changes to it.

1 Double-click the inserted worksheet object in the document.

Double-click an object to edit or modify it.

The Excel program opens inside of the Word document, as shown in Figure 12-4. Notice that Excel menus and toolbars replace the Word toolbars and menus. Now you can make changes to the worksheet object.

2 Click cell B5—the cell containing the $500 Chicago Booth expense—to select it.

With the cell selected, you can replace the cell's data simply by typing.

3 Type 515, then press Tab.

The number 515 replaces the number 500, and Excel moves to the next cell.

4 Select the entire Detroit row by clicking the gray 6 row heading.

The entire row is selected. Next, insert a new row.

5 Select Insert → Rows from the menu.

A new row is inserted immediately above the Detroit row. Now enter the data for the new row.

6 Select the first cell in the new row, type Milwaukee, and press Tab to move to the next cell.

7 Type the following, pressing Tab after making each entry: 470 Tab 135 Tab 110 Tab 25 Tab

Now that you have entered the data for this row, you must calculate its total.

8 Select the numbers you just entered in the Milwaukee row. Click the Σ AutoSum button on the Standard toolbar.

Excel makes an educated guess about what cells you want to calculate the total for and selects them—in your case, Excel guesses correctly.

9 Press Enter to accept the formula.

Excel calculates the row total and moves to the next cell. Notice that after you inserted a new row, the bottom total row is no longer displayed. Resize the Excel worksheet object so that the entire worksheet is displayed.

10 Position the pointer over the lower-right sizing handle, until the pointer changes to a ↘, click and hold the left mouse button and drag the mouse diagonally down and to the right until you can see the bottom row of the worksheet, and then release the mouse button.

The entire worksheet object should now be visible in the document window.

11 Click anywhere outside the worksheet object to stop modifying it and return to Word.

The standard Word menu and toolbars replace the Excel menu and toolbars. Compare your table to the one in Figure 12-4.

12 Save your work.

It can be confusing getting to know the differences between linked and embedded objects. Table 12-1 compares each of these methods for inserting information created with other programs into Word documents.

Table 12-1. Embedded Versus Linked Objects

Object	Description
Embedded	An embedded object is actually saved within the Word document. Word document files with embedded objects are larger than files with linked objects. The advantage of using embedded objects is the objects are actually saved inside the Word document, and you don't have to worry about any attached files becoming erased or moved.
Linked	A linked object is not saved in the Word document. Instead, a link contains information on where to find the source data file. The advantage of using linked objects is when the source file is changed, the linked object in the Word document is automatically updated to reflect the changes.

QUICK REFERENCE

TO MODIFY AN EMBEDDED OR LINKED OBJECT:

1. DOUBLE-CLICK THE EMBEDDED OBJECT.

2. WHEN YOU HAVE FINISHED EDITING THE OBJECT, CLICK ANYWHERE OUTSIDE THE OBJECT TO RETURN TO THE HOST PROGRAM.

TO MOVE AN EMBEDDED OBJECT:

• CLICK THE WORKSHEET TO SELECT IT AND THEN DRAG THE WORKSHEET TO A NEW LOCATION.

TO RESIZE AN EMBEDDED OBJECT:

• CLICK THE WORKSHEET TO SELECT IT AND DRAG THE WORKSHEET'S SIZING HANDLES UNTIL THE WORKSHEET IS THE SIZE YOU WANT.

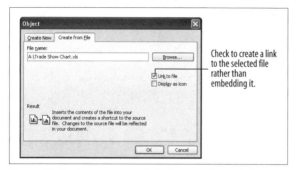

Figure 12-5. You can insert a linked Microsoft Excel chart.

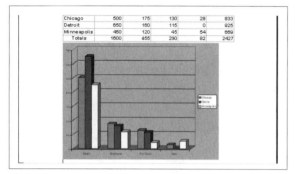

Figure 12-6. A linked Excel chart

So far, you have been working with an *embedded* Excel worksheet. This lesson mixes things up a bit. You will still be inserting information created in other programs, but in this lesson you will be inserting a *linked* Excel chart. Remember when you insert an *embedded* object, you are actually storing and saving the object in the Word document. A *linked* object maintains a connection or link between the inserted object source file and the Word document. The linked object in Word is automatically updated whenever the source file is modified. A linked object is not stored and saved in the Word document.

1 Now press Ctrl + End to move to the end of the document.

2 Press Enter twice to add two blank lines.

Now insert the linked chart object.

3 Select Insert → Object from the menu and click the Create from File tab if it does not appear in front.

Now you must specify the name and location of the file you want to insert into your document.

4 Click the Browse button.

The Browse dialog box appears, allowing you to find and locate the file you want to insert into your document.

5 If necessary, navigate to your Practice folder.

The file list box is updated to show all the files on the Practice folder.

6 Select the Trade Show Chart file.

Notice that the icon for the Trade Show Chart file indicates that it is a Microsoft Excel file.

7 Click Insert.

The Browse dialog box closes and you return to the Create from File tab of the Object dialog box. Notice the "Trade Show Chart" file name and location now appears in the File name text box, as shown in Figure 12-5.

8 Click the Link to file check box.

Checking the Link to file checkbox only inserts a link to the specified file in the Word document instead of inserting an embedded copy of the file. You should use Link to file if you want to display any changes made to the original file in your document.

9 Click OK.

Word accesses the Excel chart and then inserts a link into the document at the insertion point.

10 Resize the Chart object so it is similar in size to the one shown in Figure 12-6.

11 Save your work, then close the document.

QUICK REFERENCE

TO INSERT A LINKED OBJECT FILE:

1. PLACE THE INSERTION POINT WHERE YOU WANT TO INSERT THE LINKED OBJECT AND SELECT INSERT
   → OBJECT FROM THE MENU.

2. MAKE SURE THE LINK TO FILE CHECK BOX IS SELECTED IN THE CREATE FROM FILE TAB, AND THEN SPECIFY THE FILE YOU WANT TO INSERT AND CLICK OK.

Opening and Saving Files in Different Formats

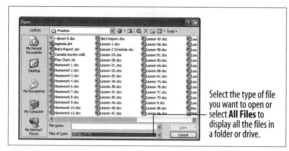

Select the type of file you want to open or select **All Files** to display all the files in a folder or drive.

Figure 12-7. You can open different file formats in Word.

Computer programs save files in different formats. Fortunately, Word can read and write in other word processing formats. See Table 12-2 for common file formats Word can read and write.

This lesson shows how you can open different file formats in Word and how to save files in different formats.

1 Click the Open button on the Standard toolbar.

The Open dialog box appears. Next, you must locate the file you want to open. In this case, the file is in WordPerfect format.

2 If necessary, navigate to your Practice folder.

The file list is updated to display the contents of the Practice folder, as shown in Figure 12-7.

3 If the Files of type list doesn't say "All Files," click the Files of type list arrow and select All Files.

The file list is updated to display all the files, regardless of their type, in the Practice folder.

4 Find and click the file Sample.

You may notice that there is no icon representing the file.

5 Click Open.

When Word opens the file, it immediately sees it is not a standard Word document file. Depending on how your computer is configured, Word will either automatically convert the file, or else prompt you to install the WordPerfect conversion files. You may have to insert the Word 2003 or Office 2003 CD-ROM into your computer to do this.

6 Click Yes to install the necessary components. If prompted, insert the Office 2003 CD-ROM into your computer's CD-ROM drive.

The WordPerfect file is converted and opened in the main document window.

> NOTE   *Word usually converts simple WordPerfect files that contain only text and basic formatting perfectly. WordPerfect documents that contain macros, graphics, and other advanced formatting elements can cause problems, and are often not converted properly. Problems can also arise when a document is formatted with fonts that are available on one computer but not on another. When Word does not convert a document properly you will have to touch-up and reformat the WordPerfect document, then save it as a Word document.*

Now save the document—since it is a converted WordPerfect document file, you have to pay a little more attention than when you normally save a file. You will be saving the file twice—first as a WordPerfect file and second as a Word file.

7 Select File → Save As from the menu.

The Save As dialog box appears.

8 Click the Save as type list arrow, scroll down, and select WordPerfect 5.1 for DOS.

9 Verify the File name is Sample, then click Save. Click Yes to confirm the necessary steps.

Word saves the document as a WordPerfect file.

10 Select File → Save As from the menu.

The Save As dialog box appears.

11 Click the Save as type list arrow, scroll down, and select Word Document.

12 In the File name text box, type Sample-Word and click Save.

Word saves the document as a Word document file.

13 Exit Word.

Table 12-2. Common File Formats Word Can Read and Write

File Format	File Extensions
Microsoft Word 6.0/95	.DOC
WordPerfect 5.x for DOS	Varies—some older documents may not have extensions.
WordPerfect 5.x / 6.x for Windows	.WPD
Text Files	.TXT
Rich Text Files	.RTF
Works 4.0 for Windows, Works 2000	.WPS
HTML Files	.HTM
XML Documents	.XML

QUICK REFERENCE

TO OPEN A FILE OF A DIFFERENT FORMAT IN WORD:

1. CLICK THE OPEN BUTTON ON THE STANDARD TOOLBAR.

2. CLICK THE FILES OF TYPE LIST ARROW AND SELECT ALL FILES TO DISPLAY ALL FILES.

3. FIND AND DOUBLE-CLICK THE FILE YOU WANT TO OPEN.

TO SAVE A FILE IN A DIFFERENT FILE FORMAT IN WORD:

1. SELECT FILE → SAVE AS FROM THE MENU.

2. CLICK THE SAVE AS TYPE LIST ARROW AND SELECT THE FILE FORMAT YOU WANT TO SAVE THE FILE IN.

3. ENTER A NEW NAME FOR THE FILE, IF YOU WANT, AND CLICK OK.

Chapter Twelve Review

Lesson Summary

Inserting an Excel Worksheet into a Word Document

To Insert an Embedded Excel Worksheet into a Word Document: Place the insertion point where you want to insert the worksheet and select Insert → Object from the menu. Click the Create from File tab to use an existing spreadsheet file, or click the Create New tab to create a new spreadsheet. Specify the Excel worksheet file you want to insert (if you selected Create from File), or else create the worksheet from scratch (if you selected Create New).

Modifying an Inserted Excel Worksheet

To Modify an Embedded or Linked Object: Double-click the embedded object. When you have finished editing the object, click anywhere outside the object to return to the host program.

To Move an Embedded Object: Click the worksheet to select it and then drag the worksheet to a new location.

To Resize an Embedded Object: Click the worksheet to select it and drag the worksheet's sizing handles until the worksheet is the size you want.

Inserting a Linked Excel Chart

To Insert a Linked Object File: Place the insertion point where you want to insert the linked object and select Insert → Object from the menu. Make sure the Link to File check box is selected in the Create from File tab, and then specify the file you want to insert and click OK.

Opening and Saving Files in Different Formats

To Open a File in a Different Format in Word: Click the Open button on the Standard toolbar. Click the Files of type list arrow and select All Files to display all files. Find and double-click the file you want to open.

To Save a File in a Different File Format in Word: Select File → Save As from the menu. Click the Save as type list arrow and select the file format you want to save the file in. Enter a new name for the file, if you want, and click OK.

Quiz

1. What is the difference between an embedded and linked object?

   A. An embedded object is saved within the file; a linked object is a hyperlink to another file.

   B. An embedded object is saved within the file; a linked object is not saved in the file—instead, a connection to the file is inserted.

   C. An embedded object can be inserted on the same page as other text or information; a linked file must be placed on its own separate page.

   D. An embedded object is saved in a separate file; a linked object is saved within the file into which it was inserted.

2. You double-click an embedded or linked object to modify it. (True or False?)

3. Which of the following statements is NOT true?

   A. When you insert an object, you can either insert an existing file or you can create a new file.

   B. Clicking the Link to file check box inserts a link to the file instead of embedding the file.

   C. You can resize an embedded object by selecting the object and dragging its sizing handles.

   D. If the program an embedded object was created in is not installed on your computer, the object won't be displayed.

4. In order to open and save in different file formats, you need to purchase a special conversion program. (True or False?)

5. How do you save a document in a different file format?

   A. Click the Save As button on the toolbar and select the file format from the Save as type list.

   B. Word can't save files in different formats.

   C. Select Tools → File Format Wizard from the menu and follow the on-screen instructions.

   D. Select File → Save As from the menu and select the file format from the Save as type list.

6. You are trying to open a .TXT (text file) but can't seem to find it in the Open dialog box. You know that you're in the right folder, so why can't you see the file?

   A. Text files are invisible to Microsoft Word.

   B. You need to select All Files from the Files of type list.

   C. You need to click the Open As button on the Standard toolbar instead of the Open button.

   D. Word can't open text files.

Homework

1. Open the Homework 12 presentation and save it as "Fleas."

2. Place the insertion point in the blank line below the sentence, "Here is the summer attendance for my travelling flea circus you wanted:"

3. Select Insert → Object from the menu, click the Create from File tab, click Browse, navigate to your Practice folder, click the "Flea Chart" file, click Insert, and click OK.

4. Make sure the chart is selected and then resize it. (Select Format → Object, select the Size tab, and set the size of the chart at 50 percent.)

5. Save your work.

6. Exit Microsoft Word.

Quiz Answers

1. B. An embedded object is saved within a file. A linked object is not actually saved within a file but points to the inserted file.

2. True. Double-clicking an object lets you modify it.

3. D. You can still view and print an embedded object even if you don't have the program that created it installed on your computer. You *will* need to have the program that created the embedded object installed to modify it, however.

4. False. Word can read and write in most word processing file formats.

5. D. To save a document in a different file format, select File → Save As from the menu and select the file format from the Save as type list.

6. B. In the Open dialog box, select All Files from the Files of type list to display all the files in a folder.

CHAPTER 13

WORKING WITH FORMS

CHAPTER OBJECTIVES:

Creating a new form, Lesson 13.1

Adding text fields to a form, Lesson 13.2

Adding check boxes to a form, Lesson 13.3

Adding drop-down fields to a form, Lesson 13.4

Assigning help to form fields, Lesson 13.5

Performing calculations in a form field, Lesson 13.6

Saving and filling out a form, Lesson 13.7–13.9

CHAPTER OBJECTIVES: CREATE A CUSTOM SATISFACTION FORM

Prerequisites

- **How to open and save a document**
- **How to use menus, toolbars, and dialog boxes**
- **How to work with tables**

A form created in Word is very similar to a paper form you fill out with a pen or pencil. However, Word forms have several major advantages over the traditional paper type of forms. The greatest benefit of a Word form is that you can complete it in Word—saving you time, effort, and paper. You also don't have to worry about trying to read bad penmanship! Another advantage of a Word form is you can provide the user with information and prompts to help them complete the form.

Word forms can include fill-in-the-blank fields and check box fields, just like their paper counterparts. In addition, you can include a list of options from which the user can choose to complete the form.

By now you're probably anxious to create and use your own online forms. Let's get started…

Figure 13-1. The Templates dialog box.

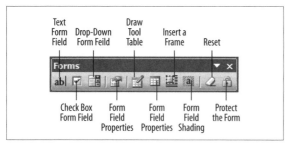

Figure 13-2. The Forms toolbar.

North Shore Travel		
Tour Satisfaction Questionnaire		
Client's Name:		**Please Rank the Following:**
Date:		Price:
Trip Cost:		Helpful Staff
Purpose:		Flight:
First Class:		Overall:

Figure 13-3. A table to be used in a form.

When you create a form, you usually start by creating a template that contains the text on the form that doesn't change, the formatting, and a table to line everything up neatly. By using a template as the basis for a form, users can fill out the form without changing the text or formatting of the form itself. Think of the template as a blank form when putting it together.

This lesson explains how to create a template that you can use to create new blank forms. Hopefully, most of the material in this lesson, such as working with formatting, creating templates, and working with tables, will be a review for you.

Some of the tools you use when creating a form include:

- **Templates:** Forms are normally saved as templates so that they can be used again and again.

- **Form Fields:** Form Fields are the areas where users input information in a form. There are three types of form fields you can use: Text fields, Check Box fields, and Drop-Down fields. We'll learn more about form fields in several upcoming lessons.

- **Tables:** Tables are often used in forms to align text and form fields, and to create borders and boxes.

- **Protection:** Forms are protected so that users can complete the form without changing the text and/or design of the form itself.

Let's get started!

1 Start Word.

2 Select File → New from the menu.

The New Document task pane appears.

3 Click the On my computer link in the Templates section of the task pane.

The Templates dialog box appears, as shown in Figure 13-1.

Since you want to create a form, you must create a new template.

4 Select the Template option in the Create New section in the lower right-hand corner of the dialog box and click OK.

The dialog box closes and a new document appears.

5 Save the template as Form Template.

First, let's add a title to the form.

6 Click both the Center button and Bold button on the Formatting toolbar, then type North Shore Travel and press Enter.

7 Type Tour Satisfaction Questionnaire and press Enter.

8 Click the Align Left button and Bold button on the Formatting toolbar, and then press Enter twice.

Next, you need to display the Forms toolbar, which contains buttons that make it easier to create a form.

9 Click View → Toolbars → Forms from the menu.

Another way to display the Forms toolbar is to right-click any toolbar and select Forms.

The Forms toolbar appears, as shown in Figure 13-2. Many forms, such as invoices, require a table.

10 Click the Insert Table button on the Forms toolbar, drag across the grid to select four rows down by four columns across, and then click the mouse button.

The table appears in the document window.

11 Select the two cells in the top row and third and fourth columns of the table.

You need to merge these two cells into a single cell—you'll see why later on.

12 Select Table → Merge Cells from the menu.

The two selected cells are merged into a single cell.

13 Using Figure 13-3 as a guide, type in the text labels for the form just as they appear in the figure.

Remember to press Tab to move forward to the next cell and Shift + Tab to move backward to the previous cell.

14 Click the Save button on the Standard toolbar to save your template when you're finished.

The form is saved as a template in the Microsoft Office Template folder.

Now that you've created the template the form will be based on, you can start entering the fields where the user fills out the form—and that is the topic of the next lesson.

QUICK REFERENCE

TO CREATE A TABLE:

- CLICK THE INSERT TABLE BUTTON ON THE STANDARD TOOLBAR OR THE FORMS TOOLBAR, DRAG INSIDE THE GRID TO SELECT THE NUMBER OF COLUMNS AND ROWS YOU WANT.

OR...

- SELECT TABLE → INSERT → TABLE FROM THE MENU, SPECIFY THE NUMBER OF ROWS AND COLUMNS YOU WANT, AND CLICK OK.

TO MOVE FROM CELL TO CELL IN A TABLE:

- PRESS TAB TO MOVE THE INSERTION POINT FORWARD ONE FIELD OR CELL, OR PRESS SHIFT + TAB TO MOVE THE INSERTION POINT BACK ONE FIELD OR CELL.

TO DELETE TEXT IN A CELL:

- SELECT THE CELL(S), THEN PRESS THE DELETE KEY.

Figure 13-4. You can insert a text field.

Figure 13-5. The Text field Options dialog box.

Now that you have created the template your forms will be based on, you can start inserting the fields the user needs to fill out. There are three types of fields you can use in a Word form: text fields, check box fields, and drop-down fields.

1 If it's not already shaded, click the Form Field Shading button **on the Forms toolbar.**

TIP

Another way to display field shading is to select Tools → Options from the menu, click the View tab, click the Field shading list arrow, select Always, and click OK.

This will add shading to your form fields, which makes them easy to see. Field shading appears on the screen but does not print.

2 Place the insertion point in the cell to the right of the Client's Name **label in the first row, and click the** Text Form Field button **on the Forms toolbar.**

A shaded field appears in the cell, as shown in Figure 13-4. This is a text field.

Next, add a text field for the date.

3 Place the insertion point in the cell to the right of the Date **label in the second row and click the** Text Form Field button **on the Forms toolbar.**

A new text field appears at the insertion point. You can make an online form foolproof by formatting the text box form field to accept only dates. You can also specify how you want the text box form field to display the dates.

4 Double-click the gray text field **in the Date row.**

TIP

Another way to change the properties of a text field is to right-click the form field and select Properties from the shortcut menu.

The Text Form Field Options dialog box appears, as shown in Figure 13-5. The Text Form Field Options dialog box allows you to specify the type of information that can be entered in a field and how that information should be formatted. See Table 13-1 for a description of the various options.

5 Click the Type **list arrow and select** Date **from the list.**

This will cause the text field to only accept dates when a user is entering information in the field. You can also specify how the date should be formatted.

6 Click the Date format **list arrow, select** M/d/yy **from the list, and click** OK.

Dates entered in this field will be displayed in M/d/yy format, such as 5/8/04.

7 Place the insertion point in the cell to the right of the label Trip Cost **in the third row and click the** Text Form Field button **on the Forms toolbar.**

A new text field appears at the insertion point.

Next, we'll format the field so that the Trip Cost field only accepts numbers.

8 Double-click the Trip Cost text field to open the Text Form Field Options dialog box.

9 Click the Type list arrow and select Number from the list.

This will cause the text field to only accept numbers when a user is entering information in the field. You can also specify how the number should be formatted.

10 Click the Number format list arrow, and select $#,##0.00;($#,##0.00) from the list, and click OK.

This will format the numbers a user enters in a currency format, like $1,000.00.

11 Add text fields to the empty cells to the right of Price, Helpful Staff, Flight, and Overall. Format these text fields so they accept only numeric input (see Steps 8 and 9 if you need help).

Table 13-1. Text Form Field Options

Option	Description
Type	The type of information that can be entered. You can choose from text, date, number, current date, current time, and calculation types.
Default	Data entered in this box will appear in the field by default.
Maximum Length	The maximum number of characters that can be entered in a field. For example, you could specify 2 characters as the maximum length for a stated field.
Format	Specifies how the selected information type should be formatted.
Run Macro on	Allows you to run a macro when the user either enters or exits the field.
Bookmark	Assigns a bookmark to the field.
Fill-in enabled	Users will not be able to enter information in the field if this check box is not checked.
Calculate on exit	Select this option if you want to use the field in a calculation.
Add Help Text	Provides the user with help and instructions.

QUICK REFERENCE

TO VIEW FIELD SHADING:

- CLICK THE FORM FIELD SHADING BUTTON ON THE FORMS TOOLBAR.

OR...

- SELECT TOOLS → OPTIONS FROM THE MENU, CLICK THE VIEW TAB, CLICK THE FIELD SHADING LIST ARROW, SELECT ALWAYS, AND CLICK OK.

TO INSERT A TEXT FIELD:

- PLACE THE INSERTION POINT WHERE YOU WANT TO PLACE THE FIELD AND CLICK THE TEXT FORM FIELD BUTTON ON THE FORMS TOOLBAR.

TO VIEW AND/OR CHANGE A TEXT FIELD'S OPTIONS:

- DOUBLE-CLICK THE TEXT FIELD.

Using Check Box Fields

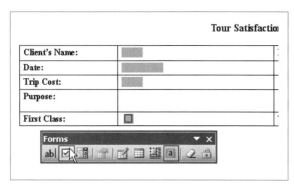

Figure 13-6. You can insert a Check Box form field.

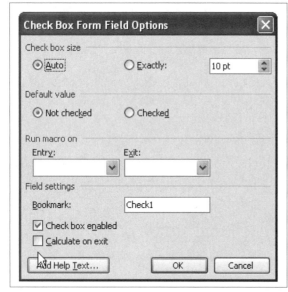

Figure 13-7. The Check Box Form Field Options dialog box

Check boxes in fields are just like the check boxes you find in dialog boxes. You can use check boxes when you want to ask the user a single-answer question, like a yes or no.

1 Place the insertion point in the cell to the right of the First Class label.

2 Click the Check Box Form Field button on the Forms toolbar.

A shaded check box appears in the cell, as shown in Figure 13-6. As with text box form fields, we can specify options for the check box field. See Table 13-2 for a description of the check box options.

3 Double-click the Check Box Form Field you just created to open the Check Box Form Field Options dialog box.

 Another way to change the properties of a check box field is to right-click the check box and select Properties from the shortcut menu.

The Check Box Form Field Options dialog box appears, as shown in Figure 13-7. Here, you can specify options for the check box, such as the size of the check box and if the check box is checked or not checked by default.

You don't need to make any changes to the check box form field, so close the dialog box.

4 Click OK to close the Check Box Form Field Options dialog box.

5 Save your work.

Table 13-2. Check Box Options

Option	Description
Check box size	Changes the size of the check box. The Auto option automatically sizes the check box based on the surrounding font size.
Default value	Specifies by default whether or not the check box should be checked.
Run macro on	Allows you to run a macro when the user either enters or exits the field.
Bookmark	Assigns a bookmark to the field.
Check box enabled	If this option is not selected, users will not be able to change the check box.
Calculate on exit	Select this option if you want to use the field in a calculation.
Add help text	Provides the user with help and instructions.

QUICK REFERENCE

TO INSERT A CHECK BOX FIELD:

- PLACE THE INSERTION POINT WHERE YOU WANT TO PLACE THE FIELD AND CLICK THE CHECK BOX FORM FIELD BUTTON ON THE FORMS TOOLBAR.

TO VIEW AND/OR CHANGE A CHECK BOX FIELD'S OPTIONS:

- DOUBLE-CLICK THE CHECK BOX FIELD.

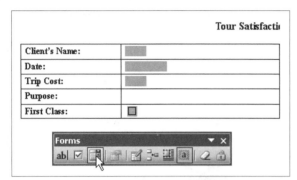

Figure 13-8. You can insert a Drop-down field in a form.

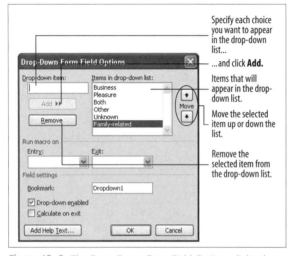

Figure 13-9. The Drop-Down Form Field Options dialog box.

Specify each choice you want to appear in the drop-down list...

...and click **Add.**

Items that will appear in the drop-down list.

Move the selected item up or down the list.

Remove the selected item from the drop-down list.

Drop-down lists are used when you want to provide the user with a list of several choices. When the user fills out the form, they see an arrow next to the drop-down field. The user clicks the arrow to display a list of options from which to choose, and then selects the desired option.

1 If necessary, navigate to your Practice folder and open Lesson 13A. **Save the file as** Form Template.

If you don't know where your practice files are located, ask your instructor for help.

2 Place the insertion point in the cell to the right of the Purpose **label.**

3 Click the Drop-Down Form Field button **on the Forms toolbar.**

A shaded drop-down field appears in the selected cell, as shown in Figure 13-8. Next, we'll take a look at the available options for a drop-down field.

4 Double-click the Drop-Down form **field you just created to open the Drop-Down Form Field Options dialog box.**

Another way to change the properties of a drop-down field is to right-click the drop-down field and select Properties *from the shortcut menu.*

The Drop-Down Form Field Options dialog box appears, as shown in Figure 13-9. Here, you can specify what options you want to appear in the drop-down list.

5 In the Drop-down item **text box type** Business **and click** Add.

The item "Business" appears in the Items of the drop-down list box to the right. Let's add some more items to the drop-down form field.

6 Continue adding the following items to the Drop-down item **text box, making sure to click** Add **after typing each option:**

Pleasure
Both
Other
Unknown
Family-related

The first item that appears in the "Items in drop-down list" will be the first item that appears in the field when a user fills out the form. You can rearrange the item list so that the "Unknown" item appears as the default option instead of the "Business" item.

7 Select the Unknown item from the "Items in drop-down list" box, then click the Move up arrow **until Unknown appears at the top of the list.**

If for some reason you decide you no longer need an item to appear in a drop-down list, you can remove the item. You decide to remove the "Family-related" item from the item list because it is covered by the "Pleasure" item.

8 Select the Family-related item from the "Items in drop-down list" box, then click the Remove button.

The "Family-related" item is deleted from the list. We're done working with the drop-down field, so we can close the dialog box.

9 Click OK.

The dialog box closes.

10 Save your work.

See Table 13-3 for a list of drop-down options and their definitions.

Table 13-3. Drop-Down List Options

Option	Description
Drop-down item	Type an item you want to appear in the drop-down list and click Add.
Items in drop-down list	Shows the items that will appear in the drop-down list.
Remove	Removes the selected item from the drop-down list.
Move	Use the arrow buttons to move the selected item up or down the drop-down list.
Run macro on	Allows you to run a macro when the user either enters or exits the field.
Bookmark	Assigns a bookmark to the field.
Drop-down enabled	If this option is not selected, users will not be able to select an option from the list.
Calculate on exit	Select this option if you want to use the field in a calculation.
Add help text	Provides the user with help and instructions.

QUICK REFERENCE

TO INSERT A DROP-DOWN FIELD:

- PLACE THE INSERTION POINT WHERE YOU WANT TO PLACE THE FIELD AND CLICK THE DROP-DOWN FORM FIELD BUTTON ON THE FORMS TOOLBAR.

TO VIEW AND/OR CHANGE A DROP-DOWN FIELD'S OPTIONS:

- DOUBLE-CLICK THE DROP-DOWN FIELD.

Figure 13-10. The Form Field Help Text dialog box.

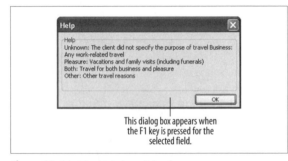

Figure 13-11. The Help key dialog box.

Figure 13-12. Help text for the selected field displayed in the Status bar.

Another way you can make forms easier to fill out and use is by providing the users with online instructions and help. There are two different ways to provide online help:

- **Status bar:** When a user selects a field, brief instructions or help for that field is displayed in the bar—up to 138 characters.
- **Help Key (F1):** When a user selects a field, they can press the F1 Help Key to display a longer help message or instructions—up to 255 characters.

You will get a chance to use both types of help in this lesson.

1 Double-click the text field for the Client's Name.

The Text field Options dialog box appears.

2 Click the Add Help Text button and click the Status Bar tab if it is not in front.

The Form Field Help Text dialog box appears, as shown in Figure 13-10. Here, you can provide to a user help in filling out your form.

3 Click the Type your own option and type Enter the Client's Name (Last, First) in the text box.

Now, whenever a user selects this form, the message "Enter the Client's Name (Last, First)" will appear in the status bar.

4 Click OK to close the Form Field Help Text dialog box, then click OK again to the Text Form Field dialog box.

The dialog box closes.

5 Double click the text field for Price.

The Text Form Field Options dialog box appears.

6 Click the Add Help Text button.

The Form Field Help Text dialog box appears.

7 Click the Type your own option and type On a scale from 1 to 5, where 1 = excellent, 5 = poor in the text box, as shown in the status bar of Figure 13-12.

8 Click OK, OK to close both dialog boxes.

9 Repeat Steps 5-8 for the text fields Helpful Staff and Flight so that they display the same help message on the status bar.

You can save some typing if you copy and paste the text from Step 7.

Status bar help messages are great for displaying a short informational message to the user as they complete the form, but they are limited to only 130 characters of text. Sometimes, however, you may want to provide the user with a more detailed message or instructions. They must access this by pressing the F1 help key. In those cases, you must type your help message in the Help Key (F1) section of the Form Field Help Text dialog box.

10 Double click the drop-down field for Purpose.

11 Click the Add Help Text button.

The Form Field Help Text dialog box appears.

12 Click the Help Key (F1) tab.

13 Click the Type your own option button, and type the following in the text box:

Unknown: The client did not specify the purpose of travel Business: Any work-related travelPleasure: Vacations and family visits (including funerals)Both: Travel for both business and pleasureOther: Other travel reasons

Now when the user selects this field and presses the F1 help key, the text you just entered will appear in a message box similar to what's shown in Figure 13-11.

14 Click OK, OK to close both dialog boxes.

The Drop-Down Form Field Options dialog box closes.

15 Save your work.

QUICK REFERENCE

TO ADD STATUS BAR HELP TEXT:

1. DOUBLE-CLICK THE FORM FIELD.

2. CLICK THE ADD HELP TEXT BUTTON AND CLICK THE STATUS BAR TAB.

3. CLICK THE TYPE YOUR OWN OPTION, AND TYPE THE HELP MESSAGE YOU WANT TO APPEAR ON THE STATUS BAR IN THE TEXT BOX.

TO ADD F1 HELP KEY TEXT:

1. DOUBLE-CLICK THE FORM FIELD.

2. CLICK THE ADD HELP TEXT BUTTON AND CLICK THE HELP KEY (F1) TAB.

3. CLICK THE TYPE YOUR OWN OPTION, AND TYPE THE HELP MESSAGE YOU WANT TO APPEAR WHEN THE USER PRESSES THE F1 KEY.

Performing Calculations in a Form Field

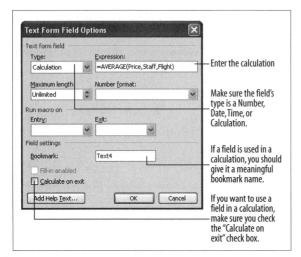

Text Form Field Options

Text form field
Type: Expression: — Enter the calculation
Calculation   =AVERAGE(Price,Staff,Flight)

Maximum length: Number format: Make sure the field's
Unlimited   type is a Number,
                                               Date, Time, or
Run macro on   Calculation.
Entry: Exit:

Field settings   If a field is used in a
Bookmark: Text4   calculation, you should
                                               give it a meaningful
  Fill-in enabled   bookmark name.
  Calculate on exit

Add Help Text...   OK   Cancel   If you want to use a
                                               field in a calculation,
                                               make sure you check
                                               the "Calculate on
                                               exit" check box.

Figure 13-13. The Text Form Field Options dialog box.

Another advantage Word forms have over their paper counterparts is that they can calculate any numbers a user enters in them. No more calculators or scrawled calculations on your forms! The only problem with form calculations is that they can be rather hard to set up, especially if you're used to the simplicity of spreadsheet programs like Microsoft Excel.

1 **Double-click the text field for** Price.

The Text Form Field Options dialog box appears, as shown in Figure 13-13.

You need to check the "Calculate on exit" option so Word knows that you want to use its information in a calculation. Although it isn't absolutely necessary, you should also give the field a more meaningful bookmark name so you can easily reference the field later on.

2 **Click the** Calculate on exit **check box, replace the existing text in the** Bookmark **box with the bookmark name** Price **and click** OK.

If you plan on using a form field in a calculation, you need to check the "Calculate on Exit" box.

Now Word will automatically update calculations that use the information entered in the Price field. You need to make the same changes to the Helpful Staff and Flight to include them in a calculation.

3 **Repeat** Step 2 **for the** Helpful Staff **and** Flight **fields—giving them bookmark names of** Staff **and** Flight.

Next, specify the calculation or formula to be performed in the field.

4 **Double-click the field for** Overall.

This is the field in which you want to display the results of a calculation. In order to do this, you need to create a *formula*.

A *formula* performs calculations—such as adding, subtracting, and multiplying. All formulas must start with an equal sign (=). The equal sign tells Word you want to perform a calculation.

Once you have entered an equal sign, you must specify two more pieces of information: the values you want to calculate, and the arithmetic function(s) you want to use to calculate the values. Formulas can contain explicit values, such as the numbers 5 or 8, but they will more often reference the values contained in other fields. For example, the formula =Price+Staff would add the values in the Price and Staff fields.

You can reference formula information two ways:

• **Table References:** Your formulas can include references to the cell or cells in a table. Some examples would be =SUM(ABOVE) or =A2*B3. See the "Making Calculations in a Table" lesson in the chapter on tables for more information.

• **Bookmark Reference:** Your formulas can include references to the bookmark names of other fields in the form. An example would be =Staff+Flight.

For your formula, you will include reference to the bookmark names of the other fields.

5 **Select** Calculation **from the** Type **list and type** =AVERAGE(Price,Staff,Flight) **in the** Expression **text box, as shown in Figure 13-13.**

The "Overall" field will now calculate and display the average of the three customer satisfaction fields.

6 Click OK.

The dialog box closes.

7 Save your work.

Refer to Table 13-4 when you start creating your own formulas. It contains examples of formulas, and the most common operators and functions used in formulas.

Table 13-4. Examples of Operators and Formulas and Their Displayed Results

Operator or Function Name	Purpose	Example
=	All formulas must start with an equal sign.	
+	Performs addition between values.	=Price+Flight
-	Performs subtraction between values.	=Price-Flight
*	Performs multiplication between values.	=B4*2
/	Performs division between values.	=B2/C2
SUM	Adds all the numbers in a range of fields.	=SUM(Price,Staff,Flight)
AVERAGE	Calculates the average of all the numbers in a range of fields.	=AVERAGE(A2:A5)

QUICK REFERENCE

TO INCLUDE A FIELD IN A CALCULATION:

- DOUBLE-CLICK THE FIELD AND MAKE SURE THE CALCULATE ON EXIT CHECK BOX IS SELECTED. YOU MAY ALSO WANT TO GIVE THE FIELD A MEANINGFUL BOOKMARK NAME.

TO CREATE A CALCULATION FIELD:

1. DOUBLE-CLICK THE FIELD IN WHICH YOU WANT TO DISPLAY THE RESULTS OF A CALCULATION.
2. SELECT CALCULATION FROM THE TYPE LIST.
3. ENTER THE FORMULA IN THE EXPRESSION TEXT BOX.

Preparing and Filling Out an Online Form

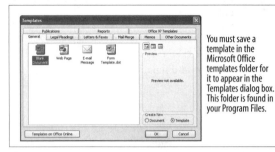

Figure 13-14. The Templates dialog box.

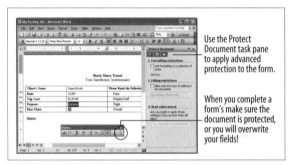

Figure 13-15. A filled out online form and the Protect Document task pane.

Before you can use or complete a form, you must *protect* it. Protecting the form makes it ready for data entry and allows the user to move to and enter text in the form fields *only*. Text or information can be added, modified, and deleted in the form fields, but not anywhere else in the document. If you want to make changes to other items in the document, you first must unprotect the form.

This lesson shows you how to protect and then fill in a form.

1 If necessary, navigate to your Practice folder and open Lesson 13B. Save the file as Form Template in your Microsoft Office templates folder.

2 Click the Protect Form button on the Forms toolbar.

> TIP **Another way to protect a form is to select Tools → Protect Document from the menu and apply more advanced protection using the Protect Document task pane.**

> TIP **Forms need to be protected before they can be used or filled in.**

Protecting a form prevents users from making any changes to the form's structure. You can also protect a form by selecting Tools → Protect Document from the menu. This method lets you assign a password so that only you can unprotect the form later on.

> NOTE **Trying to complete an unprotected form is a disaster! Word will delete and replace your form fields with whatever you type instead of filling in the fields. Always make sure you have protected a form before completing it.**

3 Click the Save button on the Standard toolbar to save the template.

Since we've finished creating the template that will be used for our forms, you can close it.

4 Close the form template.

Now you can creat a new, blank form based on the form template you have created.

> NOTE **You must save the template in the Microsoft Office templates folder so it will appear in the Templates dialog box.**

5 Select File → New from the menu.

The New Document task pane appears. We want to create a new document based on the Form Template.

6 Click the On my computer link in the Templates section of the New Document task pane. Select the Document option in the Create New section in the lower right-hand corner of the dialog box. Select the Form Template and click OK.

A new, blank form appears. Notice that the Protect Form button on the Forms toolbar is shaded, indicating that the form is protected.

7 In the Client's Name field, type your own name.

Your name appears in the Client's Name field. Move on to the text field.

8 Press Tab to move to the next field, Date, and type today's date.

TIP

When working with Windows fields, Tab moves to the next field and Shift + Tab moves to the previous field.

Today's date appears in Date field. Notice that Word will not allow you to enter any invalid characters in this field since we specified it should only accept date input in a previous lesson.

9 Press Tab to move to the next field, Price, and type 4.

Notice the help text you entered in a previous lesson appears in the status bar and the calculated value in the "Overall" field is updated to show the average of the three client satisfaction fields.

10 Press Tab to move to the next field, Trip Cost, and type 1999.

The number 1999 appears in the Trip Cost and is formatted as $1,999.00.

11 Press Tab to move to the next field, Helpful Staff, and type 5.

The "Overall" field is updated to show the average of the two values in the client satisfaction fields.

12 Press Tab to move to the next field, click the Purpose list arrow and select Business from the list.

The option "Business" appears in the drop-down list. Next, display the help information you typed for this field.

13 Press the F1 key.

The help information you typed for this field appears in a Help window.

14 Click OK to close the Help window, press Tab to move to the next field, Flight, and type 4.

Notice the calculated field "Overall" is updated to display the average of the values in the three client satisfaction fields.

15 Press Tab to move to the next field and click the First Class check box. Your online form should look something like Figure 13-15.

Now that you have completed the form, you can save it.

16 Click the Save button on the Standard toolbar and save the completed form as My Survey.

QUICK REFERENCE

- FORMS MUST BE PROTECTED BEFORE THEY CAN BE COMPLETED.

TO PROTECT A FORM:

- CLICK THE PROTECT FORM BUTTON ON THE FORMS TOOLBAR.

OR...

- SELECT TOOLS → PROTECT DOCUMENT FROM THE MENU AND APPLY MORE ADVANCED PROTECTION USING THE PROTECT DOCUMENT TASK PANE.

TO UNPROTECT A FORM:

- FOLLOW THE PREVIOUS STEP.

TO FILL OUT A FORM:

- PRESS TAB TO MOVE TO THE NEXT FIELD; SHIFT + TAB TO MOVE TO THE PREVIOUS FIELD.

Working with Multiple Sections in Forms

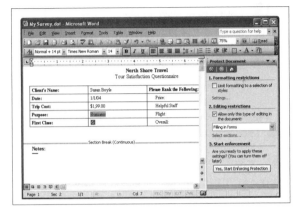

Figure 13-16. Protecting the form in the Protect Document task pane.

Figure 13-17. The Section Protection dialog box.

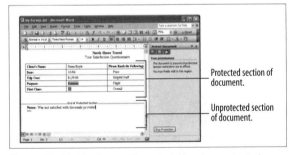

Protected section of document.

Unprotected section of document.

Figure 13-18. The form with protected and unprotected sections.

You must protect a form before you can use it or fill it out. Protecting a form restricts users from adding, modifying, or changing anything in the document except for the information in the form fields. Sometimes the protection can be restrictive. For example, you might want a user to enter information in the form fields in the top half of a document and also type several lengthy paragraphs in the bottom half. This lesson explains how you can break a document into different sections, allowing

you to protect one section (the section that contains the form fields) while leaving another section unprotected.

1 Unprotect the form by clicking the Protect Form button on the Forms toolbar.

Another way to protect a form is to select Tools → Protect Document from the menu and apply more advanced protection using the Protect Document task pane.

You want to create an area on the form where the user isn't restricted to entering information only in the form fields. To accomplish this feat, you need to create a new section in the document.

2 Now press Ctrl + End to move to the end of the document.

You want the end of the form to be unprotected, so that the user can type notes freely into the document. You need to insert a section break here.

3 Press Enter to add a blank line, then select Insert → Break from the menu.

The Break dialog box appears. Since you want the unprotected section to appear on the same page, you need to select a Continuous Section break.

4 Select Continuous under the Section break section and click OK.

View the document in Normal View to see the breaks inserted in the document.

Word inserts a continuous section break at the insertion point. The section above the break will be protected and the section below the break won't be protected, so that you can add and format freeform text.

Add a notes label in the second section of the document.

5 Type Notes:

It's time to protect the form document again. Since you will only be protecting the first section, you must use the Protect Document command from the menu instead of the Protect Document button on the Forms toolbar.

6 Select Tools → Protect Document **from the menu.**

The Protect Document task pane appears, as shown in Figure 13-16. Here, you can specify how you want to protect your document and which sections you wish to protect.

7 **Check the** Allow only this type of editing in the document **check box. Click the drop-down list arrow and select** Filling in forms **from the list.**

Now specify which sections in your document you want to protect.

8 **Click the** Select sections **link in the task pane.**

The Section Protection dialog box appears, as shown in Figure 13-17.

9 **Make sure the** Section 1 **check box is checked and that the** Section 2 **check box is unchecked, then click** OK.

Now you're ready to apply this protection.

10 **Click the** Yes, Start Enforcing Protection button **in the task pane. Click** OK.

The dialog box closes, and Word protects only the first section of the document. Figure 13-18 shows the form with protected and unprotected sections.

Let's see if the protection worked.

11 **Press** Ctrl + Home **to move to the beginning of the document.**

This is the protected section of the document—you shouldn't be able to type anything except in the form fields.

12 **Press** Tab **repeatedly to move through the form fields in the protected section of the document.**

You should be able to type text freely in the unprotected section of the document under the Notes heading. Try it!

13 **Press** Ctrl + End **to move to the end of the document, press the** Spacebar **and type** Was not satisfied with meals provided.

To unprotect the document, you would select Tools → Unprotect Document or else click the Protect Document button on the toolbar.

14 **Save your changes.**

The multiple section method for creating less restricted forms works great if there are only two or three protected and unprotected sections. Manipulate any more than that and it can become too difficult and confusing to create and work with the form.

There is another "unofficial" method of creating forms that lets you use and enter information into fields without having to protect the document—turn the page and we'll look at it.

turn the page and we'll look at it.

QUICK REFERENCE

TO PROTECT/UNPROTECT ONLY A SECTION OF A FORM:

1. SELECT INSERT → BREAK FROM THE MENU AND SELECT THE TYPE OF SECTION YOU WANT (USUALLY CONTINUOUS TO KEEP THE FORM ON THE SAME PAGE).

2. SELECT TOOLS → PROTECT DOCUMENT FROM THE MENU.

3. CHECK THE ALLOW ONLY THIS TYPE OF EDITING IN THE DOCUMENT CHECK BOX.

4. CLICK THE DROP-DOWN LIST ARROW AND SELECT FILLING IN FORMS.

5. CLICK THE SELECT SECTIONS LINK IN THE TASK PANE.

6. SELECT THE SECTION(S) YOU WANT TO PROTECT AND CLICK OK.

7. CLICK THE YES, START ENFORCING PROTECTION BUTTON IN THE TASK PANE AND CLICK OK.

The "Empty Field" Alternate Method to Creating Forms

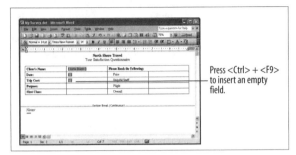

Figure 13-19. You can create a form by inserting blank fields.

No, this lesson isn't about a disgruntled farmer and a failed harvest. This lesson looks at an "unofficial" way to create forms that lets you enter information into fields without having to protect the document: the "empty field" method. This method is superior to protected forms, because you can exercise much more freedom and control in the form.

Start off by removing the form fields you entered in the previous lessons.

1 Unprotect the form by clicking the Protect Form button on the Forms toolbar.

2 Delete all the form fields you created in the previous lessons.

Now you're ready to recreate your form using the "empty field" method.

3 Place the insertion point in the cell to the right of the label Client's Name in the first row, and press Ctrl + F9.

Word inserts an empty field in the cell, as shown in Figure 13-19. This field may look a lot like the text field you already learned about, but it's really quite different. See Table 13-5 to read about the differences. The two most important differences to remember are:

• You can only use a text field type.

• You can fill in the form without protecting it.

4 Repeat Step 3, adding blank fields for the Date and Trip Cost.

You've entered enough blank fields to get an idea of how this method of creating a form works. Now try completing the form, but be careful! The procedure for completing a form created using the "empty field" method is completely different from completing a protected form.

5 Move to the beginning of the document.

You don't have to protect a document to complete it using the "empty field" form method.

6 Press F11 to move to the first field.

> TIP
> Press F11 to move to the next field, and Shift + F11 to move back to the previous field when filling in a form created by the "empty field" method.

Instead of the Tab key, you need to press the F11 key to move to the next field when you fill out a form created by the "empty field" method.

7 Click between the brackets. Type your name and press F11.

Word jumps to the next field. To move back to the previous field, press Shift + F11. Shift + F11 works just like Shift + Tab does in protected forms.

8 Press Shift + F11 to move back to the previous field.

The major advantage of using the "empty field" method of creating forms is you don't have to protect the document; you can make changes to the rest of the document, not just the form fields.

9 If you want, try modifying other parts of the form. Exit Word without saving your changes when you're finished.

Table 13-5 compares the two methods of creating forms, so you can decide which method works best for you.

Table 13-5. The Protected Form Method Versus the Blank Field Code Method

Comparison	Protected Form Method	"Empty Field" Method
Insert Fields By	Using the Forms toolbar	Pressing Ctrl + F9
Types of Fields Available	Text fields, check box fields, and drop-down list fields	Text fields only
To Move Between Fields	Tab moves to the next field;Shift + Tab moves to the previous field	F11 moves to the next field; Shift + F11 moves to the previous field.
Can Assign Help?	Yes	No
Can Assign Macros?	Yes	No
Can Calculate Fields?	Yes	No
Can Assign Default Value?	Yes	No
Requires Protection?	Yes—can only edit form fields.	No—can edit the rest of the document.

QUICK REFERENCE

TO INSERT AN EMPTY FIELD:

- PLACE THE INSERTION POINT WHERE YOU WANT THE FIELD AND PRESS CTRL + F9.

TO MOVE BETWEEN "EMPTY" FIELDS:

- PRESS F11 TO MOVE TO THE NEXT FIELD, SHIFT + F11 TO MOVE TO THE PREVIOUS FIELD.

Chapter Thirteen Review

Lesson Summary

Creating a New Form

It's usually a good idea to create a template for the form. Use a table to align the form's text and fields.

To Create a Table: Click the Insert Table button on the Standard toolbar or the Forms toolbar, drag inside the grid to select the number of columns and rows you want. Or, select Table → Insert → Table from the menu, specify the number of rows and columns you want, and click OK.

To Move from Cell to Cell in a Table: Press Tab to move the insertion point forward one field or cell, or press Shift + Tab to move the insertion point back one field or cell.

To Delete Text in a Cell: Select the cell(s), then press the Delete key.

Using Text Fields

To View Field Shading: Click the Form Field Shading button on the Forms toolbar, or select Tools → Options from the menu, click the View tab, click the Field shading list arrow, select Always, and click OK.

To Insert a Text Field: Place the insertion point where you want to place the field and click the Text Form Field button on the Forms toolbar.

To View and/or Change a Text Field's Options: Double-click the text field.

Using Check Box Fields

To Insert a Check Box Field: Place the insertion point where you want to place the field and click the Check Box Form Field button on the Forms toolbar.

To View and/or Change a Check Box Field's Options: Double-click the check box field.

Using Drop-Down Fields

To Insert a Drop-Down Field: Place the insertion point where you want to place the field and click the Drop-Down Form Field button on the Forms toolbar.

To View and/or Change a Drop-Down Field's Options: Double-click the drop-down field.

Assigning Help to Form Fields

To Add Status Bar Help Text: Double-click the form field, click the Add Help Text button, click the Status Bar tab, click the Type your own option, and type the help message you want to appear on the Status bar in the text box.

To Add F1 Help key text: Double-click the form field, click the Add Help Text button, click the Help Key (F1) tab, click the Type your own option, and type the help message you want to appear when the user presses the F1 key.

Performing Calculations in a Form Field

To Include a Field in a Calculation: Double-click the field and make sure the Calculate on exit check box is selected. You may also want to give the field a meaningful bookmark name.

To Create a Calculation Field: Double-click the field in which you want to display the results of a calculation, select Calculation from the Type list, and enter the formula in the Expression text box.

Preparing and Filling Out an Online Form

You must protect a form in order to use it. Protecting a form allows users to enter and change information in the form, but prevents them from modifying the form's design.

To Protect a Form: Click the Protect Form button on the Forms toolbar or select Tools → Protect Document from the menu and apply more advanced protection using the Protect Document task pane.

To Unprotect a Form: Follow the previous step.

To Fill Out a Form: Press Tab to move to the next field; Shift + Tab to move to the previous field.

Working with Multiple Sections in Forms

If you find that protecting an entire document is too restrictive for creating a form, you can break the document into different sections, protecting some sections and not protecting others.

To Protect/Unprotect Only a Section of a Form: Select Insert → Break from the menu and select the type of break you want (usually Continuous, to keep the form on the same page). Select Tools → Protect Document from the menu. Check the Allow only this type of editing in the document check box, click the drop-down list arrow and select Filling in forms. Click the Select sections link in the task pane, select the section(s) you want to protect and click OK. Click the Yes, Start Enforcing Protection button in the task pane and click OK.

The "Empty Field" Alternate Method of Creating Forms

You can use this method to create a form that contains fields where users can enter information without having to protect the form. The disadvantage is that users can modify the form's design if they wish.

To Insert an Empty Field: Place the insertion point where you want the field and press Ctrl + F9.

To Move Between "Empty" Fields: Press F11 to move to the next field; Shift + F11 to move to the previous field.

Quiz

1. It's usually best if you create a _____ to create and fill-in blank forms.
   A. Style
   B. Macro
   C. Data source
   D. Template

2. Which of the following is NOT a type of field you can add to a Word form?
   A. Check box field.
   B. Drop-down field.
   C. Multiple choice field.
   D. Text field.

3. Which of the following statements is NOT true?
   A. Forms must be protected before a user can complete them.
   B. You can restrict the type of information that can be entered in a field by double-clicking the field to open the Field Options dialog box and selecting the type of information from the Type list.
   C. Fields are easy to see and are identified by the text "[Form Field]".
   D. You can add helpful prompt text that appears on the Status bar when the user selects the field.

4. Which of the following statements is NOT true?
   A. If a field is used in a calculation, you must select the Calculate on exit box in the Field Option dialog box.
   B. To make it easier to reference a field in a calculation, you should give it a Bookmark name in the Field Option dialog box.
   C. All formulas and calculations must start with the = (equal sign).
   D. Fields must be placed inside a table in order to be used in a calculation.

5. You're trying to create a customer satisfaction survey. You want to protect the top half, which has several fields, but you want the bottom half of the document to be unprotected so the user can type anything they want. How would you accomplish this?
   A. You can't have a free-form text area in the document. You need to protect a document in order to complete the form.
   B. Separate the two sections with a continuous section break. Protect the document by selecting Tools → Protect Document from the menu and protect the first section of the document in the task pane.
   C. Create a message that will appear in the Status bar telling the user to unprotect the document when they need to complete the free-form section.
   D. Create the form in a table—you can protect and unprotect the table's cells individually.

6. How do you modify a field?

   A. Select the field and click the Format Field button on the Standard toolbar.

   B. Select the field and select Tools → Forms → Modify Field from the menu.

   C. Select the field and press Ctrl + M.

   D. Double-click the field.

7. You can assign help text to appear in the status bar or when a user presses F1. (True or False?)

8. How do you protect a form? (Select all that apply.)

   A. Click the Protect Form button on the Forms toolbar.

   B. Select File → Save As from the menu and check the Protected box.

   C. Select Tools → Protect Document from the menu, check the "Allow only this type of editing in the document" check box, then click the drop-down list arrow and select Filling in forms. Click the "Yes, Start Enforcing Protection" button in the task pane and click OK.

   D. Select File → Protect Form from the menu.

9. All types of forms need protection before they are filled out. (True or False?)

Homework

1. Create a template file to be used for a form: Select File → New from the menu, click On my computer from the Templates section of the task pane, select the Template option in the lower right corner Create New box, and click OK.

2. Create a 9 × 2 (9 columns by 2 rows) table.

3. Format the table: Place the insertion point anywhere in the table, select Table → Table AutoFormat from the menu, select a formatting scheme that you like, and click OK.

4. Merge the table's top and bottom rows: Select the cells in the top row and select Table → Merge cells from the menu. Do the same for the bottom row.

5. Enter the following text into the table:

IRS New Simplified Form 1040

1. Date:

2. Name:

3. Address:

4. City/State/Zip Code:

5. Sex:

6. How much money do you make?

7. Send it in.

We appreciate your business!

---

6. Summon the Forms toolbar: Select View → Toolbars → Forms from the menu.

7. Make sure the Form Field Shading button on the Forms toolbar is activated.

8. Insert a text form field for the date.

9. Restrict what can be entered in the date field: Double-click the date field, select Date from the Type list, and click OK.

10. Add text fields in the cells next to "Name," "Address," and "City/State/Zip Code" cells.

11. Add a drop-down list field: Click the cell next to "Sex" and click the Drop-Down Form Field button on the Forms toolbar.

12. Add items to the drop-down list: Double-click the Sex field, type "Male," click Add, type "Female," click Add, and click OK.

13. Add a check box field: Click the cell next to "Send it in" and click the Check Box Form Field button on the Forms toolbar.

14. Protect the form: Click the Protect Form button on the Forms toolbar.

15. Save the template as "Form 1040," and close the file.

16. Create a form based on the "Form 1040" template.

17. Complete the form.

18. Save the document as "My Taxes" and exit Microsoft Word.

Quiz Answers

1. D. Normally you will want to create a template that you can use to create new blank forms.

2. C. The three types of fields you can insert are text fields, check boxes, and drop-down fields.

3. C. A form's fields are invisible unless you specify you want them shaded by clicking the Form Field Shading button on the Forms toolbar.

4. D. Tables make it easier to align and organize your form, but they aren't necessary to perform calculations.

5. B. Separate the two sections with a continuous section break. Protect the document by selecting Tools → Protect Document from the menu and protect the first section of the document in the task pane.

6. D. Double-click a field to modify it.

7. True. You can assign help text to appear for a field in the status bar or when a user presses F1.

8. A or C. You can use either of these methods to protect a form.

9. False. A form created using the empty fields method does not need protection.

CHAPTER 14

CREATING WEB PAGES WITH WORD

CHAPTER OBJECTIVES:

Creating a Web page, Lesson 14.1

Modifying a Web page, Lesson 14.2

Converting an existing Word document to a Web page, Lesson 14.3

Adding hyperlinks to a Web page, Lesson 14.4

Viewing a Web page in a Web browser, Lesson 14.5

Applying a theme to a Web page, Lesson 14.6

Working with frames, Lesson 14.7

CHAPTER OBJECTIVES: CREATE A SIMPLE WEB SITE

Prerequisites

- **Windows basics: how to use menus, toolbars, dialog boxes, and shortcut keystrokes**
- **Familiarity with Web pages and using a Web browsing program**
- **How to edit and format text**
- **Familiarity with Word's styles**

What does the Internet mean to a word processor? More and more, documents are never printed on paper, but are read online as e-mail or as Web pages on the World Wide Web instead. Realizing this, Microsoft added some Web-related features to Word. You can use Word to create and modify Web pages so that other users can read them over the Internet or corporate Intranet. You can add hyperlinks to your documents to link them to another document, a file created in another program, or even a Web page. This chapter will cover all these topics and more.

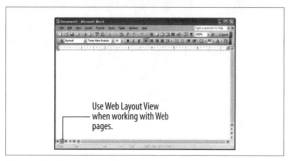

Figure 14-1. A new Web page.

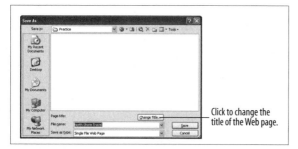

Figure 14-2. The Save As dialog box.

Though Web pages work and act much differently from a document, creating a new Web page is just as easy as creating a new Word document.

1 Start Word.

2 Select File → New from the menu.

The New Document task pane appears.

3 Click the On my computer link in the New Document task pane.

The Templates dialog box appears.

4 Double-click Web Page template in the General tab.

A new blank Web page appears, as shown in Figure 14-1.

You might think you just created another Word document. But if you look closer, you'll notice that you're in Web Page Layout view.

One of the major differences between Web pages and documents is how they are saved. When you save a Word document, everything you see on the page is saved in one file. For example, if you have inserted clip art in your document, the clip art file is embed-

ded in the document; it's not saved as a separate file outside of the document.

Web pages do not use embedded files. Each element of a Web page—the text and graphics—are saved in a separate file. For example, if you want to use a picture in your Web page, you have to define the image source, or where the file is saved on the Internet, in the Web page. All of these files required for a Web page are normally saved together in their own Web site folder.

Word 2003 saves you from some of this confusion with MHTML, a special type of file that encapsulates all the elements of a Web page into one file, just like a Word document. The drawback of this file type is increased file size, but it's very convenient.

Now that you basically know how Web pages are saved, let's try it.

5 Click the Save button on the Standard toolbar.

The Save As dialog box appears, as shown in Figure 14-2.

6 Type North Shore Travel in the File name box.

Any text you type in the Web page will be stored in this file.

Another difference between Web pages and documents is the Page Title. When a Web page is viewed in a Web browser, the Page Title appears in the title bar of the browser.

7 Click the Change Title button in the Save As dialog box.

The Set Page Title dialog box appears.

8 Type North Shore Travel, Inc. and click OK.

The Page Title you just entered appears in the Save As dialog box.

Notice that Single File Web Page appears in the Save as type area of the dialog box. This is the MHTML file that saves all the elements of the Web page in a single file.

Now tell Word where to save your Web page.

9 Navigate to your Practice folder and click the Save button.

The Web page is saved as a single file in your Practice folder.

Most of the time you will save a Web page in a Web site folder with all the other pages and files in the site.

⁝ NOTE ⁝

Microsoft Word is not the best tool to use for creating and designing Web pages. If you want to get really serious about creating your own Web site, use FrontPage, the Web design tool for Microsoft Office.

QUICK REFERENCE

TO CREATE A WEB PAGE:

1. SELECT FILE → NEW FROM THE MENU.

2. CLICK THE ON MY COMPUTER LINK IN THE NEW DOCUMENT TASK PANE.

3. DOUBLE-CLICK THE WEB PAGE TEMPLATE IN THE GENERAL TAB.

OR...

1. SELECT FILE → NEW FROM THE MENU.

2. CLICK THE WEB PAGE LINK IN THE NEW DOCUMENT TASK PANE.

TO SAVE A WEB PAGE:

1. CLICK THE SAVE BUTTON ON THE STANDARD TOOLBAR.

OR...

SELECT FILE → SAVE FROM THE MENU.

2. CLICK THE CHANGE TITLE BUTTON TO ADD A PAGE TITLE.

3. TYPE A FILE NAME FOR THE PAGE IN THE FILE NAME BOX.

4. CLICK THE SAVE BUTTON.

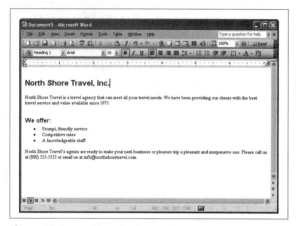

Figure 14-3. Modify and edit a Web page just as you would modify or edit a Word document.

Once you have created a Web page, you're ready to add its content. This lesson will show you how to do just that.

1 **Type** North Shore Travel, Inc. **in the Web page.**

Working with a Web page isn't very different from working with a Word document. Just be careful when you start formatting your Web page. Web pages can be formatted, but not to the same extent as some of the more advanced formatting features that Word supports, such as multiple columns and animated text.

Just like Word documents, Web pages frequently use *Styles* to format paragraphs. Styles are especially useful for applying heading styles in Web pages.

2 **Select the** North Shore Travel, Inc. **text. Click the** Style **list arrow from the Formatting toolbar and select** Heading 1 **from the list.**

The formatting of the selected text is changed to the Heading 1 style.

Now that we have a page heading, let's enter body text for the page. First, go back to the Normal style.

3 **Make sure the text is not selected. Press** Enter **twice. Click the** Style **list arrow from the Formatting toolbar and select** Normal **from the list.**

4 **Type:**

North Shore Travel is a travel agency that can meet all your travel needs. We have been providing our clients with the best travel service and value available since 1975.

Next, let's add a bulleted list to our Web page. We'll need a heading to start off the list…

5 **Press** Enter, **click the** Style **list arrow on the Formatting toolbar, select** Heading 3, **type** We offer: **and then press** Enter.

Now we can add the bulleted items.

6 **Click the** Bullets button **on the Formatting toolbar and add the following paragraphs:**

Prompt, friendly service
Competitive rates
A knowledgeable staff

Let's finish adding the text for the current Web page.

7 **Press** Enter, **click the** Bullets button **on the formatting toolbar to toggle the bulleting, press** Enter **and type the following paragraph:**

North Shore Travel's agents are ready to make your next business or pleasure trip a pleasant and inexpensive one. Please call us at (800) 555-5555 or email us at info@northshore-travel.com.

Although it's no masterpiece, we've finished creating the home page for our new Web site. Compare your document to Figure 14-3.

8 **Close all open documents without saving your changes.**

QUICK REFERENCE

TO EDIT A WEB PAGE:

• EDITING A WEB PAGE IS NO DIFFERENT FROM
  EDITING THE TEXT OF A WORD DOCUMENT.

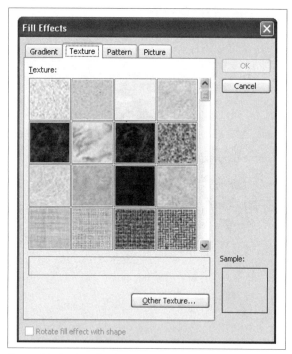

Figure 14-4. The Fill Effects dialog box.

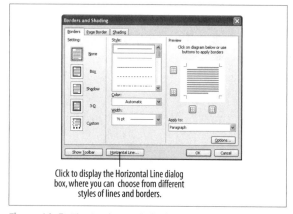

Click to display the Horizontal Line dialog box, where you can choose from different styles of lines and borders.

Figure 14-5. The Borders and Shading dialog box.

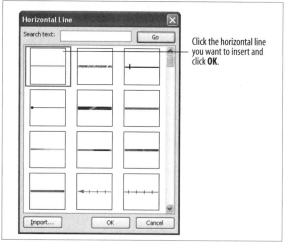

Click the horizontal line you want to insert and click **OK**.

Figure 14-6. The Horizontal Line dialog box.

There is no need to create a new document if you already have a Word document that you would like to use as a Web page. Word does a pretty good job of converting any document into HTML, even documents with embedded graphics. However, advanced formatting is often lost when documents are converted to Web pages.

1 **Open** Lesson 14A.

This document is an itinerary for a board of directors meeting for North Shore Travel. You need to convert it from Word document format to Web page or HTML format.

2 **Select** File → Save as Web Page **from the menu.**

The Save As dialog box appears.

3 **In the File name box, type** Board Meeting **and click** Save.

Word saves the document "Lesson 14A" as a Web Page named "Board Meeting."

Web Pages use a variety of predefined styles to make formatting more simple and straightforward. Make the title of the document more readable by applying the style "Heading 1."

4 **Place the insertion point anywhere in the** Board of Directors Meeting **line, click the** Style **list arrow on the Formatting toolbar, and select** Heading 1.

The title "Board of Directors Meeting" is formatted with the Heading 1 style.

5 Place the insertion point anywhere in the The Month in Review line, click the Style list arrow on the Formatting toolbar, select Heading 2.

The heading is formatted with the Heading 2 style. Now, move on to the next step and finish applying the Heading 2 style to the remaining headings in the document.

6 Repeat Step 5 for each of the remaining headings in the document.

The remaining headings are formatted with the Heading 2 style. Next, make the document more visually attractive by adding a background.

7 Select Format → Background → Fill Effects from the menu and click the Texture tab.

The Fill Effects dialog box appears, as shown in Figure 14-4. You can select a background texture from the various options listed and previewed here, or you can select and use a graphics file as a background.

8 Select the first background fill option Newsprint and click OK.

The Fill Effects dialog box closes and the Newsprint texture is added as a background to the document. Next, add a horizontal line under the document title.

9 Place the insertion point at the end of the Board of Directors Meeting line and select Format → Borders and Shading from the menu.

The Borders and Shading dialog box appears, as shown in Figure 14-5. You can select an ordinary border from this dialog box, or you can select a more interesting horizontal line by clicking the Horizontal Line button.

10 Click the Horizontal Line button.

The Horizontal Line dialog box appears, as shown in Figure 14-6. You can select a horizontal line from the ones listed and previewed.

11 Select a horizontal line and click OK.

The Horizontal Line dialog box closes and the selected horizontal line appears below the page title.

12 Click the Save button to save your work.

It's important to note that Web pages don't support as many formatting features as a Microsoft Word document. When Word saves a document as a Web page, it preserves these additional Word-specific formatting options by embedding them inside the Web page, in a language known as XML. You can reduce the size of a Web page by filtering out the XML tags by selecting File → Save as Web Page from the menu, clicking the Save as type list, and selecting Web Page, Filtered.

See Table 14-1 for web formats and their descriptions.

Table 14-1. Web Page Format Options

Format	Description
Single File Web Page	(Default) Encapsulates all the elements of the Web page (text, graphics, etc.) in a single file.
Web Page	Saves a document as a Web page and preserves all Word-specific document formatting by embedding it using XML tags—at the cost of large file sizes.
Web Page, Filtered	Saves a document as a Web page without preserving any Word-specific formatting. Filtered Web pages are much smaller in size.

QUICK REFERENCE

TO SAVE A WORD DOCUMENT AS A WEB PAGE:

• OPEN THE WORD DOCUMENT AND SELECT FILE → SAVE AS WEB PAGE FROM THE MENU.

TO FORMAT A WEB PAGE:

• FORMATTING CHARACTERS AND PARAGRAPHS IN WEB PAGES IS VERY SIMILAR TO FORMATTING CHARACTERS AND PARAGRAPHS IN A NORMAL DOCUMENT, EXCEPT THAT YOU DON'T HAVE AS MANY FORMATTING OPTIONS.

TO USE STYLES IN A WEB PAGE:

• SELECT THE CHARACTERS OR PARAGRAPH, CLICK THE STYLE LIST ARROW AND SELECT THE STYLE.

TO CHANGE THE WEB PAGE'S BACKGROUND:

• SELECT FORMAT → BACKGROUND FROM THE MENU AND SELECT THE BACKGROUND YOU WANT TO USE.

TO INSERT A HORIZONTAL LINE:

• SELECT FORMAT → BORDERS AND SHADING FROM THE MENU. CLICK THE HORIZONTAL LINE BUTTON TO ADD A GRAPHICAL HORIZONTAL LINE.

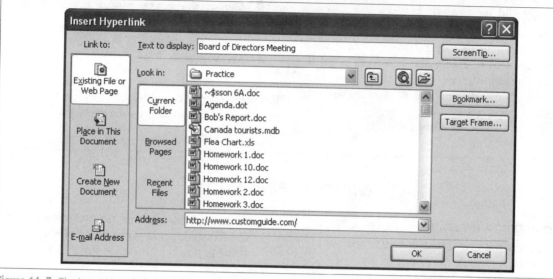

Figure 14-7. The Insert Hyperlink dialog box.

In this lesson, you will learn how to use hyperlinks in Word. A *hyperlink* points to a file, a specific location in a file, or a Web page on the Internet or on an Intranet. Whenever you click a hyperlink, you jump to the hyperlink's destination. A hyperlink is usually indicated by colored and underlined text. If you have ever been on the World Wide Web, you've used hyperlinks all the time to move between different Web pages.

Here's how to insert a hyperlink:

1 Scroll to the end of the document, press Enter twice, and type Board of Directors Meeting.

The text "Board of Directors Meeting" will contain a hyperlink to the Web page "Board of Directors Meeting."

2 Select the Board of Directors Meeting text you just typed and click the Insert Hyperlink button on the Standard toolbar.

 TIP *Another way to insert a hyperlink is to select Insert → Hyperlink from the menu, or press Ctrl + K.*

The Insert Hyperlink dialog box appears, as shown in Figure 14-7. Here, you can specify a Web address or name and location of a file you want to add as a hyperlink. If you know the location and name of the file or Web address, you can type it directly in the dialog box; otherwise, you can navigate to the file.

There are three different buttons in the Insert Hyperlink dialog box that let you browse for four different types of Hyperlink destinations.

- **Existing File or Web Page:** Create a link that takes you to another Word document or to a file created in another program, such as a Microsoft Excel worksheet, or to a Web page on the Internet.

- **Place in This Document:** Takes you to a bookmark in the same document.

- **Create New Document:** Creates a new Microsoft Word document and then inserts a hyperlink to it.

- **E-mail Address:** Creates a clickable e-mail address.

3 Click the Existing File or Web Page button.

The Look in dialog box appears, which displays a list of files that you can use as the destination for your hyperlink.

You can also create a link to another Web page on the Internet.

4 Click in the Address box. Type http://www.customguide.com and click OK.

The dialog box closes and you return to the Web page. Notice the text "Board of Directors Meeting" appears blue and underlined, signifying that it's a hyperlink.

Once you create a hyperlink, you can easily edit it to change its title or target, copy it, or delete it by right-clicking it.

5 Right-click the hyperlink.

A shortcut menu with the most frequently used hyperlink commands appears. Here, you could select Edit Hyperlink to change the hyperlink's target or Select Hyperlink to edit the hyperlink's title. Your hyperlink is fine the way it is, so close the shortcut menu.

6 Click anywhere in the window to close the shortcut menu.

7 Save your work.

In the next lesson, you will get a chance to use the hyperlink you just created, and see how you can browse Web pages and linked documents using the Web toolbar.

QUICK REFERENCE

TO INSERT A HYPERLINK:

I. SELECT THE TEXT YOU WANT TO USE FOR THE HYPERLINK AND CLICK THE INSERT HYPERLINK BUTTON FROM THE STANDARD TOOLBAR.

OR...

SELECT THE TEXT YOU WANT TO USE FOR THE HYPERLINK AND SELECT INSERT → HYPERLINK FROM THE MENU.

OR...

PRESS CTRL + K.

2. EITHER SELECT A FILE (USE THE BROWSE BUTTONS TO HELP YOU LOCATE THE FILE), OR TYPE A WEB ADDRESS FOR THE HYPERLINK'S DESTINATION AND CLICK OK.

TO EDIT A HYPERLINK:

• RIGHT-CLICK THE HYPERLINK AND SELECT EDIT HYPERLINK FROM THE SHORTCUT MENU.

Viewing a Web Page

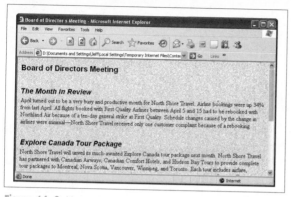

Figure 14-8. You can preview how a Web page created in Word will look in a Web browser.

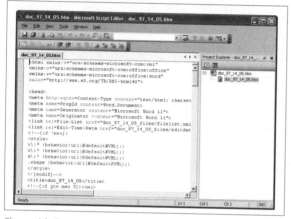

Figure 14-9. You can view a Web page's HTML source code.

Most people use a program called a *Web browser* to surf the Web and view Web pages. More than 95 percent of people use one of two different Web browsers: Netscape Navigator and Microsoft Internet Explorer. Whichever program you use, it is a good idea to view Web pages you create in Word using the actual Web browsing programs. Web pages look different in the actual browser than they do in Word. Table 14-2 shows Web toolbar buttons and their descriptions.

1 Verify that the Board Meeting Web page appears in the active document window, and select File → Web Page Preview from the menu.

Your computer's Web browser program opens and the Web page appears in the browser's window, as shown in Figure 14-8.

When you preview the page in a browser, it's a good opportunity to check your links and see if they work properly.

2 Click the Board of Directors Meeting link on the bottom of the page.

If the link works, the CustomGuide home page appears in your browser.

Now that you've seen how your Web pages appear online and checked your links, you can close your Web browser.

3 Click your Web browser's Close button.

The browser closes and you are back in Microsoft Word.

You can also view and navigate Web pages directly in Microsoft Word by clicking on hyperlinks and using the Web toolbar.

Web pages are stored in a text-based language called HTML. If you are familiar with HTML, you can directly view and edit the HTML source for Web pages in Word.

4 Select View → HTML Source from the menu.

The HTML source code for the Web page appears in a separate window, as shown in Figure 14-9. If you're like most people, HTML coding will look like Greek, but if you are familiar with HTML, you could directly edit your Web page's HTML source code here.

5 Click the Microsoft Script Editor Close button.

The HTML source code disappears.

Table 14-2. The Web toolbar buttons

Button	Description
	Brings you back to the previously viewed Web page.
	Brings you forward to the next viewed Web page.
	Stops loading a Web page.
	Reloads or refreshes the current Web page.
	Brings you to your home page.
	Searches the Web for specified information.
Favorites ▾	Quickly brings you to Web pages that you have bookmarked and use frequently.
Go ▾	Displays a list of Web commands that also appear on the Web toolbar.
	Toggles whether toolbars other than the Web toolbar should be displayed or hidden.
www.customguid ▾	Type in a file name and location or a Web URL to open a Web page or file. Clicking the Address list arrow displays a list of the last 10 documents or Web pages you've visited or opened.

QUICK REFERENCE

TO PREVIEW A WEB PAGE IN YOUR WEB BROWSER:

- SELECT FILE → WEB PAGE PREVIEW FROM THE MENU.

TO VIEW THE WEB TOOLBAR:

- SELECT VIEW → TOOLBARS → WEB FROM THE MENU.

OR...

- RIGHT-CLICK ANY MENU OR TOOLBAR AND SELECT WEB FROM THE SHORTCUT MENU.

TO VIEW A WEB PAGE'S HTML SOURCE CODE:

- SELECT VIEW → HTML SOURCE FROM THE MENU.

TO BROWSE WEB PAGES IN WORD:

- USE THE WEB TOOLBAR BUTTONS.

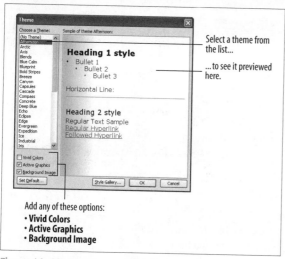

Select a theme from the list...

... to see it previewed here.

Add any of these options:
- **Vivid Colors**
- **Active Graphics**
- **Background Image**

Figure 14-10. The Theme dialog box.

A theme is a set of coordinated design elements and colors for background images, bullets, fonts, horizontal lines, and other document elements.

When you apply a theme to a document, Word customizes the following elements for that document:

- Background color or graphics
- Body and heading styles
- Bullets
- Horizontal lines
- Hyperlink colors
- Table border color

You can apply a theme by using the Theme command on the Format menu. This lesson explains how to apply themes to your documents.

1 If necessary, open the Lesson 14B document and save it file as Board Meeting.

Here's how to select and apply a theme:

2 Select Format → Theme from the menu.

The Theme dialog box appears, as shown in Figure 14-10. Word comes with a wide assortment of themes, from no-nonsense corporate themes to whimsical and playful ones. Each time you select a theme from the list, Word displays a sample of how your document will look with that theme.

The Theme dialog box has three options of which you should be aware—they are:

- **Vivid Colors:** Changes the color of styles and table borders to a brighter setting and changes the document background color.

- **Active Graphics:** Displays animated graphics when the theme contains them. You can see the animation when you view the page in a Web browser.

- **Background Image:** Sets the background of the current theme as the background for the document or file. Clear this check box to apply a background color instead. This option is selected by default.

3 Browse through the list of themes until you find one you like and click OK.

Word applies the theme you selected to the document.

4 Save your changes.

Most people use Word's themes for Web pages, but you can also use them in a Word document.

QUICK REFERENCE

TO APPLY A THEME:

1. SELECT FORMAT → THEME FROM THE MENU.

2. SELECT THE DESIRED THEME FROM THE LIST AND CHECK ANY ADDITIONAL OPTIONS, SUCH AS VIVID COLORS OR ACTIVE GRAPHICS.

3. CLICK OK.

Working with Frames

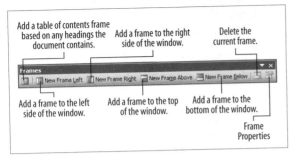

Add a table of contents frame based on any headings the document contains.

Add a frame to the right side of the window.

Delete the current frame.

Add a frame to the left side of the window.

Add a frame to the top of the window.

Add a frame to the bottom of the window.

Frame Properties

Figure 14-11. The Frames toolbar

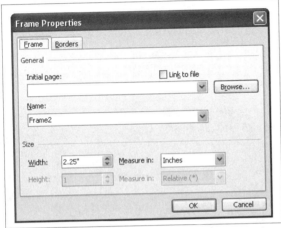

Figure 14-12. The Frame tab of the Frame Properties dialog box.

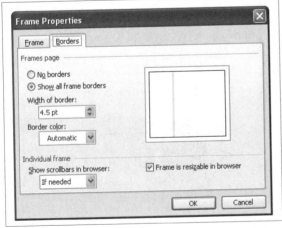

Figure 14-13. The Borders tab of the Frame Properties dialog box.

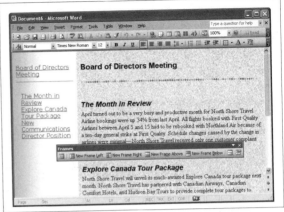

Figure 14-14. The updated document with a table of contents frame and the Frames toolbar.

Frames help organize information in your Web pages and make it easy to access. Just as a window can be broken up into separate sections, so can a single Web page be broken into sections or frames that display separate Web pages.

Frames are sometimes used in Web sites to make information easier to access, or to show the contents of a Web site that has multiple pages. Frames can be used to display a header for a Web site without having to reopen the Web page that displays the header each time the user changes pages. Frames can also be used to create a table of contents that stays on the screen while you go to different pages in the Web site. The easiest way to work with frames is with the Frames toolbar.

1 **Display the Frames toolbar by selecting** View → Toolbars → Frames **from the menu.**

Another way to display the Frames toolbar is to right-click any toolbar and select Frames.

The Frames toolbar appears, as shown in Figure 14-11.

One of the most common uses for frames is to create a Table of Contents to the left side of the page to access other Web pages or sections of the current Web page. If the current Web page uses heading styles, you can use the table of contents in Frame button to add a frame and create a table of contents based on the current Web page's headings.

2 Click the Table of Contents in Frame button on the Frames toolbar.

> TIP *Another way to add a table of contents frame is to select Format → Frames → Table of Contents in Frame from the menu.*

Word inserts a frame to the left side of the Web page and fills it with a table of contents based on the heading styles it finds in the main Web page. Clicking one of the hyperlinks in the table of contents frame will take you to that heading in the main Web page.

Once you have broken a Web page into frames, you can format the frame's size, its borders and scroll bars, and more.

3 Place the insertion point in the Table of Contents frame and click the Frame Properties button on the Frames toolbar.

> TIP *Another way to format a frame is to select Format → Frames → Frame Properties from the menu.*

The Frame Properties dialog box appears with the Frame tab selected, as shown in Figure 14-12. Here, you can specify which Web page you want to use in the selected frame and how wide that frame should be. You can measure width in inches or by a percent of the screen.

4 Click the Measure in list arrow and select Percent, then type 25% in the Width box.

Let's take a look at the Borders tab before we leave.

5 Click the Borders tab.

The Borders tab appears, as shown in Figure 14-13. Here, you can specify if the selected frame should include a border and/or scroll bar.

6 Make sure the No borders option is selected and click OK.

The dialog box closes and Word makes the changes to the selected frame.

It's important for you to realize that each frame is really a separate Web page; so, if you make changes to one frame, you aren't necessarily making changes to any of the other frames on the page or the Web site.

7 Make sure the insertion point is still in the table of contents frame and select Format → Background → and a color of your choice from the menu.

Word applies the selected color to the table of contents frame but not anywhere else. Figure 14-14 shows the updated document with a table of contents frame and the Frames toolbar.

8 Exit Microsoft Word without saving any of your changes.

Word's Web editing features make a usable Web page, it's not well equipped to create an entire Web site. For more professional Web development, you might want to consider taking a look at Microsoft FrontPage—the Web publishing component of Microsoft Office.

QUICK REFERENCE

TO VIEW THE FRAMES TOOLBAR:

- SELECT VIEW → TOOLBARS → FRAMES FROM THE MENU.

OR...

- RIGHT-CLICK ANY TOOLBAR AND SELECT FRAMES.

TO ADD A FRAME:

- CLICK THE APPROPRIATE FRAME BUTTON ON THE FRAMES TOOLBAR.

OR...

- SELECT FORMAT → FRAMES → AND THE DESIRED FRAME FROM THE MENU.

TO FORMAT A FRAME:

- CLICK THE FRAME PROPERTIES BUTTON ON THE FRAMES TOOLBAR.

OR...

- SELECT FORMAT → FRAMES → FRAME PROPERTIES FROM THE MENU.

Chapter Fourteen Review

Lesson Summary

Creating and Saving a Web Page

To Create a Web Page: Select File → New from the menu, click the On my computer link in the New Document task pane, and double-click the Web Page template in the General tab. Or, select File → New from the menu and click the Web Page link in the New Document task pane.

To Save a Web Page: Click the Save button on the Standard toolbar or select File → Save from the menu. Click the Change Title button to add a Page Title, type a file name for the page in the File name box, and click the Save button.

Modifying a Web Page

Editing a Web page is no different from editing the text of any other document.

Converting a Word Document to a Web Page

To Save a Word Document as a Web Page: Open the Word document and select File → Save as Web Page from the menu.

To Format a Web Page: Formatting characters and paragraphs in Web pages is very similar to formatting characters and paragraphs in a normal document, except that you don't have as many formatting options.

To Use Styles in a Web Page: Select the characters or paragraph, click the Style list arrow and select the style.

To Change the Web Page's Background: Select Format → Background from the menu and select the background you want to use.

To Insert a Horizontal Line: Select Format → Borders and Shading from the menu. Click the Horizontal Line button to add a graphical horizontal line.

Adding and Working with Hyperlinks

A hyperlink is a colored and underlined text that you click to jump to a file, to a location in a file, to a Web page on the World Wide Web, or to a Web page on an Intranet.

To Insert a Hyperlink: Select the text you want to use for the hyperlink and click the Insert Hyperlink button from the Standard toolbar, or select Insert → Hyperlink from the menu, or press Ctrl + K. Select the destination file or type a Web address for the hyperlink's destination, and click OK.

To Edit a Hyperlink: Right-click the hyperlink and select Edit Hyperlink from the shortcut menu.

Viewing a Web Page

To View a Web Page: Select File → Web Page Preview from the menu.

To View the Web Toolbar: Select View → Toolbars → Web from the menu, or right-click any menu or toolbar and select Web from the shortcut menu.

To View a Web Page's HTML Source Code: Select View → HTML Source from the menu.

You can browse or navigate Web pages in Microsoft Word using the Web toolbar buttons, just like you would when using a Web browser.

Applying a Theme to a Web Page

To Apply a Theme: Select Format → Theme from the menu, select the desired theme from the list, and check any additional options, such as vivid colors or active graphics, and click OK.

Working with Frames

To View the Frames Toolbar: Select View → Toolbars → Frames from the menu, or right-click any toolbar or menu and select Frames.

To Add a Frame: Click the appropriate Frame button on the Frames toolbar, or select Format → Frames → and the desired frame location from the menu.

To Format a Frame: Click the Frame Properties button on the Frames toolbar, or select Format → Frames → Frame Properties from the menu.

Quiz

1. Which of the following statements is NOT true?

    A. To save a document as a Web page, select File → Save as Web Page from the menu.

    B. A hyperlink is a link that takes to you to a different destination when clicked.

    C. MHTML (Single File Web Page) file format allows you to save all the elements of a Web page in a single file.

    D. MHTML is the code used to create Web pages.

2. When you save a Word document as an HTML file, some of the document's formatting may be lost. (True or False?)

3. Which Word feature makes it easy to create a Web page?

    A. The HTML Conversion Wizard.

    B. The File → Send To → HTML file command.

    C. The MHTML file format.

    D. It's not very easy to create Web pages in Word—or in any other program, for that matter!

4. A hyperlink, when clicked, can take you to which of the following locations? (Select all that apply.)

    A. A Web page on the Internet.

    B. A different location in the same Web page.

    C. A different Word document file.

    D. A file created in another program.

5. How can you insert a hyperlink in a document? (Select all that apply.)

    A. If the hyperlink's destination is a Web page on the Internet, simply type its address—Word will recognize it as a Web address and format the text into a hyperlink.

    B. Select Tools → Hyperlink from the menu.

    C. Click the Insert Hyperlink button on the Standard toolbar.

    D. Select the text that you want to use as your hyperlink, right-click it and select Hyperlink from the shortcut menu.

6. You can edit a hyperlink by right-clicking it and selecting Edit Hyperlink from the shortcut menu. (True or False?)

7. Just like Microsoft Word documents, Web pages can use predefined styles to format text and paragraphs. (True or False?)

Homework

1. Create a new Web page.

2. Enter your own personal information (name, address, phone number, company name and title) for the Web page's content.

3. Place the insertion point near the bottom of the screen and type "Contact Me."

4. Insert a Hyperlink: Select the "Contact Me" text you just entered and click the Insert Hyperlink button on the Standard toolbar.

5. Type your e-mail address in the Link to File or URL box and click OK.

6. Save the Web page: Select File → Save from the menu.

7. Save your Web page as "My Home Page." Exit Microsoft Word when you're finished.

Quiz Answers

1. D. HTML (HyperText Markup Language), not MHTML, is the code used to create Web pages.

2. True. Web pages can contain lots of formatting options, just not as many as a Word document.

3. C. The MHTML file format encapsulates all the elements of a Web page (text, graphics, etc.) into a single file.

4. A, B, C, and D. A hyperlink can take you to any of these destinations.

5. A and C. You can use either of these methods to insert a hyperlink.

6. True. To edit a hyperlink, right-click it and select Edit Hyperlink from the shortcut menu.

7. True. Web pages can use predefined styles to format text and paragraphs.

CHAPTER 15
ADVANCED TOPICS

CHAPTER OBJECTIVES:

Adding and removing toolbars, Lesson 15.1

Creating custom toolbars, Lesson 15.2

Sending a fax, Lesson 15.3

Creating and working with AutoText entries, Lesson 15.4

Creating and working with AutoCorrect entries, Lesson 15.5

Changing Word's default options, Lesson 15.6

File properties and finding a file, Lesson 15.7

Recording a macro, Lesson 15.8

Playing a macro, Lesson 15.9

Editing a macro's Visual Basic source code, Lesson 15.10

Using Detect and Repair, Lesson 15.11

CHAPTER OBJECTIVES: CUSTOMIZE WORD

Prerequisites

- **How to use menus, toolbars, dialog boxes, and shortcut keystrokes**
- **How to open and save a document**

This chapter explains how you can tailor Word to work the way you do. You are already familiar with toolbars and how they make it easy to access frequently used commands. In this chapter, you will get to create your very own toolbar and add the commands you use most often to it.

Next, you'll move on to working with and creating *AutoText* and *AutoCorrect* entries. AutoText lets you store and insert text or graphics that you use again and again, such as a mailing address or phrase you use often. AutoCorrect is the same feature that instantly corrects common spelling and typing errors, such as changing "teh" to "the." This chapter will explain how to create your own custom AutoCorrect entries.

The last topic covered by this chapter is *macros*. A macro helps you perform routine tasks by automating them. Instead of manually performing a series of time-consuming, repetitive actions in Word, you can record a single macro that does the entire task, all at once.

Hiding, Displaying, and Moving Toolbars

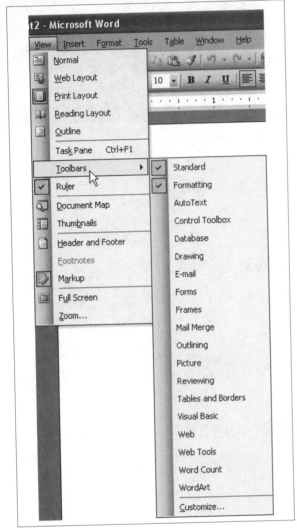

Figure 15-1. It's easy to select a toolbar to view.

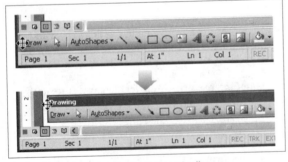

Figure 15-2. An example of moving a toolbar.

When you first start Word, two toolbars—Standard and Formatting—appear by default. As you work with Word, you may want to display other toolbars, such as the Drawing toolbar or the Chart toolbar, to help you accomplish your tasks. Soon, your screen is covered with more buttons than NASA's mission control room. This lesson explains how to remove all that clutter by moving Word's toolbars to different positions on the screen, or by removing them altogether.

1 Select View → Toolbars from the menu.

> **TIP**
> *Another way to hide or display a toolbar is to right-click any toolbar and select the toolbar you want to hide or display from the shortcut menu.*

A list of available toolbars appears, as shown in Figure 15-1. Notice that check marks appear next to the Standard and Formatting toolbars—this indicates that the toolbars already appear on the screen.

2 Select Formatting from the toolbar menu.

The Formatting toolbar disappears.

You can hide a toolbar if you don't need to use any of its commands, or if you need to make more room available on the screen to view a document.

3 Select View → Toolbars → Formatting from the menu.

The Formatting toolbar reappears. Another way to add and remove toolbars is to right-click anywhere on a toolbar.

4 Right-click the Standard toolbar or the Formatting toolbar.

A shortcut menu appears with the names of available toolbars.

5 Click Drawing from the Toolbar shortcut menu.

The Drawing toolbar appears along the bottom of the Word screen (unless someone has previously moved it). You can view as many toolbars as you want; however, the more toolbars you display, the less of the document window you will be able to see.

6 Move the pointer to the move handle, , at the far left side of the Drawing toolbar. Click and drag the toolbar to the middle of the screen, then release the mouse button.

The Drawing toolbar is torn from the bottom of the screen and floats in the middle of the document window, as shown in Figure 15-2. Notice that a title bar appears above the Drawing toolbar. You can move a floating toolbar by clicking its title bar and dragging it to a new position. If you drag a floating toolbar to the edge of the program window, it becomes a docked toolbar.

7 Click the Drawing toolbar's title bar and drag the toolbar down until it docks with to the bottom of the screen.

The Drawing toolbar is reattached to the bottom of the Word screen.

8 Right-click any of the toolbars and select Drawing from the shortcut menu.

The Drawing toolbar disappears.

QUICK REFERENCE

TO VIEW OR HIDE A TOOLBAR:

- SELECT VIEW → TOOLBARS FROM THE MENU AND SELECT THE TOOLBAR YOU WANT TO DISPLAY OR HIDE.

OR...

- RIGHT-CLICK ANY TOOLBAR OR MENU AND SELECT THE TOOLBAR YOU WANT TO DISPLAY OR HIDE FROM THE SHORTCUT MENU.

TO MOVE A TOOLBAR TO A NEW LOCATION IN THE WINDOW:

- DRAG THE TOOLBAR BY ITS MOVE HANDLE (IF THE TOOLBAR IS DOCKED) OR TITLE BAR (IF THE TOOLBAR IS FLOATING) TO THE DESIRED LOCATION.

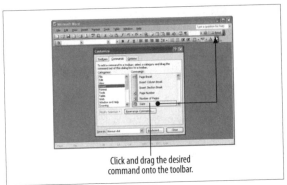

Click and drag the desired
command onto the toolbar.

Figure 15-3. Select the command you want to add to the
toolbar from the Customize dialog box, and drag it to the
desired location on the toolbar.

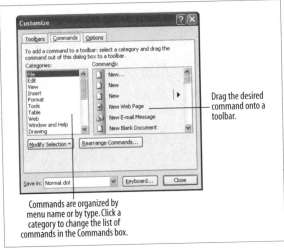

Drag the desired
command onto a
toolbar.

Commands are organized by
menu name or by type. Click a
category to change the list of
commands in the Commands box.

Figure 15-5. The Customize dialog box.

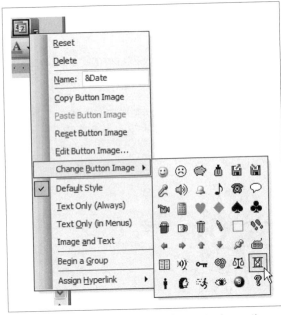

Figure 15-4. Right-click any toolbar button to change the
button's text and/or image.

The purpose of Word's toolbars is to provide buttons for
the commands you use most frequently. If Word's built-
in toolbars don't contain enough of your frequently used
commands, you can modify the toolbars by adding or
deleting their buttons. You can even create your own custom toolbar.

In this lesson, you will learn how to modify Word's toolbars.

1 **Select** View → Toolbars → Customize **from the
menu.**

The Customize dialog box appears, as shown in
Figure 15-3. You can select toolbars you want to view,
or create a new custom toolbar in this dialog box.

2 **Click the** Commands **tab.**

The Commands tab appears in front of the Customize
dialog box, as shown in Figure 15-5. Here, select the
buttons and commands you want to appear on your
toolbar. The commands are organized by category,
just like Word's menus.

3 **In the Categories list, scroll to and click the** Insert
category.

Notice that the Commands list is updated to display
all the available commands in the "Insert" category.

4 In the Commands list, click and drag the Date button to the end of the Standard toolbar, as shown in Figure 15-3.

The Date button appears in the Standard toolbar.

It's easy to change the image or text that appears on a toolbar button.

5 Right-click the Date button on the toolbar and select Change Button Image → hourglass, as shown in Figure 15-4.

You're finished modifying the toolbar!

6 Click Close to close the Customize dialog box.

Notice that the hourglass icon appears on the new Date button on the Standard toolbar. When you no longer need a toolbar button, you can remove it.

7 Select View → Toolbars → Customize from the menu.

The Customize dialog box appears, as shown in Figure 15-5. To remove a button, simply drag it off the toolbar, back to the Customize dialog box.

8 Click and drag the Date button off the toolbar into the Customize dialog box.

9 Click Close to close the Customize dialog box.

Adding your frequently used commands to a toolbar is one of the most effective ways you can make Microsoft Word more enjoyable and faster to use.

QUICK REFERENCE

TO ADD A BUTTON TO A TOOLBAR:

1. SELECT VIEW → TOOLBARS → CUSTOMIZE FROM THE MENU.

   OR...

   RIGHT-CLICK ANY TOOLBAR AND SELECT CUSTOMIZE FROM THE SHORTCUT MENU.

2. CLICK THE COMMANDS TAB.

3. SELECT THE COMMAND CATEGORY FROM THE CATEGORIES LIST, FIND THE DESIRED COMMAND IN THE COMMANDS LIST AND DRAG THE COMMAND ONTO THE TOOLBAR.

TO CHANGE A BUTTON'S TEXT OR IMAGE:

1. SELECT VIEW → TOOLBARS → CUSTOMIZE FROM THE MENU.

   OR...

   RIGHT-CLICK ANY TOOLBAR AND SELECT CUSTOMIZE FROM THE SHORTCUT MENU.

2. RIGHT-CLICK THE BUTTON AND MODIFY THE TEXT AND/OR IMAGE USING THE SHORTCUT MENU OPTIONS.

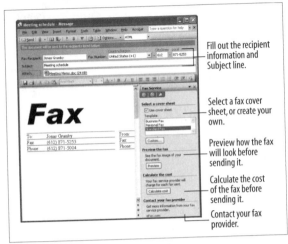

Fill out the recipient information and Subject line.

Select a fax cover sheet, or create your own.

Preview how the fax will look before sending it.

Calculate the cost of the fax before sending it.

Contact your fax provider.

Figure 15-6. The fax message window.

A new feature in Word 2003 is the ability to send faxes right from the program. Instead of scanning paper copies into a fax machine, Word creates (.TIF) image files of the document and cover letter. These image files are then sent to the fax service provider in an e-mail. When the fax message is received, the fax service sends the image files through the telephone wires to the fax machine.

If none of that made sense, all you really need to know is that the new fax feature saves time and a lote of paper, and is incredibly easy to use.

> ⋮ NOTE ⋮ *You must have Outlook and Word installed to use the fax service, and Outlook must be open to send your fax. If Outlook is not open and you click Send, the fax will be stored in your Outbox until the next time you open Outlook.*

1 Open the file you want to fax.

If you don't have the file open you can always attach it, just as you would attach a file to an e-mail message.

2 Select File → Send to → Recipient using Internet Fax Service from the menu.

An e-mail message window opens, as shown in Figure 15-6.

> ⋮ NOTE ⋮ *If you do not have a fax service provider installed on your computer, you will be prompted to sign up with a provider over the Internet. It's very easy to sign up; just follow the instructions to choose a provider and sign up for the fax service. Many providers offer a free 30-day trial in case you're trying to decide whether or not you want this service.*

Complete the information in the fax message window.

3 Enter the recipient's name and fax number at the top of the window.

You can send the same fax to multiple recipients by clicking the Add More button at the end of the row.

4 Type the fax subject in the Subject line.

Once you have entered the fax message information, fill out the cover letter.

5 Select the Business Fax cover sheet template in the Fax Service task pane.

The template appears. Replace the template text with information that applies to the fax being sent.

> ⋮ NOTE ⋮ *The information you include on your cover sheet may require some extra thought if you are sending the fax to multiple recipients.*

Once you've completed the cover letter, check out other options in the Fax Service task pane.

6 Click the Preview button in the Fax Service task pane.

The FaxImage window appears with a preview of the pages in the fax.

You can also get an estimate of how much the fax is going to cost you from your fax service provider.

7 Click the Calculate Cost button **in the task pane.**

A browser window opens with an estimate of what your provider will charge you for sending the fax.

8 **Close the browser window.**

Once you're satisfied with how your fax is going to look, you're ready to send it.

9 Click the Send button **in the fax message window.**

The fax e-mail is sent, and the recipient will receive the fax in no time.

You should also receive an e-mail from your provider, telling you whether or not the fax was successful.

QUICK REFERENCE

TO USE THE FAX SERVICE:
- YOU MUST BE SIGNED UP WITH A FAX SERVICE PROVIDER.

AND...
- YOU MUST HAVE WORD AND OUTLOOK 2003 INSTALLED ON YOUR COMPUTER.

TO SEND A FAX:
1. OPEN THE DOCUMENT YOU WANT TO FAX.
2. SELECT FILE → SEND TO → RECIPIENT USING INTERNET FAX SERVICE FROM THE MENU.
3. ENTER THE FAX INFORMATION: RECIPIENT NAME AND FAX NUMBER, AND A SUBJECT.
4. CHOOSE THE TYPE OF COVER SHEET YOU WANT TO USE IN THE FAX SERVICE TASK PANE AND FILL IT OUT.
5. CLICK THE SEND BUTTON.

TO PREVIEW THE FAX:
- CLICK THE PREVIEW BUTTON IN THE FAX SERVICE TASK PANE.

TO CALCULATE COST OF FAX:
- CLICK THE CALCULATE COST BUTTON IN THE FAX SERVICE TASK PANE.

TO FAX MULTIPLE FILES:
- CLICK THE ATTACH BUTTON IN THE FAX MESSAGE WINDOW AND ATTACH EACH FILE YOU WANT TO FAX.

Creating and Working with AutoText Entries

Figure 15-7. The Create AutoText dialog box.

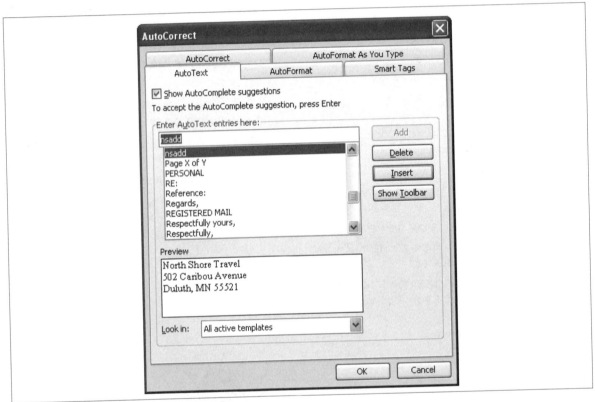

Figure 15-8. An AutoComplete tip box for an AutoText entry.

Figure 15-9. The AutoText tab of the AutoCorrect dialog box.

If you find yourself typing the same text again and again, you could save a lot of time by using an *AutoText* entry. AutoText lets you store the text and graphics you use frequently, such as a return address or canned paragraph. Once you have created and stored an AutoText, you can insert the AutoText entry by typing the AutoText entry's name and pressing Enter. It is worthwhile knowing that Word stores AutoText entries in template files (usually in the default NORMAL.DOT), so that your AutoText entries are available in every document created from the template.

1 Type North Shore Travel's address as follows:

North Shore Travel
502 Caribou Avenue
Duluth, MN 55621

2 Press Enter twice to add a line of space under the address, then select the entire address.

You want to create an AutoText entry for the selected text.

3 Select Insert → AutoText → New from the menu.

The Create AutoText dialog box appears, as shown in Figure 15-7.

Word suggests a name for the AutoText entry based on its content. You can use Word's suggested name for an AutoText entry, or you can enter one of your own.

4 Type nsadd in the Please name your AutoText entry text box, and click OK.

The Create AutoText dialog box closes and the new AutoText entry "nsadd" is stored in Word's default document template, which will be available in any future documents you create.

You can insert an AutoText entry two different ways. One way to insert an AutoText entry is by typing the name of the AutoText Entry you wish to insert and using Word's AutoComplete feature.

5 Type nsadd.

An AutoComplete tip box containing the AutoText entry you just typed appears, as shown in Figure 15-8. Word sees that you have just typed the name of an AutoText entry and is asking if you want to insert the AutoText entry.

6 Press Enter to insert the nsadd AutoText entry.

The AutoText entry "nsadd"—North Shore Travel's address appears, saving you a lot of typing. If you hadn't wanted to insert the AutoText entry, you would have continued typing at the AutoComplete prompt instead of pressing Enter.

Now that you know how to insert an AutoText entry using AutoComplete, let's undo the AutoText insertion.

7 Click the Undo button.

AutoComplete works great if you know the name of the AutoText entry you wish to insert. However, sometimes you may not remember the exact name of the AutoText entry you want inserted. When this happens, you can use the menu to view all available AutoText entries and insert the one you want.

8 Select Insert → AutoText → AutoText from the menu.

The AutoText tab of the AutoCorrect dialog box appears, as shown in Figure 15-9. Here, you can view and select the AutoText entry you want inserted into your document.

9 Scroll down the list of AutoText entries, select nsadd, and then click Insert.

The AutoText entry "nsadd"—North Shore's address—is inserted into the document.

You can easily delete any AutoText entries that you no longer need.

10 Select Insert → AutoText → AutoText from the menu.

The AutoText tab of the AutoCorrect dialog box appears.

11 Scroll down the list of AutoText entries, select nsadd, and then click Delete.

The "nsadd" AutoText entry is deleted from the list of AutoText entries, and will no longer be available in documents you create.

12 Click OK.

QUICK REFERENCE

TO INSERT AN AUTOTEXT ENTRY:

- TYPE THE FIRST FEW LETTERS OF THE NAME OF THE AUTOTEXT ENTRY AND PRESS ENTER WHEN A POP-UP WINDOW APPEARS WITH THE AUTOTEXT ENTRY'S NAME.

OR...

- SELECT INSERT → AUTOTEXT → AUTOTEXT FROM THE MENU, SELECT THE AUTOTEXT ENTRY YOU WANT, AND CLICK INSERT.

TO CREATE AN AUTOTEXT ENTRY:

1. SELECT THE TEXT YOU WANT TO USE AS THE AUTOTEXT ENTRY AND SELECT INSERT → AUTOTEXT → NEW FROM THE MENU.

2. ENTER A NAME FOR THE AUTOTEXT ENTRY AND CLICK OK.

TO DELETE AN AUTOTEXT ENTRY:

- SELECT INSERT → AUTOTEXT → AUTOTEXT FROM THE MENU, SELECT THE AUTOTEXT ENTRY YOU WANT TO DELETE, AND CLICK DELETE.

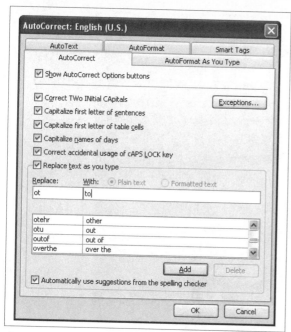

Figure 15-10. The AutoCorrect tab of the AutoCorrect dialog box.

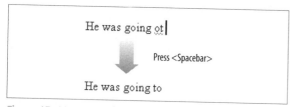

Figure 15-11. An example of using AutoCorrect.

AutoCorrect automatically corrects many common typing and spelling errors as you type. For example, Auto-Correct will change the mistyped words "hte" to "the," or "adn" to "and." AutoCorrect also corrects simple grammar mistakes, such as capitalization problems. For example, it would change "GOing" to "Going" or capitalize the first letter in sentences.

AutoCorrect is a feature that is shared across the Microsoft Office suite—so any additions or changes you make to AutoCorrect in one program, such as Word, will appear in all the Microsoft Office programs, like Excel. This lesson will show you how you can easily add errors that you commonly make to the list of AutoCorrect entries.

1 Type He was going ot the store.

Make sure you type *ot*—an obvious typo. You could spell check this mistake, but since it's one you make frequently, you decide to add the word (ot) and the correction (to) to AutoCorrect.

2 Select Tools → AutoCorrect Options from the menu.

The AutoCorrect dialog box appears with the Auto-Correct tab in front, as shown in Figure 15-10. Here, you can change the AutoCorrect options and add, change, or remove the AutoCorrect entries.

3 In the Replace text box, type ot and in the With text box, type to, then click Add and OK.

Now see if your new AutoCorrect entry works.

4 Repeat Step 1, making sure to type the word "ot."

AutoCorrect automatically changes the mistyped word "ot" to "to" the second you type it and press the Spacebar, as shown in Figure 15-11.

⁞ NOTE ⁞ *Use AutoCorrect like you've used it in this lesson—to correct common spelling and typing errors. Some users add each and every spelling error they make as an Auto-Correct entry and eventually bog down their system.*

Besides correcting common typing and spelling mistakes, many people use AutoCorrect as a "shorthand" feature. For example, you can create an AutoCorrect entry that would automatically replace the text "rdi" with "Regional Developing Chemical and Agricultural Industries, Inc.". You could also create this example using an AutoText entry, except it would take a second longer to insert the text because you have to press Enter after typing "rdi."

QUICK REFERENCE

TO USE AUTOCORRECT:

* TYPE THE WORD OR CHARACTERS FOR THE AUTOCORRECT ENTRY AND PRESS THE SPACEBAR.

TO CREATE AN AUTOCORRECT ENTRY:

1. SELECT TOOLS → AUTOCORRECT FROM THE MENU.

2. TYPE THE WORD OR CHARACTERS YOU WANT TO REPLACE IN THE REPLACE TEXT BOX, TYPE THE CORRECTION IN THE WITH TEXT BOX, CLICK ADD AND THEN OK.

TO DELETE AN AUTOCORRECT ENTRY:

* SELECT TOOLS → AUTOCORRECT OPTIONS FROM THE MENU, SELECT THE AUTOCORRECT ENTRY YOU WANT TO DELETE, AND CLICK DELETE.

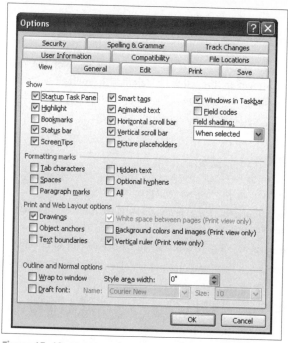

Figure 15-12. The View tab of the Options dialog box.

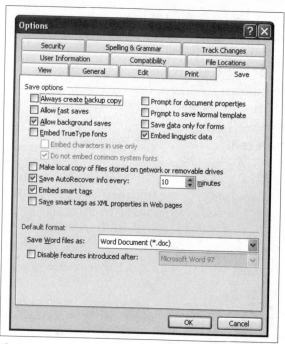

Figure 15-14. The Save tab of the Options dialog box.

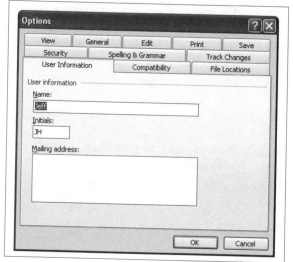

Figure 15-13. The User Information tab of the Options dialog box.

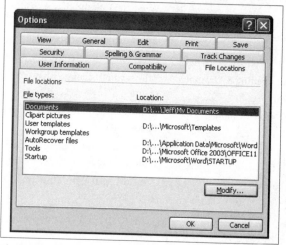

Figure 15-15. The File Locations tab of the Options dialog box.

Microsoft spent a lot of time and research when it decided what the default settings for Word should be. However, you may find that the default settings don't always fit your own needs. For example, you might want to change the default folder where Word saves your workbooks from C:\My Documents to a drive and folder on the network.

This lesson isn't so much an exercise as it is a reference on how to customize Word by changing its default settings.

1 Select Tools → Options **from the menu.**

The Options dialog box appears. Figure 15-12 shows the View tab of the options dialog box, Figure 15-13

the User Information tab, Figure 15-14 the Save tab, and Figure 15-15 the File Locations tab.

2 Refer to Table 15-1, and click each of the tabs shown in the table to familiarize yourself with the Options dialog box. Click OK when you're finished.

Table 15-1. The Options Dialog Box Tabs

Tab	Description
Compatibility	Options for making Word compatible with other word processing programs.
Edit	Controls Word's editing options, such as if typing replaces selected text and whether features such as Click & Type and Drag & Drop are enabled or not.
File Locations	Allows you to change the default location where Word saves documents and looks for templates.
General	Controls Word's default settings for more general options, such as the default unit of measurement used.
Print	Controls what gets printed, such as a document's properties and any comments. You can also specify whether Word should update any fields such as cross-references, table of contents, or indexes before printing.
Save	Allows you to change how Word saves documents, such as if a backup copy of every document is created, if Word should prompt you to enter properties for a document before you save it, and if Word 2003 should disable features not supported by earlier versions of Word when saving a document.
Security	Allows you to password protect your documents. For example, you could specify that a user must enter a password to either open or modify a document.
Spelling & Grammar	Allows you to change what types of errors Word flags when looking for spelling and grammar errors.
Track Changes	Controls Word's revisions features, such as the color Word uses to indicate changes made to a document.
User Information	Enter your name and address here. Word will use this information when printing envelopes, in its built-in AutoText entries, and to indicate who saved or modified a document.
View	Controls what Word displays in a document, such as nonprinting characters, field codes, and graphical objects.

QUICK REFERENCE

TO CHANGE WORD'S DEFAULT OPTIONS:

• SELECT TOOLS → OPTIONS FROM THE MENU,
  CLICK THE APPROPRIATE TABS, AND MAKE THE
  NECESSARY CHANGES.

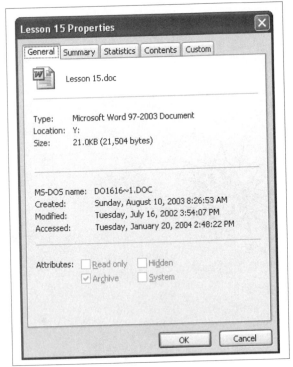

Figure 15-16. The File Properties dialog box.

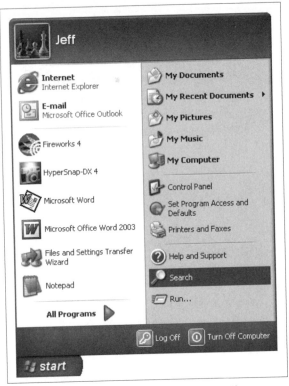

Figure 15-17. Search for Word documents using the Windows Search command.

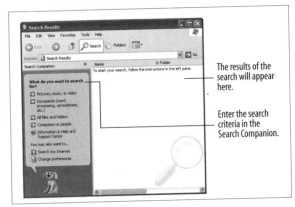

Figure 15-18. The Search Results window.

The first topic covered in this lesson is file properties. File Properties contain information about the size of a document, when it was created, when it was last modified, and who created it. The File Properties dialog box also has custom fields, such as Subject and Category, so you can add your own information to your workbooks.

The second topic covered in this lesson is how to find a file. It is just as easy to misplace and lose a file in your computer as it is to misplace your car keys—maybe easier! Luckily, Windows comes with a great search feature that can track down your lost files. Search can look for a file, even if you can't remember its exact name or location.

1 Open any document, select File → Properties from the menu, and click the General tab.

The General tab of the Properties dialog box appears, as shown in Figure 15-16. The General tab of the Properties dialog box tracks general information about the file, such as its size, its location, when the file was created, and when it was last accessed or modified.

2 Click the Summary tab.

The Summary tab of the Properties dialog box lets you enter your own information to describe and summarize the file, such as the author, subject, keywords, and category. You can use the information in the Summary tab to help you search for files.

3 Click Cancel and close the current document without saving any changes.

Let's move on and figure out how to find a file. The Search feature is part of Windows and can be used to find any type of file—not just those created in Microsoft Word.

4 Click the Windows Start button and select Search, as shown in Figure 15-17.

The Search Results window appears, as shown in Figure 15-18.

⊰ NOTE ⊱ *The instructions for accessing the Search feature process may differ, depending on what operating system you use.*

5 Click the Documents (Word processing, spreadsheet, etc.) option in the Search Companion pane. Select the Don't remember option and type Homework in the All or part of the document name text box.

This will search for any document that contains the word "Homework," such as "Homework 1," "Homework 8," and so on. If you only know part of the file name, you can enter the part of the file name that you

know. Searches are even more effective if you can remember the time frame of the document.

6 Click Search.

A list of files that match the criteria you entered appear in the open dialog box.

7 Double-click the Homework 2 file.

The Homework 2 file opens in Microsoft Word.

QUICK REFERENCE

TO VIEW A DOCUMENT'S PROPERTIES:

• SELECT FILE → PROPERTIES FROM THE MENU.

TO FIND A FILE:

1. CLICK THE WINDOWS START BUTTON AND SELECT SEARCH FROM THE START MENU.

2. ENTER THE SEARCH CONDITIONS AND WHERE TO LOOK IN THE SEARCH COMPANION.

3. CLICK SEARCH TO START SEARCHING FOR THE FILE(S).

Recording a Macro

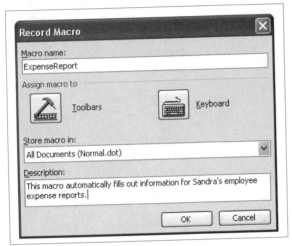

Figure 15-19. The Record Macro dialog box.

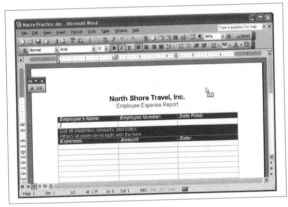

Figure 15-20. An example of recording a macro.

If you find yourself frequently doing the same task, you might be able to produce the same document much faster by creating a *macro*. A macro is a series of Word commands and instructions that are grouped together and executed as a single command. Instead of manually performing a series of time-consuming, repetitive actions in Word, you can create and run a single macro to perform the task for you.

There are two ways to create a macro: by recording them or by writing them in Word's built-in Visual Basic programming language. This lesson will show you how to create a macro by recording the tasks you want the macro to execute for you.

1 **Open the document** Lesson 15 **and save it as** Macro Practice.

This document is an employee expense summary, which Sandra has to fill out several times a week. Because Sandra fills this form in with the same information on a regular basis, she decides to record a macro to perform some of the repetitive work of filling out the form for her.

2 **Select** Tools → Macro → Record New Macro **from the menu.**

The Record Macro dialog box opens, as shown in Figure 15-19. Here, you must give your new macro a name and description.

3 **In the Macro name box, type** ExpenseReport. **In the Description box, type** This macro automatically fills out information for Sandra's employee expense reports.

Macro names can be no longer than 25 characters and cannot include spaces.

4 **Click** OK.

The Record Macro dialog box disappears and you are returned to the document. Notice that the macro toolbar and a new pointer appear in the document window, as shown in Figure 15-20.

The macro pointer indicates that Word is currently recording everything you type and every command you issue into the ExpenceReport macro. Do the next several steps very carefully—you don't want to make a mistake and record it in your macro!

> ⁞ NOTE ⁞   *You cannot use the mouse to edit and select text as you normally would while recording a macro—you have to use the keyboard instead. You can still use the mouse to access Word's menus and toolbars, however.*

5 **Select** Edit → Go To **from the menu.**

The Go To dialog box appears. This document contains a single bookmark named EmployeeName. You want to jump to that bookmark.

6 In the Go to what list, select Bookmark.

Since the EmployeeName bookmark is the only one in the document, it appears in the Enter bookmark name list.

7 Click Go To and click Close.

The dialog box closes and the insertion point jumps to the EmployeeName bookmark—located in the cell under titled Employee's Name.

8 Type Sandra Willes, then press Tab to move to the next cell, under the heading Employee Number.

9 Type 10369, and then press Tab to move to the next cell, under the heading Date Filed.

10 Select Insert → Date and Time from the menu.

The Date and Time dialog box appears.

11 Select the third date format from the top and click OK.

The current date is inserted in the cell.

12 Press the Tab key.

Now you are ready to start manually entering the expenses for the expense report. This is the last step we want in our macro, so we have to stop it from recording.

13 Click the ▣ Stop button on the Macro Record toolbar.

The Macro toolbar closes and the pointer returns to its normal shape, indicating that you are not longer recording a macro.

In the next lesson, you will learn how to play the macro you just recorded.

QUICK REFERENCE

TO RECORD A MACRO:

1. SELECT TOOLS → MACRO → RECORD NEW MACRO FROM THE MENU.

2. ENTER A NAME AND DESCRIPTION FOR THE MACRO.

3. (OPTIONAL) CLICK THE KEYBOARD BUTTON AND ASSIGN A SHORTCUT KEYSTROKE TO YOUR MACRO.

4. CLICK OK AND CAREFULLY PERFORM THE ACTIONS YOU WANT TO INCLUDE IN YOUR MACRO.

5. CLICK THE STOP BUTTON ON THE MACRO RECORD TOOLBAR WHEN YOU'VE FINISHED RECORDING YOUR MACRO.

Running a Macro

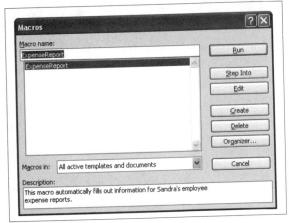

Figure 15-21. The Macros dialog box.

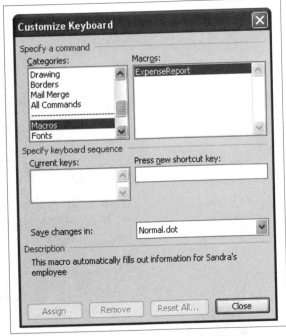

Figure 15-22. The Customize Keyboard dialog box.

In this lesson you get to play the macro you recorded in the previous lesson. Once you have created a macro, you can make it easy to access by adding the macro as a button on a toolbar, or even assigning a keystroke shortcut, such as Ctrl + F to the macro.

1 Select the second row in the table that contains Sandra Willes; Sandra's employee number, 10369; and the current date. Press Delete to delete all the information in this row.

The information you entered in the previous lesson is deleted. Now you can see how macros can save you time.

2 Select Tools → Macro → Macros from the menu.

The Macros dialog box appears, as shown in Figure 15-21. The Macro dialog box displays the available macros you can run.

3 In the Macro Name list, click the ExpenseReport macro and click Run.

The ExpenseReport macro you recorded in the previous lesson runs, automatically entering Sandra's name, employee number, and the current date.

If you use a particular macro frequently, you can assign it to a keyboard shortcut.

4 Select Tools → Customize from the menu.

The Customize dialog box appears.

5 Click the Keyboard button.

The Customize Keyboard dialog box appears, as shown in Figure 15-22. Here you can assign a keystroke combination to your macro.

6 In the Categories list, scroll to and click Macros.

A list of available macros appears in the Macros box.

7 In the Macros list, select the ExpenseReport macro.

Normally, custom keystroke shortcuts are stored in the default document template so they are available in all documents. Since you only need to use the ExpenseReport macro in the "Macro Practice" document, save it there instead.

8 Click the Save changes in list arrow, then select Macro Practice.

Word will save the custom keyboard shortcut that you will assign only to the document "Macro Practice."

Next, assign a shortcut key for the ExpenseReport macro.

9 Place the insertion point in the Press new shortcut key box and press Ctrl + F.

Now, any time you press the keystroke Ctrl + F in the "Macro Practice" document, Word will run the ExpenseReport macro.

10 Click Assign, then Close, and then Close again.

The dialog box closes.

11 Repeat Step 1 to clear the information from the second row in the table.

With the information cleared from the form, you can test the new custom keystroke shortcut.

12 Press Ctrl + F.

The ExpenseReport macro runs again, automatically filling out the top of the Employee Expense form.

QUICK REFERENCE

TO RUN A MACRO:

1. SELECT TOOLS → MACRO → MACROS FROM THE MENU.

2. SELECT THE MACRO YOU WANT TO PLAY AND CLICK RUN.

TO ASSIGN A SHORTCUT KEYSTROKE TO A MACRO:

1. SELECT TOOLS → CUSTOMIZE FROM THE MENU AND CLICK THE KEYBOARD BUTTON.

2. SELECT MACROS FROM THE CATEGORIES LIST AND SELECT THE MACRO YOU WANT TO ASSIGN A SHORTCUT KEYSTROKE.

3. PLACE THE INSERTION POINT IN THE PRESS NEW SHORTCUT KEY BOX AND PRESS THE SHORTCUT KEYSTROKE YOU WANT TO ASSIGN TO THE MACRO.

4. CLICK ASSIGN, THEN CLOSE.

TO DELETE A MACRO:

1. SELECT TOOLS → MACRO → MACROS FROM THE MENU.

2. SELECT THE MACRO AND CLICK DELETE.

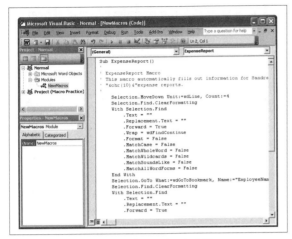

Figure 15-23. The Microsoft Visual Basic Editor.

This lesson introduces the Visual Basic programming language: the code Word used to record macros in. You might be thinking, "You can't be serious! I can't even program my VCR!" Relax. This lesson is meant to help you become familiar with the Visual Basic language and the Visual Basic editor, so you can make *minor* changes to your macros once you have recorded them. If you want to pursue Visual Basic further than the basic concepts introduced in this lesson, you will have to do so on your own.

1 Select Tools → Macro → Macros from the menu.

The Macros dialog box appears.

2 In the Macro Name list, click the ExpenseReport macro and click Edit.

The Microsoft Visual Basic Editor program appears, as shown in Figure 15-23. Yikes! You're probably thinking "What is all of that complex programming code doing on my screen?!" That funny-looking programming language is actually the written code of the macro you recorded earlier. Whenever you record a macro, Word writes and saves the macro in a language called *Visual Basic*.

Don't worry, you don't have to learn Visual Basic to be proficient at Word, but knowing the basics can be helpful if you ever want to modify an existing macro.

3 Find the line of code that says Selection.TypeText Text:="Sandra Willes".

Believe it or not, this is the piece of code that automatically enters the name "Sandra Willes" in the Employee's Name cell. Try changing the code so that it inserts the name "Brad Johnson" instead.

4 In the same line of code, replace the text "Sandra Willes" with the text "Brad Johnson", verifying that the name is enclosed with quotations.

The macro will now insert Brad Johnson's name instead of Sandra Willes' name in the document. Next, change the code that automatically inserts the employee number.

5 Find the line of code that says Selection.TypeText Text:="10369".

Now replace Sandra's employee number with Brad's employee number.

6 In the same line of code, replace the number "10369" with the number "12561", verifying that the name is enclosed with quotations.

That's it! You've made the necessary modifications so that your macro will enter Brad Johnson's employee information.

7 Close the Visual Basic Editor by selecting File → Close and Return to Microsoft Word from the menu.

The Visual Basic Editor window closes and you return to Word.

Try out your newly modified macro to see if it works. First, you will have to clear the existing information from the current form.

8 Select the second row in the table that contains Sandra Willes; Sandra's employee number, 10369; and the current date. Press Delete to delete all the information in this line.

The information you entered in the previous lesson is deleted.

9 Select Tools → Macro → Macros from the menu.

The Macro dialog box appears.

10 In the Macro Name list, click the ExpenseReport macro, then click Run.

The modified ExpenseReport macro runs, this time automatically entering Brad Johnson's name, employee number, and the current date.

11 Close the document without saving changes.

QUICK REFERENCE

TO VIEW AND/OR EDIT A MACRO'S VISUAL BASIC SOURCE CODE:

1. SELECT TOOLS → MACRO → MACROS FROM THE MENU.

2. SELECT THE MACRO AND CLICK EDIT.

3. EDIT THE MACRO'S VISUAL BASIC CODE AS NEEDED AND CLOSE THE VISUAL BASIC EDITOR WINDOW WHEN YOU'RE FINISHED.

Using Detect and Repair

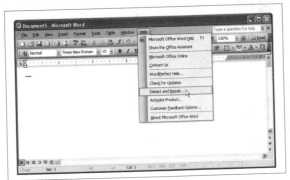

Figure 15-24. Select Detect and Repair from the Help menu.

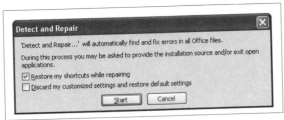

Figure 15-25. The Detect and Repair dialog box.

It's a sad fact of life. The more complicated programs get, the less stable they are. Programs sometimes become corrupted and have to be reinstalled in order to make them work right again. Fortunately for you and your network administrator, Microsoft has made this process relatively painless with the *Detect and Repair* feature. Detect and Repair searches for corrupted files and incorrect settings in any Microsoft Office applications and then finds and reinstalls the appropriate files.

Should your installation of Microsoft Word become corrupted or buggy, this lesson explains how you can use Detect and Repair to fix the problem.

1 Make sure the Office 2003 CD is inserted in your computer's CD-ROM drive, or is available through the network.

If you are connected to a large corporate network, hopefully your friendly network administrator will have made the Office 2003 files available to everyone on the network so that you can use the Office 2003 detect and repair feature. The only way you can find out if the Office 2003 installation files are available is to run Detect and Repair.

2 Select Help → Detect and Repair from the menu, as shown in Figure 15-24.

The Detect and Repair dialog box appears as shown in Figure 15-25.

To perform a standard detect and repair, do not select any of the options in the dialog box. But if you want to add them, here's what they do:

Restore my shortcuts while repairing: This restores application shortcuts to the Start menu.

Discard my customized settings and restore default settings: This option will reset such features as the Office Assistant, menu and toolbar customizations, security levels, and view settings.

Here we go…

3 Click Start.

If Word finds the Office 2003 installation files, it begins looking for and repairing any problems it finds with any Office 2003 programs. This might be a good time for you to take a coffee break, as Detect and Repair takes a long time to fix everything.

Detect and Repair doesn't only fix problems with Microsoft Word, but with all your Microsoft Office 2003 applications, such as Microsoft Excel and Microsoft PowerPoint.

QUICK REFERENCE

TO USE DETECT AND REPAIR:

- SELECT HELP → DETECT AND REPAIR FROM THE MENU.

Chapter Fifteen Review

Lesson Summary

Hiding, Displaying, and Moving Toolbars

To View or Hide a Toolbar: Select View → Toolbars from the menu and select the toolbar you want to display or hide. Or, right-click any toolbar or menu and select the toolbar you want to display or hide from the shortcut menu.

To Move a Toolbar to a New Location in the Window: Drag the toolbar by its move handle (if the toolbar is docked) or title bar (if the toolbar is floating) to the desired location.

Customizing Word's Toolbars

To Add a Button to a Toolbar: Select View → Toolbars → Customize from the menu, or right-click any toolbar and select Customize from the shortcut menu. Click the Commands tab and select the command category from the Categories list. Find the desired command in the Commands list and drag the command onto the toolbar.

To Change a Button's Text or Image: Select View → Toolbars → Customize from the menu, or right-click any toolbar and select Customize from the shortcut menu. Right-click the button and modify the text and/or image using the shortcut menu options.

Sending Faxes

To Use the Fax Service: You must be signed up with a fax service provider, and you must have Word and Outlook 2003 installed on your computer.

To Send a Fax: Open the document you want to fax and select File → Send to → Recipient using Internet Fax Service from the menu. Enter the fax information: recipient name and fax number, and a subject. Choose the type of cover sheet you want to use in the Fax Service task pane and fill it out. Click the Send button.

To Preview the Fax: Click the Preview button in the Fax Service task pane.

To Calculate Cost of Fax: Click the Calculate Cost button in the Fax Service task pane.

To Fax Multiple Files: Click the Attach button in the fax message window and attach each file you want to fax.

Creating and Working with AutoText Entries

AutoText lets you quickly store and retrieve text and graphics you use frequently. AutoText entries are stored in document templates.

To Insert an AutoText Entry: Type the first few letters of the name of the AutoText entry and press Enter when a pop-up window appears with the AutoText entry's name. You can also select Insert → AutoText → AutoText from the menu, select the AutoText entry you want, and click Insert.

To Create an AutoText Entry: Select the text you want to use as the AutoText entry and select Insert → Auto-Text → New from the menu, enter a name for the AutoText entry in the text box, and click OK.

To Delete an AutoText Entry: Select Insert → AutoText → AutoText from the menu, select the AutoText entry you want to delete, and click Delete.

Using and Customizing AutoCorrect

AutoCorrect automatically corrects common typing and spelling errors as you type. For example, AutoCorrect will change the mistyped word "hte" to "the."

AutoCorrect corrects/replaces words when you press the Spacebar. You can also use AutoCorrect as a shorthand feature—so you can type quick abbreviations and have AutoCorrect replace them with words or phrases.

To Use AutoCorrect: Type the word or characters for the AutoCorrect entry and press the Spacebar.

To Create an AutoCorrect Entry: Select Tools → Auto-Correct from the menu, type the word or characters you want to replace in the Replace text box, and type the correction in the With text box and click Add then OK.

To Delete an AutoCorrect Entry: Select Tools → Auto-Correct Options from the menu, select the AutoCorrect entry you want to delete, and click Delete.

Changing Word's Default Options

You can change Word's default options by selecting Tools → Options from the menu.

File Properties and Finding a File

To View a Document's Properties: Select File → Properties from the menu.

To Find a File: Click the Windows Start button and select Search from the Start menu. Enter the search conditions and where to look in the Search Companion. Click Search to start searching for the file(s).

Recording a Macro

A macro is a series of Word commands and instructions that are grouped together and are executed as a single command, saving a lot of time.

To Record a Macro: Select Tools → Macro → Record New Macro from the menu, and enter a name and description for the macro. If you want, click the Keyboard button and assign a shortcut keystroke to your macro. Click OK and carefully perform the actions you want to include in your macro. Click the Stop button on the Macro Record toolbar when you're finished recording your macro.

Running a Macro

To Play a Macro: Select Tools → Macro → Macros from the menu, select the macro you want to play, and click Run.

To Assign a Shortcut Keystroke to a Macro:
Select Tools → Customize from the menu and click the Keyboard button, select Macros from the Categories list, and select the macro you want to assign a shortcut keystroke. Place the insertion point in the Press new shortcut key box and press the shortcut keystroke you want to assign to the macro, and click Assign, then Close.

To Delete a Macro: Select Tools → Macro → Macros from the menu, select the macro and click Delete.

Editing a Macro's Visual Basic Code

Macros are recorded/written in the Visual Basic programming language.

To View and/or Edit a Macro's Visual Basic Source Code: Select Tools → Macro → Macros from the menu, select the macro, and click Edit. Edit the macro's Visual Basic code as needed and close the Visual Basic Editor window when you're finished.

Using Detect and Repair

To Use Detect and Repair: Select Help → Detect and Repair from the menu.

Quiz

1. Which of the following statements is NOT true?

    A. You can change the position of a toolbar by dragging it by its move handle (if it's docked) or title bar (if it's floating).

    B. You can display a toolbar by selecting View → Toolbars and selecting the toolbar you want to display from the list.

    C. You can display a toolbar by clicking the Toolbar button on the Standard toolbar and selecting the toolbar you want to display from the list.

    D. Toolbars attach or "dock" to the sides of the program window.

2. Which of the following statements is NOT true?

    A. You can customize a toolbar by right-clicking any toolbar or menu and selecting Customize from the shortcut menu.

    B. You can customize a toolbar by selecting View → Toolbars → Customize from the menu.

    C. Once the Customize dialog box is open, you can add buttons to a toolbar by double-clicking on the toolbar where you want to insert the button.

    D. If the Customize dialog box is open, you can add buttons to a toolbar by dragging them from the Commands list onto the toolbar.

3. You can modify Word's built-in toolbars, and you can create your own toolbars. (True or False?)

4. What is required to send a fax in Word 2003? (Select all that apply.)

   A. Word 2003 and Outlook 2003.

   B. A fax modem.

   C. A fax machine.

   D. A fax service provider.

5. Which of the following statements is NOT true?

   A. AutoCorrect automatically checks for and corrects common typing errors, such as replacing the typo "hte" with the word "the."

   B. AutoCorrect checks every word you type as soon as you press the Spacebar.

   C. AutoText lets you store text you frequently use, such as a return address or canned paragraph.

   D. The fastest and easiest way to insert an AutoText entry is to select Insert → AutoText → AutoText from the menu, select the AutoText entry you want to use, and click Insert.

6. Only menu and toolbar commands are recorded when you record a macro. (True or False?)

7. Which of the following statements is NOT true?

   A. Word records macros in Visual Basic language.

   B. Macro names can be up to 25 characters long, including spaces.

   C. You start the macro recorder by selecting Tools → Macro → Record New Macro from the menu.

   D. You can assign a keystroke shortcut to a macro to make it quicker to access.

Homework

1. Start Microsoft Word.

2. Select Tools → Customize from the menu and click "New" to create a new toolbar. Name the toolbar "My Commands."

3. Click the Commands tab, browse through the various Categories and Commands, and drag the commands you think you will use frequently onto the new "My Commands" toolbar.

4. Delete the My Commands toolbar when you're finished (click the Toolbars tab, select the My Commands toolbar and click Delete).

5. Add an AutoText Entry: Type your name and address, highlight it, and select Insert → AutoText → New from the menu.

6. Accept the default AutoText name and click OK.

7. On a new line, start typing your name. Press Enter to insert the AutoText entry when Word prompts you.

8. Record a macro called NewTable that inserts a 5×5 table into the document, format the new table with Grid style borders, and place the insertion point in the first cell.

9. Click the Stop button to stop recording the macro.

10. Create a new document and run the NewTable macro.

11. Exit Word without saving any of your changes.

Quiz Answers

1. C. There isn't a toolbar button in Word.

2. C. Once the Customize dialog box is open, you can add buttons to a toolbar by dragging commands from the commands list to the desired location on the toolbar—not by double-clicking.

3. True. You can modify Word's existing toolbars and you can create your own custom toolbars.

4. A and D. You must have Word and Outlook 2003 and a fax service provider to send a fax in Word 2003.

5. D. While you can insert an AutoText entry using this method, it's much faster to simply type the first few letters of the AutoText entry and press Enter as soon as a pop-up window appears with the AutoText entry's name.

6. False. Everything is recorded—every menu you select, button you click, everything you type—even any mistakes you make!

7. B. Macros can't have spaces in them.

INDEX

Colophon

Our look is the result of reader comments, our own experimentation, and feedback from distribution channels. Distinctive covers complement our distinctive approach to technical topics, breathing personality and life into potentially dry subjects.

Sarah Sherman was the production editor and the proofreader for *Word 2003 Personal Trainer*. The cover image is an original illustration by Lou Brooks. Claire Cloutier provided quality control. Julie Hawks wrote the index.

The art of illustrator Lou Brooks has appeared on the covers of *Time* and *Newsweek* eight times, and his logo design for the game Monopoly is used throughout the world to this day. His work has also appeared in just about every major publication, and it has been animated for MTV, Nickelodeon, and HBO.

Emma Colby designed and produced the cover of this book with Adobe InDesign CS and Photoshop CS. The typefaces used on the cover are Base Twelve, designed by Zuzana Licko and issued by Emigre, Inc., and JY Comic Pro, issued by AGFA Monotype.

Melanie Wang designed the interior layout. Emma Colby designed the CD label. This book was converted by Andrew Savikas to FrameMaker 5.5.6 with a format conversion tool created by Erik Ray, Jason McIntosh, Neil Walls, and Mike Sierra that uses Perl and XML technologies. The typefaces are Minion, designed by Robert Slimbach and issued by Adobe Systems; Base Twelve and Base Nine; JY Comic Pro; and TheSansMono Condensed, designed by Luc(as) de Groot and issued by LucasFonts.

The technical illustrations that appear in the book were produced by Robert Romano and Jessamyn Read using Macromedia FreeHand MX and Adobe Photoshop CS.

Related Titles Available from O'Reilly

Personal Trainers

Access 2003 Personal Trainer

Excel 2003 Personal Trainer

Microsoft Project 2003 Personal Trainer

Outlook 2003 Personal Trainer

PowerPoint 2003 Personal Trainer

Windows XP Personal Trainer

Word 2003 Personal Trainer

Windows Users

Windows XP Home Edition: The Missing Manual

Windows XP Pro: The Missing Manual

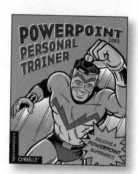

O'REILLY®

Our books are available at most retail and online bookstores.

To order direct: 1-800-998-9938 • *order@oreilly.com* • *www.oreilly.com*

Online editions of most O'Reilly titles are available by subscription at *safari.oreilly.com*

Keep in touch with O'Reilly

1. Download examples from our books

To find example files for a book, go to:

www.oreilly.com/catalog

select the book, and follow the "Examples" link.

2. Register your O'Reilly books

Register your book at *register.oreilly.com*

Why register your books?
Once you've registered your O'Reilly books you can:

- Win O'Reilly books, T-shirts or discount coupons in our monthly drawing.
- Get special offers available only to registered O'Reilly customers.
- Get catalogs announcing new books (US and UK only).
- Get email notification of new editions of the O'Reilly books you own.

3. Join our email lists

Sign up to get topic-specific email announcements of new books and conferences, special offers, and O'Reilly Network technology newsletters at:

elists.oreilly.com

It's easy to customize your free elists subscription so you'll get exactly the O'Reilly news you want.

4. Get the latest news, tips, and tools

www.oreilly.com

- "Top 100 Sites on the Web"—PC Magazine
- CIO Magazine's Web Business 50 Awards

Our web site contains a library of comprehensive product information (including book excerpts and tables of contents), downloadable software, background articles, interviews with technology leaders, links to relevant sites, book cover art, and more.

5. Work for O'Reilly

Check out our web site for current employment opportunities:

jobs.oreilly.com

6. Contact us

O'Reilly & Associates
1005 Gravenstein Hwy North
Sebastopol, CA 95472 USA

TEL: 707-827-7000 or 800-998-9938
(6am to 5pm PST)

FAX: 707-829-0104

order@oreilly.com
For answers to problems regarding your order or our products. To place a book order online, visit:

www.oreilly.com/order_new

catalog@oreilly.com
To request a copy of our latest catalog.

booktech@oreilly.com
For book content technical questions or corrections.

corporate@oreilly.com
For educational, library, government, and corporate sales.

proposals@oreilly.com
To submit new book proposals to our editors and product managers.

international@oreilly.com
For information about our international distributors or translation queries. For a list of our distributors outside of North America check out:

international.oreilly.com/distributors.html

adoption@oreilly.com
For information about academic use of O'Reilly books, visit:

academic.oreilly.com